Educational Psychology
A Problem-Based Approach

Educational Psychology
A Problem-Based Approach

Elizabeth A. Jordan

University of British Columbia

Marion J. Porath

University of British Columbia

PEARSON

Boston   New York   San Francisco
Mexico City   Montreal   Toronto   London   Madrid   Munich   Paris
Hong Kong   Singapore   Tokyo   Cape Town   Sydney

Senior Editor: Arnis E. Burvikovs
Series Editorial Assistant: Kelly Hopkins
Marketing Manager: Tara Kelly
Production Editor: Janet Domingo
Editorial Production Service: Nesbitt Graphics, Inc.
Composition Buyer: Linda Cox
Manufacturing Buyer: Andrew Turso
Electronic Composition: Nesbitt Graphics, Inc.
Interior Design: Nesbitt Graphics, Inc.
Photo Researcher: Sarah Evertson, Image Quest
Cover Administrator: Linda Knowles

For related titles and support materials, visit our online catalog at www.ablongman.com.

Between the time Web site information is gathered and then published, it is not unusual for some sites to have closed. Also, the transcription of URLs can result in typographical errors. The publisher would appreciate notification where these errors occur so that they may be corrected in subsequent editions.

Library of Congress Cataloging-in-Publication Data

Jordan, Elizabeth Anne.
    Educational psychology : a problem-based approach / Elizabeth Jordan and Marion Porath.
        p. cm.
    Includes bibliographical references and index.
    ISBN 0-205-35912-4
     1. Educational psychology. I. Porath, Marion. II. Title.

LB1051.J635 2006
370.15—dc22   2005048056

Printed in the United States of America

10 9 8 7 6 5 4 3 2 1   VHP   09   08   07   06   05

Contents

CHAPTER 1

Educational Psychology   1

CHAPTER **2**

Development: A Holistic Preview   15

Learning and Cognition: Developmental and Sociocultural Perspectives

CHAPTER 3

69

CHAPTER **4**

Learning and Cognition: Expanding Our Perspectives   97

CHAPTER **5**

Learning and Cognition: Applications for Diverse Classrooms   **117**

CHAPTER **6**

Understanding Our Learners: Social and Emotional Development   **136**

CHAPTER 7

Understanding Our Learners: Society and Culture   181

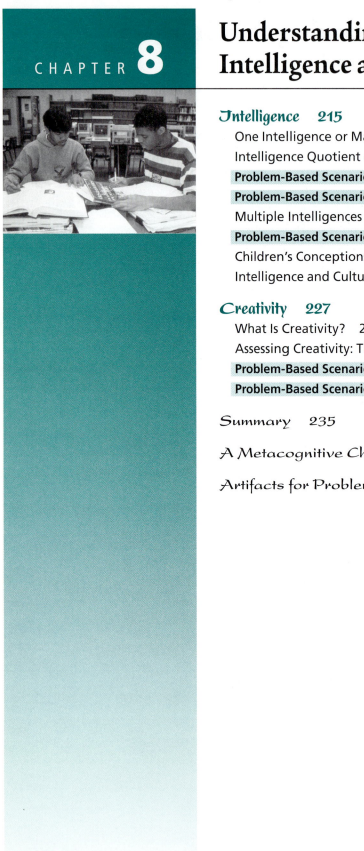

CHAPTER **8**

Understanding Our Learners: Intelligence and Creativity   **214**

CHAPTER **9**

Understanding Our Learners: Motivation   245

CHAPTER **10**

Understanding the Learning Context: The Supportive Classroom   279

CHAPTER **11**

Understanding the Learner in Context: Assessing Learning   306

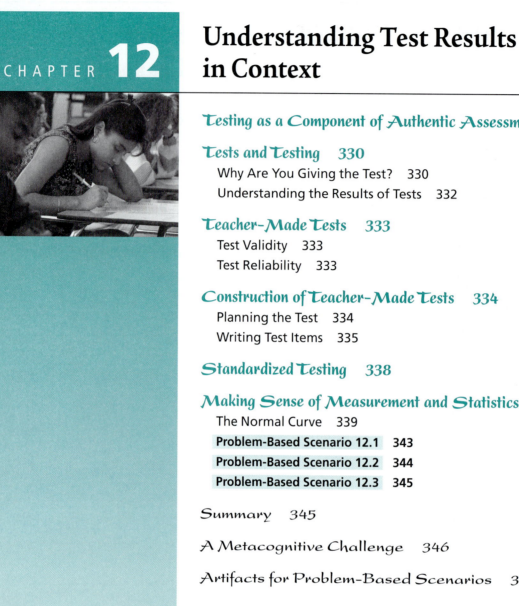

CHAPTER 12

Understanding Test Results in Context   329

Problem-Based Scenarios

K-5   6-8   9-12   SpEd

K-5   6-8   9-12   SpEd

Preface

This book reflects the significant changes evident in today's education of preservice teachers. Within a generation, access to knowledge has grown exponentially. This means that traditional ideas of what it means to teach need to take into account the amount of information available to teachers and the skills necessary to access it. Traditionally, educational psychology was about providing theories and research with the intention that future teachers would be able to apply theory in their classrooms. Looking back on many years of teaching experience, we realized that this model didn't really prepare us for actual classroom situations. For both of us, the students in our classrooms provided the real learning experience.

Working with students in public schools and at the university level, we developed teaching strategies that reflected a greater understanding of how people learn and an appreciation for individual variations. This required the applied approach to theory and research that you will find in this book. People construct knowledge of their world by sharing experiences and building on the knowledge that they already have. This text provides you with opportunities to share experiences with a teacher in an actual teaching situation. The model used is *problem-based learning*. Interspersed throughout the text are scenarios based on real classroom situations. As you are introduced to theories and research, think about what they may mean in the classroom. Why is Fred acting that way? Why can't Mary understand the directions? What should their teacher do to support them? It is only by actively participating in the scenario that you will acquire a deeper understanding of theory and research, allowing them to become "real" for you, as a future teacher.

The skills required to work through the problem-based scenarios will make you selective consumers of information. Easily accessed electronic information networks require teachers to be knowledgeable and skilled in selection and use. Since every classroom situation is unique, we feel that preservice teachers should be provided with the skills to define educational problems, select the most plausible theory to help understand the situation, carefully select the most appropriate information to help make an informed decision, and finally, interact with the individual(s) in the most positive and effective manner possible. We hope that this text will help you to develop these skills. Teaching is a collaborative effort between teacher and student. It often takes the form of a *conversation* in which ideas are shared. We chose a narrative style for this book to reflect the world of teaching. We hope it will help you to engage in the fascinating world of education.

Both of us have been teaching within the field of educational psychology at the university level for over fifteen years. During that time a number of major research advances have occurred that allow us greater insight into the learning process. As we adjusted our teaching to accommodate those broader understandings of how people learn, we noticed we had a greater dissatisfaction with available textbooks. While current research was noted and explained in detail, textbooks did not reflect the changes that were being discussed. This left us with texts that reflected a more traditional format while our classes featured a more collaborative style of knowledge construction.

The approach we use in our classes, and in this textbook, is based on constructivist theory. Constructivist theory provides us with an understanding of how knowledge is constructed. While most individuals can memorize facts, it is only when the facts are applied to an actual situation that they develop into meaningful concepts. Discussions with colleagues allow us the opportunity to enrich and broaden our understanding of a concept. What started as a set of memorized facts becomes a more flexible concept that has greater use and may be applicable in more situations. This means that knowledge is both individually and socially constructed—we make personal meaning of facts through discourse with others. Knowledge building requires not only factual information, but an opportunity to discuss and manipulate the ideas in a meaningful situation.

Also related to the constructivist approach we take in this text is our focus on problem-based learning. In order to learn about the realities of teaching children and adolescents, it is necessary to think about what happens in real classrooms. A problem-based approach allows for engagement with genuine teaching situations. We have incorporated problem-based learning into our teaching of educational psychology for a number of years. Both of us have considerable experience in public school teaching and we brought the stories of our lives as teachers to our university classrooms.

Problem-Based Learning

Problem-based learning works differently than traditional approaches to teaching and learning. *Problem-based learning* is a strategy that creates a "culture of inquiry" in which, rather than learning in a rote and isolated manner and making rapid judgments, individuals engage in defining problems, seek ways of addressing those problems, collaborate with others, and become curious about the work that they do. Problem-based learning presents learners with real-life "problems" to solve. As in actual teaching practice, problem-based learning presents professional problems that need to be identified. Life as a teacher presents "fuzzy" problems; that is, there often is no clear or immediate solution to many situations that teachers encounter. The problems need to be clarified and strategies generated, often with the help of colleagues.

The problem-based learning approach allows learners to begin with authentic information and then to construct meaning and directions for practice from that information. Rather than proceed from theory to practice in an abstract way, problem-based learning begins with practice-based situations that facilitate the linking of theory to practice through consideration of the questions inherent in the problem. Teachers need to understand the developmental and educational needs of all the students in their classroom. To achieve this objective, it is critical to think about real-life teaching situations. As you prepare to become a teacher, learning experiences from the real world of school are critical.

Our goal was to write a text that:

- Presents information that is not only up to date and research-focused but balanced by the art of teaching. Throughout the text, we acknowledge the art of teaching as that creative, intuitive flair necessary to transform curricula into developmentally appropriate opportunities for student learning.

- Is written in a *narrative format* which reflects the style of discussion in social construction of knowledge.

- Uses a *developmental approach* to understanding children and adolescents. Since everyone matures and develops in unique ways, it is more realistic to understand the broader aspects of development. This will allow teachers to understand development as an ongoing progression. For this reason we introduce problem-based scenarios that cover elementary, middle school, and high school age groups. We encourage instructors to have students read scenarios that cover all age groups. In this way elementary preservice teachers have insight into the future development of their students and secondary preservice teachers can get a sense of the elements that contributed to the background their students bring to secondary classrooms.

- Focuses on the student as part of a *community of learners*. We emphasize the integral and complex nature of individual experiences, interpersonal interactions, and environmental influences that form the learning community of a classroom.

- Uses *problem-based learning* to allow preservice teachers an opportunity to engage in real educational problems. All of the scenarios in the book are based on the authors' actual experiences. The experiences we bring to the text allow students to have insight into actual school situations.

- Slowly introduces the problem-based approach in the first few chapters of the text by providing starting points, hints, and questions. After a couple of chapters, these supplements end. This allows preservice teachers a chance to start clarifying situations and finding plausible solutions on their own. The goal is to make students self-sufficient teachers with skills that allow them to *problem solve* and *think critically* about classroom situations. They also develop an understanding that there is often no "right answer" but rather "plausible solutions" to many situations.

- Encourages preservice teachers to reflect on their professional practice within the classroom through the use of narrative. Becoming a *reflective practitioner* is a necessary and integral part of the teaching profession.

- Introduces topics in a *holistic* way. Topics are woven together rather than divided into compartmentalized sections. Classrooms are complex settings where multiple influences interact, resulting in unique learning communities. The narrative style and the problem-based scenarios present situations that represent the "story" of classroom life.

- Uses *Surfing Terms* to acknowledge that most students are adept at searching the Internet for information. One goal for our own classes is to make our students critical consumers of the wealth of information so readily available to them over the Internet. For this reason, search terms are given rather than actual Web sites. By accessing a search term, students often find large numbers of sites. A necessary skill for any teacher is to "weed out" those sites that are actually useful from those that contain a biased view or are selling something. As students find sites, it is worthwhile to have them share good Web sites with the rest of the class.

- Incorporates the reality of *inclusive education* in today's classrooms. This means that most every classroom has students who have either identified or unidentified special needs. This text recognizes that most teachers will encounter students with special needs in their regular classrooms. We have attempted to incorporate many topics from the area of special education as part of the narrative. The text's approach does not eliminate the need for students to take a course in special education, but rather reflects the reality of today's regular classroom situation.

- Selects specific topics that reflect the essential elements of knowledge in educational psychology that students need to become effective classroom teachers. Educational psychology is too broad a field to cover in depth in a traditional text format. Further, we recognize that the educational needs of urban and rural areas also include local issues such as poverty, parental pressure for university entrance, second language needs, infrastructure problems, and numbers of itinerant students, to name a few. By providing the essentials within a topic, we are allowing the university instructor an opportunity to tailor the course to his or her own unique geographic area or situation. This means instructors can emphasize one topic over another by using the Surfing Terms to delve into specific areas in greater depth. We would also like to encourage instructors to add locally developed materials such as policy statements, forms, local terminology, and so on.

■ Reflects the set of skills and competencies identified in state and provincial certification standards for effective teachers. Throughout the text we have emphasized what is considered to be *best practice* within education.

■ Provides preservice teachers with materials that reflect the current certification process within many states and provinces, namely the PRAXIS-type examinations. These examinations use a case-based segment where students are required to analyze a situation and apply research-based solutions. By working through the problem-based scenarios in this text, students develop the set of problem-solving skills that are tested on praxis exams.

Understanding Learners as the Central Concept

We feel that understanding the learner is the central component of effective teaching. For this reason we have written the text to reflect some key concepts of educational psychology.

■ What motivates our students?
■ How do they conceive of themselves as learners?
■ How do they understand the purposes of schooling?
■ Do they feel safe and secure as learners in an educational community?
■ How do other factors in their lives influence their learning?
■ How do they change and grow throughout childhood and adolescence, and how does this change influence their learning?
■ What strategies do they use to learn?
■ How do they respond to different ways of teaching?
■ How do I, as a teacher, interact with my students in the most effective, supportive ways?
■ How do I manage my class when it includes a child with special needs?

Key Features of the Text

In addition to the above goals, we have developed key features in the text to assist the instructor and the students to make the most efficient use of this book.

■ **Narrative Writing Style.** Our students have found that a narrative style is easier to read and understand than a more formal writing style. This narrative style also allows us to introduce the problem-based scenarios as a natural extension of the information/research-based text material. The scenarios are woven into the narrative as examples of the current topic under discussion.

■ **Advanced Graphic Organizers.** Each chapter begins with an Advanced Graphic Organizer. As a visual form of an advanced organizer the graphic provides a cognitive structure to which new learning can be anchored. Particularly when students are new to the field of educational psychology, an advanced organizer provides a context for relating and connecting relevant topics and information to the overall concept. The graphic format allows the complexity of the field of educational psychology to be presented in a visually meaningful way that is easy to understand and remember.

Problem-Based Scenario 2.3

K-5   6-8   **9-12**   SpEd

Student: Sean
Teacher: Marilyn

Marilyn had had a very long week. She had spent three nights meeting parents. The parent interviews were great because you got to know your students better, but they were also tiring. She had known that her ninth-grade English class was going to be a challenge this year, even before meeting the parents.

Sean Murphy was endearing and exasperating at the same time. He seemed to have boundless energy, but none of it was directed at his English assignments. After talking to his parents, Marilyn had a bit more insight into some of the difficulties that lay ahead. Sean was a gifted hockey player, with a sharp eye and great skills. Marilyn knew this, since hockey was the only topic Sean would write or talk about. Mr. Murphy seemed convinced that Sean's future lay in the National Hockey League and was already lining up scouts to have a look at his boy. What he talked about during the interview centered on how the parents and Marilyn would work to improve Sean's grades in English. Without good grades, Sean's chances for a university hockey scholarship decreased considerably.

From Marilyn's perspective, the drawback didn't seem to be grades, but rather that both Mr. and Mrs. Murphy weren't any taller than her 5'7". Sean seemed to favor his mother in that he was short in stature and small boned. While there were instances of short NHL hockey players, from his bruises it was apparent that Sean was already getting knocked around on the ice by bigger players. Even though he was working out with weights, Marilyn was skeptical about a lot of future growth. When she tried to direct the conversation toward university or other future professions (Mr. Murphy was a plumber), only Mrs. Murphy responded. The conversation always returned to the hockey scholarship.

Apply

■ How would knowledge of development help Marilyn in communicating with Mr. and Mrs. Murphy in this parent interview?

■ How could Marilyn use Sean's interest in hockey to motivate him in English?

FIGURE 2.3

■ **Problem-Based Scenarios.** These are based on actual classroom situations. They often contain artifacts such as memos, student worksheets, test results, and the like that might be contained in a folder on the teacher's desk. They are ill-structured problems that reflect not only the reality of a classroom but individual personalities. Rarely are classroom problems clearly identified. Instead they tend to be "messy" with "hidden issues" often brought into schools from outside situations. By providing preservice teachers with this reality, they are given opportunities to develop appropriate problem-solving skills.

■ **Icons Used in Problem-Based Scenarios.** The Problem-Based Scenarios in the text have identifying icons to situate the case within an elementary, middle, or secondary school narrative. Because schools work on a philosophy of inclusion, there is also a code to specifically identify those scenarios that deal with students who have special needs within a particular grade area. We encourage readers to peruse each situation, as time allows, since the text narrative encourages a holistic view of development and the teaching–learning process. However, the grade icons may assist instructors' planning and permit students to focus directly on one particular age group.

Surfing Terms 2.4

Social constructivism
Community of learners
Dynamic assessment
Hidden curriculum
Peers
Popular children
Neglected children
Rejected children
School–family partnership

■ **Surfing Terms.** This is a list of terms or the names of specific researchers associated with certain topics. In order to develop the ability to become critical consumers of information, students must have opportunities to search the Internet and determine the utility of Web sites. By providing search terms rather than specific Web sites, students gain experience with researching information. Instructors are of course encouraged to supplement searches with local and national Web site information where applicable.

■ **Info Bytes.** Throughout the text we have attempted to provide some additional detail on a specific topic that is strictly informational. We have done that through the use of small segments that do not interrupt the narrative or the problem-based scenarios. These small segments of information provide an enhancement of the topic within the narrative without detracting from the flow of the reading.

INFO BYTE 2.1

Fetal alcohol syndrome (FAS) as a clinical diagnosis did not exist until 1973. Until then, children were put into an "unknown" category, despite earlier warnings that were ignored. FAS is a medical diagnosis with specific characteristics that include growth deficiencies, physical abnormalities, and central nervous system damage. It manifests in mental and physical developmental delays. Fetal alcohol effect (FAE) exists when the child has some, but not all, of the characteristics. Children with FAE appear to have missed the damaging effects of alcohol, but often face more difficulties because their problems are not as apparent. They face issues such as learning disabilities, behavioral problems, hyperactivity, and social and emotional problems (Soby, 1994).

FAS and FAE are also known as fetal alcohol spectrum disorder and alcohol-related neurodevelopmental disorder (Streissguth & Kanter, 1997).

A Metacognitive Challenge

You should now be able to reflect on the following questions:

■ How do I define development?
■ What do I know about physical development? How does it influence the social and academic lives of students?
■ What do I know about language development? Could I explain the connection between language acquisition and thought development?
■ What do I know about cognitive development?
■ How do social and emotional development affect learning?

■ **Metacognitive Challenges.** At the end of each chapter we have provided students with an opportunity to synthesize the information they have learned by asking thought-provoking questions. The term *metacognitive* is used specifically to focus on the cognitive skills necessary to integrate information, manipulate it with reference to an individual age group or community situation, and provide answers or opinions that can be supported by valid rationales. The questions could be used as examples of the types of questions found on teacher certification exams.

Supplemental Support Material

Student Supplements

- **Resource Manual: Building Expertise as a Teacher.** This booklet should be considered as an extension of the textbook, rather than a study guide, and will be packaged with the text. It provides information on writing a teaching philosophy, developing a professional portfolio, hints for working in a team or group situation, and tools for working with the problem-based scenarios. The chapter activities allow students to expand their understanding of textual material with thought-provoking questions or PRAXIS-type questions. Chapter activities are referenced to PowerPoint slide numbers for convenience.

- **Companion Web Site.** A Web site, **www.ablongman.com/jordan1e,** is provided for students that includes additional problem-based scenarios, Web links, and sample test questions.

- **MyLabSchool** From video clips of teachers and students interacting to sample lessons, portfolio templates, and standards integration, Allyn & Bacon brings students the tools needed to succeed in the classroom—with content easily integrated into your existing courses. Delivered within Course Compass, Allyn & Bacon's course management system, Blackboard, or on the Web, this program gives students powerful insights into how real classrooms work and a rich array of tools that provide support on the journey from the first class to the first classroom. MyLabSchool is an optional supplement that requires an access code that can be requested by your instructor. MyLabSchool.com includes a direct connection to Research Navigator.

- **Research Navigator.** In order to assist with research prompted by Surfing Terms, Allyn & Bacon provides the Research Navigator. This powerful research tool allows you to investigate key concepts and terms from the book using a collection of resources available to you online, including EBSCO's ContentSelect Academic Journal Database and *The New York Times.* When the MyLabSchool supplement is requested by your instructor, purchase of this book allows you free access to this exclusive pool of information and data.

Instructor Supplements

- **Instructor's Resource Manual.** This manual provides information concerning problem-based learning, including research background and how to work with a problem-based scenario. Each chapter from the text is outlined in PowerPoint slides that extend text material. Each slide in turn is tied to corresponding questions in *Resource Manual: Building Expertise as a Teacher* and MyLabSchool video clips. Synopses of each problem-based scenario are provided, along with lesson objectives and additional sets of thought-provoking questions. A brief glossary of Special Education terms and additional problem-based scenarios are included.

- **PowerPoint Slides.** The slides highlight topics within individual chapters. They contain not only informational material but questions for class discussion. They provide an opportunity for active learning and engagement during class. Slides relevant to problem-based scenarios give helpful hints and ask relevant thought-provoking questions. These questions are an excellent source of PRAXIS-type questions for class discussion.

- **MyLabSchool** As described above under Student Supplements, MyLab-School provides video clips of teachers and students interacting, sample lessons, portfolio templates, and standards integration that complement the text and problem-based scenarios. Video clips have been referenced to PowerPoint slides and chapter activities. MyLabSchool is available free, but needs to be specifically requested so that access codes are included with the text package.

- **Companion Web Site.** A Web site is provided for students that includes additional problem-based scenarios, Web links, and sample test questions.

- **Computerized Test Bank** The printed Test Bank is also available electronically through our computerized testing system: TestGen EQ. Instructors can use TestGen EQ to create exams in just minutes by selecting from the existing database of questions, editing questions, or writing original questions. The test bank contains a variety of testing items including multiple choice, true/false, matching, and essay questions. The essay questions are based on PRAXIS-type questions and are similar to those found on the PowerPoint slides or within the *Resource Manual: Building Expertise as a Teacher.*

Using Research Navigator

This text is designed to integrate the content of the book with the valuable research tool, Research Navigator, a collection of research databases, instruction, and contemporary publications available to you online through www.mylabschool.com.

In each chapter the Surfing Terms provide special research prompts cueing you to visit the Research Navigator Web site to use the terms to expand upon the concepts of the text and to further explore the work being done in the field of educational psychology. To gain access to Research Navigator, go to www.mylabschool.com and log in using the passcode you'll find on the inside front cover of your text. RN learning aids include:

EBSCO's ContentSelect Academic Journal Database

Contains scholarly, peer-reviewed journals. These published articles provide you with specialized knowledge and information about your research topic. Academic journal articles adhere to strict scientific guidelines for methodology and theoretical grounding. The information obtained in these individual articles is more scientific than information you would find in a popular magazine, newspaper article, or on a Web page.

The New York Times Search by Subject Archive

Newspapers provide contemporary information useful, or even critical, for finding up-to-date information to support specific aspects of your topic. Research Navigator™ gives you access to a one-year, "search by subject" archive of articles from one of the world's leading newspapers—*The New York Times.*

"Best of the Web" Link Library

Link Library, the third database included on Research Navigator™, is a collection of Web links, organized by academic subject and key terms. Searching on your key terms will provide you a list of five to seven editorially reviewed Web sites that offer educationally relevant and reliable content. The Web links in Link Library are monitored and updated each week, reducing your incidence of finding "dead" links.

In addition, Research Navigator™ includes extensive online content detailing the steps in the research process including:

- Starting the research process
- Finding and evaluating sources
- Citing sources
- Internet research
- Using your library
- Starting to write

For more information on how to use Research Navigator go to **http://www.ablongman.com/aboutrn.com**

Acknowledgments

This book required the help and cooperation of a large number of people. We would like to thank all those who went out of their way to answer questions and share materials with us. We would like to offer our most sincere appreciation and thanks to:

Iris Schneider
Mary Brown
Rosie Steeves
Davinder Hothi
Janet Jamieson
Anne and Chris Page
Divya Henderson
Nathan Anderson
David Nicks
Lisa Maio
Lorelli McKay
Jo-Anne Naslund
John Jordan
Tristan Jordan
Merv Porath
Dave and Cathy Taff
Stuart and Lietta Turnbull
Ramona Mar and Mark Sachs
Constantine and Getrude Ngara
Sayed Haider Abbas and Sayeda Bano
Lisa Turpin
Lacey Dougherty
Laura Zajac

Reviewers who provided invaluable comments and advice are: Patricia Arlin, California State University–San Bernardino; Donna C. Browning, Mississippi State University; Jerrell C. Cassady, Ball State University; Mary Ruth Coleman, University of North Carolina; Anastasia D. Elder, Mississippi State University; Vicky Farrow, Lamar University; Muktha B. Jost, North Carolina Agricultural & Technical State University; Kit Juniewicz, University of New England; David J. Magleby, Brigham Young University Idaho; Dona Matthews, University of Toronto; Stacey Neuharth-Pritchett, University of Georgia; William F. Ritchie, Tunxis Community College; Sam Securro, Marshall University; and Vianne Timmons, University of Prince Edward Island.

We would particularly like to thank the editors at Allyn & Bacon: Arnis Burvikovs, Kelly Hopkins, Janet Domingo, Adam Whitehurst, and Judith Hauck. We also are grateful for Allison Aydelotte's editing, Tom Conville's project management, and Melissa Olson's design. The enthusiasm of all these individuals for this project and their guidance through the publication process were invaluable. We hope that we have included all the people who helped us develop this book. If we have omitted anyone, please accept our apologies and know that the omission was not intentional.

Coverage of Interstate New Teacher Assessment and Support Consortium (INTASC) Standards for Beginning Teacher Licensing and Development

Below is a listing of the INTASC standards on education and a correlation of where those standards are addressed within *Educational Psychology: A Problem-Based Approach*. Because of the holistic approach of the textbook, the standards below are woven into all chapters. Chapter Coverage identifies the chapters in which particular INTASC standards are addressed specifically.

INTASC STANDARD		CHAPTER COVERAGE
Standard 1	*Knowledge of Subject Matter:* The teacher understands the central concepts, tools of inquiry, and structures of the subject being taught and can create learning experiences that make these aspects of subject matter meaningful for students.	Chapters 2 and 3
Standard 2	*Knowledge of Human Development and Learning:* The teacher understands how children learn and develop, and can provide learning opportunities that support their intellectual, social, and personal development.	Chapters 2, 3, and 4
Standard 3	*Adapting Instruction for Individual Needs:* The teacher understands how students differ in their approaches to learning and creates instructional opportunities that are adapted to diverse learners.	Chapters 3, 5, 6, 7, and 8
Standard 4	*Multiple Instructional Strategies:* The teacher uses various instructional strategies to encourage students' development of critical thinking, problem solving, and performance skills.	Chapters 3 and 5
Standard 5	*Classroom Motivation and Management:* The teacher uses an understanding of individual and group motivation and behavior to create a learning environment that encourages positive social interaction, active engagement in learning, and self-motivation.	Chapters 5, 8, and 9
Standard 6	*Communication Skills:* The teacher uses knowledge of effective verbal, nonverbal, and media communication techniques to foster active inquiry, collaboration, and supportive interaction in the classroom.	Chapters 7 and 10
Standard 7	*Instructional Planning Skills:* The teacher plans instruction based upon knowledge of subject matter, students, the community, and curriculum goals.	Chapters 4, 7, and 10
Standard 8	*Assessment of Student Learning:* The teacher understands and uses formal and informal assessment strategies to evaluate and ensure the continuous intellectual, social, and physical development of the learner.	Chapters 11 and 12
Standard 9	*Professional Commitment and Responsibility:* The teacher is a reflective practitioner who continually evaluates the effects of his/her choices and actions on others (students, parents, and other professionals in the learning community) and who actively seeks out opportunities to grow professionally.	Chapters 1 and 7
Standard 10	*Partnerships:* The teacher fosters relationships with school colleagues, parents, and agencies in the larger community to support students' learning and well-being.	Chapters 1 and 10

Educational Psychology
A Problem-Based Approach

Educational Psychology

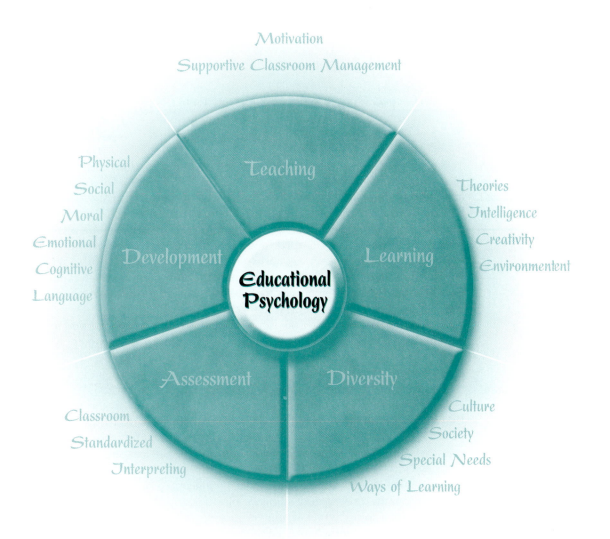

Motivation

Supportive Classroom Management

Physical
Social
Moral
Emotional
Cognitive
Language

Theories
Intelligence
Creativity
Environmentent

Teaching

Development

Learning

Educational Psychology

Assessment

Diversity

Classroom
Standardized
Interpreting

Culture
Society
Special Needs
Ways of Learning

Welcome to the study of Educational Psychology. Educational psychology helps us understand learning and teaching and how development and differences among individuals influence the process of learning. Learning and teaching are highly interrelated, and the study of educational psychology helps us make informed decisions about how our students learn best. It helps us reflect on our own learning and, at the same time, informs our educational practice. As teachers faced continually with the complexities of professional practice, you will learn exactly how interwoven teaching and learning can be. In this chapter, we lay the groundwork for your involvement with educational psychology.

In this text we take a developmental approach to understanding how children and adolescents grow, change, and learn. Development is critical in the study of educational psychology, and we discuss the topic from a variety of perspectives. Age and experience affect children's knowledge of and ways of engaging in academic subjects, social relationships, and moral dilemmas. Physical and emotional development also affect children's ways of understanding. Thus, teaching strategies need to be responsive to the ways in which children and adolescents think about things.

Teaching as Both Art and Science

There is a complex interrelationship between teaching and learning. The process of teaching is a combination of art and science. The art of teaching requires talent, creativity, flair, and intuition. A teacher must be attuned to other people and be able to read emotions and feelings. He or she must be able to perceive the nuances of students' reactions. At the same time, the science of teaching relies on reproducible knowledge that provides direction for instruction; in other words, teachers rely on the experience of others who have taught successfully. What has worked for others, especially if backed up by the close scrutiny of research, gives us information on the teaching strategies that provide students with opportunities to learn. The learner is central to teaching.

Too often, however, the learner is forgotten in the endeavor of learning to teach. This tendency is especially evident when we observe preservice or novice teachers. They are so busy with the act of teaching that they sometimes overlook the students themselves. This is a natural and common occurrence when one is concentrating so hard on mastering a new skill. For example, most children are very careless when learning to ride a bicycle. They are working so hard at riding the bike that they forget about the cars and pedestrians sharing the street with them.

Learning, on the other hand, tends to be a personal enterprise. No one else can learn something for you. When conditions for the learner are appropriate, learning can occur whether a teacher is present or not. Think of the number of things that you know about the world that you learned simply by watching a television program or observing someone else. There was no teacher present, and yet you learned something. Learning occurs naturally. The act of teaching builds on this innate capability and enhances learning. To facilitate the learning process, this book is designed not only to introduce concepts connected with effective teaching and the influences affecting the learner, but also to help preservice teachers understand the learner's perspective. This understanding is vital if you are to make the learner your primary focus in teaching.

Educational Psychology: Theory and Practice

Educational psychology is a discipline concerned with the overall teaching–learning process. Broadly defined, it can be separated into two distinct but highly related areas: theory and practice. Throughout this book you will be

FIGURE 1.1
Theory–Practice Continuum

introduced to concepts that often have what appear to be two or more opposing viewpoints. In almost all instances, however, we urge you to think not in terms of two different, opposing frameworks, but rather in terms of two concepts on either end of a continuum. Education is seldom a choice between two concepts; more often it is a compromise based on our knowledge of the learner, the context of the learning situation, and the necessary learning goals. On the theory–practice continuum, a teacher can typically be found somewhere in the middle of the continuum, depending on the learner and the learning situation (Figure 1.1).

Theory: A Scientific Framework for Understanding Learners

Psychologists analyze what it means to be a human, whereas educational psychologists, with the use of theories and principles, analyze what it means to be a learner. These theories provide teachers with an understanding of the learner generalized from many individuals' experiences. From among the numerous theories that exist, the teacher selects the concepts that most closely match the learner in question. The teacher then uses intuition (the "art" of teaching) combined with the theory to achieve a better understanding of the unique learner and situation. In this way, theories are a critical part of the teaching process. For example, a teacher notices that a ninth-grade student is very concerned with comparing his marks to others in the class. The teacher knows that social comparison theory will help her understand this, combined with talking to the student and his parents to see if other pressures are affecting him. Or a grade 3 student is constantly seeking teacher attention, leading the teacher to question why the child is so needy. Is the child emotionally and socially immature? Does she lack self-confidence? Has she had enough opportunities to experience mastery?

Practice: Combining Science with the Art of Teaching

On the other end of the theory–practice continuum, practice provides teachers with a series of concrete strategies and activities that have proved to be effective teaching tools. Often these strategies and activities are handed down from practitioners who have developed and tested their repertoires over years of experience—one of the reasons that a student teaching experience with a master teacher is so important (Photo 1.1). Master teachers create their repertoire from theoretical building blocks. They understand important theoretical concepts and use them to design instructional strategies that engage students and facilitate their academic achievement. The art of teaching can be learned only in a classroom, and it is learned most effectively with someone who shares a rich, well-informed repertoire of experience.

Working along the Theory–Practice Continuum

The development of a theory without any intention of putting it into practice makes it nothing more than an interesting exercise in psychology. A comment sometimes heard in school staff rooms is that a teacher's proven repertoire has value, whereas theories are just for those in universities or "ivory towers"—not those of us in the "trenches." As one of the authors illustrates,

> "When my son was in grade 4, he was placed in the school's Challenge Program. We lived in a very small community in which the local school was only kindergarten to grade 3, so when he changed to the larger elementary school we were delighted to see this program for gifted students continuing. But soon my son started to "hide" by being very busy and quiet when it was time to leave his class to go to this program. He wanted no part of it. After talking to him, I met with the teacher who worked with the Challenge Program to explain that all the children who came from the primary school had already completed the unit on magic that this teacher was now doing. The teacher explained that, although she knew some children had already completed the unit, she had already prepared the worksheets and materials and was proceeding with teaching it. She noted that there wasn't any additional material for the children to cover in this program. Her teaching assignment was a result of scheduling, and she had had no opportunity to acquire an understanding of theories of giftedness. Such an opportunity would undoubtedly have made her approach very different."

This example illustrates that both theory and practice are necessary for education to function. Theory and practice *interact* to inform each other, and a teacher needs to work back and forth along the theory–practice continuum to find the best mix for a specific teaching–learning situation. Likewise, educational psychologists learn a great deal from what happens in classrooms.

As you work through the various theories of development and learning presented in this text, you will quickly realize that no single theory can explain all the variations that occur in the children and adolescents you encounter. The developmental approach we use in this text is actually a combination of many theories, since human development is an open and complex dynamic system. The major challenge to developing a comprehensive theory is human nature itself.

PHOTO 1.2

Classrooms are dynamic social communities in which the particular mix of learners affects the learning that takes place. We learn in both social and individual ways. Classrooms are unique social communities, often called *communities of learners*, that contribute to the development of knowledge.

Theory and Practice in the Classroom Community

Theories help us grasp some of the nuances of human nature. Theories tend to be succinct and based on the integration of a large research base. They provide us with starting points to understand the learner as a human being and with ideas that can be used to try to find the best fit between our teaching goals and the learners in our classroom. Each learner is an individual with particular learning styles and needs that must be taken into account in our teaching. Classrooms, however, are also dynamic social communities in which the particular mix of learners affects the learning that takes place (Photo 1.2). We learn in both social and individual ways. Classrooms are unique social communities, often called communities of learners, that contribute to the development of knowledge.

Community of Learners: The Social Construction of Knowledge

What we learn is influenced both by our individual characteristics as learners and by our interactions with others. Knowledge is socially constructed, a point to which we will return in more detail. For now, we emphasize two points.

- *Teachers are both learners and teachers.* It is their responsibility to impart knowledge, but they do this most effectively when they learn from their students. If they learn how students understand the curriculum, for example, they can help students build on their current understanding to acquire more complex forms of knowledge.
- *Learners take on dual roles as well.* This is an important corollary to the concept of a teacher as both learner and teacher. In addition to the obvious relationship between students and their teachers, students also learn in their relationships with each other. Students are part of a *community of learners* (see also Chapter 6). They learn from the experience of teaching each other and working together on problems and projects. If teachers are open to the experience, they also teach their teachers innumerable lessons. Detailing the teaching–learning experience and the variety of influences that bear on this experience is central to educational psychology.

Core Principles and Concepts of Educational Psychology

Understanding the learners in our classrooms is central to the educational enterprise. Without this understanding, we cannot make informed decisions about how best to support our students. As teachers, we need to ask ourselves a number of key questions to ensure that we understand our students as fully as we can. These questions reflect the core principles and concepts of educational psychology:

- What motivates our students?
- How do they conceive of themselves as learners?
- How do they understand the purposes of schooling?
- Do they feel safe and secure as learners in an educational community?
- How do other factors in their lives influence their learning?
- How do they change and grow throughout childhood and adolescence, and how do these changes influence their learning?
- What strategies do they use to learn?
- How do they respond to different ways of teaching?
- How do I, as a teacher, interact with my students in the most effective, supportive ways?
- How do I manage my class when it includes a child with special needs?

Educational psychology is concerned with these and other related questions. The discipline focuses on the critical intersections among the minds and actions of the learner, teacher, and educational community.

Educational Psychology in the Classroom

In this textbook we discuss the following core principles and central concepts of educational psychology:

- Learning
- Cognitive development
- Social and emotional development
- Moral development
- Physical development
- Social–cultural context
- Children with special learning needs
- Intelligence and creativity
- Motivation
- The learning context
- Assessment and evaluation of learning

We consider how these principles and concepts bear on understanding learners at different stages of their development and with varying capabilities. The relationship between understanding learners and educational practice is paramount in this text. As teachers, we must understand *why* we do what we do. This understanding will enable us to provide a sound rationale for our practice to parents and school administrators. More important, though, this understanding is fundamental to best practice. *Best practice* refers to the provision of an environment and learning challenges that allow each student to achieve his or her full potential.

Examples from Early Childhood

Throughout the text, we include examples to illustrate key concepts of educational psychology. These examples are intended to help you make the connections between educational psychological theory and practice. A number of these examples are from early childhood, such as the following from Vivian Paley's (1981) book, *Wally's Stories*. Wally highlights better than we can the reasons for emphasizing examples from early childhood.

Wally:	People don't feel the same as grown-ups.
Teacher:	Do you mean "Children don't"?
Wally:	Because grown-ups don't remember when they were little. They're already an old person. Only if you have a picture of you doing that. Then you could remember.
Eddie:	But not thinking.
Wally:	You never can take a picture of thinking. Of course not. (p. 4)

Wally's comments on thinking remind us that, as adults, we have forgotten a lot about how we used to think when we were children. There is more of a gap between the thinking of adults and young children than there is between the thinking of adults and older children and adolescents. However, even at these later periods of development, adults are sometimes challenged to understand how older children or adolescents think. For example, a sixth-grader responded in the following way to a question on a social studies test:

Why is the Rhine River known as the "sewer of Europe"?
Because Cologne is on the Rhine, and that's where they make toilet water.

Students rarely are being "smart." They are genuinely trying to answer the question they *thought* you asked. Teachers need to ask what may have been meant by a student's response or action. By asking this question, you will become better prepared to think through the possible meanings of your students' thoughts and actions during all stages of development.

Examples from High School and College

We also use examples from high school and college. As adults, we sometimes forget what it is like to be a novice in a field or area of specialization. We often overlook the struggles we went through in learning—and that these experiences often changed the way we understand our world. In a college physics class, for example, Dykstra (1996) analyzed students' discussions during a laboratory session on forces. After observing another student's demonstration of forces canceling out each other, Mike responds, "Okay, I see how what you're saying can work. It sure isn't what I was thinking and I'm not sure it feels right, but I think I see what you mean" (p. 197). Mike's comment illustrates how novices often depend on what "feels right" when solving scientific problems. They struggle when they see evidence that is counterintuitive. Mike's teacher listened to their conversations to help students build scientific knowledge. When students reach the "I think I see what you mean" stage, they need opportunities to build solid understanding. They are starting to consolidate a concept; this is a perfect "teachable moment." Only by listening to what they are saying will you recognize these moments.

In many instances you will find the examples from young children to be clearer than those from high school or college. This is because young children tend to be more open socially when speaking or asking questions; the examples are not complicated by subject area topics, and the social–emotional situation may not be as complex. Throughout this book, however, we provide examples of students from a range of ages to demonstrate that each age group has unique, yet related, challenges.

Integrating Education and Psychology

Educational psychology is considered to include "the development and application of psychological principles to education, as well as the adoption of psychological perspectives on education" (O'Donnell & Levin, 2001, p. 73). What will this mean to you as a teacher? First, it is important to note that the relationship between psychology and education is not unidirectional. While educational psychology has drawn on psychology to inform education, education has just as much to offer to psychology. Education offers the realistic learning and teaching situations that challenge psychological theory (Mayer, 2001; O'Donnell & Levin, 2001). It is in the real world that students and teachers engage in thinking and learning. This is why educational psychology is meaningful to teachers. Mayer (2001) argued, "There is nothing as beneficial to practice as a good theory" (p. 87). Theory provides the conceptual underpinnings for teachers' work. Since the early 1900s, educational psychology has been concerned with the following topics (O'Donnell & Levin):

1. Measuring intelligence and relating intelligence to other variables (e.g., gender and achievement)
2. The reliability and validity of tests, the development of tests, and the evaluation of teaching
3. Influences on learning, including different sorts of instruction and different sorts of learning tools (e.g., types of text, computers)
4. Teacher behavior (e.g., how teachers praise students, how teachers respond to problem behaviors)
5. The influence of motivation on learning
6. Students' attitudes, self-esteem, self-concept, and personality
7. Students' classroom behavior

Self-Regulated Learning

The third and fifth topics in the preceding list can be expanded to include research that has taken place since the 1970s on *self-regulated learning* (Paris & Paris, 2001). Self-regulated learning includes effective strategies for learning, reflection on one's own thinking and learning (metacognition), and motivation and engagement with school tasks. The social support that students receive in classrooms enhances self-regulated learning. Students who are self-regulated tend to take charge of their learning. Educational psychology has been helpful in articulating the characteristics of self-regulated learners and the classroom practices that support self-regulation and teaching self-regulatory strategies.

Classroom Management

An additional area of inquiry in educational psychology is classroom management. How teachers organize and manage classrooms is central to establishing

PHOTO 1.3
Educational psychologists study what it means to have a learning or developmental disability, be developmentally advanced, demonstrate behavior problems, or have a physical or sensory impairment that affects learning.

and maintaining a supportive educational environment. Because teachers work in such complex environments, they need to be aware of research on students' psychological needs, positive teacher–student and peer relationships, and effective responses to behavioral problems (Emmer & Stough, 2001).

Exceptional Learning Needs

Another critical area studied by educational psychologists is exceptional learning needs. They study what it means to have a learning or developmental disability, be developmentally advanced, demonstrate behavior problems, or have a physical or sensory impairment that affects learning (Photo 1.3). They also study the sorts of learning tasks and environments that are most supportive of students with exceptional learning needs. An examination of development, behavior, and learning that differ from the norm helps inform our understanding of more typical development, behavior, and learning (Robinson, Zigler, & Gallagher, 2000).

Transition to Learner-Centered Classrooms

Contemporary education shows an increasingly *learner-centered* focus (Fried, 2001). This focus is a significant change from the way many of us were educated, in teacher-centered classrooms. *Learner-centered classrooms* focus on the needs and capabilities of the students as starting points for instruction. *Teacher-centered classrooms* focus on a curriculum and the delivery of predetermined knowledge to students. The change from teacher-centered to learner-centered classrooms requires two major considerations:

1. *How we conceptualize education and schooling:* Many of us "cling to the image of the teacher as the fixed source of knowledge" (Fried, 2001, p. 136) and resist the more reciprocal focus of learner-centered education.
2. *How we foster passionate learners:* Young children have an innate passion for learning, and educational psychology is key to keeping this passion alive throughout their years of formal schooling. Its principles are central to the learning process.

Translating Core Principles and Concepts into Practice

To present educational psychology in a way that facilitates its translation into practice, we emphasize two directions for this book:

1. *Presentation of background material in a narrative style:* We have found (and our students agree) that the use of textbooks fosters a fragmented type of thinking. Teachers need to think in a much more holistic way and consider the multiple influences on and meanings of learning for each student. We understand that classrooms are complex, and we present theory in a way that reflects the "story" of classroom life.
2. *Incorporation of problem-based learning into the text:* To learn about children and adolescents and the lives of those who teach them, it is necessary to think about real-life teaching. A problem-based approach allows for engagement with genuine teaching situations (Murray, 2000).

Problem-Based Learning

Problem-based learning works differently than traditional approaches to teaching and learning. *Problem-based learning* is a strategy that creates a "culture of inquiry" in which, rather than learning in a rote and isolated manner and making rapid judgments, individuals engage in defining problems, seeking ways of addressing these problems, collaborating with others, and being curious about the work that they do. Problem-based learning presents learners with real-life problems to solve (Photo 1.4). Unlike most problem-solving endeavors, however, such learning also requires that students first identify and characterize the problem to be solved. As in actual teaching practice, problem-based learning presents students with professional problems that need to be identified (*found* or *set*).

Donald Schon (1983) made an important distinction between *problem solving* and *problem finding* or *setting* that is particularly relevant to teaching. If the teaching profession is viewed as a problem-solving endeavor, it ignores the critical activity of problem setting, which Schon defines as

> the process by which we define the decision to be made, the ends to be achieved, the means which may be chosen. In real-world practice, problems do not present themselves to the practitioner as givens. They must be constructed from the materials of problematic situations which are puzzling, troubling, and uncertain. . . . When we set the problem, we select what we will treat as the "things" of the situation, we set the boundaries of our attention to it, and we impose upon it a coherence. . . . (p. 40)

The problem-based learning approach allows learners to begin with authentic information and then to construct meaning and directions for practice from this information. Rather than proceed from theory to practice in an abstract way, problem-based learning begins with practice-based situations that facilitate the linking of theory to practice through consideration of the questions inherent in the problem. Teachers need to understand the developmental and educational needs of all the students in their classroom. To achieve this objective, it is critical to think about real-life teaching situations.

PHOTO 1.4
The problem-based learning approach allows learners to begin with authentic information and construct meaning and directions for practice from this information.

As you prepare to become a teacher, learning experiences that are matched to the real world of schools are critical (Blumberg, 2000). Preservice teachers typically find that their practical experiences in schools are the most valuable features of their programs. This book provides a complement to those experiences. It engages you in linking theories to the real world of practice. Simply reading about or listening to theories of development and learning and how they are connected to practice is not enough. This approach represents a naïve view of learning (Duch, Groh, & Allen, 2001), not one that is appropriate for beginning teachers. Our complex society requires that professionals have not only a solid knowledge base, but also the ability to apply their knowledge to the solution of complex problems (Dochy, Segers, Van den Bossche, & Gijbels, 2003). As teachers, you need to be proactive lifelong learners (Kelson, 2000).

Using Problem-Based Learning to Become an Effective Teacher

Consistent with current research on effective learning (Donovan, Bransford, & Pellegrino, 1999), you will learn about teaching practice in a way that facilitates the monitoring of your own growth in understanding the concepts and issues concerned with educational psychology. As teachers, you will come face to face with problems daily, often in situations for which the problem has no clear solution. These open-ended problems are called *ill-structured problems*. That is, in many instances you don't really know all the factors related to the problem situation, or the problem setting may change while you are trying to figure out a solution. Sometimes the problem isn't really solved; it is just put on hold while the student is in the school environment. In any event, this is the reality of working with people and complex situations.

If you live in a province or state where praxis examinations or something similar are required for certification as a teacher, the types of problem-based scenarios included in this book provide solid preparation for the exam. The exams include scenarios that require you to develop plausible solutions with a theoretical base.

This book uses examples from our experience as teachers—Elizabeth in middle and secondary schools and Marion in elementary schools. We have altered all identifying information to protect students' confidentiality, but the dilemmas are

INFO BYTE 1.1

Since this text does not go into the specific details of many theories, it is necessary for you and your group to decide what theories might be the most relevant and then to research more details. In this book we give you *Info Bytes* to assist in your information searches. By researching theories in the library and on the Internet, you will soon become efficient at looking up information. You will also become selective consumers of the huge amount of material at your disposal. The Internet will allow you to access information that is up to date and valid, but this information is also meant to sell products or give global coverage to personal bias. As a teacher, you must be able to identify the information that is based on solid research from reputable sources. The strategies used in this text will allow you to practice these skills.

real. They represent the real world of teaching, with all its complexity, excitement, challenges, and unknowns. The problem-based learning strategy involves working in cooperative groups to think about the real world of teaching. In general, people seldom attempt to solve problems by themselves; instead, they usually ask others for information, opinions, and advice. By working in groups, you will find that information searches are more manageable. Furthermore, the collaboration required in a group to find a possible or probable solution reinforces and reflects the collaborative nature of the teaching profession.

Features of This Text

This text has two unique features. First, theory is presented the way we like to teach it—through stories of development, learning, and teaching. We all make meaning of our lives through narrative (Bruner, 1986, 1996). Stories reflect individuals' construction of the meaning of events in their lives. Teachers spend a great deal of their professional lives in the "narrative mode" (Bruner, 1986), both listening to their students' stories and telling and retelling their own as they try to understand their practice.

Theory-Based Narration

In each chapter, narrative-style text introduces you to relevant theory by presenting key theoretical concepts and examples of what these concepts mean in the real world. Consistent with a problem-based approach to learning, the presentation of theoretical concepts contains key information, but does not include exhaustive detail. To supplement the theory-based narration, we have included features called *Info Bytes* and *Surfing Terms*. These features provide additional relevant information to help you to find and set the problem and also to expand your ideas on how to solve the problem.

At the end of each of the following chapters, you will find a section called *A Metacognitive Challenge*. This is your opportunity to synthesize the information you have learned. In Chapter 4 you will learn more about metacognition and discover why this section has the title it does. This section contains questions that provoke personal reflection.

Problem-Based Scenarios

INFO BYTE 1.2

In addition to previews of relevant information to help you find, or set, the problem, we have included lists, entitled Surfing Terms, to help you find more in-depth information. They will help you search the Internet and library catalogues. The lists are not all-inclusive. You often will need to narrow your searches, since the terms sometimes target general information about a topic.

Second, *problem-based scenarios* reinforce principles of theory by introducing you to teachers, students, parents, principals, and other school personnel. Many of these scenarios contain two parts: the first describes the context, and the second is a collection of artifacts such as might be contained in a folder on a teacher's desk: memos, student work samples, test results, and the like. Only some of the scenarios contain artifacts, since it is often the case that teachers are confronted with issues that are immediate and for which no relevant data have been gathered. The problem-based scenarios are situated in elementary, middle, and secondary school contexts. Also, some narratives focus on students with special educational needs. Each narrative is coded with an icon to identify the particular context (Figure 1.2).

Because development, learning, and teaching are multifaceted, you will revisit various students and teachers as you move through the different topics in the book. For example, the first time you meet a student, his or her teacher may be focused on a cognitive developmental question to meet academic needs. Later you

Elementary school narrative

 Middle school narrative

 Secondary school narrative

SpEd   Problem-based scenario that focuses on the consideration of special learning needs in a regular classroom

FIGURE 1.2

Icons Used in Problem-Based Scenarios

might learn more about that student's motivation, peer relationships, and family life to determine how a teacher might help this student function successfully at school. Problem-based scenarios demonstrate the interconnectedness of different facets of development, learning, and teaching.

Using the Problem-Based Scenarios

In many instances, you will find that a topic is introduced but omits the lengthy detail often found in educational psychology texts. One goal of problem-based learning is for you, as the student, to detail not only the problem, but also the type of information necessary for its solution. For each problem-based scenario, you will need to actively engage in setting (defining) the problem and then determining where and how to gather the necessary information related to your focus of action.

The first several scenarios in this text provide additional help in the form of quick questions and hints to focus you on the problem to be solved. For example, suppose a sixth-grade teacher noticed that one of his best students, Peter, began to turn in incomplete work and appear disinterested in school. Several questions need to be considered. Is this a motivational issue (Peter isn't challenged enough), a hearing problem (perhaps made worse by a severe cold), a result of peer influence, an indication of an emotional issue at home, or some other cause? Teachers talk to each other, offer advice on where to find information, and swap articles and addresses. In other words, they work together as a collaborative unit, gathering and analyzing information to find probable and possible solutions.

Focus on the Classroom

Teachers often consider students' development on an individual basis. But it also is the case that a teacher needs to consider student needs within the context of all the learners in the classroom. Some chapters conclude with classroom scenarios in which the learners you met earlier in the book join their classmates. These scenarios challenge you to apply principles of educational psychology to meeting individual needs within the classroom setting. Teaching is both a challenging and a rewarding profession. It requires hundreds of decisions a day, and these decisions often involve consideration of a variety of factors. Educational psychology will help you make informed decisions. It also will add to the excitement of teaching by giving you new frameworks for interpreting students' thoughts and behaviors. Ultimately, we hope that the use of educational psychology leads you to innovative practice and engaged learners—two invaluable rewards of the profession.

Development:
A Holistic Preview

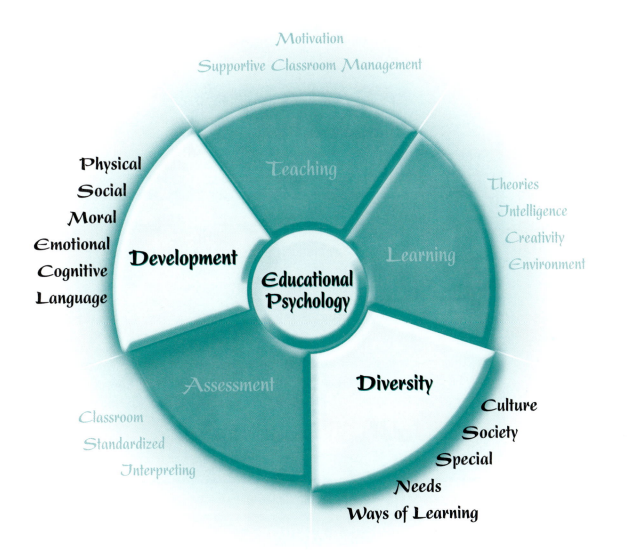

Motivation

Supportive Classroom Management

Teaching

Theories

Intelligence

Creativity

Environment

Physical
Social
Moral
Emotional
Cognitive
Language

Development

Learning

**Educational
Psychology**

Culture

Society

Special

Needs

Ways of Learning

Assessment

Diversity

Classroom

Standardized

Interpreting

In this chapter, central ideas about development and the relationship between development and education are presented. A holistic approach to an individual's development requires an attempt to understand the individual within an overall context of what it means to be human. We need to simultaneously consider aspects of a person's development, such as physical condition, maturity, emotional and social development, and reaction to the environment (Photo 2.1). To provide

PHOTO 2.1

Children of different ages use play as a way to socialize.

this context and its influence on education, a definition of the term *development* is provided, followed by an introduction to several types of development:

- Physical development, including puberty
- Language development
- Cognitive development
- Social and emotional development

Later, these topics are discussed within the context of the classroom community. At this point, however, certain topics, such as moral development, are not on the list. This chapter's intent is to provide a basic background for discussing some of the characteristics that a student brings to an educational setting. Once we have this basic knowledge, we can then move into other areas of a student's development, such as moral development and the development of motivation to learn.

Development as a Central Concept in Education

As teachers, you probably already have some intuition about what development means to you on a daily basis in the classroom. You have probably heard or said things like "He's big for his age," "Puberty has hit this class big time," "I can't understand why they didn't get the idea," or "I should probably put her in another learning group." Observations about how children and adolescents develop underlie all these comments. These observations, together with theories of development, can help teachers find ways to support optimal growth in their classrooms.

Development takes many forms. We develop cognitively; that is, our thinking changes in form, content, and complexity as we mature and participate in formal education. We develop socially, forming relationships with family, peers, friends, teachers, partners, and colleagues. Within this social framework of relation-

PHOTO 2.2

Children naturally accommodate each other's physical development during games.

ships, we become increasingly adept at understanding abstract concepts, such as fairness and justice (Photo 2.2).

Our sense of who we are, our *self*, also develops over time, as does our ability to understand our own and others' emotions. Similarly, physical growth follows a developmental pattern. Where all this fits into education is the focus of this chapter.

Fairness and *justice* are considered part of moral development (see Chapter 6)

Controversies Surrounding Development

A big question in educational psychology is this: Why do we need to understand development? Before asking the question, however, it is important to be sure we are all working with the same concept of development. As with any word, different definitions and interpretations exist, depending on the field of study or the context in which the word is used. The importance of providing a clear definition of development will become more evident later in the chapter when we introduce you to the constructivist philosophy on which this text is based. To define d*evelopment*, then, we first need to understand some of the controversies surrounding it. These include the following:

- Nature versus nurture
- Continuity versus discontinuity
- Early versus late experience

FIGURE 2.1

Nature–Nurture Continuum

Nature versus Nurture (Controversy 1)

One early argument in psychology centered on whether people physically inherited all their defining features (nature, or genetics) or whether it was possible to change people through education and experience (nurture, or the influence of environment). This is called the *nature–nurture controversy* (Figure 2.1). As with any debate, this controversy can be easy to discuss as a dichotomy (i.e., black or white, right or wrong, left or right). Instead, we ask you to consider all the debates presented in this text as continua, with opposing viewpoints on either end and varying viewpoints along the continuum. Most people tend to fall somewhere along the continuum, accepting some aspects of one idea, but leaning toward the opposite idea in other respects. The majority of people may accept one or two aspects of an issue that make one side more valid than the other. This is why a continuum is such a reasonable approach: it allows one to have an opinion or preference without completely denying the validity of the other viewpoint.

On one side of the nature–nurture controversy, it is argued that one's genetic makeup determines the strengths, weaknesses, and outcomes for the individual. On the other side, it is argued that the way in which an individual is brought up and the environment and people encountered ultimately shape the person.

Development and Risk-Taking Behaviors

For example, a conference on behavior problems in adolescence discussed research that looked at a connection between genetics and adolescent risk-taking behaviors. Part of the conclusion was that genetic predisposition should be given more emphasis when looking at risky behaviors (Rowe, 1994). If we do not view this notion from the perspective of a continuum and instead assume that risk-taking behavior always leads to criminal behavior, we might conclude that nothing can be done with these teenagers.

Our society and culture hold as a basic tenet the idea that people can change if they are given the opportunity (nurture). For many of us, then, statements on the exclusive role of nature make us uncomfortable. On the other hand, researchers at this conference provided considerable support for their findings on the role of nature. Perhaps, then, some people are *hardwired* for problem behavior and no amount of support can change their final outcomes.

Fetal Alcohol Syndrome

Another example of the nature–nurture issue is fetal alcohol syndrome (see Info Byte 2.1). We now know that one effect of alcohol consumed by the mother before birth is a condition in the child known as fetal alcohol syndrome or fetal alcohol effect (FAS/FAE), also referred to as fetal alcohol spectrum disorder. Alcohol consumed by the mother enters the fetus and interferes with biological development, resulting in injury to the nervous system or physical deformities. This is not a genetic problem, but rather one caused by an environmental factor. Children born with this disorder can exhibit a range of difficulties, from physical deformities (particularly facial) to mental retardation. In some instances, however, there may be no outward physical problems (FAE).

Until recently, children with FAE were thought to have escaped the influence of maternal alcohol consumption. We now know this is not the case. A distinctive characteristic of FAS/FAE is the inability to understand and remember consequences. Children with FAS/FAE may have perfectly normal physical development (although they tend to be small in stature), but have behavior problems. These children can tell you what the punishment will be if they misbehave, explain that they don't want the punishment, and then immediately misbehave. Thus, a large number of children, adolescents, and adults, no matter what the punishment, will continue to repeat illegal and immoral acts. This recidivism has become a major judicial issue (Conry & Fast, 2000). How do you deal with someone whom you know does not have the ability to comprehend consequences?

Not every person with FAS or FAE is a criminal, however. Many are productive citizens in our community—evidence that FAS/FAE does not automatically lead to criminal behavior. How have some individuals with FAS/FAE been able to control themselves in the face of a seemingly hardwired condition? Considerable time and effort are spent on training children with FAS/FAE to behave appropriately. In other words, their environment has become a major factor in how they develop as individuals in a community.

Genetic Determinism

The nature–nurture controversy has blurred over the years due to our increasing understanding of genetics, heredity, and the influence of environmental forces. The Human Genome Project (Kitcher, 1996) is an international work designed to map the DNA structure and sequences of humans. The intent is to better understand heredity and thereby predict, control, and possibly treat diseases that are caused by chromosomal irregularities. Knowing that a certain gene carries the likelihood of a disease, however, has raised certain medical, social, and ethical issues. *Genetic determinism* is the belief that, if you have a certain gene or gene abnormality, you are bound to contract the related disease. This, of course, is not always the case, since in many instances a disease can be the result of environmental factors, such as life-style (Plomin & Rutter, 1998).

For example, in phenylketonuria (PKU) an individual is born with an inability to normally metabolize an amino acid, phenylalanine, in milk and high-protein foods such as meat. As a result, a normal diet will build up nonmetabolized products in the blood. This eventually results in convulsions, severe mental retardation (developmental delays), and behavioral problems. However, by restricting the intake of the amino acid phenylalanine, these symptoms and severe mental retardation are prevented. This is why babies are systematically tested for PKU. Although the genetic factor is present, a change in the environment, specifically in the diet, can change the outcome for a person.

As you delve more into the issues surrounding genetics and environment, you will find that although an individual may be born with a certain genetic potential, or *genotype*, it may be the environment that affects the expression of this potential, or *phenotype* (see Info Byte 2.2). This dynamic is called the genotype–environment interaction (Photo 2.3) (Bergman & Plomin, 1989). As a simple example, a child may be born with a genetic potential (genotype) to be tall, but due to illness or malnutrition (environment) remains short as an adult (phenotype).

Because genetics–environment interactions are complex, it is difficult to determine whether some characteristic is genetic in origin or the result of envi-

PHOTO 2.3

Identical twins still have unique physical characteristics.

INFO BYTE 2.2

THE IMPORTANCE OF ENVIRONMENT

If we provide the right experiences for children and adolescents, we can "open up the lock of nature" (Brazelton & Greenspan, 2000) and help them reach their potential. Educational environments are critical in providing the experiences that optimize potential. Teachers in the world-renowned schools of Reggio Emilia, Italy, refer to the environment as the "third teacher" (Strozzi, 2001). In addition to the teacher and learning materials (books, computers, paint, clay, etc.), the structure, complexity, and esthetics of educational environments can facilitate learning and awake learners to new possibilities in learning. The way we arrange our classrooms (considering space, light, and design) and display materials has implications for how we "open the lock of nature."

Are our classrooms esthetic places? Do they convey a sense of welcome and invite students to engage in learning? Are materials arranged provocatively? For example, are art materials arranged in ways that invite experimentation and foster creativity?

If we provide complexity in educational environments, we allow for complex determination of ability (Jackson, 2000). In other words, if children have not been exposed to new ideas and materials, creatively presented, then we have no idea of just how able they might be. Creativity and high commitment to task will only be observed if children have the benefit of rich environments that afford them opportunities to demonstrate their abilities (Renzulli, 2002).

---

ronmental factors. For any teacher with a student who has a constant learning or behavior problem, the issue may be so complex that determining "why" the behavior exists (genetics vs. environment) is strictly an academic exercise. A more constructive approach for a teacher is to focus on ideas and solutions. Problem-Based Scenario 2.1, on Jay, gives you the opportunity to think about possible strategies for dealing with such behavior issues. As you consider Jay's development, also take into account the social issues that arise from our increased knowledge of genetics and environment. Sensitivity toward social and environmental concerns is sometimes as important for you to consider as finding ways to help the student.

Continuity–Discontinuity (Controversy 2)

As in the nature–nurture debate, there are different viewpoints on whether we grow and change slowly over time (continuity) or in distinct stages of growth (discontinuity), like a caterpillar changing into a butterfly. Many theorists discuss development in terms of discrete and very distinct stages or levels. As you will see in Chapters 3, 4, and 5, theorists have proposed different stages of human development, yet there is continual controversy about aspects of these theories. Once again, we have limitations on our ability to understand something as complex, interdependent, and interrelated as development.

In some instances, the idea of stages might be a very useful way to approach the topic of development. It allows us a chance to discuss major characteristics and teaching techniques without including too many variables at any one time. In other instances, an approach such as this may cause us to ignore opportunities or signs of growth. Here is one example. "As a friend was explaining to me that my son was too young to ride the tricycle he received for his second birthday, my

Problem-Based Scenario 2.1

Student: *Jay*
Teacher: *Vicky*

It's interesting how some names become known to teachers even before the student shows up in their class. Jay was one of those students that everyone on the staff knew about. He had been involved in truancy, mouthing off to teachers, breaking into someone's locker on a dare, leaving tests just as they got started, and leaving the school grounds after getting off the bus to spend the day at the mall, to name just a few examples. He was also suspected of putting a dead snake in the girl's change room after lunch on Monday. While he was always in some kind of trouble, the most frustrating thing was that he could be so charming as well.

Vicky was a teacher who, despite Jay's reputation, just could not believe he was the same person everyone talked about. As a grade 9 English teacher, Vicky figured she could handle Jay's behavior problems. He was always polite and, with his good looks and charming smile, seemed to be willing to turn his energy to more productive activities. All this ended abruptly when she learned it was Jay who put oil all over her car windows. He didn't even try to do it secretively, but rather showed all the kids how much of a mess you could make with olive oil. When she spoke to Jay about it, he apologized and seemed genuinely sorry. The next day, however, it happened again.

That day, after school, the counselor had a meeting with all of Jay's teachers. Apparently, Jay had been in a lot more trouble at home. He had broken into the neighbor's house while they were away and essentially trashed the kitchen (explaining where he found the olive oil). He was well known to the local police and social services, so his situation at school was not a surprise to them.

There had been considerable effort by the school and social workers to conduct testing to determine the exact nature of Jay's problem. Jay's father always blocked the testing. The counselor had known the family for many years and understood the situation well. He had shared very confidential information with the teachers and requested that all the teachers maintain that confidentiality as a personal favor to him.

Jay's mother had been an alcoholic and had gone to a clinic when Jay was 2 years old. Since that time, she had always been supportive of her family, a loving wife and mother and an avid community volunteer. The father felt there was too much "family baggage" to allow testing or an Individualized Education Plan (IEP) to be written on Jay. Instead, the father had asked the counselor to see if there was some other way to control Jay in school. The idea was that if he could be controlled in school the same technique might work at home too. This was the reason for the meeting.

At the meeting, the counselor suggested that a contract be set up between the teachers and Jay. All his teachers were to write up what they wanted from him in terms of their class (see Figure 2.2 on pages 57–58). The counselor would organize the contract and conditions. The alternative was suspension from school and further involvement with the police and social services.

Vicky now had to figure out what she wanted from Jay and how she was going to deal with him in her classroom. She knew that the last thing she needed was to make an enemy of Jay. So, even with the contract, it would be important to have additional ideas and techniques ready to use in class.

Apply

- Are there strategies that might help Jay to meet behavioral expectations in Vicky's class? For example, would a watch with an alarm help him to be on time for class?
- Would a checklist of books and materials help him to keep organized?
- Could Jay contribute to thinking about strategies?

Source: Jordan, Porath, and Jamieson (2000). *Problem-Based Learning in Inclusive Education.* Pearson Canada. Reprinted with permission of the publisher.

son went riding by. No one told him he was too young to accomplish that task, so he just did it on his own." By using the concept of a continuum, we can work with theories that define growth in terms of stages, at the same time realizing that life is a continuous progression.

Early–Late Experience (Controversy 3)

Burton White's 1975 book, *The First Three Years of Life*, became extremely popular since it was the first written for the general population. The book introduced parents to the work of Jean Piaget and other current theorists on human development. White's premise was that the most crucial time in the development of a child was the first 3 years. He stated that if a child did not receive appropriate nurturing during the first 3 years it was essentially too late for the child to catch up. This claim led to considerable upset among parents with older children, because they were just becoming aware of the importance of early experience for infants.

The book further added to the controversy about when in a child's life the most essential experiences occur—in infancy and early childhood or later? Both sides of this controversy are fiercely debated. If a child has had limited experiences before the age of 5, is it really too late? (Photo 2.4). What about children from disadvantaged backgrounds who have been exposed to enriched environments when they enter school and excel beyond expectations?

PHOTO 2.4

Young children who are exposed to enriched environments have a better chance of success at school.

If we return to our previous discussion of nature–nurture, we could argue that a child born with musical skill and talent will need opportunities and a supportive environment for this potential to be expressed. But is there a time limit on genetics? For example, we do know that time is a necessary factor for physical development, so is it also reasonable to conclude that there are age limitations on the expression of musical talent and skill? An elderly person with arthritis provides an obvious example in which age is a limiting factor. But how old is too old? Does something happen at 5 years of age to limit the potential for the expression of a genetic talent? If we adhere to a strict interpretation of stage theory, then the answer is yes. But there are 12-year-olds who are beginning music lessons and have considerable talent. One author's son began guitar in grade 10 and continues to play this instrument as an adult. Again, what this demonstrates is the need to work within the context of a continuum in dealing with controversial issues or theories.

Defining Development

As we have been discussing various controversies and themes about development, you have probably been thinking about your own understanding of this term. In this text we use a generic, more flexible definition that allows us to introduce you to numerous ideas without being constrained by personal viewpoints. It also allows us to introduce a range of ideas within a topic so that you may start to build your own understanding of what development means to you.

> As used in this text, **development** is a pattern of change that continues throughout the life-span, encompassing cognitive, physical, moral, and social-emotional elements.

As explained earlier, few things in life can be approached from a single perspective. The complexity of an individual, with his or her unique genetic complement, singular personal experiences, and innermost thoughts and aspirations, makes it unreasonable to exclude developmental perspectives from our concepts of learning. Even identical twins are not really the same in anything other than genetic makeup.

Using a Developmental Perspective in the Classroom

By taking a developmental perspective as a teacher, you open yourself to an understanding of people from an individual, holistic viewpoint. Children and adolescents in a classroom exemplify this point. Each has progressed to a particular, and probably unique, point along the continuum of social, emotional, physical, and cognitive development in his or her life on any particular day. For a teacher, the challenge is to meet the needs of each student as an individual (Photo 2.5).

However, as you begin to understand students from an individual, holistic perspective, you begin to realize that education and learning also need the same kind of perspective. If you have ever purchased a sweater that is advertised as "One size fits all," you will know that this just isn't true. The garment never really fits right because it was made for someone who only exists in a statistical composite. If we approach learning and education with this same "one size fits all" philosophy, we will find very few students who will actually thrive; most will get by, but others will fail. This is another reason why we have introduced you to the idea of using a continuum to study development.

Surfing Terms 2.1

Heredity

Genetic determinism

Environment

Resilience

Fetal alcohol spectrum disorder

Alcohol-related neurodevelopmental disorder

Phenotype

Genotype

Fine-motor skills

Gross-motor skills

Nutritional deficiencies

Adjusting Curricula to Developmental Needs

A developmental philosophy provides us with an understanding of learning and education that allows us to have some idea of where a student sits on that developmental continuum. As teachers, we then can adjust our curriculum to best suit the needs of that student, a process called *curriculum matching*. Using this process, a teacher starts with the curriculum he or she needs to present and then adapts it to the abilities and interests of a student. In this way, students have a chance to succeed and be challenged by education; it allows education to become a natural component of a student's life, rather than an artificial social enterprise constructed without consideration of the recipients. This philosophy emphasizes and reflects the continuity of life by taking into account previous characteristics as well as future potential. More simply, it allows us to respect the student as an individual person.

Physical Development

Physical changes are one of the most obvious things we notice about people. Children tend to grow rapidly, so even after a short time away from a child we often see jumps in their growth. Although physical changes are generally predictable, the variations that occur are the result of biological processes that make growth a personal, individual event. The *growth process* is influenced by several variables that need to be taken into consideration, such as the genetic makeup of the person, his or her environment, and the cultural group into which the child is born. However, *maturation* is the regular, orderly sequence of growth determined by the child's genetic makeup. Although other factors, such as malnutrition, can influence this orderly growth, maturation occurs on its own time line. As a result, teachers see an incredible variation in physical height and weight even within one classroom.

Problem-Based Scenario 2.2, on Dylan, gives you a chance to think about the practical implications of variations in physical development. It is also an opportunity to think about individual profiles of development. Students'

Problem-Based Scenario 2.2

Student: Dylan
Teacher: Shelley

Dylan towers over his classmates. At 7, he is barely distinguishable from the fifth-graders on the playground. He holds his own with the older boys pretty well, too. Besides being tall, he is muscular. Nothing the older boys can dream up seems beyond him. He tackles, runs, climbs, and handles a hockey stick like a pro. He enjoys recess and lunch breaks; in fact, they seem to be the highlight of his first-grade experience. He can barely wait for the recess or lunch bell to ring so that he can join the older boys. In the spring of first grade, though, he seemed to lose his enthusiasm. Just after recess one day, his teacher, Shelley Lim, heard the other children call her, "Dylan's crying, Miss Lim!" She crouched next to him to ask him what the matter was. Dylan sobbed, "They won't let me play! It's not fair. It's not fair."

Apply

- Is Dylan's physical maturity affecting other areas of his development?
- What is the first thing you would do if you were Shelley? Why?

physical development often presents unexpected problems for teachers. Handling situations appropriately requires adept interpersonal skills, considerable diplomacy, and quick thinking to assess what is going on. Dylan, for example, is a big boy physically, yet he is still a grade 1 student on a cognitive, social, and emotional level. Because of his size, however, his peers see him differently.

If you will be teaching adolescents, Problem-Based Scenario 2.3, on Sean, gives you the opportunity to think about how profiles of development may affect career planning. This scenario also raises questions about the roles of teachers and parents in guiding adolescents toward certain professions. The prospect of small stature may have an influence on Sean's future. At issue here is the effect this particular situation will have not only on Sean, but on his entire family. You may want to revisit this scenario when you encounter the topic of self-esteem.

Periods of Physical Development

Physical development can be organized into periods with characteristic growth patterns. As with any aspect of development, these periods should be considered only as points along a continuum. Here we describe the following stages of physical development:

- Infancy
- Early childhood
- Middle and late childhood
- Adolescence

Infancy

Infancy is the period from birth until about 18 months to 2 years. This period is characterized by vigorous growth. At birth, a human baby has a differentially large head that makes up about a quarter of its overall length. As a general principle, growth occurs from the top down (head to tail); that is, the head and trunk

Problem-Based Scenario 2.3

K-5   6-8   **9-12**   SpEd

Student: *Sean*
Teacher: *Marilyn*

Marilyn had had a very long week. She had spent three nights meeting parents. The parent interviews were great because you got to know your students better, but they were also tiring. She had known that her ninth-grade English class was going to be a challenge this year, even before meeting the parents.

Sean Murphy was endearing and exasperating at the same time. He seemed to have boundless energy, but none of it was directed at his English assignments. After talking to his parents, Marilyn had a bit more insight into some of the difficulties that lay ahead. Sean was a gifted hockey player, with a sharp eye and great skills. Marilyn knew this, since hockey was the only topic Sean would write or talk about. Mr. Murphy seemed convinced that Sean's future lay in the National Hockey League and was already lining up scouts to have a look at his boy. What he talked about during the interview centered on how the parents and Marilyn would work to improve Sean's grades in English. Without good grades, Sean's chances for a university hockey scholarship decreased considerably.

From Marilyn's perspective, the drawback didn't seem to be grades, but rather that both Mr. and Mrs. Murphy weren't any taller than her 5'7". Sean seemed to favor his mother in that he was short in stature and small boned. While there were instances of short NHL hockey players, from his bruises it was apparent that Sean was already getting knocked around on the ice by bigger players. Even though he was working out with weights, Marilyn was skeptical about a lot of future growth. When she tried to direct the conversation toward university or other future professions (Mr. Murphy was a plumber), only Mrs. Murphy responded. The conversation always returned to the hockey scholarship.

Apply

- How would knowledge of development help Marilyn in communicating with Mr. and Mrs. Murphy in this parent interview?
- How could Marilyn use Sean's interest in hockey to motivate him in English?

FIGURE 2.3

Cephalocaudal growth: Top-down growth

Proximodistal growth: Growth from the center outward

develop first and then the arms and legs. This is called *cepahlocaudal growth*. Then growth continues from the center parts outward, called *proximodistal growth*, with the limbs developing first and the fingers and toes last. This pattern of growth results in the differentially proportioned body of a newborn. Parents are always amazed at the diminutive size of a newborn baby's fingers and toes.

Disproportionately large head size and the placement of small eyes somewhat lower down on the head are what characterize the "cuteness" of babies and young animals. Konrad Lorenz (1971) found that it was this cuteness that triggered impulses in adults to nurture and take care of babies. In his study, both men and women responded in a nurturing way to figures with disproportionately large heads and low-set features that were described as cute.

Between 10 and 18 weeks of gestation, the majority of neurons are formed. With some rare exceptions, this means the brain of an infant contains all the neurons it will ever have, due to the inability of these very specialized types of cells to reproduce after birth (Todd, Swarzenski, Rossi, & Visconti, 1995). But the baby's brain does continue to grow. Growth occurs as a result of the myelination of neurons (the coating of neurons with a fatty substance called myelin), the reproduction of glial cells that support and nourish the neurons, and the branching and pruning of synapses (connections between neurons) (Tanner, 1978).

Early Childhood

Early childhood spans from about 2 to 5 or 6 years of age. Physical growth during this period is slower than during infancy. Usually, this leads to a reduction in the amount of food children need (and much concern on the part of parents) as babies grow out of being toddlers. The most noticeable change, however, is in the body proportions and overall appearance of the child. Limbs grow longer than the torso, which in turn grows more than the head, so the child starts to lose the top-heavy look of an infant. As children continue to grow, they require less sleep, so by 5 years of age naps may no longer be necessary.

As children grow, they gain control over their bodies. They learn to control their bladder muscles, for example, allowing them to sleep throughout the night without needing to urinate. Motor skills improve due to increased body awareness. Activities such as running and jumping become automatic with increase in muscle development (Photo 2.6). At about 18 months of age,

PHOTO 2.6

Early challenges help children to develop coordination.

approximately two-thirds of children have already started to show a preference for being either right-handed or left-handed (Archer, Campbell, & Segalowitz, 1988). This leads to an understanding of left and right by the time children enter school.

Middle and Late Childhood

Middle and late childhood ranges from about 6 to 11 or 12 years of age. From 6 to 9 years of age, there is steady growth, producing on average an additional 2 to 3 inches in height and 4 to 6 pounds in weight per year. The larger trunk, with more room for internal organs, leads to a reduction of the bulging stomach characteristic of early childhood (Photo 2.7). With the exception of the onset of puberty, when physical differences become apparent, both boys and girls appear to be relatively equivalent in physical capabilities. *Puberty* is defined as the age range during which an adolescent undergoes sexual maturation.

From approximately 9 years of age, both girls and boys tend to add about 8 to 10 pounds per year until around age 12. At about 9 years old, girls start to show early signs of puberty, which is characterized by exuberant growth, most notably in height gains. Intermediate teachers find the girls towering over the boys and are often not really prepared for this change, since the students are still in elementary school. There is a tendency for teachers to mistakenly think that puberty is a characteristic of students in secondary school. For this reason it is important for elementary teachers to familiarize themselves with the characteristics of puberty and adolescence. One author worked in a middle school where a very upset male teacher had to deal with a young grade 7 girl who had not noticed she had blood on her white jeans until she stood up to do work on the chalkboard. Not only was the young girl embarrassed, but the teacher was not prepared for an event like this. He hadn't thought about puberty because he had always dealt with elementary students. Luckily, one of the girl's friends saw what had happened and stood up behind her quickly, and they both left the room. Most of the class was unaware of the incident.

Puberty: Age range during which an adolescent undergoes sexual maturation

PHOTO 2.7

In middle and late childhood, physical development and socialization become interrelated.

Likewise, it is important for secondary teachers to understand late-childhood development, since new teachers who are assigned an eighth-grade group of boys and girls are often unprepared for the characteristics of eighth-graders. The physical transition that characterizes early adolescence is one aspect of the rationale for separate middle schools in many communities.

Adolescence

Adolescence ranges from puberty until adulthood and is characterized by vigorous growth. In general, adolescence begins at about 12 years of age for girls and 14 years of age for boys and lasts until about 18 to 20 years of age. The timing of adolescence is a very individual affair and often becomes the source of stress for those adolescents who mature late. This is a time when teenagers attain most of their adult height, undergo sexual maturation, and develop secondary sex characteristics, such as underarm hair, as the result of the production of sex hormones. Secondary sex characteristics distinguish boys from girls, but are not directly involved in reproduction; for example, for boys, secondary sex characteristics are the growth of facial hair or a deepening voice and, for girls, changes in hips and thighs.

It comes as a bit of a surprise to a teacher to find a boy in ninth grade with the beginnings of a beard and mustache (see Info Byte 2.3). Although we understand what is happening, for some reason we assume it will occur in older students, not in our younger classes. When changes do occur in younger students, it is extremely important to remember that the student may be mature physically, but at a different point in his or her cognitive and social development.

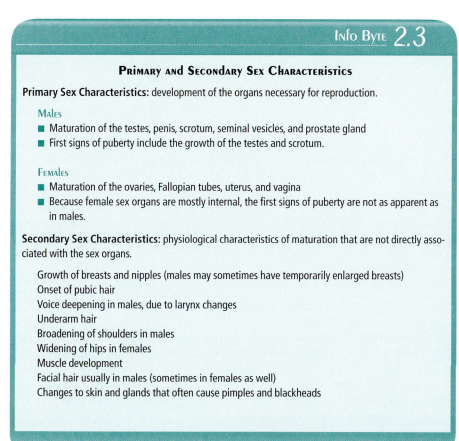

INFO BYTE 2.3

PRIMARY AND SECONDARY SEX CHARACTERISTICS

Primary Sex Characteristics: development of the organs necessary for reproduction.

MALES
- Maturation of the testes, penis, scrotum, seminal vesicles, and prostate gland
- First signs of puberty include the growth of the testes and scrotum.

FEMALES
- Maturation of the ovaries, Fallopian tubes, uterus, and vagina
- Because female sex organs are mostly internal, the first signs of puberty are not as apparent as in males.

Secondary Sex Characteristics: physiological characteristics of maturation that are not directly associated with the sex organs.

Growth of breasts and nipples (males may sometimes have temporarily enlarged breasts)
Onset of pubic hair
Voice deepening in males, due to larynx changes
Underarm hair
Broadening of shoulders in males
Widening of hips in females
Muscle development
Facial hair usually in males (sometimes in females as well)
Changes to skin and glands that often cause pimples and blackheads

Distal–proximal growth:
Growth from the ends inward

Since by adolescence the brain and head are already at adult size, the biggest growth occurs in the body. As any parent of a teenager can tell you, the body parts that grow first are the hands and feet. Earlier we mentioned the growth pattern of a developing fetus, in which development occurred from the trunk outward (proximodistal). With adolescents, this pattern is reversed and occurs in a *distal–proximal* direction, from the ends inward.

Changes during Adolescence   A distal–proximal pattern of growth often leads to a certain amount of clumsiness in young adolescents. Feet that appear to have grown a couple of sizes overnight often trip on stairs or fall over things. It takes a while for the legs and arms to catch up to the size of the hands and feet. The trunk is the last body part to gain adult size. Facial proportions change: the forehead becomes wider and higher, the nose longer, and the chin more prominent. An increase in the activity of sweat glands leads not only to pimples, but also to the production of sweat and resulting body odor.

During puberty, social, emotional, and cognitive complexities are associated with the biological process. In some instances, it refers specifically to the age when a male first produces live sperm, or *spermarche*, and when a girl has her first menstrual period, or *menarche*. At this point, an individual could reproduce (although there is often an actual lag in time from the first production of sperm and eggs and physically being able to conceive).

Sexual Development in Girls   In North America, girls on average reach menarche at about 12 years of age. Over the past couple of centuries, the age of menarche has steadily declined due primarily to increased nutrition and better general health. Menarche is triggered by the percentage of body fat to height. Since the trigger is body fat and not muscle, it is not unusual for athletes to have delays in the onset of their first period.

After their first period, girls continue to add height for about 2 years and then generally stop growing. For early maturing girls, this means that they may attain their adult height earlier than their later developing peers, although there may be no differences in the final adult height in either group. Often the only physical difference that may occur with the age of menarche is in leg length, in which later developing girls have slightly longer legs due to a longer growth period. An increase in breast size and changes in hip shape are aided by the addition of increased body fat. This is a time when many girls are upset by the weight gains caused by body fat and often become devoted to dieting. Body image is a crucial issue at this point in development.

A level of stress is associated with the timing of maturational events. For girls, early maturation may mean not only shorter stature, but a heavier appearance that is seen as undesirable and may lead to excessive dieting (Biro et al., 2001; Peterson, 1988). As you will see later, the timing of puberty can have an influence on adolescents' academic and social lives. A short list of research results is given in Info Byte 2.4.

Sexual Development in Boys   Boys begin to show signs of puberty around 12 years of age, usually with an increase in the size of the testes and penis. The first viable ejaculation, *spermarche*, usually occurs at approximately 14 years of age. Some facial hair may begin to appear, but beard growth is a late developing characteristic. The sex hormones cause shifts in the pitch of the voice, an increase in the prominence of the Adam's apple, and, for some boys, an embarrassing slight swelling of breast tissue. As with girls, the timing of puberty can lead to problems both socially and academically.

INFO BYTE 2.4

Early and Late Maturing Boys and Girls

Early Maturing Boys

- Considered more attractive and masculine
- Often more adept at athletics, thus tend to be more popular
- More confident, greater self-esteem (Graber et al., 1997)
- More likely to have behavior problems due to association with older boys
- Tend to become less curious and less active as they get older (Duncan et al., 1985; Peskin, 1973)

Late Maturing Boys

- Considered less attractive, childish
- Appear to peers as dependent, less leadership ability (Brooks-Gunn, 1988)
- Tend to become more assertive and flexible in later life (Alasker, 1995)

Early Maturing Girls

- More vulnerable to peer pressure
- More likely to get into trouble and take risks
- More independent
- Unhappy about body image
- Lower grades than late maturing girls (Ge et al., 1997)

Late Maturing Girls

- Few problems with parents and teachers
- More gregarious and self-confident (Graber et al., 1997)
- Tend to be taller and thinner (Simmons & Blyth, 1987)

Language Development

While physical development is certainly a focus of new parents, there is also the accompanying emphasis on communication with the baby. *Infant-directed speech*, or "motherese," normally consists of low-spoken, variably pitched short words and sentences (Littlewood, 1984). Research done on the interaction that occurs between mothers and infants found that the general reason for communication is to provide a social–emotional connection (Trainor, Austin, & Desjardins, 2000), as well as to enhance language development (Kuhl & Meltzoff, 1997). While cultural variations occur in parent–child interaction (Rogoff, Mistry, Göncü, & Mosier, 1993), our human desire to connect with each other for social and emotional reasons makes communication a necessity (Photo 2.8).

Communication among Other Animals

It has often been said that language is the defining difference between humankind and the rest of the animal kingdom. However, we know that animals have language in the form of body language, vocalizations, or other forms

PHOTO 2.8

"Motherese" is an important contributor to language development and social-emotional connections.

of communication. These forms of communication are used among animals to signal individual and group needs. Bees, for example, dance to indicate the direction in which food can be found, and chimpanzees hoot to signal the danger of a snake in the area. Thus the idea of language being the defining difference of humankind requires a more detailed look at the structure and function of language.

Features of Human Language

One unique aspect of human language in general is our ability to pass along thousands of years of collective experience to the next generation. This information extends beyond our own environment and range of experiences to that passed along to us by our ancestors and neighbors. Research on mazes and problem solving has demonstrated that the concept of planning for the future exists even in chimpanzees. Although this planning is limited, it does exist in rudimentary form (Gazzaniga, 1998). For humans, the concept of planning allows us to extend time and ideas into the future. For example, the space station has been a dream of humankind for generations.

The concept of planning over time exemplifies a totally unique human capability. It involves taking an abstract idea from one person, giving it form in the structure of verbal and written language, having other people add to it, and then passing it along to another generation to be carried out. As we look at this capability, the complexity of the structure of language requires branching off into a variety of topics and areas that need to be synthesized if we are to comprehend this uniquely human characteristic.

Theories of Language Development

To better understand the structure of human language and how humans acquire the ability to communicate, we introduce three important theories of language development:

- *Piaget:* Language use depends on our ability to use symbols and map categories and relationships onto the brain
- *Vygotsky:* Thought and language are independent until 2 years of age
- *Chomsky:* An innate capability allows humans to learn language

Piaget: Language and Cognition

The Swiss psychologist Jean Piaget (1896–1980) stressed the aspect of thought, or cognition, over the verbal production of language. He felt that, for an object to become more than just a word or label, cognitive-structural information was necessary to map the categories and relationships pertinent to the object. Piaget believed that for the first 2 years of their lives children are engaged in developing the cognitive structure necessary to apply the symbolic function relayed by language. This is why for the first 2 years children usually use names of items rather than categories (e.g., "dog" rather than "animal") and sometimes call other animals by the word they are most familiar with (Photo 2.9). Once the ability to symbolize (the *semiotic function*) emerges, the ability to use language begins.

Vygotsky: Thought and Language

The Russian theorist Lev Vygotsky (1896–1934) believed that social and cultural interaction affects both the language development and cognitive development of a child. According to his theory, before the age of 2 years a child uses both language and thought, but they are independent of each other. By the time a child reaches about 2 years of age, language and thought become interrelated. Children then use language to drive their reasoning. For example, we know children will invent words and sentence formations to grasp concepts. A friend's child called a skunk a "stinky cat" because he was told a skunk looks like a cat, but has other qualities as well. As you will read later in this chapter, Piaget and Vygotsky provided insight into the development of language and thought. Rice (1989) suggested that perhaps the two domains of cognition and language are interconnected in such a way as to overlap at certain points of development. Despite the debate about language and thought, in education we depend on language to

PHOTO 2.9

Natalie insists on calling the ceramic deer a doggie.

communicate not only thoughts, but also skills. As adults, we know that there is a major difference between thought and language, even though they are connected.

The difference between thought and language can be seen in a student who has the verbal learning associated with certain words, but does not really understand the idea behind these words. This concept is exemplified by Tom, a fourth-grade boy who had recently completed the Just Say No program at school. (The program is designed to show elementary students how to deal with sexual abuse and advances.) One of the older boys in the neighborhood thought it was funny to grab younger boys by the genitals. Even though all the boys knew it was wrong, they didn't know what to do. When it was suggested to Tom that he handle it exactly as he had been taught in school, his comment was, "Oh, so that's what they meant." Tom had learned all the words and had completed the program to the satisfaction of his teachers. What he hadn't learned was the idea or concept behind the words. This is known as a *production deficiency* (Flavell, Beach, & Chinsky, 1966).

Chomsky: Language-Acquisition Device

Originally, theorists believed children learned language and concepts through exposure to adults and continued repetition and reinforcement. According to this theory, language was strictly a process of mimicking adults. Noam Chomsky (1965) rejected this idea since it could not explain how children regularly generated new sentences not heard before. He postulated an innate capability that allows humans to learn language, a *language-acquisition device.*

The language-acquisition device that Chomsky proposed is not a specific structure or area in the brain, but rather an individual's capacity to learn and understand language, as well as the need to acquire language (Photo 2.10). It programs children's brains so that they have the ability to analyze spoken language and figure out the rules. This basic need to communicate with each other is exemplified by the development of visual languages, such as American Sign Language (ASL). Today, ASL is a recognized modern language. ASL and parallel forms of sign languages around the world are similar to the variety of spoken languages. Problem-Based Scenario 2.4 gives you an opportunity to learn about not only ASL, but also about issues surrounding the cultural aspect of language development. Problem-Based Scenario 2.5 allows you to think about how you would work with students who have developed their own form of communication.

PHOTO 2.10
Sign languages are recognized forms of modern language.

Problem-Based Scenario 2.4

Student: *Yetta*

Teacher: *Dianne*

Dianne Collie was stumped. In her 15 years of teaching she had worked with students with a variety of special needs—learning disabilities, cerebral palsy, visual impairment, Down syndrome. When she learned 2 months ago, at the end of August, that a profoundly deaf student, Yetta Clarke, was to transfer from the Provincial School for the Deaf into *her* homeroom, she thought she'd have no difficulty learning about and accommodating the unique challenges to this student's learning. She had even been excited at the prospect of learning American Sign Language!

However, American Sign Language (ASL) had not proved so easy to learn, and with all the demands on her time during September, Dianne had been grateful for the easy access to communication with Yetta that Jasmine, the educational interpreter, provided. In fact, Dianne thought guiltily, she had relied on Jasmine too much, allowing her to have more contact than Dianne had with the Hearing Resource teacher and even agreeing for her to adapt the language level in the texts when necessary. Now, at the end of October, it was apparent that Yetta had settled well socially into the integrated experience, and so it was time, Dianne thought, to focus more directly on Yetta's academic performance. It was here that Dianne was baffled.

When Dianne spoke with Yetta (through Jasmine) yesterday and suggested that she focus on improving her English grammar, Yetta had been resistant—even defiant. Her hands were clearly expressing anger when she signed that she could learn only through ASL and that English grammar was important only to hearing people. Yetta accused Dianne of neither appreciating nor understanding ASL and Deaf culture. Deaf culture? What on earth did *that* mean? And what was the difference between ASL and English? Dianne didn't know the answers to these questions, but she realized that to be an effective teacher for Yetta she needed to find out . . .

Figure 2.4 appears on pages 59–61.

Apply

- How do theories of language development help you understand Yetta?
- Think about language and culture. Is there a relationship? If so, what is the nature of this relationship? What might be the educational implications?

Source: Jordan, Porath, and Jamieson (2000). *Problem-Based Learning in Inclusive Education.* Pearson Canada. Reprinted with permission of the publisher.

The inherent function of the language-acquisition device allows us to learn language without systematic instruction or reinforcement. Brown (1973), for example, studied the errors children made as they learned to speak and found that their mistakes followed the rules of language. When a 2-year-old says "they goed," instead of "they went," she is following the structural rule of putting an "ed" on the word to form the past tense (e.g., "open" to "opened"). Children rarely make grammatical mistakes with structure; the problems come from the variations in our language that result when we change the rules.

Language and the Brain

Although Chomsky opened our minds to the concept of a naturally occurring tendency toward language, the current findings in brain research complement this information by showing how language acquisition actually takes place. To

Problem-Based Scenario 2.5

Students: Hannah and Holly
Teachers: Patty and Lisa

During the first half-hour of the day in the grade 2 class, children planned their day, then chose an activity for the remaining time. It was a favorite time of day for children and teachers alike—a chance to settle in, get organized for the day, and exercise some personal choice. Team teachers Patty Inglis and Lisa Yamoto valued it because it gave them time to observe the children and to interact informally with them.

Today Lisa observed Hannah and Holly playing with puppets. The twins' identical red ponytails bobbed as they worked their hand puppets in an animated way in the class drama center. They appeared to have a shared understanding of their dramatic play. To Lisa, though, observing this activity added to her concern about the twins' development. Hannah and Holly's language was immature. They had difficulty understanding prepositional phrases like "behind the door" and "on top of the shelf." They used "on" for "in" and "over" for "in front of." Their vocabulary was limited. Patty was first alerted to just how limited the day Holly asked her if she could borrow "a write with." Vocabulary limitations affected their day-to-day comprehension of class discussions, teacher directions, conversations with peers, and stories. They often interrupted stories to ask, "What's that mean?" The puppet play indicated, once again, that something needed to be done to help with the twins' language development. While Holly and Hannah communicated with each other easily, their ability to communicate with others needed a lot of support.

Patty and Lisa also talked regularly about Hannah and Holly's reading and written language development. In the spring of grade 2, both girls were struggling with reading material geared for beginning grade 1 students and finding written language very difficult. Patty and Lisa wondered how to approach the upcoming parent conference. They wanted to offer some support to Sheila, Hannah and Holly's mother, who tried hard to help out, but really had her hands full as a single parent with a toddler at home. But Patty and Lisa worried about how to reinforce the fact that the girls needed more exposure to language. When they had met with Sheila in the fall, she'd been so proud of the fact that the girls had each other to talk to and appeared to dismiss their concerns about language development.

In addition to offering the right kind of support to Sheila, Patty and Lisa were wondering where to turn next themselves. Hannah and Holly had learning assistance support, but what more could be done?

Figures 2.5 through 2.10 appear on pages 62–68.

Apply

- How could Vygotsky's view of language development help Patty and Lisa support Hannah and Holly's mother?
- What is a strategy you could use to begin to address the twins' language development?

Source: Jordan, Porath, and Jamieson (2000). *Problem-Based Learning in Inclusive Education.* Pearson Canada. Reprinted with permission of the publisher.

communicate using language, humans must develop sufficient cognitive structure, a language-acquisition device that allows for verbal structure and mutual communication, and a physical capacity to receive and express thought.

Recent brain research has provided us with some understanding of the complex ability of language. Much of the work has been done during neurosurgery when the brain surface is exposed. In many instances the surface needs to be mapped before the surgeon can proceed with the operation. Since the brain itself has no pain receptors, a patient can be awake during the operation. The mapping usually takes the form of asking the patient questions that require verbal responses. As questions are asked and the patient responds, small areas of the brain become activated, identifying areas as speech or verbalization centers. In this way the surgeon can determine exactly where areas of language are located (Gazzaniga, 1998).

Structure of the Brain

The brain is divided into right and left hemispheres. This arrangement is called *lateralization*, with each side having specialized functions. In the left frontal region near the motor cortex is *Broca's area*, which controls the ability to speak (Figure 2.11). People with an injury in this area have difficulty speaking fluently, or *expressive aphasia*, but they can still comprehend language.

Slightly behind this area is the temporal region responsible for auditory processing. Within this area is *Wernicke's area*, where comprehension of spoken language takes place. People with injuries in this area find it difficult to understand spoken language and often speak with nonsense words. This is called *receptive aphasia* (Owens, 1996).

Annett (1973) found that children suffering injuries to Broca's and Wernicke's areas recovered language function. This demonstrates what neurologists call the *plasticity* or flexibility of the brain to compensate for injury. In some instances, other areas of the brain may take over some tasks when the usual areas become nonfunctional. For people who are deaf and use sign language, researchers have found that some areas regularly devoted to hearing become functional for visual stimuli (Bransford, Brown, & Cocking, 2000). This means that the brain has the capability to adapt to injury and changes in the environment.

Variation in Brain Structure

Everyone has slightly different areas for speech, thereby necessitating a personalized map for each patient. Some areas are devoted specifically to terminology, or the

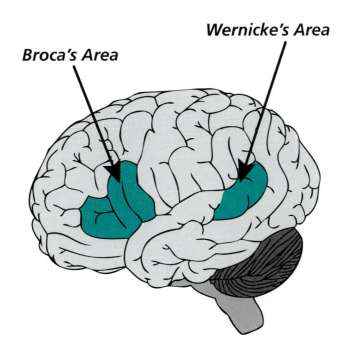

Broca's Area

Wernicke's Area

FIGURE 2.11

The brain has areas dedicated to specific tasks such as Broca's area, which controls the ability to speak, and Wernicke's area for auditory processing.

identification of items. Others are devoted to concepts or to a second language (Bransford et al., 2000). As we accumulate information on language development, we find that Chomsky's language-acquisition device is actually a complex interconnection of areas primarily in the left hemisphere of the brain. The interconnection among these areas and between the two hemispheres of the brain means that, in cases where the same type of brain injury occurs, the resulting disability can vary from patient to patient. Recently, research done on people with brain injuries has provided us with a more precise understanding of language development.

For some types of injuries, however, a precise understanding is not possible. For example, children with FAE generally have few to none of the overt characteristics of the brain damage that results from alcohol consumption during pregnancy. However, brain scans done on some of these children reveal actual holes—areas where there is no brain tissue (Conry & Fast, 2000) (Photo 2.11). If these holes occur in a language area or in a connection between areas, the student may exhibit difficulty in tasks ranging from identifying colors to putting together complete sentences with a subject, verb, and object. Due to the social implications of identifying a child with FAE, as was the case with Eve, these students are often subjected to years of frustrating remedial instruction in school, with few substantial results.

Stages of Language Development

Even though language development is a complicated process, we can artificially separate it into two parts: the structural aspect and the functional aspect. The

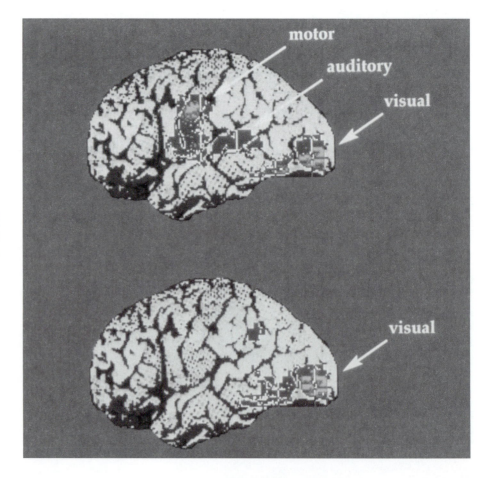

PHOTO 2.11

MRI scans show levels of activity in different areas of the brain.

structural aspect includes all the elements of grammar, as well as social and cultural rules related to communication, such as gestures and facial expressions. The *functional aspect* is the actual use of language to communicate ideas, think, and problem solve (see Info Byte 2.5).

As teachers, we also need to take into consideration the child's environment, or *speech community*. A speech community refers to the social and cultural language group within which the child lives. It influences word use, slang, intonations, sound variations, and so on. It once took one of the authors some time to understand a child when he talked about a "ruff." What he was actually talking about was a "roof." This child's particular pronunciation resulted from his speech community at home. Teachers always need to consider the speech community of the child when assessing speech and language capabilities. Without this awareness, local variations in rule systems of language could make it appear as though the student had a communication problem.

INFO BYTE 2.5

STRUCTURAL AND FUNCTIONAL ASPECTS OF LANGUAGE

STRUCTURAL ASPECT OF LANGUAGE

From a structural point of view, it is somewhat arguable exactly when the rudiments of language begin to develop. Analyses of the interaction between new mothers and infants claim a vocal interaction within 72 hours after birth (De Casper & Fifer, 1980). While this may be contested by experts, most mothers would likely confirm this bond between themselves and their infants. The time between birth and 2 years of age is devoted to acquiring the actual formation of words. The sequence of sound production generally follows this pattern:

Birth to 2 months: Infants make comforting, gurgling sounds.
2 to 4 months: Sounds are produced, but they are different from those of an adult due to the physiology of the infant's head:
4 to 7 months: Repetitious babbling (e.g., dadada). Deaf babies don't do this, suggesting experience with sound has an effect on language acquisition.
10 to 14 months: The pacing and rhythm of sound are acquired.
Approximately 13.5 months: First recognizable words are produced (e.g., Mama, Dada).

Usually, during this first year and a half babies communicate using sound (crying, cooing, etc.) and/or gestures, such as holding up their hands to indicate they want to be picked up. By the time the child has reached 24 months, she or he is capable of two-word combinations and has a vocabulary of over 200 words. At 3 years old, most children will have increased their vocabulary, expanded sentence structure, and learned to use questions and negatives. When the child has reached about 6 years of age, his mouth and palate will have developed so that the sounds produced will reflect the sounds of the adult language (Owens, 1988).

FUNCTIONAL ASPECT OF LANGUAGE

From a functional viewpoint, children absorb information about their world from the time they are born. As they interact with people, they pick up general information and place it in observable categories. For example, a child understands the category *dog* but may find the terms *collie* or *mammal* make no sense. One of the authors relates the story about a neighbor's child, Duncan, who, as a toddler, learned that his dog's name was *Daisy*. When his mother tried to teach him the names of flowers, Duncan would be sent into hysterical laughing at the patch of daisies along the road. He would very carefully explain to his mother that Daisy was a dog, not a flower. Not only does this example show us that the understanding children bring to their world relies on language, but it also underscores the importance of language in cognitive development.

Surfing Terms 2.2

Aphasia

Dialect

Apraxia

Mutism

Pragmatics

Semantics

Neurolinguistics

Sociolinguistics

Sign language

Dual language

Bilingual education

Literacy

Multiliteracies or multiple literacies

Language proficiency

Syntax

Reading

Whole-language approach

Basic skills and phonetic approach

Infinite generativity

Language versus communication

Cognitive Development

Our capacity to think and reflect on our thinking is the focus of the study of cognitive development. Two main questions drive this study (Flavell, Miller, & Miller, 1993, p. 3):

1. What does children's thinking look like at various points throughout development?   (the description question)
2. How does this development come about?   (the explanation question)

Defining Cognition   A basic definition of cognition is a dictionary definition: *cognition* refers to the process of knowing or perceiving, according to the *Concise Oxford Dictionary*. This definition provides a general overview of cognition, but does not give us much detail. In addition to knowledge and perception, cognition also includes the following:

- Memory of what we know and have perceived in the world around us
- Representation of knowledge and perceptions (e.g., in written, symbolic, or graphic form)
- Problem solving (Sternberg, 1999a)
- Intelligence, thinking, imagining, creating, planning and strategizing, classifying, and relating (Flavell et al., 1993)

Defining Cognitive Psychology   *Cognitive psychology* concerns itself with the study of the preceding concepts. It investigates the following:

- How we acquire knowledge (e.g., in mathematics, social reasoning, scientific reasoning, or narrative)
- Nature of the knowledge acquired
- How knowledge is influenced by the culture in which we live
- Ways of transmitting knowledge in that culture

Cognitive Psychology and Education   Fundamentally, cognitive psychology is concerned with "the mind as an object of study" (Sternberg, 1999a, p. viii). Educational psychology takes this study into the classroom. It asks questions about the following:

- How students represent knowledge
- How they solve problems
- How they perceive verbal and visual information
- How memory affects their learning
- How aware they are of their thought processes

Thinking about knowledge and our own and others' ways of thinking is at the heart of teaching.

Bruner's Models of Mind

Models of mind: How we think learning takes place

How we think about others' minds and how they develop is incredibly important to how we teach. Jerome Bruner (1996, pp. 53–63), an esteemed educational theorist, presented four *models of mind* and their pedagogical consequences:

1. *Children as imitative learners:* If we view children as *imitative learners* who need to acquire know-how, we assume a modeling role in teaching. We teach children the skills they need to function in particular social–

cultural settings by showing them and having them practice the skills. This model of mind does not focus on teaching for understanding (or "knowing that"), but on skill sets only. For example, if a teacher models science experiments for children and shows them how to write up the modeled experiments using the scientific method framework, the children may never come to understand the critical role of experimentation in science or learn from their own attempts to solve scientific problems. There is a serendipity to scientific discoveries that is often constrained by the need to fit science into a preset structure. The scientific method is a cultural tool. It needs to be united with children's own efforts to understand science, not the teacher's modeling of it, to encourage conceptual understanding (see model 4) (Kuhn, 1970).

2. *Learning through didactic exposure:* If we believe that children learn from *didactic exposure*, or exposure to anything that instructs, we take the position that there are knowledge sources, including the teacher's mind, that allow children to look up or hear what they need to know. In this model, "knowing how" is assumed to result from "knowing that." Thus, if we teach that area is equal to length times width, it is assumed that students will be able to calculate the area for any given surface. This model of mind sees the learner's mind as a *tabula rasa* (blank slate) waiting to be filled with facts dispensed by teachers, books, and the like.

> **Didactic:** Intended to instruct or explain

3. *Children as thinkers:* If we see children as *thinkers*, we teach in a way that reflects our curiosity about children's perspectives on learning, the curriculum, and school as a social–cultural milieu. This model of mind assumes that it is the child's capacity to reason and engage in discussion with others that results in learning (Photo 2.12). Underlying this approach to education is the teacher's effort to understand how children think, how they think about their own thinking, and how they remember and organize knowledge and learning.

In teaching young children about density, Bickerton (2000; Bickerton & Porath, 1997) engaged them in discussion about their experiences with boats. They then discussed what makes boats float before taking part in a boat contest. Their challenge was to design a boat that was seaworthy and

PHOTO 2.12

Students who are encouraged to discuss their ideas have rich insights about their learning.

could hold cargo. The children's discussion of the challenge, both with the teacher and each other, led to rich insights into the nature of their understanding and how they set about solving problems. Each child was encouraged to take on the role of scientist, including the framing and testing of hypotheses and thinking about his or her approach to boat design and sea trials.

4. *Personal versus objective cultural knowledge:* If we see children as needing to distinguish their own knowledge from the objective knowledge in their culture, we teach in a way that unites the previous perspective, children as thinkers, with study of the past. We help children understand what distinguishes personal knowledge from knowledge that has a history—"what is taken to be known" in our culture. We also strive to use children's ways of knowing in our instruction. We help them to build bridges between their own conceptions of knowledge and those of the culture.

Continuing with the previous example of density, this perspective unites the children's understanding of how boats float with study of the design of boats throughout history, including well-known nautical disasters, such as the *Titanic*. Discussion should be linked to children's observations in their own work, their experiences with boats, and their ways of solving problems involving buoyancy.

Models of Mind and Problem-Based Learning

Of the four models outlined by Bruner (1996), the fourth most closely parallels the philosophy of problem-based learning. Problem-based learning aims to help learners become aware of their own knowledge and to use this awareness to raise questions about what needs to be known in particular learning situations. It facilitates the *construction* of knowledge in terms that are meaningful to the learner.

Problem-based learning also aims to support self-directed learning by introducing learners to appropriate resources. Rather than defining teachers as dispensers of knowledge, problem-based learning incorporates tutors and resource people to help students make connections between their own understanding and the traditional knowledge of the culture.

The connection between personal knowledge and other sources of knowledge is critical. Personal knowledge based on our own experience and practice is important, but to be useful it "must be compared to knowledge from other sources, connected with knowledge based in research, and interwoven with knowledge derived from a theoretical perspective" (Snow, 2001, p. 8). As discussed in Chapter 1, the flow of knowledge is not unidirectional. The personal knowledge of excellent teachers, when made systematic, can enrich research-based and theoretical knowledge (Snow).

Theoretical Perspectives on Cognitive Development

In this section, overviews of the theories of two psychologists who played significant roles in describing cognition and learning, Jean Piaget and Lev Vygotsky, are presented. Key concepts related to each of these theories are introduced. In Chapter 3, we discuss how current work in educational psychology has built on the important work of Piaget and Vygotsky.

The principle underlying the presentation of theory in this and subsequent chapters is the degree of relevance to practice (the *theory–practice link*). Teachers need to have a rationale for the instructional, social, and behavioral support systems that they implement in their classrooms. Teachers are accountable to parents, administrators, and school boards. Understanding why you base some instruction on one theoretical approach and some on another is essential in making informed professional decisions.

Piaget's Theory of Cognition

Cognitive psychology attributes its tradition and direction as a field of study to the influence of Jean Piaget. Although his view of the nature and development of knowledge was not accepted universally, his theory and methods of investigation greatly influenced thinking and research into cognitive development. He was truly interested in why and how children think the way they do and in how thinking develops from infancy through adolescence.

Epistemology   Piaget became interested in *epistemology*, the theory of knowledge, while working in the laboratory of Theodore Simon in Paris in the early part of the 20th century. Simon, following up on work begun with Alfred Binet, was developing a test of reasoning. Piaget's task was to develop a French version of the test, which was in English (Ginsburg, 1997). This involved the administration of the test to many French children.

Piaget was fascinated by patterns in the children's test performance. Noticing that virtually all children of a particular age got the same items wrong on the multiple-choice test, he wondered what could account for their reasoning. (If they had guessed at the answers, 25% would have got the answers right simply by chance.) Rather than dismissing errors as straightforward mistakes, he posed the question of why children answered as they did: "I engaged my subjects in conversations . . . with the aim of discovering something about the reasoning process underlying their right, but especially their wrong answers" (Piaget, 1952, p. 244).

Piaget's Stages of Development

Following his work with Simon and his subsequent intense, detailed observations of his own three children from birth on (e.g., see Piaget, 1953), Piaget formulated a theory of intellectual development. The hallmark of Piaget's theory is that we progress through definite stages in cognitive development. Each stage is distinguished by the thought associated with it. Each stage builds on the previous one, integrating familiar ways of thinking with new abilities. The ages at which each of these stages are achieved are rough guidelines; their sequence, however, is believed to be invariant. Piaget outlined four stages of development (Table 2.1):

1. Sensorimotor stage
2. Preoperational stage
3. Concrete operational stage
4. Formal operational stage

Sensorimotor Stage   During infancy, thinking is simple and is bound to actions on the infant's environment. Piaget described the period from birth to approximately 2 years of age as the *sensorimotor stage*. In this stage, motor development becomes increasingly focused and purposeful, allowing infants to gain some control over their actions in their environment. Through these actions, infants come to learn about the world in which they live.

Between about 18 and 24 months of age, infants acquire a fully developed concept of *object permanence*. Before infants acquire this concept, a hidden object does not appear to exist for them. After developing object permanence,

TABLE 2.1

Piaget's Stages of Development

Stage	Approximate Age Range	Summary of Accomplishments (theoretical)	Summary of Accomplishments (practical)
Sensorimotor	Birth to 24 months	Vision coordinated with motor actions	Baby touches mobile over crib
		Reflexes refined into purposeful action as a result of experience	Baby bats mobile to get it to spin
		Efforts to learn about the world	Toddler verbally labels objects; insists on doing things independently
Preoperational	2 to 7 years of age	Symbolic–representational ability (pictures, models, words, and pretend play as standing for real objects or events)	Child builds a castle out of blocks; dresses up as mommy or daddy; draws stick figures
		Tendency to make judgments on the basis of appearance (e.g., big things are heavy)	The size of the box in which a birthday present is wrapped is the basis for judging the present's worth
		Knowledge of event sequences	Child knows the sequence of events for a visit to a fast-food restaurant
		Recognition of others' minds	Recognizes others' feelings; by the end of this stage, recognizes a relationship between thoughts, feelings, and behavior
		Simple numerical reasoning	Adds and subtracts small numbers
		Socially shared thinking	Preschoolers plan a game together
		Irreversibility of thought	Child watches as a clown shapes two equal-sized balloons into a snake for his brother and a pig for him; he cries loudly because his brother has the larger balloon
Concrete operational	7 to 11 years of age	Acquisition of operations that result in logical thinking (e.g., class inclusion)	Children now know that dogs are animals, tulips are flowers, and so on
		Operations applied to concrete objects or situations	Bundles of 10 popsicle sticks are used to teach the concept of place value
		Reversibility of thought	The child above knows that his "pig" is actually the same size as his brother's "snake." He is able to "think back" to the original balloon.
		Ability to take perspective	Children understand that others may have opinions different from their own
Formal operational	11 to 15 years of age	Ability to form hypotheses and think deductively	A student examines a science problem, hypothesizes an explanation, deduces whether the explanation is logical, then tests her theory
		Ability to reason with possibilities	An adolescent girl thinks of all the possible reasons that her friend has rejected her, then reasons that only two of the reasons are viable
		Ability to think abstractly	An adolescent sees the political implications of Orwell's *Animal Farm*

Source: Based on Flavell et al., 1993.

they actively seek out toys and other objects when they are under a blanket or behind a couch. This concept is fundamental to our beliefs about ourselves and objects in the world; if we do not believe that objects and people continue to exist when they are out of our sight, life will be irrational (Flavell et al., 1993).

Preoperational Stage   During the *preoperational stage*, from approximately 2 to 7 years of age, children begin to use *representations* to think about their world. Language, drawings, movement or gestures, and mental images are understood to stand for (or represent) objects and events (Flavell et al., 1993). Thinking is highly influenced by perception (e.g., judgments about weight are made on the basis of size: big is heavy; small is light) (Case, 1985).

Piaget believed that thinking at this stage is *egocentric*. Although it is true that young children relate events to their own experience, they are capable of understanding others' feelings or points of view (e.g., Astington, 1993; Case, 1992). However, children at this stage usually are not able to include understanding of others' feelings or points of view in explanations for their actions and behavior (Case & Okamoto, 1996; Porath, 2001).

During the preoperational stage, children demonstrate thought that is irreversible (Flavell et al., 1993). That is, appearances are everything. If one preschooler receives a cup of juice in a shallow, wide cup while her friend gets the same amount of juice in a tall, thin glass, she thinks her friend has more juice. Seeing the juice poured back into the cup will not convince her otherwise.

Egocentric: A viewpoint centered completely on one's self that ignores others' points of view (not to be confused with egotistic)

Concrete Operational Stage   During the *concrete operational stage*, from approximately 7 to 11 years of age, children acquire *operations*—"systems of internal mental actions that underlie logical thinking" (Flavell et al., 1993, p. 133). These operations include class inclusion (dogs are part of the larger concept "animal") and taking the perspective of others. They also include various types of conservation:

- *Number:* 10 beads are 10 beads whether they are placed close together or far apart.
- *Liquid quantity:* two equal amounts of water remain equal despite one being poured into a container of a different shape.
- *Length:* two strings of equal length remain equal when one is moved to the left of the other).

A classic Piagetian experiment on conservation of amount involves presenting a child with two balls of clay of the same size. One ball is rolled into a sausage shape in front of the child. The child is then asked which piece of clay is bigger. In the preoperational stage, because of their reliance on appearance, children tend to say that the sausage-shaped piece of clay is bigger, even though they agreed earlier that the pieces were the same size. In the concrete operational stage, in reaction to the same experiment, children look amazed that any adult would be so foolish as to ask the question of which piece is bigger.

During this stage, children also become capable of reversible thinking. They understand that actions can be reversed or *undone*. In the experiment just described, they understand that the clay can be returned to its original shape. Children also acquire the capacity to take another's perspective. The logical thinking that children demonstrate in this stage is applied to concrete situations. Hypothetical thinking, however, is difficult for children in the concrete operational stage of development.

Formal Operational Stage   The final stage of development hypothesized by Piaget is the *formal operational stage*. In this stage, from approximately 11 to 15 years of age, adolescents acquire the ability to think abstractly. (See Chapter 3, however, in which we discuss the low percentage of adolescents who actually acquire formal operational thinking.) Children in this stage are capable of framing hypotheses, thinking deductively, reasoning in the absence of concrete objects (Flavell et al., 1993), and thinking interpretively (Case & Okamoto, 1996). They begin to think in terms of possibilities, rather than being bound by reality, as in the concrete operational stage.

Educational Implications of Piaget's Theory

Student teachers often want to know how Piaget's theory applies to their teaching. Although Piaget's theory has been criticized for its lack of direct applicability to curriculum, in a general sense the theory informs teachers about the characteristics of thought at different age levels. Teachers' observations tell them that there is something "first-grade-like" about 6-year-olds and "seventh-grade-like" about preadolescents. School staff room conversations contain references to how teachers understand and accommodate the different stages of development in early and middle childhood and adolescence. Piaget's theory can help teachers build on this intuitive knowledge by offering specific examples of how children of different ages think.

Concrete Thinking   In the early and middle elementary years, children think concretely. They need direct experience with objects, such as counters in mathematics and meaningful materials in science. They need to have new concepts related to their own experience. This need is especially critical during the early years of formal schooling when children's thinking is tied very closely to their own experiences. One of the authors explains:

> *"A kindergarten student informed me that she would soon be six years old. Since I work regularly with a small group of children in her class on a research project and would likely be there for her birthday, I asked her when her birthday was. She replied emphatically, 'When I'm six is my birthday.' She seemed to think I just didn't get the idea of birthdays."*

Deductive and Hypothetical Reasoning   In preadolescence, children begin to acquire the ability to think in more formal, logical terms; to reason without reference to concrete objects or events, to think hypothetically; and to reason deductively. Instruction is critical in helping children acquire formal thought (Inhelder & Piaget, 1958).

Children and adolescents cannot acquire the formal knowledge of disciplines in a culture without teaching. However, the nature of the teaching is critical in building conceptual understanding of a discipline. Did you ever learn mathematical formulas or historical facts without acquiring a conceptual understanding of mathematics or history? Bruner's (1996) four models of mind are critical to remember here. To help learners truly understand a discipline, they must be respected as thinkers who have relevant questions and experiences that can be used as building blocks for the construction of conceptual understanding.

Spiral Curriculum   In addition, the hierarchical and integrative nature of Piaget's theory translates into the notion of a *spiral curriculum* (Bruner, 1996). A spiral curriculum acknowledges that concepts are revisited periodically during the period of formal schooling, with each new exposure incorporating and building on the previous one, while moving to a more sophisticated level of understanding.

Piaget's Theory of Constructivism

The core of Piaget's theory of intellectual development was that we construct knowledge through our actions on and in our environments. Children have certain ways of thinking about the world:

- When engaged in play or schooling, children *assimilate* new experiences to their existing knowledge.
- Children also *accommodate*, or modify, existing ways of thinking to incorporate new knowledge.
- Both assimilation and accommodation allow us to *adapt* to our environment; adaptation is a state of *equilibrium* between assimilation and accommodation (Piaget, 1953).

To Piaget (1981), intelligence was equilibrium. In other words, when we act intelligently, our thinking is organized so that we both assimilate and accommodate new information. Piaget saw children and adolescents as scientists engaged in thought experiments that allow successive adaptations to their intellectual worlds.

The educational analogy of this type of intellectual activity is known as *constructivism*. The constructivist philosophy of education takes into account the child's ways of thinking and learning when planning instruction. The child's ways of knowing are used as starting points for education. At its most basic level, constructivism is the common sense that says we don't teach abstract concepts like government to first-graders. However, we can present more concrete notions like community and jobs within the community, things relevant to 6-year-olds, that serve as building blocks for their eventual construction of the more abstract notions of community systems and government.

Teaching from a Constructivist Perspective

Teaching in a constructivist way involves the active engagement of learners. Because learners are seen as bringing knowledge and experience to school, their points of view are taken into account. Learners are not vessels into which knowledge is to be poured and then absorbed; instead, they are involved in a knowledge-building enterprise with educators. Learning and teaching, from the constructivist perspective, are highly active processes.

As teachers, you will need to *design* rather than *plan* lessons (Arlin, 1993). A design allows you to be flexible in responding to the learners in your classroom. It is just as well articulated as a plan, but is notable for its capacity to change as the lesson evolves. Rather than being linear in nature, a design allows for doubling back, fast forwarding, and using feedback loops. It results in a dynamic, rather than passive, learning experience.

Combining Different Philosophies of Teaching You might ask, "But, as a teacher, don't I have a responsibility to tell my students what they need to know? Doesn't constructivist teaching take up a lot of time and energy that I could use to teach children the answers they need?" The answer is yes to both questions, if you teach from a model of mind that sees children as learning from imitation or didactic exposure.

A more qualified positive answer is that, of course, some information simply needs to be given to children and adolescents. Models of mind aren't mutually exclusive. However, if children are to acquire true understanding, they need educational experiences that build in opportunities not only to acquire,

Surfing Terms 2.3

Tabula rasa

Imitation

Exemplary practice

Sensorimotor development

Preoperational stage

Concrete operations

Formal operations

Postformal operations

Perspective taking

Spiral curriculum

Schema

Assimilation

Accommodation

Animism

Centration

Transitivity

Hypotheticodeductive reasoning

Neo-Piagetian

or receive, knowledge, but also to understand, apply, analyze, synthesize, and evaluate knowledge (Bloom, 1956a) (see Info Byte 2.6). Students need to know that their own points of view are respected and that these points of view constitute valid starting places for learning (Paley, 1986). The time and energy devoted to constructivist teaching is well worth the outcome—engaged learners and teachers.

Tailoring Theories to Individual Students   One of a teacher's greatest challenges occurs with students who do not seem to develop cognitively in the manner outlined by theorists. The school curriculum is based on the work of the theorists just discussed. This means that, for a number of students, there is a mismatch between curriculum and cognitive capabilities. For Eve, the mismatch is exacerbated by the damage resulting from a birth mother with a drug and alcohol habit (see Problem-Based Scenario 2.6). Teachers need to be aware of some of the learning challenges students encounter in these circumstances. Also, they need to be prepared to make curricular modifications that consider the specific needs of an individual student. The following narrative gives you a chance to revisit some of the issues you discussed about Jay, but with an emphasis on cognitive development and school achievement.

Earlier in the chapter you met Dylan, a physically mature first-grader. The following glimpse of Dylan gives you the opportunity to think about his cognitive development (see Problem-Based Scenario 2.7). In this case, the curriculum cannot quite keep up with Dylan. Modifications for students like Dylan require a teacher as dedicated as Eve's teacher, Marilyn. Often teachers overlook students

---

INFO BYTE 2.6

Bloom's Taxonomy of Educational Objectives

In 1956, Benjamin Bloom and a number of other researchers published a Taxonomy of Educational Objectives, an organization of objectives that is still used today. The intent of the publication was to facilitate communication about educational goals. The book presented six educational objectives in a hierarchy from simple (knowledge) to complex (evaluation). The taxonomy is useful in helping teachers understand and balance the demands of different educational tasks.

- Level 1: Knowledge. Recall of specific, isolated bits of information, terminology, facts, conventions, trends, categories, criteria, methods of inquiry, and principles.

Levels 2 to 6: Intellectual Abilities and Skills

- Level 2: **Comprehension.** Lowest level of understanding. Knowledge and use of what is being communicated without relating it to other material or recognizing implications. Translation, interpretation, inference.
- Level 3: **Application.** Use of abstract concepts (e.g., general ideas or principles, theories) in specific, concrete situations.
- Level 4: **Analysis.** Recognition of assumptions; ability to distinguish fact from opinion; ability to determine whether an argument is logical; recognition of propaganda and advertising strategies.
- Level 5: **Synthesis.** Putting together elements in a coherent way; organization of ideas; planning; ability to generate hypotheses and revise them in light of new information.
- Level 6: **Evaluation.** Judgments based on internal evidence (accuracy of facts, logic of argument); judgments based on external criteria (comparison of theories or cultures; comparison to standards of excellence in a particular field).

Source: Based on Bloom, 1956, pp. 201–267.

Problem-Based Scenario 2.6

Student: Eve
Teacher: Marilyn

Marilyn enjoyed her chats with Mr. and Mrs. Dominic. Their daughter, Eve, was one of the most pleasant young ladies in the ninth-grade class, at least up until now. During eighth grade Eve was an enthusiastic student, even when she was having troubles grasping some of the more abstract ideas in class. But now, in ninth grade, things had changed. The parent interview this time included the counselor, Jeff Grimes, at the request of Eve's parents. During the discussion it became evident that Eve was having considerable trouble with abstract concepts in all her classes. In the previous grades this hadn't been a problem, since most of the curriculum was concrete and she could get by without having to manipulate the more abstract ideas.

Lately, however, problems were arising. Mr. Dominic spoke in strictest confidence to Marilyn. As Mr. Dominic put it, "This wasn't anyone's business—it stayed within the family." Eve was adopted, and at the time of the adoption knowing that Eve's birth mother was an alcoholic with a crack cocaine addic-

tion seemed irrelevant. Eve was a beautiful baby and seemed to have none of the characteristics of fetal alcohol or drug abuse. Now, however, some learning problems were surfacing. Not only was Eve having problems in school, but she had started to talk about dropping out of high school when she turned 16. Her best friend, Maria, was talking about dropping out as well, since she was having so many difficulties at school. The problem was building, and since both Eve and Maria were inseparable partners in the same English class, everyone was hoping that Marilyn could help.

Apply

- How do Piaget's stages of development help you understand Eve?
- Is the spiral curriculum a useful concept in thinking about how to help Eve?
- Are there strategies in the research on fetal alcohol abuse that would be helpful?

such as Dylan, thinking that the student will eventually work things out on his or her own. But this is not true; students such as Dylan need as much attention from their teacher as does Eve.

Vygotsky's Theory of Social Interaction and Learning

In addition to his contribution to understanding language development, Lev Vygotsky's work has been influential in our consideration of sociocultural influences on learning. Vygotsky studied the role of adults and more capable older children and adolescents in communicating the intellectual tools of the culture to younger children. Whereas Piaget focused on the individual in interaction with his or her environment, Vygotsky believed that society was an important and essential factor in shaping knowledge. For Vygotsky, social interaction played a central role in learning.

Rather than concentrating on a *static* description of children's thinking, as Piaget did, Vygotsky was interested in how far a child could progress with the help of an adult or older child. His approach is described as *dynamic* because it is concerned not simply with what children know, but with how their knowledge can be extended and elaborated with guidance. While Piaget encouraged children to elaborate on their answers to problems, his method concentrated on eliciting as full a picture as possible of children's ways of understanding without actually teaching them.

Problem-Based Scenario 2.7

K-5   6-8   9-12   SpEd

Student: *Dylan*

Teacher: *Shelley*

Dylan and his classmates were very excited about the guest speaker who was due to arrive at their first-grade classroom any minute. They were gathered on the rug in front of an armchair, all set to welcome the visitor from the zoo. The big attraction was that he was bringing a boa constrictor and a lizard. The children had just completed a science unit on reptiles. This visit was the culminating activity. Shelley told her pupils that the visitor would give them a chance to ask questions. She drilled the class on what "good questions" were and on how questions differed from "telling." As a class, they had practiced asking questions several times before the guest speaker's visit. Now all that seemed forgotten as hands waved and excited voices told of experiences with snakes and lizards.

Shelley had counted on Dylan, at least, to ask good questions or show off his knowledge a little bit, but he was far more interested in telling the guest speaker about his cousin's lizard and the time he got

to feed it. Dylan was a walking encyclopedia of knowledge about reptiles. He knew facts and figures that challenged Shelley, his teacher. She was amazed to hear him join the chorus of little voices that had to tell their guest about family members and friends that had snakes and lizards or about the reptiles they had seen in zoos.

Apply

- What would Vygotsky say about Dylan's interaction with the guest speaker?
- What model of mind did Shelley demonstrate in teaching the class about "good questions"? How might this have affected the way the children interacted with the visitor?
- How does this practice-based narrative consider special educational needs?

PHOTO 2.13

Dylan loves to talk about lizards to his friends.

The Construction Zone   Piaget used prompts and questions to draw out children's reasons for responding as they did. Their justifications for their answers were considered significant indicators of their way of thinking. Piaget was interested in the nature of children's thought, but not in terms of education. Vygotsky, in contrast, used children's knowledge as the basis for teaching. He was interested in how far children could progress from the understanding they expressed initially. In a Vygotskian approach to education, children's knowledge is taken as a starting point for instruction that continues until no further learning takes place. Vygotsky called this the *zone of proximal development*: "It is the distance between the actual developmental level as determined by independent problem solving and the level of potential development as determined through problem solving under adult guidance or in collaboration with more capable peers" (Vygotsky, 1978, p. 86).

Teachers sometimes refer to the zone of proximal development as the *construction zone*, the zone in which children can move forward in constructing knowledge.

Scaffolding   Also using the building metaphor, another kind of help offered to children by adults or capable older learners is known as *scaffolding* (Photo 2.14). Scaffolding involves providing active support during instruction, while continually taking account of the child's responses. For example, one author showed children a pattern of letters (e.g., A X B X C . . .) and then asked them to predict what letters came next:

> First, I asked the children if they had ever seen a problem like that before. If they had, they were asked how they had solved that problem

PHOTO 2.14
Adult-child interaction with literature actively supports learning.

Surfing Terms 2.4

- Social constructivism
- Community of learners
- Dynamic assessment
- Hidden curriculum
- Peers
- Popular children
- Neglected children
- Rejected children
- School–family partnership

Social responsibility: Individual wants and needs are understood in the wider social context; responsibility is taken for the good of the community

and if that solution might help them solve the current problem. If children had not seen a similar problem or if their recall of a previous problem did not yield a specific strategy, they were asked to read the letters out loud to see if patterns could be heard. If that strategy didn't help, they were asked if there were any alphabetical or repeating patterns. Finally, specific clues such as the insertion of the first missing letter were given. (Ferrara, Brown, & Campione, as cited in Porath, 1988)

Vygotsky drew our attention to the important role of social interaction in learning. Research done within a Vygotskian perspective asks the following kinds of questions:

- How do mothers' interactions with their children facilitate or impede effective problem solving?
- How do different societies approach education?
- How do different approaches to education influence what is achieved and how it is achieved?
- How do children function as a community of learners under their teacher's guidance?

Piaget's approach to understanding children's intellectual development has been characterized, perhaps unfairly, as individualistic (DeVries, 1997; Youniss & Damon, 1992). Vygotsky's approach, on the other hand, recognizes the importance of the social context of learning. Vygotsky made the link between the nature of cognition and society.

Social and Emotional Development

How we develop as social and emotional beings has consequences for how we learn. Children's temperaments, family structure, social support, early socialization experiences, and emotional well-being all contribute to their adjustment and achievement in school. Social development and academic development are intertwined. Children who begin school able to interact effectively with their peers and teachers and to adjust and adhere to school routines and procedures for conduct tend to do better academically. These children have a better chance of acquiring the prosocial behaviors necessary for effective adjustment in our complex world (Eisenberg, 1992). Their *social responsibility* also contributes to successful academic achievement (Wentzel, 1993).

Emotional and social development also are closely related, as our social experience contributes to our emotional experience (Saarni, 1999).

Emotional Intelligence   Emotional intelligence (also referred to as *emotional competence*) is critical to healthy development. *Emotional intelligence* is an awareness of one's own emotional self, that is, the ability to manage one's own emotions, read the emotions of others, and navigate the complexities of interpersonal relationships (Photo 2.15). Emotional intelligence is believed to be as important, if not more important, than IQ in determining success in school, career, and relationships (Goleman, 1995).

Emotional intelligence contributes to self-efficacy, self-awareness, self-esteem, empathy and sympathy for others, and adaptive coping (Saarni, 1999), all of which have implications for school adjustment and achievement. Teachers often question how children can learn effectively when they repeatedly arrive at

PHOTO 2.15
Emotional well-being is important to school success.

school emotionally upset. The curriculum doesn't hold much relevance for a child whose family is unstable or who has witnessed violence. Researchers have increasingly recognized the importance of emotional well-being for effective learning and overall success, leading to an increased emphasis on emotional learning in schools (e.g., Goleman, 1995; Salovey & Sluyter, 1997).

In addition to children's own social and emotional characteristics, the social and emotional contexts of schooling are themselves powerful influences on learning. Teachers' understanding of their students' social and emotional development and their design of supportive, caring classroom environments have important educational consequences. Classroom environments that emphasize autonomy, cooperation, and caring encourage children to be motivated to learn (e.g., Lickona, 1991). In addition, knowing students' perspectives on what happens in their classrooms is critical. Students' perceptions of classroom practices predict achievement and motivation far better than do teachers' perspectives (Paris & Ayres, 1994). For example, if students perceive that their teacher is interested in learning and respects their approaches to learning, they are motivated to achieve. On the other hand, if a teacher "shoots down" students' ideas, it is a signal to the student to conform to the teacher's viewpoint.

Subsequent chapters provide more detail on the various aspects of development presented here. In these later chapters, related concepts, such as intelligence, creativity, gender, exceptional learning needs, motivation, and assessment, are presented. The importance of social and cultural influences on teaching and learning also are considered. For now, Problem-Based Scenario 2.8 gives you a chance to think about social–emotional development and its effect on learning.

As you meet Mike in his ninth-grade science class, think about the social–emotional consequences of his misunderstanding the lesson being taught. Consider in Mike's case how cognition and social development can interact. During planning sessions, teachers take into consideration the curriculum and the cognitive stages of their students, as we discussed earlier. But students often throw curves at teachers in some other area of development. The social–emotional aspect of students' lives needs to be considered, especially during adolescence, when peers are so prominent in their lives.

Problem-Based Scenario *2.8*

Student: *Mike*

Teacher: *Marilyn*

The teacher's staff room was always noisy at lunchtime. Marilyn was sitting beside Barry, the ninth-grade science teacher. Several teachers were laughing as Barry talked about his second-period class. It seems that Mike Dawson really "blew it" in front of his friends today. At 6'1", Mike was not only tall for his age, but also sought after by the ninth-grade girls due to what Marilyn's grandmother would have called "rugged good looks." Being on the basketball team only added to the leading social position he held in the high school.

Barry had been covering asexual reproduction in molds during the class. He explained that he had not only given out diagrams, but had also put quite a bit of information on the board. Everything was going well, so Barry thought, when Mike raised his hand. Barry called on him to ask his question. Apparently, Barry had to ask him several times to repeat or rephrase the question. It just didn't make sense. Unfortunately, at the same moment that it dawned on Barry what was being asked, it also dawned on the class. The question referred to human sexual reproduction, not molds. That's when the laughing began.

Barry had tried to calm the class down. Even though he asked to see Mike after class, it was too late. The other students told Mike that human reproduction was different from molds and "how couldn't he know that!" Mike didn't stick around after class. The question, which Marilyn missed, elicited a lot of laughing around the lunch table as well. Barry was going to try to track Mike down after he ate so that things could get cleared up. Barry also wondered out loud how many other students really didn't understand what was being done in the class.

Marilyn thought about how she was struggling with metaphors in English, a classic abstract concept, and wondered if this could be the same thing. And what about her afternoon class with Mike? Was she assuming her students understood, just like Barry had in his science class? How could she find out without causing the social–emotional chaos that occurred by accident in the science class? There had to be some way to find out before she continued with her planned lesson. There certainly was no use having them write their own metaphors if they really didn't understand what one was to start with. And how about Mike? This had to have been devastating to him.

Apply

- What would Piaget say about Mike's experience?
- As a teacher, Marilyn needs to consider making some alterations to her plans because of an incident earlier in the school day. Teachers often need to take the entire day's events into their planning, particularly in secondary schools where there might be a tendency to consider only the subjects being taught, not the students who come into these classes. If you were Marilyn, how would you approach Mike to talk about what had happened in science class?

Problem-Based Scenarios 2.9 and 2.10 allow you to apply your knowledge of development to the context of the whole classroom. In the first of these scenarios, Dylan's first-grade classmates complain about his behavior. In Problem-Based Scenario 2.10, Sean, Eve, and Maria are part of a ninth-grade English class in which students present a variety of learning needs. Both scenarios present the challenge of balancing students' individual needs with the group needs of the classroom.

Problem-Based Scenario *2.9*

Student: *Dylan*
Teacher: *Shelley*

Shelley Lim worked hard the 2 weeks before spring break to get new learning centers organized for after the holiday. Her students now were very comfortable with this way of learning, and she was proud of the way they had grown in independence. However, Dylan was always in the back of Shelley's mind as she did her planning. She felt that, despite all her thinking and trying of various strategies, she still hadn't really reached Dylan in a way that made a difference to his adjustment to school.

Shelley could hear the all too familiar comments in her head. They were most evident as the children worked in partners at centers or in groups during science activities. "Ms. Lim, Dylan's bossing me around. He won't listen." "Does Dylan have to work with us? He's mean." "Dylan says we're dumb. He's going to do his own science." Dylan had no friends in the class. Was it his size? His aggression? What was going on anyway?

Apply

- Are there other questions Shelley could ask to help her focus her thinking about Dylan?
- What might Dylan's perspective be? How could you find out?

Problem-Based Scenario *2.10*

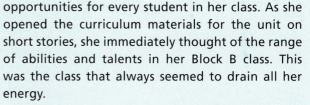

Students: *Sean, Eve, and Others*
Teacher: *Marilyn*

Marilyn had been teaching ninth-grade English for 6 years. Each year had become easier in certain respects. The curriculum was so familiar that she could anticipate problems, and in most instances she had a small bag of tricks to tackle these moments. What had started to take time lately was trying to reach more students who needed the extra help and attention. For the first couple of years, many of them just coasted through her class. While Marilyn was aware of these students, she was so busy trying to keep up with the curriculum, the rest of the students in the class, and all the ongoing paperwork that these students had taken a bit of a back seat.

Over the summer Marilyn had taken a course on students with special needs and had started to compile a resource file for students with various types of needs. Although her file was starting to look pretty complete, it quickly became apparent that putting all these ideas into a lesson plan for the entire classroom wasn't as easy as the books implied. However, Marilyn was determined to write lessons that provided opportunities for every student in her class. As she opened the curriculum materials for the unit on short stories, she immediately thought of the range of abilities and talents in her Block B class. This was the class that always seemed to drain all her energy.

Marilyn thought back to the parent interviews she had had the week before. The Block B English class had included Sean Murphy, Eve Dominic, and her friend, Maria Gonzaga, as well as 27 other students. How could she design a unit to accommodate not only these students, but also the three exceptionally bright (and often bored) boys, the five girls who sat at the back of the room and did as little as possible, and the three ESL students?

All these students did the assigned work, but Marilyn wasn't sure how interested they were in her course. How could she convey some of the passion she had for literature? What could she design for this unit that would span the variety of talents and interests of these students? After the unit on metaphors, Marilyn

(continued)

Problem-Based Scenario 2.10 *(continued)*

realized there was about a quarter of the class who had little difficulty with abstract thinking. But others in the class struggled gamely by memorizing and just doing the best they could with the unit text. And, finally, what about all the information she had obtained during the parent interviews? Could she use any of it?

Apply

- Marilyn has quite a few questions about how to teach her class and a lot of different learning needs in the class. What might be a realistic start?
- How can Marilyn evaluate the teaching strategies she tries? When should she do this?

Summary

Throughout this chapter you saw how complex it is to discuss only one aspect of an individual's development. You also found that the definitions used for various forms of development can vary depending on the viewpoint of the author or researcher. As a result, a teacher must work along a continuum of competing theories, finding from among the extremes a balance that most closely resembles the student. The student, and not the theory, thus becomes the focus of the teacher's thinking.

A Metacognitive Challenge

You should now be able to reflect on the following questions:

- How do I define development?
- What do I know about physical development? How does it influence the social and academic lives of students?
- What do I know about language development? Could I explain the connection between language acquisition and thought development?
- What do I know about cognitive development?
- How do social and emotional development affect learning?

Artifacts for Problem-Based Scenarios

FIGURE 2.2 ■ Artifact for Problem-Based Scenareo 2.1

To: Ralph Tsortis, Counselor
From: Vicky McElvy
Re: Jay Thomas
Date: Oct. 14, 1998

Enclosed is the list of behaviors I expect from Jay in English 9.

• Must be on time to class.

• Must have books and materials.

• Must complete all in-class and homework assignments.

• Must not interfere or interrupt other students working.

• Must work cooperatively with others during group work.

• Must not leave the room without permission and must come back
  in a specified time.

In the past I have found Jay responds well to the following "rewards" for
appropriate behavior. But these rewards lose their appeal quickly.

• Getting to do his work differently from other students; e.g., using
  colored paper or writing in point form.

• Getting to go to the library or deliver a message for me.

• Being allowed to give or to read a report first.

FIGURE 2.2 ■ Artifact for Problem-Based Scenario 2.1 (continued)

Jay does not seem to respond to praise or to an appeal for personal satisfaction. While he can be very charming, he does not appear to have a desire to please anyone unless it seems to serve his own needs.

P.S. Despite all that has happened, I still like Jay. Please let me know how I can help. He is an intelligent young man with a lot of potential, which makes it so hard to see him headed in such a self-destructive direction.

FIGURE 2.4 ■ Yetta's Individualized Education Plan (IEP)

North Ashland School Board
INDIVIDUALIZED EDUCATION PLAN

Date: _October 1999_

Name (last /first):

Clarke , Yetta

Birthdate: _84/04/22_   Age: _15_   Sex: _F_

Home Address:

237 Parkhurst Drive

North Ashland

School: _Ashland Secondary_

Grade or Program: _10_

Classroom Teacher: _Dianne Collie_

Parent / Guardian:

Carol & Mark Clarke

Hearing Res. Teacher: _Joanne Embleton_

Transportation: _n/a_

Parent / Guardian Phone #:

_635 - 2114_

Emergency Phone #:

639 - 8212 (Dad's work)

Parent Signature: _Carol Clarke_

First Language: _English / ASL_

School History: _For Preschool Yetta attended the Mt. Seymour Deaf Children's Development Centre. She has attended the Provincial School for the Deaf since kindergarten._

Siblings / Ages: _Calvin 13 yr._

Social Factors:

Group/Foster Home & Phone #:

Social Worker & Phone #:

Medical Alert/Conditions:

Yetta has a profound bilateral sensorineural hearing loss which she acquired at the age of 3½ due to meningitis.

Support Services & Specialized Equipment:

Yetta receives full-time support services from the educational interpreter, as well as direct services from the Hearing Resource Teacher and the Skills Development Teacher.

FIGURE 2.4 ■ Yetta's Individualized Education Plan (IEP) (continued)

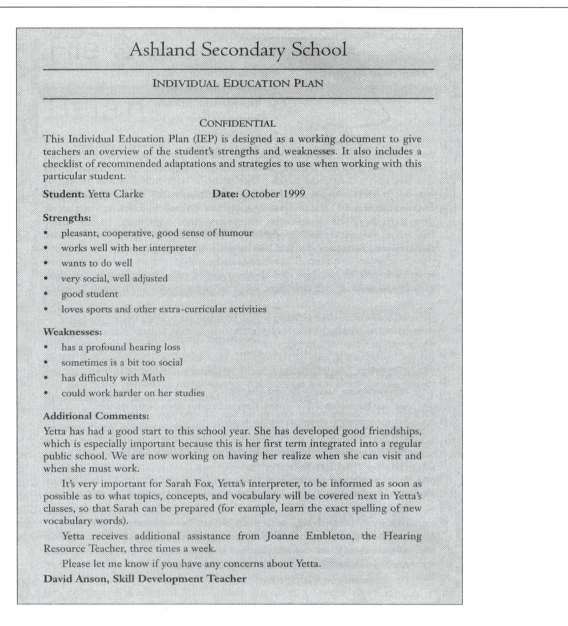

Ashland Secondary School

INDIVIDUAL EDUCATION PLAN

CONFIDENTIAL

This Individual Education Plan (IEP) is designed as a working document to give teachers an overview of the student's strengths and weaknesses. It also includes a checklist of recommended adaptations and strategies to use when working with this particular student.

Student: Yetta Clarke   **Date:** October 1999

Strengths:

- pleasant, cooperative, good sense of humour
- works well with her interpreter
- wants to do well
- very social, well adjusted
- good student
- loves sports and other extra-curricular activities

Weaknesses:

- has a profound hearing loss
- sometimes is a bit too social
- has difficulty with Math
- could work harder on her studies

Additional Comments:

Yetta has had a good start to this school year. She has developed good friendships, which is especially important because this is her first term integrated into a regular public school. We are now working on having her realize when she can visit and when she must work.

It's very important for Sarah Fox, Yetta's interpreter, to be informed as soon as possible as to what topics, concepts, and vocabulary will be covered next in Yetta's classes, so that Sarah can be prepared (for example, learn the exact spelling of new vocabulary words).

Yetta receives additional assistance from Joanne Embleton, the Hearing Resource Teacher, three times a week.

Please let me know if you have any concerns about Yetta.

David Anson, Skill Development Teacher

FIGURE 2.4 ■ Yetta's Individualized Education Plan (IEP) (continued)

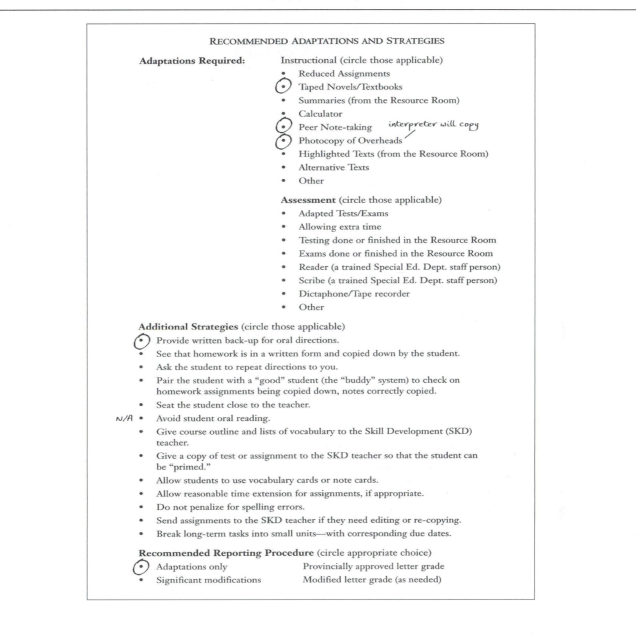

RECOMMENDED ADAPTATIONS AND STRATEGIES

Adaptations Required: Instructional (circle those applicable)

- Reduced Assignments
- (•) Taped Novels/Textbooks
- Summaries (from the Resource Room)
- Calculator
- (•) Peer Note-taking   *interpreter will copy*
- (•) Photocopy of Overheads
- Highlighted Texts (from the Resource Room)
- Alternative Texts
- Other

Assessment (circle those applicable)

- Adapted Tests/Exams
- Allowing extra time
- Testing done or finished in the Resource Room
- Exams done or finished in the Resource Room
- Reader (a trained Special Ed. Dept. staff person)
- Scribe (a trained Special Ed. Dept. staff person)
- Dictaphone/Tape recorder
- Other

Additional Strategies (circle those applicable)

- (•) Provide written back-up for oral directions.
- See that homework is in a written form and copied down by the student.
- Ask the student to repeat directions to you.
- Pair the student with a "good" student (the "buddy" system) to check on homework assignments being copied down, notes correctly copied.
- Seat the student close to the teacher.
- *N/A* • Avoid student oral reading.
- Give course outline and lists of vocabulary to the Skill Development (SKD) teacher.
- Give a copy of test or assignment to the SKD teacher so that the student can be "primed."
- Allow students to use vocabulary cards or note cards.
- Allow reasonable time extension for assignments, if appropriate.
- Do not penalize for spelling errors.
- Send assignments to the SKD teacher if they need editing or re-copying.
- Break long-term tasks into small units—with corresponding due dates.

Recommended Reporting Procedure (circle appropriate choice)

- (•) Adaptations only   Provincially approved letter grade
- Significant modifications   Modified letter grade (as needed)

FIGURE 2.5 ■ Student Background Form: Hannah

Student Background

Name: Hannah Page

Age: 7

Address: 62 Ryder Lane #201

Phone: 555-0011

Mother's Name: Sheila Lundquist

Address (if different from above): _____

Work: _____ Home: 555-0011

Father's Name: Ted Page

Address (if different from above): Unknown

Work: _____ Home: _____

Legal Guardian: _____

Work: _____ Home: _____

Family Information: Younger brother, age 2

School	Year	Grade	Placement
Rivercrest Elementary	1996-97	K	Full day
Rivercrest Elementary	1997-	1	Multi-age K-2
Pearson Elementary	1998	1	1/LAC 1x/wk.
Pearson Elementary	1998-99	2	2/LAC 3x/wk.

FIGURE 2.6 ■ Student Background Form: Holly

Student Background

Name: Holly Page

Age: 7

Address: 62 Ryder Lane #201

Phone: 555-0011

Mother's Name: Sheila Lundquist

Address
(if different from above):

Work: _____   Home: 555-0011

Father's Name: Ted Page

Address
(if different from above): Unknown

Work: _____   Home: _____

Legal Guardian: _____

Work: _____   Home: _____

Family Information: Younger brother, age 2

School	Year	Grade	Placement
Rivercrest Elementary	1996-97	K	Full day
Rivercrest Elementary	1997-	1	Multi-age K-2
Pearson Elementary	1998	1	1/LAC 1x/wk.
Pearson Elementary	1998-99	2	2/LAC 3x/wk.

FIGURE 2.6  **Student Background Form: Holly (continued)**

Medical History: *Normal development reported by mother. Healthy.*

Medications: *None.*

FIGURE 2.7 ■ Formal Assessment Record: Hannah

Hannah P.
Div. 16

Formal Assessments

Type	Evaluator	Date
PPVT-R	Lana Van Dyck (LAC)	May 12, 1998

Result
79th. percentile

Type	Evaluator	Date
Woodcock-Johnson	Lana Van Dyck (LAC)	May 19, 1998

Result		
Letter-word identification	81	(10th. percentile)
Word attack	76	(5th. percentile)
Passage comprehension	82	(12th. percentile)

Type	Evaluator	Date

Result

Type	Evaluator	Date

Result

FIGURE 2.8 ■ Formal Assessment Record: Holly

Holly P.
Div. 16

Formal Assessments

Type	Evaluator	Date
PPVT-R	Lana Van Dyck (LAC)	May 12, 1998

Result   79th percentile

Type	Evaluator	Date
Woodcock-Johnson	Lana Van Dyck (LAC)	May 19, 1998

Result
Letter-word identification   77 (6th percentile)
Word attack   70 (2nd percentile)
Passage comprehension   85 (16th percentile)

Type	Evaluator	Date

Result

Type	Evaluator	Date

Result

FIGURE 2.9 ▧ Portfolio Reflections: Hannah

Portfolio Reflections

Student Name: _Hannah_   Date: _Nov 14/98_

I was pleased that my child

Writes
Draws
Knows numbers

Questions I have about my child's progress:

Parent/Guardian Signature: _Sheila L._

FIGURE 2.10 ■ Portfolio Reflections: Holly

Portfolio Reflections

Student Name: _Holly_   Date: _Nov 14/98_

I was pleased that my child

Writes

Knows numbers

Questions I have about my child's progress:

Where is her drawing?

Parent/Guardian Signature: _Sheila L._

Learning and Cognition: Developmental and Sociocultural Perspectives

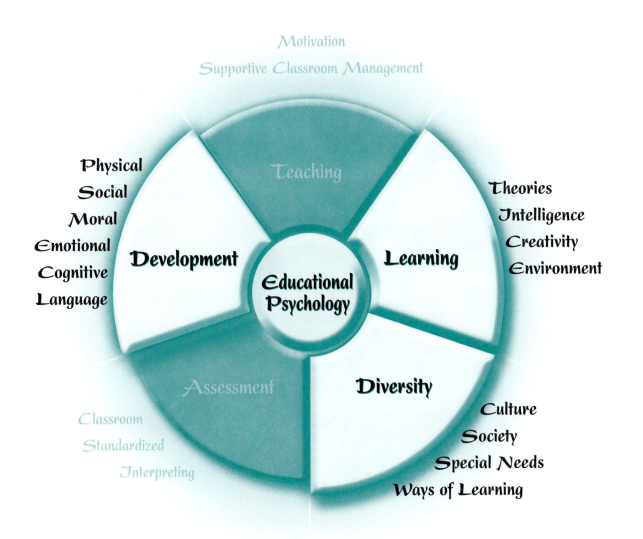

Motivation

Supportive Classroom Management

Physical
Social
Moral
Emotional
Cognitive
Language

Development

Teaching

Educational Psychology

Learning

Theories
Intelligence
Creativity
Environment

Assessment

Diversity

Classroom
Standardized
Interpreting

Culture
Society
Special Needs
Ways of Learning

In this chapter, contemporary theories of learning and cognitive development are presented. Each theory provides an approach that is useful in certain educational contexts. This chapter includes theories that are relevant to the practice of teaching. Teachers are accountable to parents, administrators, and school boards (Photo 3.1). Understanding why, as a teacher, you should base some instruction on one theoretical approach and some on another is essential in making informed professional decisions.

CHAPTER

3

Educational psychology is a relatively new field of study, beginning in the early 1900s (Good & Levin, 2001). The historical milestones in research on learning and cognitive development help us understand contemporary research. In this chapter, major contributors to educational psychological theory and research are discussed, beginning with contemporary theories that evolved in response to Piaget's theory of child and adolescent development. Piaget's seminal work has had a lasting influence on teaching and curriculum development. You will be introduced to a number of other theorists and their contributions to our understanding of learning in later chapters.

PHOTO 3.1
Teachers base their instruction on a variety of theoretical approaches.

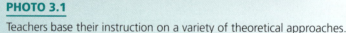

Piaget and the Cognitive Revolution

Cognitive science: The discipline that explains how the mind works as we think and learn.

Contemporary theories of cognition owe their origins to the *cognitive revolution* of the 1970s, when a new discipline, *cognitive science*, began to describe the mechanisms of thinking in detail and search for explanations for *how* the mind works (Gardner, 1985; Larkin, 1994). Since the cognitive revolution, research in educational psychology has concerned itself to a much greater degree with how the mind works in real-world settings. Research came out of the lab and into schools and classrooms and addressed several variables:

- Mental processes
- Strategies for learning
- Effective teaching
- Motivation to learn
- Individual differences in learning
- Effect of classroom and school contexts on achievement

This type of research related directly to the learner and the learning environment. Studies examined how the brain and mind function in a variety of circumstances, as well as in the social context of education.

Critical Response to Piaget's Theory of Development

Piaget defined broad stages of development, each characterized by a certain type of thought. (These stages were described in Chapter 2.) According to Piaget (Photo 3.2), during each stage children were believed to master certain abilities as a result of constructing the type of thinking associated with the stage. During the concrete operational period, for example, children acquired logical operations such as class inclusion, one-to-one correspondence, and the conservation of number, weight, and volume. Piaget believed that each of these operations shared the same logical characteristics. He reasoned that competence in executing these operations stemmed from the emergence of a general capability—concrete operational thinking. In other words, once children entered a new stage, they became capable of doing the sort of thinking associated with this stage within a variety of contexts.

Piaget believed that a child makes a transition to a new stage when his or her current mental structures no longer explain events in their world. A state of *disequilibrium* results, and children are motivated to restore *equilibrium* in their thinking. That is, they construct a new way to conceptualize events, and thus they adjust their way of thinking to new circumstances (Case, 1985). This involves *equilibration*—balancing one's thinking.

Disequilibrium: A Turning Point   One author recounts the following story of Duncan, whom you met before when he had trouble understanding that Daisy could be the name of a flower as well as a dog's name.

> "At 4 years old, Duncan was the youngest of the group of eight boys in the neighborhood. They all tended to get along quite well, and Duncan was tolerated within the group, even though he was seen as a baby. When they all arrived in the kitchen wanting something to drink, I would get out my mismatched set of glasses and start pouring juice or milk. Part of the tradition that developed was the older boys singling out 'Duncan's glass.' The glass was tall and narrow, while theirs were a bit shorter but wider. It was crucial to this group of boys that when I finished pouring juice all the levels be the same.
>
> For the longest time, Duncan was quite pleased with this arrangement. He didn't even notice that the boys laughed as they deliberately handed him 'his glass.' One day, however, Duncan became aware that something was going on around him, but he wasn't sure exactly what. Shortly after this, he asked one of the older boys what they were laughing at. Ken replied, 'Look stupid, you don't have the same amount as we do because the glass is tall and skinny.' Duncan stared at the glass for a long time as he worked to figure out what all of this meant."

At this moment, Duncan's understanding was being challenged within a social context. This was a turning point in his understanding of the world—what Piaget would call *disequilibrium*.

PHOTO 3.2

Piaget outlined distinct stages of development during which children mastered specific cognitive abilities.

Achieving Equilibrium   The process of equilibration takes time because the type of thinking involved is very broad—it provides the "big picture" of conceptual understanding—and because children must do their own reflection and construction to achieve equilibrium. Consider the 5-year-olds in Paley's (1986) kindergarten classroom who wanted to measure a rug for a class play. The children had a notion of how measurement worked and used their classmates as the "units" with which to measure the rug. They found that repeated measurement with children lying end to end did not always work. After much discussion, the children concluded that their classmate Warren was just the right size for a "rug measurer." They resisted the teacher's attempts to introduce formal units of measurement.

Teacher:	So this rug is ten rulers and two dolls long? (*Silence.*) Here's something we can do. We can use one of the rulers over again, this way.
Eddie:	Now you made *another* empty space.
Teacher:	Eddie, you mentioned a tape measure before. I have one here. (*We stretch the tape along the edge of the rug, and I show the children that the rug is 156 inches long. The lesson is done. The next day Warren is back in school.*)
Wally:	Here's Warren. Now we can really measure the rug.
Teacher:	Didn't we really measure the rug with the ruler?
Wally:	Well, rulers aren't really real, are they? (Paley, 1981, pp. 15–16)

While the children had acquired a fundamental idea, that units of measurement are needed, they were not yet "disequilibrated" enough to begin thinking about the formal conventions of measurement in our society. Their methods were appropriate to them and made far more sense than conventional approaches to measurement. This is a good example of why it is important for a teacher to understand children's thinking. By about age 7, after *experience with* and *reflection on* situations in which measurement is important, the children will likely be ready to incorporate standard units of measurement into their thinking.

Adolescent Thinking: Becoming Specialists   As children grow older and adopt social and cultural conformities (e.g., they want to look good in front of their peers or do what adults expect), these moments of disequilibrium become harder to spot. However, teachers often notice on school assignments how this lack of understanding is a drawback to learning the prescribed curricula. A grade 8 teacher was shaking her head and had no idea what to do with students who were having major problems drawing maps correctly. Some students just couldn't get the spatial understanding necessary to place cities, mountains, and rivers in appropriate, proportionally correct alignment. This is an ideal example of the mismatch that often occurs when teachers are confronted with curricular topics that may not match the student's level of cognitive development. The challenge for many teachers is to be sure they are cognizant of the level of thinking that the topic requires (e.g., concrete or abstract) and then adjust their teaching strategies in such a way that the students grasp the basic understanding necessary to accomplish classroom tasks. This is called *curriculum matching* and will be discussed in more detail later.

Strengths of Piaget's Theory

Piaget's theory was strong in that it emphasized several points:

- *Lower-order thinking contributes to more complex, or higher-order, thought.* So Wally and his classmates, in the preceding example, having experimented with and discussed the advantages and disadvantages of different ways of measuring things (lower-order thought), acquired an important foundation for more complex (higher-order) ways of thinking about measurement.
- *Development takes time.* Certain kinds of conceptual understanding can be achieved only once a child has constructed the kind of logical reasoning required for this understanding. Similarly, children can only profit from certain types of experiences once they are developmentally ready (Case, 1985).
- *The individual plays an active role in achieving understanding.* Thus, children do not simply receive knowledge from adults or older children in a way that necessarily makes sense to them; rather, their minds must be actively engaged with knowledge for it to be meaningful to them.

Building on Piaget's Theory: A Neo-Piagetian Approach

As more research examined children's acquisition of Piagetian thinking, a number of problems surfaced. Researchers found that the categories of abilities believed to be typical of a certain type of thinking actually bore little relationship to each other. Proficiency in concrete operational tasks such as conservation, classification, and seriation was not necessarily achieved at the same time, as would have been expected given Piaget's predictions. Children who scored well on one task might receive a low score on others.

All these developmental tasks were believed to depend on the broad capability of concrete operational thought—a child who could accomplish one task should have been able to accomplish the others. The inconsistency in the patterns of performance raised questions about Piaget's theory.

Staggered Skill Acquisition   Additionally, some children acquire particular abilities over a number of years, whereas Piaget believed that these abilities should emerge all at once. Researchers have shown that children grasp ideas about the conservation of number at about 6 years of age, but do not understand the conservation of liquid volume tasks until 7 or 8 years old or the conservation of weight tasks until the age of 9 or 10 (Case, 1985).

Studies also found that children could think in fairly complex ways at younger ages than Piaget had described. For example, Piaget showed preschool children a model of mountains, houses, and people and asked them to predict what someone would see from various places. They were unable to describe what someone would see from different vantage points. Piaget thus believed that preschoolers were incapable of perspective taking. Margaret Donaldson (1978), on the other hand, found that when teddy bears at a tea party were the context, preschoolers were quite capable of taking a perspective other than their own.

Emphasis on Scientific Reasoning   Piaget also conceived of children as "little scientists" (Astington, 1993). The image evoked by Piaget was that of a child individually and consciously engaged in scientific experimentation by conducting intellectual experiments with little input from others. Piaget was interested in general patterns in the development of intelligence and knowledge—the "big picture" of thinking—rather than in how individuals are influenced by context (Ginsburg, 1997).

Similarly, the tasks Piaget devised to assess thinking reflected a scientific frame of reference. These tasks had an obvious link to science and mathematics instruction, but the implications for other areas of the curriculum were not so clear. Educational psychologists raised important questions (Photo 3.3):

- How does modeling thought processes in scientific and mathematical terms translate to understanding how children acquire the abilities to read, write, draw, understand their social worlds, and understand themselves?
- How do we explain development in those children whose *logical–mathematical thinking* is weak, but whose abilities in other areas are strong?

> **Logical–mathematical thinking:** Thinking that is structured and sequential or patterned

> **Hypothetical–deductive thinking:** Thinking that involves forming a hypothesis and judging relevant evidence; the *scientific method*

Multiple Paths to Learning   Toward the end of his career, Piaget (1972) did consider that there might be other ways of developing intellectually than those that he had mapped out. He recognized that specialization in development that begins to take place in adolescence might mean that formal thinking takes different forms in different people. That is, an adolescent might be able to think in a *hypothetical–deductive* way for English class, but not necessarily in science.

The possibility of individualized paths of learning may help explain the rather discouraging finding that many adults do not acquire formal operational thinking, as measured by Piagetian tasks (Crain, 2000). In a number of studies, only half of the participating adolescents and young adults demonstrated formal thought (Larivée, Normandeau, & Parent, 2000). However, if opportunities are offered to demonstrate formal thinking in ways other than the logical–mathe-

PHOTO 3.3
One criticism of Piagetian theory is that it fails to consider important areas of aptitude and learning such as art, writing, and emotional intelligence.

matical mode and in ways that are gender sensitive, more learners are judged as able to think hypothetically (de Lisi & Staudt, 1980; Peskin, 1980). Early studies of Piagetian thinking foreshadowed research on cultural and gender differences in achievement, a topic we discuss in Chapter 6.

Hypothetical Thinking   Middle school teachers see clear evidence of students' struggles to think hypothetically. Their students are in a transitional stage between concrete and formal thinking. Like the social studies teacher who wondered how to help students with map drawing, teachers of all subjects find transitions between concrete and formal thinking a challenge to their teaching and ingenuity.

Often students struggle, not quite understanding the material, as they work through assignments. From the concept of metaphors in English to understanding density in science, students are forced to think abstractly and hypothetically. These formal concepts are, at first, barriers to students' thinking. One author remembers, "I once told a group of 10- and 11-year-olds to 'pull up their socks' when they were misbehaving. However, they all immediately did just what I'd asked—pulled up their socks. On another occasion, we had a guest speaker who mentioned that we all probably have 'skeletons in our closets.' The children looked extremely scared." With time, equilibration, and opportunities to demonstrate their thinking in different ways, however, conceptual structures may be developed that allow students to move into the next stage (formal level) of thinking. Figure 3.1 shows eighth graders' use of metaphors. It is apparent that the students are transitional in their understanding; there is a grasp of the concept, but it is usually expressed in fairly concrete ways.

Postadolescent Stages of Development   Piaget's (1972) later thinking also included the possibility of development beyond adolescence, a possibility with obvious implications for postsecondary education. Contemporary researchers

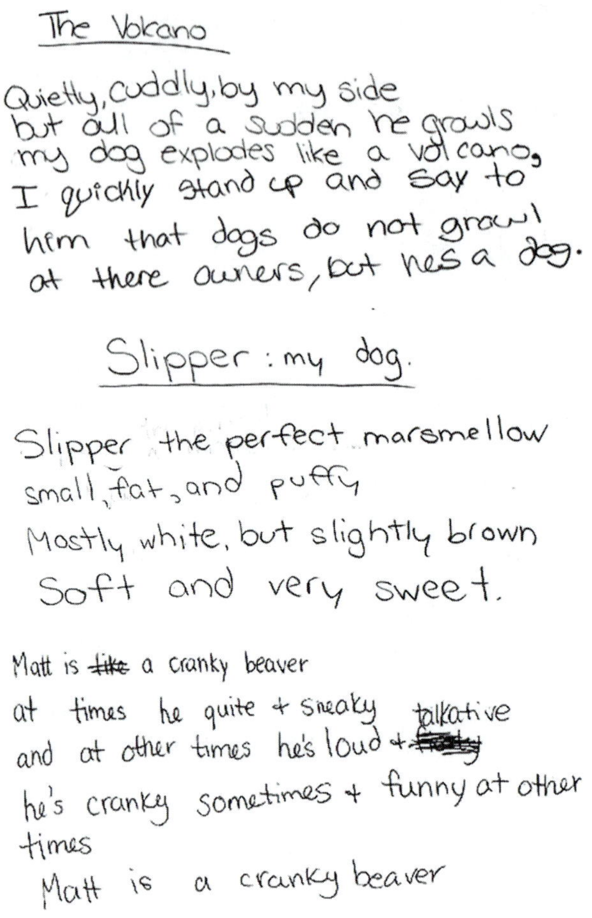

The Volcano

Quietly, cuddly, by my side
but all of a sudden he growls
my dog explodes like a volcano,
I quickly stand up and say to
him that dogs do not growl
at there owners, but hes a dog.

Slipper : my dog.

Slipper the perfect marsmellow
small, fat, and puffy
Mostly white, but slightly brown
Soft and very sweet.

Matt is ~~like~~ a cranky beaver
at times he quite + sneaky
and at other times he's loud + ~~friendly~~ talkative
he's cranky sometimes + funny at other
times
Matt is a cranky beaver

FIGURE 3.1

Grade 8 Students' Use of Metaphors Is Fairly Concrete

have focused on the nature and course of development in adulthood, finding that thinking becomes more reflective as adults come to understand the complexity of many issues and the conditional nature of knowledge (see, e.g., Alexander & Langer, 1990; Arlin, 1989; Commons, Demick, & Goldberg, 1996). Further development in adulthood also has implications for secondary education. Just as elementary teachers think ahead to the kinds of demands their students will face in high school, so secondary teachers can think ahead to the demands their students will face in the worlds of postsecondary education, work, serious relationships, and child rearing.

Building on Piaget's Theory: Neo-Piagetian Approaches to Development

Some psychologists and educators have left Piaget's work behind entirely, while others maintain the view that development is stagelike and that there are characteristic ways of thinking associated with each stage. The latter group of theorists, in analyzing Piaget's work, has evolved new ways of viewing developmental stages. Their work is known as *neo-Piagetian* (see, e.g., Case, 1992; Demetriou &

Efklides, 1988; Fischer, 1980; Halford, 1993.) This work has built on the strengths of Piaget's theory, drawing on contemporary educational psychological research in information processing and the social and cultural context of development.

Kurt Fischer and Robbie Case are two neo-Piagetian theorists whose work is relevant to understanding the ways in which children and adolescents think. Both theorists and their colleagues investigated the way children's understanding developed over time and conducted their investigations in a broader context than that used by Piaget. Fundamental to their work, however, was the principle that stages of development build on each other, a distinctly Piagetian notion. Fischer and Case added to this notion more detailed analyses of how reasoning unfolds across levels of competence. They also informed these analyses by considering developmental contexts like experiences at home, level of education, and social and cultural factors.

Fischer's Roles and the Importance of Context

Fischer, Hand, Watson, Van Parys, and Tucker (1984) studied how children of different ages acted out parental and occupational roles. Four-year-olds demonstrated a *behavioral role*, focusing on the actions typical of each role. This sort of role is evident in preschoolers' play in the "house corner" or "dress-up center" in their classrooms as they imitate the actions of parents or story characters (Photo 3.4). Six-year-olds in Fischer et al.'s study acted out a "true role" in which internal motivation was considered, but limited to a single role. This level of understanding of role is evident in the following anecdotes.

Six-Year-Olds   *A Limited Understanding of Roles.* Todd arrived at the door of his first-grade classroom in tears, unable to understand how his mother could have taken a job. As far as he was concerned, she had a job already: she was his mother. How could she be his mother *and* a nurse? Vivian Paley (1981) noted the same

PHOTO 3.4

Young children typically focus on the behaviors that characterize a particular role.

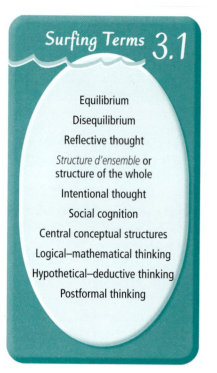

Surfing Terms 3.1

Equilibrium
Disequilibrium
Reflective thought
Structure d'ensemble or structure of the whole
Intentional thought
Social cognition
Central conceptual structures
Logical–mathematical thinking
Hypothetical–deductive thinking
Postformal thinking

sort of understanding in her kindergarten students when they decided that soaking beans overnight was the reason they didn't grow. Overnight was too long and someone needed to be there, *at school*, to oversee the soaking.

> The children preferred not to think of me or the beans in another place. I had soaked the beans in the classroom and that is where the beans—and I—belonged. The children could not envision my life away from school and had difficulty coordinating events in the classroom with those in my house. (p. 57)

Ten-Year-Olds   *An Understanding of Multiple Roles.* In contrast, 10-year-olds display an understanding that one can have multiple interacting roles at once. A parent can be both a doctor and a Girl Scout leader at the same time, for example. In the school context, by the end of their elementary school experience, not only can children envision other roles for their teachers (Fischer et al., 1984), but they can also understand and appreciate that the teachers have lives outside school. One author remembers the day in sixth grade when her teacher, a Catholic nun, mentioned an incident that occurred when the Sister had been a child. "I distinctly remember coming to a complete 'stop,' with the clear understanding that this nun had been a child at one time. Looking back I think it had never entered my mind that this person had had a life outside the school and convent. To me, the nuns had always just been there."

Case's Substages of Development

Like Kurt Fischer, Case (1985, 1992) broke down the broad stages defined by Piaget into substages. Both Fischer and Case noted that children's thinking changes incrementally during the periods of early childhood, middle childhood, and adolescence. Thus, while a broad descriptor of thinking characterizes each of these periods (much like Piaget described preoperational, concrete operational thinking, and formal operational thinking), within each stage notable changes take place.

In thinking about what motivates others to act the way they do, children between the ages of about 5 and 11 understand that other people have *intentions* (Case, 1996; Goldberg-Reitman, 1992). Their thought during this broad stage of development can be described as *intentional* (McKeough, 1992). However, there are noticeable differences between a 6-year-old's and a 10-year-old's intentional thinking.

- *Six-year-olds* simply coordinate an action and its underlying motivation (e.g., a peer hit someone because he was angry at having his ball taken away).
- *By 10 years of age*, children have a more general understanding of why people behave as they do. They can give more complex explanations involving two or more underlying motivations. For example, they might say that a peer hit someone because he was angry and frustrated and that people sometimes react like this when they are upset.

Knowing how an understanding of others develops can help teachers understand situations that arise on the playground or in learning groups. Children in the primary grades have a much more rudimentary understanding of others' intentions than do upper elementary and middle school students. They need to be supported in acquiring more sophisticated knowledge of motivations for actions. (This topic is covered in more depth in Chapter 4.)

Comparison of Piagetian and Neo-Piagetian Theories

The examples just presented concern *social cognition,* or knowledge about the social world. They highlight important differences between Piaget's work and that of neo-Piagetian theorists.

Piaget: Structure of the Whole   Piaget believed in a *structure d'ensemble* (structure of the whole), a general structure of mind that influenced one's thinking in a variety of contexts. As discussed earlier, once adolescents acquired the structure of the whole of formal operational thinking, they were believed to be able to apply this across subject areas.

Neo-Piagetians: Development of Multiple Structures   Neo-Piagetians retained the idea of structure, but theorized that we develop a number of such structures. Case's research group has investigated several of these (see Case, 1992; Case & Okamoto, 1996):

- Social understanding (including understanding of self and others)
- Mathematical understanding
- Scientific understanding
- Understanding of spatial relationships

So, rather than developing one way of thinking at each stage of development that shapes how we understand various aspects of our world, we develop along a number of different pathways, each with unique characteristics. This view of development has important educational implications.

- Children and adolescents differ from each other in their rates of development in mathematics, reading, science, and other areas of the school curriculum.
- Each child or adolescent also has his or her unique developmental profile. An adolescent may be much better at English than math, for example.

Table 3.1 summarizes the differences between Piagetian and neo-Piagetian views of development and the respective educational implications of these differences.

Educational Implications

Knowing the differences in conceptual understanding for various subject areas allows teachers to design meaningful learning experiences for their students.

A Conceptual Approach to Teaching

When we attempt to discover *how* our students understand key concepts, we can use what we learn to make meaningful links to the curriculum. For example, a student may possess social skills like taking turns and requesting permission to use classroom materials, yet still not have the conceptual understanding that "glues" these skills together. That is, in situations that require some understanding of others' motivations, the student just doesn't appear to get the concept that thoughts and actions are related, so he or she may not use social skills appropriately.

In planning instruction, keeping key conceptual understanding at the center of our thinking can help in unifying learning activities. It leads to education that consists of and results in meaningfully related knowledge, rather than isolated skills. Later in this chapter, we present more on this idea in a discussion of what

TABLE 3.1

Comparison of Piagetian and Neo-Piagetian Views of Development

	Piagetian	Neo-Piagetian
Age/stage relationship	Four broad stages—infancy, early childhood, middle childhood, adolescence	Four broad stages—infancy, early childhood, middle childhood, adolescence
Qualitatively different type of thinking at each stage	Broadly defined: Sensorimotor, preoperational, concrete operational, formal operational. Stage transitions not well explained.	Each stage broken down into substages and type of thinking described in detail. Transitions between stages described and explained.
Higher stages include and build on earlier stages	New stage of thought builds on and incorporates the type of thinking previously demonstrated.	Each stage and substage builds on and incorporates earlier forms of thought. This happens separately in different domains of thinking.
Effect of new stage of thought	New way of thinking applied to all situations ("structure of the whole")	Different domains have independent developmental trajectories. *Form* of thought is parallel across domains, but *content* differs.
View of the child	Child as scientist or logician[1]	Child as user of cultural tools, processor of information, and problem solver[1]
Recognition of individual differences	Little; more interest in universal forms of thought	Roles of experience, motivation, instructional support, socioeconomic status, and culture recognized. Inter- and intra-individual differences considered.[2]

[1]Case (1985).
[2]Case (1987).

it means to be an expert at something. For now, let's use the mental number line as an example of a core understanding.

Development of Mathematical Understanding: The Number Line

One important goal of education is to help children acquire mathematical understanding, or *numeracy*. Knowing how children's conceptual understanding of mathematics develops is critical for planning appropriate instruction. Case (1992; Case & Okamoto, 1996) described the core feature of a mathematical structure as the "mental number line."

Picture a numbered line in your head that allows you to understand that if you have 3 objects and someone gives you 4 more you have moved forward along the line to 7. Conversely, if you lose 2 of those objects, you move backward on the line

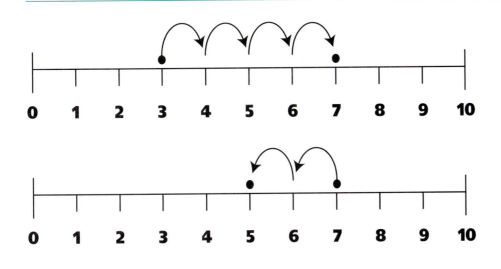

FIGURE 3.2

**The Mental Number Line Helps
Children to Develop Number Sense**

to 5. The *mental number line* (Figure 3.2) captures concepts in mathematics that are critical to achievement in early mathematics curricula. The mental number line also helps children compare quantities and understand the nature of mathematical notation, in general, to develop number sense. If the mental number line is well understood in early childhood, children have a sound foundation on which to develop more complex, related understandings that also can be explained by the number line structure. These include rational numbers (fractions, percentages, and decimals) and functions (e.g., Kalchman & Case, 1998; Moss & Case, 1999).

If children enter school with no understanding of the mental number line, they are at risk of failure in mathematics (Griffin, Case, & Siegler, 1994). Unfortunately, many children of poverty enter school without this understanding (Case, Griffin, & Kelly, 1999). When children are given number line training by engaging in activities that develop their knowledge of the number line, they not only greatly improve in their number line knowledge, but also in their overall mathematics achievement (Griffin & Case, 1996). Children who engage in real-world "take-away" operations, such as counting backward for a pretend rocket blast-off, build a conceptual understanding of subtraction (Griffin & Case, 1996). Similar work that builds *conceptual bridges* for children and adolescents as they learn about rational numbers and functions results in mathematical knowledge that is well understood and applied fluently to a variety of problems (Kalchman & Case, 1998; Moss & Case, 1999).

Mathematics: Using a Conceptual Approach

Using children's experiences with percentages, such as school marks, sales tax, and the number ribbon displayed when a computer file is being transferred, Joan Moss developed a curriculum for fractions, decimals, and percentages that used children's prior knowledge, experience, and conceptual understanding (Moss & Case, 1999). Rather than simply covering the curriculum as presented in the textbook, Moss *uncovered* children's conceptual understanding.

Elementary mathematics curriculum generally presents fractions first, followed by decimals and percentages. Children have meaningful experiences with percentages, but not fractions and decimals (Moss & Case, 1999). Therefore, children learned percentages first; then their understanding of percentage is used as a basis for teaching decimals and fractions. The following example illustrates the effectiveness of a conceptual approach to teaching rational numbers.

In response to the question, *"Another student told me that 7 is 3/4 of 10. Is it?"* a child who was taught using the conceptual approach answered, *"No, because one half of 10 is 5. One half of 5 is 2 1/2. So if you add 2 1/2 to 5, that would be 7 1/2. So 7 1/2 is 3/4 of 10, not 7."*

Problem-Based Scenario 3.1

Student: *Sammy*

Teacher: *Emma*

Emma got to the last math exercise book in the pile. She was marking after dinner and had done what she usually did with Sammy's book—put it at the bottom of the pile. Not only was the work messy and disorganized, but in trying to reach Sammy, Emma had exhausted all the strategies in her math education collection. She had serious concerns about his academic achievement in general, but she somehow felt better equipped to deal with other areas of the curriculum than with math. She tried to figure out how Sammy thought about math, both by poring over his written work and by listening to his responses in class. But, so far, she felt she had failed dismally.

Sammy was one of Emma's 25 third-grade pupils. It became clear to her early in the school year that Sammy was at a terrible disadvantage in mastering the third-grade math curriculum. He could recall only the simplest basic facts. At first, Emma had quizzed him. "What is five plus seven, Sammy?" "Nine! Three! Eleven!" Emma had to credit him. He knew how to read the look on her face and respond with another attempt at an answer. Emma had tried a variety of aids from fingers to counters, to no avail. Sammy just didn't know what to do first.

Emma thought back to her math education class when her professor had put a huge arrow under his arm and marched back and forth on the number line that was tiled into the classroom floor. Emma didn't have such a line in her classroom, so she tried using a ruler instead. "Where's the 5, Sammy? OK, now count 7 more." Sammy could do this if they counted together, but could not use the strategy on his own. When Emma tried a counting backward strategy with the ruler to help him with subtraction, Sammy fell apart. This experience, combined with his distractibility and frustration during math classes, left her wondering where to turn next.

Figures 3.3 and 3.4 appear on pages 94 and 95.

Apply

- How could neo-Piagetian theory help Emma support Sammy in learning math? Think of two activities you would do based on this theory and be prepared to justify them to your principal.
- How is the social context of learning relevant to helping Sammy learn?

In contrast, a child taught using textbook exercises responded, "*No . . . 7 is not right because it is an odd number so 6 would be right.*"

Notice the quality and the depth of the first response; it reflects a conceptual understanding of elementary mathematics.

In some instances, teachers are challenged to understand the way children "have concepts." Emma, a third-grade teacher, struggled to understand the nature of the problems one of her students, Sammy, was having in math. Her attempts to match curriculum and instruction to his way of understanding were not succeeding (see Problem-Based Scenario 3.1).

Fostering Expertise

Another useful framework for thinking about how knowledge of development translates to practical educational considerations is the *novice–expert* distinction. Research in this tradition shares certain characteristics with contemporary developmental theory:

- Novices have simpler knowledge structures than those of experts, which are complex (Bereiter & Scardamalia, 1986). Novices not only have less information to work with than experts, but they tend to have this information "in pieces" (diSessa, 1988).
- Experts have integrated, cohesive knowledge. Because experts' knowledge is well organized, they acquire and remember new knowledge effectively. New knowledge is also retrieved and used efficiently (Spoehr, 1994).

Novice: Learners who are encountering new material or who do not understand familiar material at a deep level. *Expert:* Learners who have developed a rich understanding of concepts.

Using a Novice–Expert Framework

Applied research done within the novice–expert framework shows that if we teach only skills we create more proficient novices (Bereiter & Scardamalia, 1986), rather than experts who understand at a meaningful, conceptual level. In fact, a focus on skills alone can lead to cumulative deficits in achievement, because children never get the chance to understand and appreciate underlying concepts (Griffin et al., 1994; Meichenbaum & Biemiller, 1998). Novices say things like "I don't get it" and "I'm stuck" or ask questions like "Can you show me how to do this?" These comments and questions indicate that they have only a superficial understanding of what they are learning. Even this superficial understanding may be partial at best. Experts, on the other hand, ask questions such as "I've done problems like this before and I think I'm going wrong here. Could you have a look and give me a clue?"

This is not to say that skills are unimportant. Rather, without a conceptual support for skills, knowledge remains fragmented. One author calls this an *educational overlay*. That is, it is a set of skills learned at school that never gets incorporated into our thinking in a meaningful way. All of us have educational overlays that were often learned for tests and then quickly discarded or forgotten. The reason they were discarded was that they had no meaning.

Meichenbaum and Biemiller (1998) noted additional important differences between experts and novices:

- *A degree of familiarity with the situation and motivation*. Experts do best in familiar situations because they process information efficiently (Meichenbaum & Biemiller, 1998).
- A *"nurturant resourceful environment"* (Meichenbaum & Biemiller, 1998, p. 13) to support high motivation.

Nurturant resourceful environment: An environment that nurtures learners' needs through appropriate resources, stimulating experiences, encouragement, and support.

These differences also are important from the point of view of instruction. Children need to be helped and supported to be interested expert learners (Bereiter & Scardamalia, 1986). The discussion of the importance of a supportive learning environment and the motivation to learn is continued in Chapters 8 and 9.

Conceptual Bridging

Conceptual bridging is an instructional approach that teaches both skills and conceptual understanding (Griffin et al., 1994; McKeough, 1992). This approach includes activities that are based on understanding children's conceptual development in a domain and the sequence of this development. By knowing children's current level of conceptual understanding and the next step in the developmental sequence, a conceptual bridge can be built between these levels of understanding.

This approach requires analysis of the material to be learned, in addition to honoring learner's ways of understanding. For example, Moss and Case (1999) taught rational numbers to fourth-graders in reverse order to the traditional textbook presentation (percentages, decimals, fractions, rather than fractions, decimals, percentages) based on the following analysis:

- Children have intuitions about proportions and numbers to 100 by the fourth grade. Beginning with percentages rather than fractions allows them to coordinate these intuitions.
- Children are familiar with number ribbons on computers that show percentages.
- Comparison of ratios with different denominators, a complex and unfamiliar task, is postponed until children have had the opportunity to develop their own ways of calculating and comparing.
- It is easier to compute fractional or decimal equivalents for percentages than to do the opposite. Beginning with percentages allows a solid foundation for understanding the equivalence of rational numbers.
- Children have experience with percentages (e.g., sales tax, price reductions). (Moss & Case, 1999)

Using Students' Intuitive Knowledge

Hunt and Minstrell (1994) described an approach to teaching introductory high school physics that takes students' intuitive knowledge of the natural world as the starting point. "We see instruction as fostering reconstruction of understanding and reasoning, rather than as the memorization of correct procedures and answers" (Hunt & Minstrell, p. 56). Hunt and Minstrell incorporated a number of constructivist principles into their instruction:

- Honoring students' understandings as starting points for instruction
- Bridging the gap between "students' physics" and "scientists' physics" (p. 51)
- Teaching as conversation, that is, talking to students about their ideas and using these ideas as points of departure for instruction or opportunities to consolidate their understanding

Teachers can have conversations with their students that will lead to better understanding of how students think, as well as to instruction that is more appropriately matched to students' needs (Arlin, 1990) (Photo 3.5). Think back

PHOTO 3.5

Informal conversation is an effective way of assessing students' understanding of concepts.

to the group of kindergarteners who could only measure a rug when Warren was at school (Paley, 1986). When her attempts to introduce formal measurement failed, their teacher had conversations with the children to help her understand their conceptions of measurement. Similarly, rather than just teaching her students how to compute averages, a fifth-grade teacher probed their understanding of averages, starting with the question "What is an average anyway?" (Arlin, p. 83). The students' responses allowed her to see their misconceptions and to engage them in discussion about the concept. She did not correct misconceptions, but instead had the children experiment to test their ideas. This approach allows children to develop a solid understanding of concepts and become intellectually autonomous (Kamii; as cited in Arlin).

In another example, an eighth-grade science class was studying the Earth's rotation. It was a windy day, and one of the students commented, "You can really see it spinning today." This comment could be viewed as funny or completely lacking in understanding. Instead we can view it as a starting point for instruction—showing respect for the student's thinking and also optimizing the chances for successfully moving the student to a more sophisticated level of understanding. Some guidelines for "listening to what the children say" (Paley, 1986) in conversations about academic subjects and social relationships are summarized in Figure 3.5.

The guidelines in Figure 3.5 may also help you think about how you would approach the situations presented in Problem-Based Scenarios 3.2 and 3.3. Both situations are highly emotional and culturally influenced. The scenarios also present situations that are rarely discussed in teacher education. They require thoughtful consideration not only of children's points of view, but also of your own ideas and beliefs.

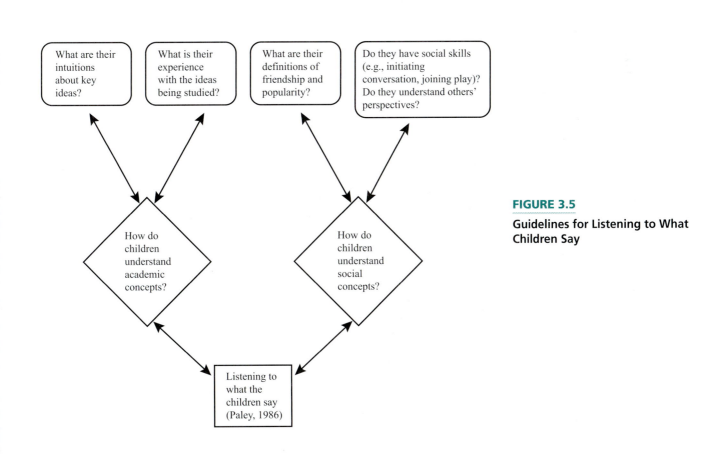

FIGURE 3.5

Guidelines for Listening to What Children Say

Problem-Based Scenario 3.2

Student: Sara
Teacher: Greg

It was 8:30 in the morning and Greg Norris had been at school since 7 organizing the day. Marked exercise books were in their slots, the kids' artwork was framed and ready to hang, science materials were set up for the afternoon, and test booklets and answer sheets were all set for the district assessment scheduled for the morning. All fourth-graders were taking a reading achievement test this year as part of a district literacy initiative.

A soft tap on the door interrupted Greg's thoughts about how his pupils would cope with the unfamiliar process of lengthy group testing. Anna O'Neill, teacher librarian at Mountainview Elementary, approached his desk. She was obviously very upset.

"Greg, Toni Desrosiers just came in to tell me she wouldn't be able to help out in the library for awhile. Sara was with her. Greg, I can't believe it. Sara just told me her daddy died last night. Toni said it was a heart attack. Sara won't be back in school until next week."

Greg sat in a state of shock. What a terrible thing for Sara and her mom. What could he do to support Sara? What *should* he do? How should he break the news to Sara's classmates? He had never had to deal with death in his 7 years of teaching or, for that matter, in his own life.

Apply

- What do theories of cognitive development tell you about how Sara may understand death?
- How is the concept of a "community of learners" relevant to supporting Sara?
- You decide to write your ideas about breaking the news to Sara's classmates and show them to a senior colleague. What will you write and how will you justify it to your colleague?

Problem-Based Scenario 3.3

Student: Alice
Teacher: Ruth

Driving along and hearing the news broadcast about the TV star who had committed suicide last night, Ruth knew that there would be problems today in school. Alice was a ninth-grade student who adored this star. Her entire locker was covered in pictures and memorabilia. Every episode of the show was taped and replayed continuously. It was the kind of adoration Ruth remembered seeing on old tapes of Elvis Presley shows.

Walking down the hall toward her room, Ruth encountered Mary Winters, who taught in the room next to hers. Mary told Ruth she had just had a talk with "that foolish girl, Alice," who was "sitting in the corner crying." Mary said, "I just told her, it's a movie star, get up and go to your class." As Mary waved her hand in Alice's direction, she said "Anyway, she didn't react—maybe you can get her to move." With that Mary walked to her room.

Ruth just stood there. Alice was sitting in the corner by the lockers, curled in a fetal position, sobbing. A couple of girls were standing near Alice, but they didn't seem to know what to do either. Ruth could hear Alice telling the girls that this person didn't have to commit suicide. If he had come to her, she would have loved him. It was affecting the whole group of girls. Now that additional damage had been done and the bell was about to ring, what would she do with Alice? And what about the other girls? And Mary!?

Apply

- What should Ruth do to help Alice?
- Should Ruth use the same approach to support the other girls?
- What should Ruth do about Mary's reaction to Alice?

Concept Mapping

The examples of developmentally based instruction just given are from mathematics and science, subjects in which the developmental progression of fundamental concepts is relatively clear. Spoehr (1994) noted that conceptual organization in the humanities is less clear. Rather than make reference to universal laws, as in science and mathematics, teachers can help students search for patterns of knowledge and foster "discrimination and informed judgment about the relationships between parts of the knowledge base" (p. 79).

One example of fostering this type of thinking is through concept mapping (Figure 3.6). For example, students might read a number of poems written in the 1960s and look for common themes and modes of expression. In the humanities, the "conceptual neighborhood" (Spoehr) is a useful way of defining central conceptual knowledge.

Teachers often engage their students in *webbing* or *mapping* to help them reflect on key concepts and construct their own organizing frameworks. Brownlie, Close, and Wingren (1990) provided helpful guidelines for teachers to use in supporting students to map concepts (Table 3.2):

- Read examples of visually based text to the students. For example, Brownlie et al. used an image from a sixth-grade science text: "*See the tarantula . . . Feel the fangs . . . exoskeleton . . . Notice the stinger . . . punctured abdomen . . . See the female . . . large . . . The male is lighter . . .*" (p. 91).
- Have the students then write down their thoughts about the topic.
- Once their thoughts are in writing, have them use this text to create a map of the concepts.

The central objective of developmentally based instruction is "tuning the learning environment to the knowledge to be conveyed as well as to the learning capabilities of the students" (Larkin, 1994, p. xii). In accomplishing this objective,

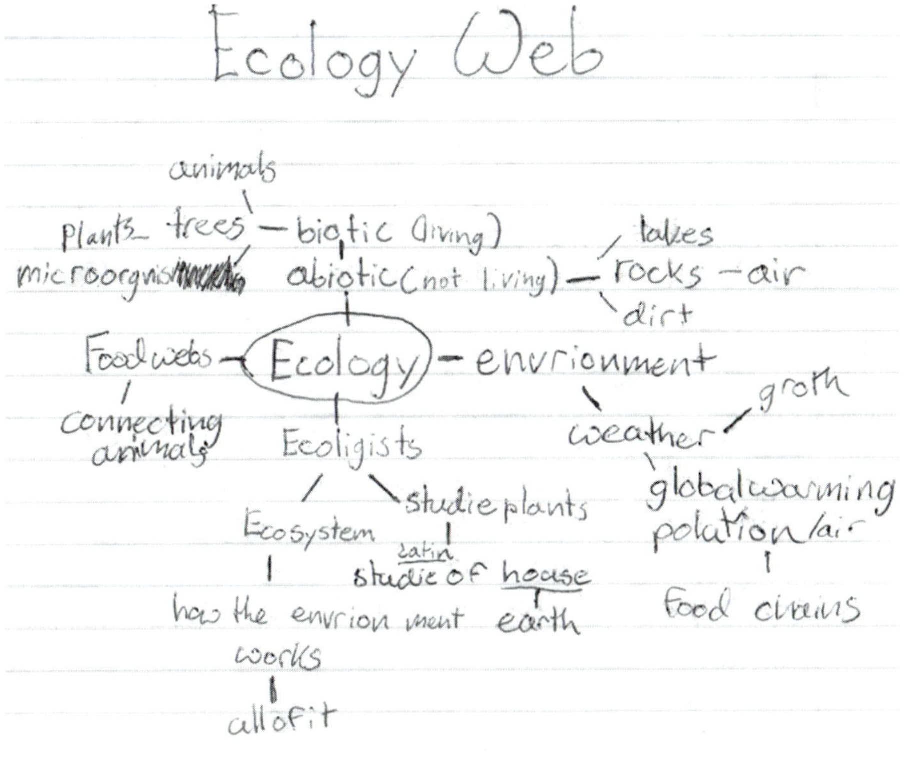

FIGURE 3.6

Example of a Concept Map: Ecology Web by Bruce, Eighth Grade

TABLE 3.2

Guidelines for Concept Mapping

1. Read an image created from an experience, text, or topic sequence.
2. Talk to a partner about how it felt being "in the topic."
3. Exchange impressions with the entire class.
4. Write for five minutes to show, not tell, what has been learned.
5. Listen to drafts and build criteria for effective writing.
6. List the "big ideas" of the text.
7. Choose two important ideas to begin the concept map.
8. Link these ideas with a word that shows the context of the text, the connection between the ideas, and/or an application of the information.
9. Map and link the "big ideas," crossing out the ideas used as they are connected into the map.
10. Make cross-links between words.
11. Work with a partner or individually to list "big ideas" and to create a concept map.

Source: Based on Brownlie, Close, and Wingren, 1990, p. 99.

you achieve an *"optimal match"* between school and the learners' minds (Donaldson, 1979).

Implicit in the developmentally based approaches discussed in this chapter is the important role of the learning environment and how it is matched to learners' capabilities. The sociocultural approach to learning and development offers a theoretical perspective that assigns primary importance to the environment. This perspective has its roots in the work of Vygotsky (see Chapter 2). A central tenet is that social interaction is a critical component in learning.

Sociocultural Psychology and Education

The sociocultural approach to development, like cognitive psychology, is a product of the 1970s revolution in the study of cognitive development (Gauvain, 2001). The approach evolved because the *social and cultural context* of cognitive development was perceived to be missing in previous accounts of intellectual development. Piaget's work, particularly, was criticized as focusing too much on individuals and not enough on the environment in which they developed.

Research in non-Western cultures (e.g., Cole, Gay, Glick, & Sharp, 1971) and the writings of Vygotsky were influential in highlighting the roles of social and cultural contexts in development and learning (Gauvain, 2000). (see Info Byte 3.1). Sociocultural psychologists believe that structures of mind are first constructed socially and then reconstructed by the individual (Scardamalia, Bereiter, & Lamon, 1994). In contrast, Piaget emphasized the role of individual mental activity in constructing knowledge.

Socially Shared Cognition

As discussed in Chapter 2, an important concept in Vygotsky's theory is the *zone of proximal development.* Starting from the child's or adolescent's level of

Surfing Terms 3.2

Novice
Expert
Concept mapping
Conceptual change
Constructivist teaching

understanding, the emphasis is on *how far* the individual can progress with assistance. Taking a dynamic view of development, Vygotsky emphasized the role of the culture, particularly that of adults and capable peers, and the tools used in the culture in shaping knowledge. Current applications of Vygotsky's perspective focus on *socially shared cognition*. This focus is evident in Brown and Campione's (1994) approach to education.

Distributed Expertise in Communities of Learners   The social nature of learning takes the form of *distributed expertise*. Children become experts in an area, and their knowledge is then combined with others' knowledge to make a whole. They teach their material to others and prepare questions for a test that all will take. "The essence of teamwork is pooling varieties of expertise" (Brown & Campione, 1994, p. 235).

Zones of Proximal Development   Brown and Campione conceived of the classroom as composed of "multiple zones of proximal development through which participants can navigate via different routes and at different rates" (p. 236) (Photo 3.6). Scaffolding learning through a zone of proximal development can be accomplished through interactions with adults and children, "but it can also include artifacts such as books, videos, wall displays, scientific equipment, and a computer environment intended to support intentional learning" (Brown & Campione, 1994, p. 236).

Incorporating Individual Variation   In a community of learners, children learn from adults and other children; adults also learn from children. Students' questions and prior knowledge give meaning to curriculum. For example, fifth- and sixth-graders were asked the following questions about a unit in biology: Do large amounts of DDT depress immune function? If a human has malaria, can it be transmitted? Can a baby get it inside the body [of its mother]? (Brown & Campione, 1994, p. 242). These questions informed the design of the biology unit.

INFO BYTE 3.1

As we combine words to describe complex ideas, such as combining *social* and *cultural* into *sociocultural*, it helps us to clearly understand the individual terms. *Society* ("socio") refers to people, in general, living within a community. This community can consist of many layers that may be seen as divisions within the larger group. For example, we often hear about socioeconomic status. This term refers to societal layers that have been divided on economic, educational, and/or occupational characteristics.

Culture refers to behaviors and beliefs that are passed down from one generation to the next within a group of people. Culture can transcend the layers often found within a society. In societies where there are many different cultures, celebrations are enjoyed by people who are not originally from a specific culture. A local newspaper published a picture of people lining the streets for the traditional Dragon Dance celebrating Chinese New Year. The smiling faces in the picture reflected a number of different races and ethnic backgrounds. Thus, the term sociocultural is meant to reflect the combined community in which learners live. It is the larger, multiethnic, and diverse community that shares many traditions and ideas.

PHOTO 3.6

Different opportunities for learning allow individual students to master concepts at their own pace, within their own zone of proximal development.

For teachers, distributed expertise can be seen as a creative opportunity to design effective classroom experiences that challenge all the students. Even when students *appear* to have similar capabilities, there may be individual variations that require an inventive lesson design and classroom organization. Consider Tim's experience as presented in Problem-Based Scenario 3.4.

Socially Meaningful Activities

The sociocultural approach focuses on *"socially meaningful educational activities"* (Moll, 1990, p. 8) that emphasize the underlying meaning of an educational

Problem-Based Scenario 3.4

K-5   6-8   9-12   SpEd

Student: Harry

Teacher: Tim

Tim sat down in the staff room to eat his lunch and grab a welcome cup of fresh coffee, a treat since most of the coffee sat for long periods of time. He had picked up the papers from his mailbox and used this quiet time to sort through the barrage of memos. It was the one from Marie, the school counselor, that caused him to stop and think. How was he going to run his tenth-grade history class now?

Figure 3.8 appears on page 96.

Apply

- How should Tim accommodate Harry's learning disability in his history class?

FIGURE 3.7

activity (e.g., literacy as the comprehension and communication of meaning) (Moll). The sociocultural perspective makes a critical and important distinction between *basic skills* and *basic activity* (Cole & Griffin, as cited in Moll). Basic activity concerns a much deeper level of meaning than basic skills. This distinction is similar to the novice–expert distinction discussed earlier.

Central Role of the Learner   Along with the constructivist approach outlined in this text, educational applications of sociocultural theory emphasize the central role of the learner. In a school community in Salt Lake City, children, parents, and teachers collaborate in planning educational activities (Rogoff, Bartlett, & Turkanis, 2001). That is, learning is a natural extension into the community, not something that only happens in a school with a teacher. Moreover, mutual learning takes place; children, parents, and teachers all learn from each other.

Community of Learners   Rogoff et al. (2001) emphasize, though, that a community of learners is more than "a collection of people who are learning" (p. 9):

> In our sense, "community" involves relationships among people based on common endeavors—trying to accomplish some things together—with some stability of involvement and attention to the ways that members relate to each other. In other words, a community of learners develops "cultural" practices and traditions that transcend the particular individuals involved, such as expected ways of handling conflicts and interpersonal issues and crises, as well as traditions for celebrating turning points and successes. (Rogoff et al., 2001, p. 10)

For a community of learners to function effectively, there must be mutual understanding among all participants in education—teachers, students, and parents. Tim, the grade 10 teacher you met previously, deliberated the complexities of establishing shared meaning after receiving feedback from parents about his efforts to incorporate distributed expertise in his classroom. This follow-up to Tim's initiatives is presented in Problem-Based Scenario 3.5.

Surfing Terms 3.3

Shared cognition
Distributed expertise
Scaffolding
Zone of proximal development
Basic activity
Basic skills
Multicultural education

Problem-Based Scenario 3.5

K-5   6-8   **9-12**   SpEd

Student: Tim
Teacher: Harry

Tim closed the door of his car with a sigh. It had been a long day, extending into Parent's Night. He was finally headed home at 10 P.M., but with more questions than answers. Earlier in the term he had changed around some of his teaching techniques to accommodate Harry, who had a learning disability, and two other students with learning problems. Tim had been feeling pretty proud of himself. Harry's grades and participation had improved, along with the two other students, and the class seemed to be moving along well. But tonight several parents spoke to him regarding what they saw as a "watering down" of the curriculum. This had taken him by surprise. The parents were concerned that the students were not learning the kinds of skills and background

(continued)

Problem-Based Scenario 3.5 (continued)

knowledge they would need in the next couple of years to get into a university. When Tim started to explain about different student needs, it became apparent the parents already understood these issues. In general, they were quite nice about it, but were also adamant that the class should, as one father put it, "be beefed up to challenge the brighter kids."

Now Tim had to think: Did adjusting to different students "water things down"? Was he really challenging the students to think? Did giving variety in assignments allow students to bypass learning how to work in other modalities? Does giving choice reduce skill development? And, the big question, what was he going to do now?

Apply

- Tim has a lot of questions about his teaching strategies. What could he do as a first step in answering them?
- Does accommodating different ways of learning in the classroom necessarily lead to watering down the curriculum?
- How would you adjust your teaching strategies and activities to meet different learning needs in your classroom?

Summary

In this chapter, you saw how theories grew and changed as our knowledge of development, behavior, teaching, and learning became more sophisticated. You also saw how many theories are used to explain the complex process of development. No one theoretical perspective can explain the complexity of human development and learning. Rather, as teachers, you need to understand a variety of theories so that you can make informed educational decisions about each student's needs.

- Neo-Piagetian theory describes the central conceptual understandings that are important for school success. For example, children's understanding of others' roles and the number line are critical to their broader understanding of social roles and relationships and concepts learned in elementary mathematics.

- Both conceptual understanding of a subject and related skills are necessary for expert understanding.

- Conversations with students can help you understand their perspectives on different concepts. These perspectives provide a valuable foundation for designing your instructional approaches.

- Classrooms described as communities of learners pool individual expertise to create learning environments where adults and children learn from each other and the artifacts of their culture. Meaningful educational activities are stressed.

A Metacognitive Challenge

You should now be able to reflect on the following questions:

- What do I know about children's thinking and how it develops?
- What do I know about adolescents' thinking and how it develops?
- What do I know about the social context of learning?
- How do my knowledge of thinking and the social context of learning help me to teach the learners in my classroom?

Artifacts for Problem-Based Scenarios

FIGURE 3.3 ■ Sammy's Math Worksheet

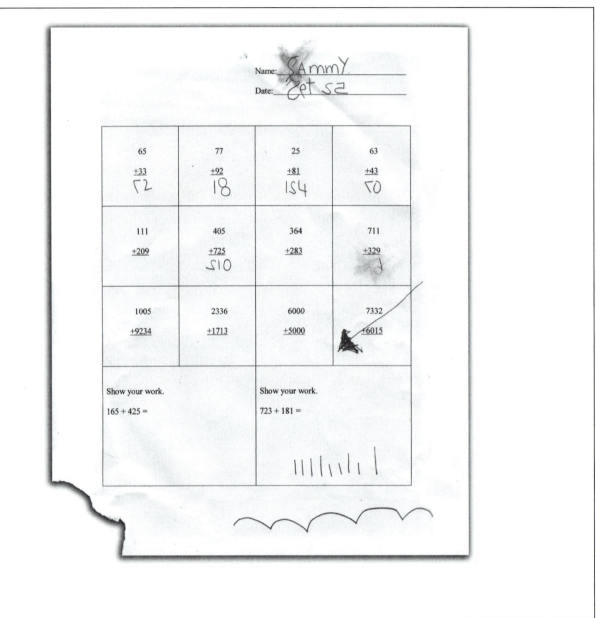

FIGURE 3.4 ■ **Artifact for Problem-Based Scenario 3.1**

```
Date:    Tuesday, October 25, 2001
Subject: Sammy
To:      Emma Anderson eandersen@sd10.whiteplains.ks.us
From:    jblythe@sd10.whiteplains.ks.us (Jack Blythe)


Hi Emma,
        Sorry to have missed you after school today.
I dropped by to talk to you about Sammy.  You know
what a struggle it's been to make a breakthrough in
math.  It continues to be, but I just had to tell
you that we did some activities in the resource
room today - making change, etc. in a "play store"
context.  Sammy was an absolute star.  As far as
planning how much to spend and figuring out change,
he really knows his stuff.  I'll try to catch you
in the next couple of days.  We should talk about
this!!
Jack

*********************************************************

Jack Blythe
Resource Room Teacher
White Plains Elementary
```

FIGURE 3.8 ■ Artifact for Problem-Based Scenario 3.4

MEMORANDUM

To: Tim Roland
From: Marie Howe
Re: Harold Williams

Tim,

I just got the results back from some testing done on Harry. You should know that there seems to be a language processing difficulty that is causing most of Harry's academic problems. He has a very hard time processing oral language. This means that it takes a lot of his energy to understand what is being said to him in a structured situation, like a classroom. He has few difficulties in social situations, so that isn't any problem. Since this is considered a Learning Disability we will be giving him extra help in the Resource Room. What this means in the classroom is not to expect him to be able to listen to lecture material and take notes at the same time.

I will get back to you later with more details.

Marie

P.S. Would you mind sitting on a School Based Team?

Learning and Cognition: Expanding Our Perspectives

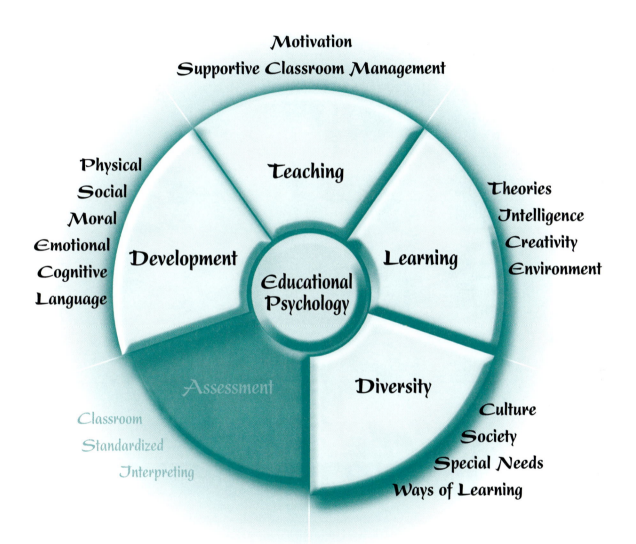

Motivation
Supportive Classroom Management

Teaching

Physical
Social
Moral
Emotional
Cognitive
Language

Development

Educational
Psychology

Learning

Theories
Intelligence
Creativity
Environment

Assessment

Diversity

Classroom
Standardized
Interpreting

Culture
Society
Special Needs
Ways of Learning

In this chapter, additional ways of understanding learning and cognition are introduced. You will see that many current educational ideas have their basis in the work of 20th-century theorists. From behaviorism to adaptive behavioral analysis, each theory provides us with additional ways of understanding influences on cognitive development, as well as on the role of the teaching–learning process in development.

As you read about each of these theories, you are encouraged to take from each the features that have the most meaning for your subject area and the age group you will be teaching. Behaviorists, for example, can help us understand why many of the techniques in classroom management are so effective, and social learning theorists help us understand the value of teaching techniques such as modeling.

PHOTO 4.1

Technology influences cognitive development.

Understanding Learning

Most of us have a basic understanding of the concept of learning. *Learning* consists of acquiring a basic level of knowledge or skills and then building on this base to master more and more complex ideas and tasks. Learning involves middle- and high-level mental processes (Sternberg, 1999a) and varied paths to acquiring knowledge.

- *Association:* We learn through mental association (e.g., the terms kingdom, phylum, class, order, family, genus, and species are linked together in the minds of most students of high school biology).
- *Perception:* Our learning is influenced by our perception of what is to be learned. If a task is perceived as difficult, we assume we cannot do it before we even try (Photo 4.2). However, the relationship between perception and what is learned is not always predictable (Nelson, 1999). Sometimes we learn better if we are challenged by a difficult task that interests us.

PHOTO 4.2
Students' perception of the difficulty of a task can often influence their success in completing it.

- *Conditioned response:* Beyond knowledge and skills, there is the learning that takes place when we acquire attitudes, beliefs, and habits. These may be learned through *conditioning* (explained later in the chapter). If children receive negative feedback on their writing, for example, they learn to avoid the task, believing that they are incompetent.
- *Social learning:* Attitudes, beliefs, and habits also can be learned through observation of those around us.

But as we contemplate our definition of learning, we can start to see its variations. For example, we were born with the ability to suck; it was an innate ability we did not have to learn. However, walking required not only mental understanding and coordination of muscle groups, but practice until the complete sequence was learned to the point of *automaticity*. Once toddlers master walking, they no longer have to concentrate intensely because walking becomes an effortless, automatic process—one they don't have to think about.

At times you realize that you have forgotten something that you once knew. What happens to things that have been learned? Do we really forget over time? "Learning is a change in human disposition or capability, which persists over a period of time, and which is not simply ascribable to processes of growth" (Gagne, 1977, p. 3). The change can be behavioral or cognitive, actual or potential (since many times learning is not immediately obvious). When a student memorizes the multiplication table for 5s and is able to pass a written quiz including items such as 5×2 and 5×6, then teachers can conclude the student has learned something. But this observation is behavioral; that is, the student has overtly demonstrated an ability to correctly answer certain questions. We do not know the depth of cognitive understanding unless we ask more probing questions. Often students know and answer superficially, such as $5 \times 2 = 10$, because the answer has been memorized. Other students may know $5 \times 2 = 10$ because it is 5 groups of 2s, or 2 groups of 5s, and it could also be 10 groups of 1s. This cognitive understanding exemplifies a depth to the learning beyond an overt, behavioral demonstration.

Our interest in learning could be considered an extension of being human. As mentioned in Chapter 2, understanding the knowledge of previous generations

> *Automaticity:* When something is done automatically, without conscious thought (e.g., brushing your teeth, locking the door when you leave the house)

and going beyond this knowledge to build and expand thought requires each generation to learn what has come before. The discussion of various perspectives on learning takes this point of view; how contemporary approaches to learning have built on and extended the work of previous theorists is discussed.

Behaviorism: Evidence of Learning in Behavior

Learning has been studied intensely only during the past 100 years. Before then most work on human learning and psychology was based on self-reflections. You will notice that many philosophers' names are listed in the Surfing Terms. This emphasis on philosophy reflects the type of writing about learning and thinking that took place prior to the 20th century. By the turn of the 20th century, advances in science and mathematics had changed the way research was done, heralding the scientific method. This in turn influenced psychology and our understanding of how we learn.

Following the trend toward scientific understanding of natural phenomena that was popular at the turn of the 20th century, psychologists undertook the study of *how* people learned. Since it was necessary to observe and record all data in a scientific manner, learning had to be defined in terms of observable behaviors. This led to an approach to studying learning that ignored anything that was not observable and the subsequent term *behaviorism*. The origins of behaviorism can be found in the work of Ivan Pavlov (1849–1936) (Sternberg, 1999b).

Involuntary Learning: Classical Conditioning

Pavlov was a physician who specialized in learning through *conditioning*, that is, repeated encounters with associated phenomena that cause an expectation that one phenomenon will result in the other happening. Pavlov (1927) worked with dogs that were trained to salivate not at the sight of food, but rather at the sound of a bell that rang when food normally appeared. This training was referred to as *classical conditioning*, since it was first described in a series of classical experiments.

An educational example of classical conditioning is when students learn to read "red" by having it paired with a picture of a red apple (Photo 4.3). Soon the teacher removes the picture of the apple, and the student has learned to identify the word *red* in written form. The type of learning investigated by Pavlov is called *involuntary learning*.

Voluntary Learning

Early behavioral psychologists studied voluntary learning. Edward Thorndike (1913) studied learning by placing animals in problem situations. For example, Thorndike would put a cat in a box from which it could escape by hitting a lever. Through trial and error (usually by accident the first few times), the cat eventually learned how to get out of the box. Since the cat used an *instrument* (a lever) to solve the problem of getting out of the box, this type of learning was called *instrumental conditioning*. Based on his work, Thorndike postulated two laws of learning:

1. The *law of exercise* states that repetition of a conditioned response strengthens the stimulus–response bond; that is, practice makes perfect.
2. The *law of effect* states that responses followed by pleasure are strengthened, while responses followed by pain or punishment are weakened.

Observable Behavior versus Mental States

Behaviorism ignored any internal influences, such as inner states of the individual (Sternberg, 1999b; Watson, 1925), focusing only on observable objects or events called *stimuli* in the physical environment of the learner. The learning that

PHOTO 4.3

Learning by association with known objects is a feature of classical conditioning.

resulted from exposure to stimuli was described in terms of *responses,* that is, observable physical movement, actions, or reactions of the learner. The central goal of *behaviorists,* as these psychologists were called, was to provide a set of simple laws that explained *all* learning.

Behaviorists are sometimes called radical behaviorists because of their disregard of internal *mental states* (Sternberg, 1999b). John Watson, generally considered to be the father of radical behaviorism, made the following claim (Watson, 1925):

> Give me a dozen healthy infants, well formed, and my own special world to bring them up in, and I'll guarantee to take any one at random and train him to become any type of specialist I might select—doctor, lawyer, artist, merchant, chief and yes, even beggarman and thief, regardless of his talents, penchants, tendencies, abilities, vocations, or race of his ancestry. (p. 82)

Watson, like other behaviorists, concentrated on shaping behavior without considering individuals' thoughts or feelings about the training or their interests and backgrounds.

Manipulating the Environment: Operant Conditioning

As psychologists developed laws for learning, they became interested in manipulating the environment to attempt to control behavior. B. F. Skinner (1938) was interested in how new behaviors were acquired. He noticed that many behaviors were not simple responses but deliberate, voluntary actions that *"operated"* on an environment (Photo 4.4). He called this process *operant conditioning.*

Mental states: Thoughts, feelings, desires, and intentions are mental states

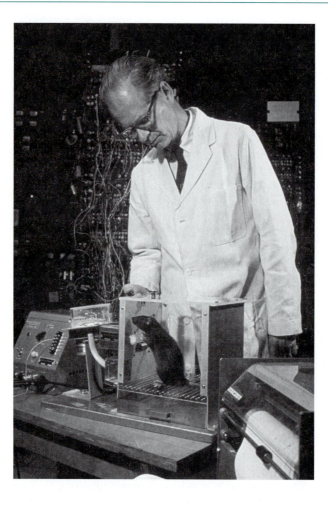

PHOTO 4.4

From Skinner's experiments we learned how to shape behavior.

By manipulating the environment, Skinner was able to shape behavior in a desired way. He expanded the law of effect by shaping a behavior so that one doesn't have to wait for the desired outcome. For example, an elementary teacher holds up his hand to indicate to the class that they must stop talking, look at him, and pay attention to what he is about to say. The teacher doesn't wait for the class to settle down by itself, but rather influences the environment by an action.

Skinner proposed reinforcing a behavior by making it contingent on something else—the principle that you get dessert if you eat your dinner. This is often referred to as "Grandma's rule" or the Premack principle, where students are more likely to do something they don't particularly like to gain a favored activity or reward (Premack, 1959). Skinner also pointed out that the behavior is established more quickly when it is reinforced immediately and that in some instances a partial reinforcement or withdrawal of a reinforcer will also produce results. When managing a classroom, for example, a teacher may get faster results by ignoring a problematic student behavior than by calling attention to the action.

Operant conditioning, like classical conditioning, requires a stimulus and a response. In classical conditioning the response is often automatic, while in operant conditioning it is usually controlled, such as learning something. Also operant conditioning adds a reinforcer to follow the response. Reinforcers are either primary, that is, basic to physiological needs like water or air, or secondary, such as praise or stickers. Secondary reinforcers are widely used in classrooms. However, caution is needed when utilizing reinforcers, since a teacher can inadvertently reinforce an undesirable response. For example, if students are given homework, the teacher needs to collect it, go over it in class, check for correctness, or acknowledge the work in some timely fashion. If a teacher does nothing with the homework, it will only take students a few assignments to figure out they don't have to do the homework. In this case the reinforcer for the behavior is the inaction of the teacher, which gives a message to the students about the importance of homework.

As children get older, the type of reinforcement needs to change. Many young children find stickers a fun thing to collect, but not all children will respond to stickers. Teachers need to observe their students and find a repertoire of reinforcements that go beyond stickers. As with stickers, a teacher should be careful with items such as grades or extra points as reinforcers. Secondary teachers often complain of students who want grades for every item they produce. In this case the reinforcer has taken a more prominent role than the activity or behavior and actually detracts from the goal of independent work.

A number of reinforcement techniques are utilized in education.

- *Group contingency:* In this instance the group is rewarded only when all members have achieved the desired behavior. This can be very effective when used judiciously with students. It relies on peer pressure to encourage a specific behavior (O'Leary & O'Leary, 1972). When students reach adolescence, they start to question the morality of using the whole group, especially for discipline purposes (e.g., the whole class is punished when only a few people are disrupting the lesson). Although, if used positively, such as in a team sport, group contingency can be extremely motivating for students.

- *Token economy:* In this instance, students are allowed to choose a reinforcer (such as free reading time or access to a computer game) as the result of collecting tokens (or poker chips) earned when an appropriate behavior is demonstrated. This is a fairly labor-intensive activity for a teacher. Keeping track of tokens, watching for specific behaviors, and teaching a whole class means that this type of reinforcement is usually relegated to students with behavior problems. Over time it is important to withdraw the tokens as the student learns to respond appropriately on his or her own. Otherwise, the tokens take on the same importance as the grades did in our earlier example.

- *Cueing:* Once students understand the desired behavior, it only requires a trigger to get them to respond appropriately. For example, if students need to clean up before they can go to lunch, the teacher just needs to comment "five minutes until the bell rings" to start students cleaning up.

Operant conditioning forms the basis for many forms of behavior control within a school. Most students respond well to various types of reinforcers and, over time, will learn behavior appropriate to social and classroom situations. However, when students misbehave, it interferes not only with everyone's learning, but it also may threaten the safety of others in the classroom. Misbehavior requires immediate attention from the teacher. For this reason, many techniques for classroom management utilize various reinforcements in terms of consequences, punishments, and rewards to achieve appropriate behavior from students. Operant conditioning originally did not have any connection to punishment, but due to the use of reinforcement to change behavior, it has naturally expanded to encompass this topic. We have chosen to give a very brief introduction to this topic. As teachers you are encouraged to understand your students and expand your repertoire of classroom management techniques to reduce the need for punishment as a means to change student behavior. For many teachers, punishment is seen as a last resort, accessed only when all other means of behavior change have failed.

Punishment is a reinforcer that decreases a behavior. Grossman (2004) discusses how teachers use the term *punishment* in two ways. If it is a mild consequence, such

Verbal reprimand: a scolding given due to some misbehavior; most effective when given quietly, unemotionally, briefly, and in a timely manner

Time-out: placing a student in a separate area for a short period of time where there is no opportunity to interact with others

Surfing Terms *4.1*

History of psychology

William James

René Descartes

John Locke

James Mill

Immanuel Kant

John Dewey

Dialectics

Contingency

Contingency contracts

Classical conditioning

Verbal reprimands

Time-out

Response cost

Extinction in classical conditioning

In-school suspension

as a *verbal reprimand* or private statement of disapproval, teachers consider it simply a negative consequence. They save the term punishment for harsher consequences, such as being removed from a class. A *time-out* often works well for many situations: the student is removed from the situation and given a chance to settle down before returning to the group. However, most teachers do not really need to distinguish between degrees of punishment, since what may seem mild to the teacher could be deemed harsh by the student.

Grossman (2004) points out factors that must be taken into consideration with any punishment:

- *Students' perceptions of consequences.* Make sure the consequences have the desired effect on the student. In some instances the consequences may actually be beneficial to a student. For example, school suspension may allow a teenager to sit at home and watch television. It actually may be an enjoyable vacation, especially if there is no reaction from parents.
- *Provide a rational cognitive structure.* Make sure students know what is wrong, why it is inappropriate, what the correct response should be, and why you are using punishment, rather than another strategy. This may be effective when a series of other techniques has failed to work. A student who continues to hit others on the playground, after numerous attempts by teachers to stop this behavior, may need to be punished by removing playground privileges for a day or two.
- *Alternative behaviors.* Sometimes students encounter situations they do not know how to handle. A young child may hit another when he doesn't get what he wants. A teacher who understands this will provide a lesson in appropriate conversation and sharing to provide the student with an alternative means to handle the situation.
- *Severity.* Caution is given here. The severity of punishment actually depends on many items, such as age of the child, ethnic background, gender, intensity, and duration. Even writing a student's name on the board may be seen as severe if it causes extreme embarrassment or stress to the student. Never give out punishments when you are angry or upset. Always make decisions in a calm, well thought-out manner.
- *Consistency.* Make sure that the punishment is consistently given when the infraction occurs. Otherwise, students become confused when a teacher sometimes reacts and at another time lets it go.
- *Timing.* Try to respond to misbehavior in a timely fashion. The exact time depends on the behavior, the student, the situation, the emotions present, extenuating circumstances, and the like. (pp. 320–324)

As you will see in the next section some more active ways to deal with antisocial and disruptive behaviors have evolved beyond the stage of punishment.

Applied Behavioral Analysis: The Influence of Environment on Behavior

Since the early 1990s, behaviorist principles have been applied to the design of *"effective environments"* (Lucyshyn, Kayser, Irvin, & Blumberg, 2002; Sugai, Horner, & Sprague, 1999). Effective environments are different than the environmental control envisioned by B. F. Skinner. Effective environments take into account a wider range of complex variables and are flexible and responsive to learners. In educational terms, such environments for learning create classrooms in which children learn skills that are valued in the culture, prosocial behaviors are modeled and encouraged, and there is little disruptive behavior (Sugai et al., 1999).

Applied behavioral analysis directs its attention to when and why disruptive or violent behaviors occur and what events maintain these behaviors (Photo 4.5). Consider the

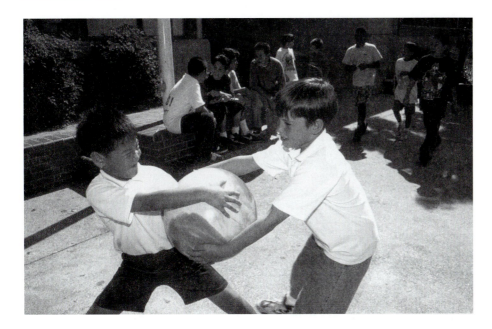

PHOTO 4.5
Applied behavioral analysis attempts to pinpoint the events or interactions that might trigger problem behavior.

following scenario. A group of boys is playing marbles at recess. One of their class-mates, Roger, observes them for several minutes, then suddenly rushes over and grabs a bag of marbles belonging to one of the boys. Roger is chased by the owner of the bag, knocked down, and kicked. The school has a zero tolerance policy on phys-ical violence. Both boys end up at the principal's office, and their parents are called to take them home. Often such events result in repetitions of this cycle.

Functional Assessment

An applied behavioral analysis approach would pose the question of *why* Roger behaved as he did. For example, did Roger desperately want to play with the other boys? What are his friendship patterns? Does he have trouble with social situations? Perhaps he simply does not know how to approach others and request entry into a play situation. Roger can be observed in different school set-tings with these questions in mind. He could also be asked for his point of view on why the marble incident happened. Such questions form the basis of a *functional assessment* (Sugai et al., 1999).

A functional assessment identifies "when, where, and why problem behaviors occur *and* when, where, and why they do *not* occur" (Sugai et el., 1999, p. 254; ital-ics in the original). Knowing when, where, and why problem behaviors do *not* occur is equally important to knowing when, where, and why they do occur.

Positive Behavioral Support

The information provided by a functional assessment allows teachers to focus on *positive behavioral support* by constructing educational environments that are sup-portive and encouraging of valued social behaviors. As Sugai et al. (1999) point out,

> There is value in knowing whether tantrums are maintained by access to teacher attention versus escape from challenging tasks. There is value in identifying that defiance and disruption are more likely when certain peers are present. There is value in understanding the features of math problems or error corrections that make the task highly aversive for a student. (p. 254)

Carr et al. (2002) emphasized that the best time to intervene with problem behavior is when the behavior is not occurring. Positive behavioral support is *proactive*, in "sharp contrast to traditional approaches, which have emphasized the use of aversive procedures" (Carr et al., p. 9) to control difficult behaviors.

Positive behavioral support: Support that focuses on *understanding* behavior and providing a positive school environment

Additional key concepts in applied behavior analysis, functional assessment, and positive behavioral support are the following:

- *Contextual fit* (Lucyshyn, Albin, & Nixon, 1997): support that is a good match between the child and the educational setting, personal competence, and environmental integrity (Carr et al., 2002)
- *Person-centered planning:* planning based on individual needs, a concept that is closely aligned to the philosophy of constructivism on which this book is based
- *Environmental integrity:* a focus on encouraging self-reliance, choice, and decision making

Key concepts of applied behavioral analysis are also part of the supportive classroom that is discussed in more detail in Chapter 9.

In Problem-Based Scenario 4.1, Jessie, a fourth-grade teacher, revisits the idea of functional assessment in the hope of figuring out what is underlying a student's disruptive behavior. For secondary teachers, students who are disruptive have usually been identified in their elementary school years. However, the basic technique of functional behavioral assessment can often be used as a tool to understand why disruptive behaviors continue to occur, as seen with Ian, an eighth-grader, in Problem-Based Scenario 4.2.

Problem-Based Scenario 4.1

K-5   6-8   9-12   SpEd

Student: *Giselle*
Teacher: *Jessie*

Jessie was at her wit's end. It had been an exceptionally tiring day and all she really wanted to do was go home. Teaching fourth grade shouldn't be this complicated! But Mrs. Poirier was waiting to speak to her. Her daughter, Giselle, was in another fight today. Mrs. Poirier was understandably concerned. This behavior had been going on for a couple of years, but now was becoming more frequent. Giselle got into fights on the playground regularly, and her behavior in class was disruptive. She was often out of her seat and invariably poked, kicked, or insulted someone as she wandered around the classroom.

Jessie was really confused. Giselle could be such a thoughtful child. She often brought small bouquets of flowers to Jessie, and she enjoyed talking to her after school. Giselle also could be very helpful to her classmates, sensing when they were upset and offering help. The other children were now very wary of these offers of help; they, too, seemed confused. How could the same child who hit them be kind to them?

Jessie thought that Giselle's disruptive behavior might be associated with her academic difficulties. Her reading level was typical of a beginning second-grader, and her written work was very immature. Giselle preferred to print. Jessie had backed off on insisting that she use cursive writing after Giselle ripped up a notebook and stormed out of class early in September. Jessie had modified the language arts curriculum for Giselle, but still the outbursts and restlessness continued.

A few months ago, Jessie had started to fill out a functional assessment form on Giselle (Figures 4.1 and 4.3 on pages 112–114). Her principal had recommended the strategy. However, too many days like this one had interfered with completing it and analyzing it to see if there were patterns to Giselle's disruptive behaviors. Jessie now searched her desk for the form. Even though it was incomplete, it might give her something concrete to talk about with Mrs. Poirier. And maybe Mrs. Poirier could offer some helpful insights. It was worth a try.

Apply

- What kinds of questions could Jessie ask Mrs. Poirier that would add to her understanding of the limited observations in the Behavioral Assessment Form?

(continued)

Problem-Based Scenario 4.1 (continued)

■ How could Jessie organize her teaching to provide for more written observations of her class, and of Giselle in particular?

Source: Based on Shippen, Simpson, & Crites, 2003, pp. 38, 40–41.

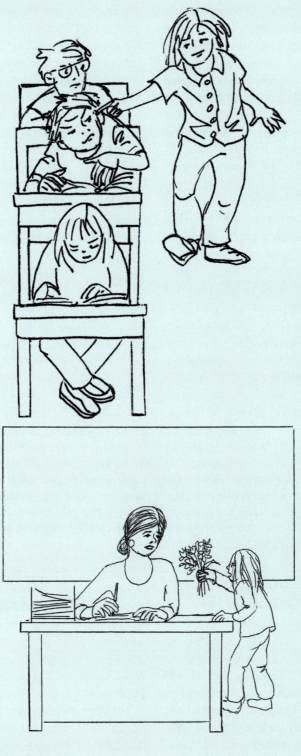

FIGURE 4.2

Problem-Based Scenario 4.2

Student: *Ian*
Teacher: *Margaret*

Margaret left the school on Friday exhausted. It had been another week of constantly fighting a "battle of wills" with Ian. He was not really such a bad kid, but at certain times he caused nothing but trouble. Even Hal, the vice-principal, seemed to have gone through every reasonable punishment and nothing worked for long. His record noted the pattern of a fairly smart kid who had been able to get past the behavior problems by doing well on tests in elementary school. It also showed that the parents stepped in only when it seemed that he was ready for more severe discipline techniques, such as an alternative school. But things were really getting out of hand. The grade 8 classes were organized on a different system from elementary schools, so what had worked in the past could not work now.

Margaret wanted to try to figure out what was behind behaviors like ripping up quizzes as they were handed out, pushing desks over during seat work, talking when she was trying to explain the day's tasks, telling her "no" when he was asked to do something, and so on. All seemed to be meant as deliberate disruptions. But were the disruptions trying to gain something or get out of something? That was the question. Hal had given her an article on Functional Behavioral Assessment. While she could not do the assessment in its entirety by herself since she was also teaching the class, Hal suggested she might be able to do some of the basics. It was certainly worth a try. Margaret set up a large file card with columns for date, time, class activity, action, and consequence. The idea was to fill in the columns as soon as possible after an incident with Ian (Figure 4.4 on page 115). In this way, Hal and Margaret would be able to analyze not only the actual incident, but, it was hoped, why Ian acted in this manner. This week the card really got filled in. Now what to do next?

Apply

- What is the next step for Margaret to take when trying to interpret a Behavioral Assessment?
- What strategies could you suggest to Margaret to try with this student?

In addition, consider the challenge that José Santos, a middle school teacher, is experiencing with Jonathan, who repeatedly eats test papers (see Problem-Based Scenario 4.3). José cannot find a way to get Jonathan to stop this behavior. Might positive behavioral support be a direction for José? The same question might be posed for Emma, an elementary teacher. Emma has tried a number of strategies to help Charlie develop better work habits, but Charlie's behaviors are getting worse rather than better (see Problem-Based Scenario 4.4).

Problem-Based Scenario 4.3

Student: *Jonathan*
Teacher: *José*

José had been teaching for two years and usually enjoyed his eighth-grade English classes. Everyone had finally settled down from the excitement of the Christmas vacation, and José thought that the routine of Friday quizzes would give him an opportunity to bring up the subject of grades. But today, standing here, watching this again, he knew that he had no idea where to even start.

As José was passing out today's quiz, Jonathan slowly started to tear the paper into strips and eat it. Of course the class was hysterical, as usual. Everyone,

(continued)

including José, watched as Jonathan finished the entire sheet. The class then turned to Mr. Santos to see what would happen, but José just turned and sat down at his desk. Slowly everyone started to work on the quiz, while Jonathan just sat there, staring out the window with a smirk on his face.

José berated himself: Why hadn't he done something or said something? Jonathan had been a problem before the holidays and seemed to be picking up where he left off. He had eaten tests before, and José had given detentions, sent him to the office, and even

spoken to his mother (who considered this a minor problem that the teacher should take care of). So as José sat there he began to wonder, where do I go now?

Apply

- Using Behavior Theory, give an explanation for this student's behavior.
- What might be at least two strategies José might try with this student?

Problem-Based Scenario 4.4

K-5   6-8   9-12   SpEd

Student: Charlie
Teacher: Emma

Emma had been preparing for the spring parent conferences for 2 weeks. She felt like she was ready for anything—anything but Charlie's parents. Not that they were difficult; on the contrary, they were pleasant, proactive, concerned parents. They were as puzzled as Emma was and as three other teachers had been before her. Now, by third grade, everyone was anxious for some concrete direction to support Charlie. Charlie Roper had a "history," but it was a strange one. Not one of his teachers could really pin down what it *really* was about Charlie. He was well mannered most of the time and always helped out with classroom chores and events. He simply didn't do any schoolwork. Emma could not think of one time that he had actually completed an assignment or even remotely approached completing one (Figure 4.5). This had been the story since kindergarten (Figure 4.6).

The support provided to Charlie included extra reading instruction in the second grade. Charlie's reading level was somewhat lower than that of his peers, but not low enough to qualify for another year of support. The school district's behavior management team had implemented a behavior modification program for Charlie focused on work completion, also in the second grade. Results were uneven and the program was discontinued. The school psychologist said that other children were in far more need than Charlie was. Testing done by the

school psychologist indicated that Charlie had average ability overall and that his academic achievement was average also, with the exception of reading.

Charlie's parents told Emma at the beginning of the year that they had taken him to a psychiatrist during the summer. However, they said she had nothing concrete to offer to help with his school problems. Charlie's parents asked for, and Emma agreed to provide, regular telephone updates on his work. Emma also suggested that they try sending a homework book home. Emma would detail what was to be done and the Ropers would oversee the work and sign the book before Charlie took it back to school. Things had gone smoothly for the first term, but began to fall apart in the winter. Emma felt that the response to her phone calls had become less than enthusiastic, and Charlie often neglected to return his homework book. Emma had to admit that she was growing tired of looking for solutions and that she was feeling pretty tense about Charlie. Probably the Ropers were, too.

Something else puzzled Emma. During the first term, Charlie had been tough to motivate, but he was pretty quiet about it. Then he began to demonstrate some "attitude"—smirking when asked to attend to his work and often looking defiant. Last week, he responded to Emma's reminder to complete

(continued)

Problem-Based Scenario 4.4 (*continued*)

his work by having a temper tantrum. He rolled on the floor, kicked his feet, and cried loudly. Emma ignored him and kept on giving instructions to the class. He composed himself quickly and went back to his desk. She wondered what might happen next and how to approach discussing this change of behavior with the Ropers.

Apply

- How would you organize the meeting with Mr. and Mrs. Roper? What kinds of questions would you ask?
- Is there anything in the literature on children's art that might help you understand Charlie better?

Social Learning Theory: Observing and Learning from Our Social Environment

As behaviorism began to expand, this question arose: How do people learn to function in their own society? In 1941, Miller and Dollard published a book, *Social Learning and Imitation*, that highlighted the importance of learning through the observation of other people. Before then, learning theorists had ignored unobservable cognitive aspects of learning, focusing instead on behavior.

Most of the credit for the work on social learning was given to Albert Bandura (1977, 1986). He combined behaviorism and cognition into *social learning theory*. He introduced the idea of *modeling*, or imitation of the actions of others. New behaviors are learned more quickly through modeling than through the trial and error process that is necessary for learning by operant conditioning. Social learning theory also introduced ideas such as *vicarious learning*, in which observing someone getting rewarded or punished indirectly teaches another person the same rules or actions.

Bandura's work on social learning touched on many aspects of classroom instruction, including

- Classroom management
- Student motivation
- Teaching concepts or skills
- Teaching social interaction
- Counteracting socially unacceptable influences

These concepts are discussed further in Chapters 6, 8, and 9.

Beyond theories of modeling, ideas of behaviorism and social learning theory guided educators in North America into the 1950s when other perspectives on learning became more prevalent. It became apparent that no neat set of laws could describe and explain this human capacity. It was time to explore the complexity of human learning.

Surfing Terms 4.2

Social learning

Modeling

Vicarious learning

Observational learning

Self-regulation

Goal-directed behavior

Response facilitation effect

Response inhibition effect

Response disinhibition effect

Behavior analysis

Summary

In this chapter you supplemented your knowledge of developmental theories with background on classical theories that explain behavior and how we respond to various social situations. These theories add to your repertoire for understanding the many ways in which learners think and behave. Use of the theories will help you plan instructional and social support for your students in a classroom.

- Behavior may offer evidence of learning. However, it also is important to consider the environmental context in which the behavior takes place and possible reasons for the behavior.

■ Operant conditioning helps us understand how we can enhance student learning through reinforcing correct and appropriate behaviors.

■ When used in a rational, humane, and controlled manner, punishment is another way of influencing problem behaviors.

■ Applied behavior analysis is a contemporary interpretation of behaviorism that takes account of how context influences behavior. Functional assessment of students' behavior can help you determine what triggers problem behavior and what supports positive behavior.

■ One way we learn is by observing and interacting in social environments. Teachers can model appropriate behaviors and work habits for their students.

A Metacognitive Challenge

You should now be able to reflect on the following questions:

■ How would I define learning?

■ What do I know about the influence of environment on behavior?

■ What do I know about learning and teaching styles?

■ What do I know about how thinking and learning are monitored by students?

■ How does my knowledge of influences on behavior and learning and regulation of learning help me to teach the learners in my classroom?

■ How can I use what I know about reinforcement and behavior to enhance the learning environment?

■ In my career as a teacher, where does punishment fit in? Or does it?

Artifacts for Problem-Based Scenarios

FIGURE 4.1 ■ Antecedent–Behavior–Consequence Sequence for Giselle

Antecedent	Behavior	Consequence
Told G to sit down and finish her work (language skills)	Sharpened pencil; poked Joey with it	Asked her to apologize
Told class they had 10 minutes to finish work	G sits down; scribbles over the worksheet	Told her she would have to finish after school
Dismissed for recess	Angry, distracted, pushes others to get out the door	Brought her back for a cool-down period
Introduced printmaking activity	Focused; created a beautiful design; helped Simone cut her lino	Praised her helpfulness and her work

FIGURE 4.3 ■ Functional Behavioral Assessment for Giselle

Baseline Data Collection

Target Behavior I *Poking classmates (pencil, finger, ruler)*

Baseline Assessment Method   Baseline Frequency of Target Behavior

Parent interview

Systematic observation

Frequency count   *about 5 times a day*

Target Behavior II *Fights on playground*

Baseline Assessment Method   Baseline Frequency of Target Behavior

Parent interview

Systematic observation

Frequency count   *about twice a week*

Target Behavior III

Baseline Assessment Method   Baseline Frequency of Target Behavior

Parent interview

Systematic observation

Frequency count

Purpose of Target Behavior I: Poking classmates

1. To obtain something?   Yes   (No)   What?

2. To escape/avoid something?   (Yes)   No   What? Avoid doing work

3. Other factors?   Yes   No   What?

FIGURE 4.3 ■ **Functional Behavioral Assessment for Giselle (continued)**

Hypothesis:

Replacement and Behavioral Goal:

Necessary Skills?   (Yes)   No   *Can be helpful and kind to classmates*

Purpose of Target Behavior II   *Fights on playground*

1. To obtain something?   Yes   No   What?

2. To escape/avoid something?   Yes   No   What?

3. Other factors?   Yes   No   What?

Hypothesis:

Replacement and Behavioral Goal:

Necessary Skills?   Yes   No

Purpose of Target Behavior III

1. To obtain something?   Yes   No   What?

2. To escape/avoid something?   Yes   No   What?

3. Other factors?   Yes   No   What?

Hypothesis:

Replacement and Behavioral Goal:

Necessary Skills?   Yes   No

FIGURE 4.4 ◼ **Baseline Data Collection for Ian**

Date	Time	Class activity	Action	Consequence
11/2	8:20	Starting to draw a graph of lab results	Wrote on partner's graph – "this is stupid"; partner reacted by swearing	Sent to Hal's office
11/3	11:35	Cleaning up –end of lab	Threw water on girls at the sink	Time out inside the prep room
11/4	1:00	Lab on temperature – beakers, thermometers and burners	Spit a half-eaten Twinkie into a beaker of water	Sat out lab in prep room and detention
11/5	2:30	Drawing graphs and discussion	Made (farting) noises with his hands during discussion to get class to laugh	Spoke to him, tried to ignore it –didn't work. Time out in prep room. Detention
11/6	8:30	Video and discussion of scientific method	Pencil tapping and humming	Asked to stop several times, no response. Sent to see Hal

FIGURE 4.5 ◼ **Artifact for Problem-Based Scenario 4.4**

FIGURE 4.6 ▦ **Artifact for Problem-Based Scenario 4.4**

```
Date:    Wednesday, February 19, 2002
Subject: Charlie
To:      Emma Anderson eandersen@sd10.whiteplains.ks.us
From:    jwong@se10.whiteplains.ks.us (Jolie Wong)


Hi Emma,
        I got your note about Charlie.  Yes - his
aversion to completing schoolwork was evident when
I taught him last year.  It got worse as the year
went on.  Nothing seemed to make a difference.  You
know how 2nd graders love stickers - not Charlie!
That was part of the problem when the behavior team
was here.  They tried to find something that Char-
lie would be interested in to use as a motivator
but he wouldn't cooperate.  Finally, they tried
some things on their own - some worked, some
didn't.  In the end we all felt like Charlie had
really learned how to work the system!
        Home-school communication was good, but not
very consistent.  I'm partly to blame, but I just
got the impression that I was becoming a bother, so
I backed off.
        Why don't you talk to Brian?  He taught
Charlie in first grade.  I think the transition to
first grade was difficult for Charlie, but Brian
could give you more details.
Good luck!
Jolie
**************************************************
Jolie Wong
2nd Grade Teacher, White Plains Elementary
```

Learning and Cognition: Applications for Diverse Classrooms

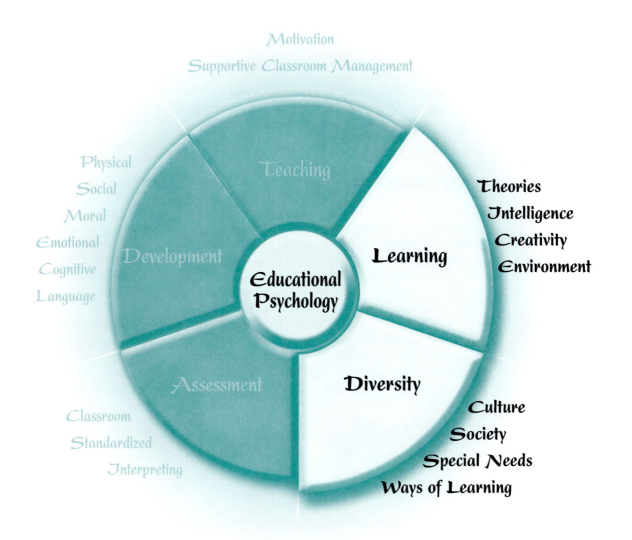

In this chapter we introduce a theory that helps us understand the complexity of human learning. Information-processing theory has informed our understanding of the many steps and subtleties that are involved in learning and applying what we know. Information-processing theorists laid the groundwork for related concepts that help us understand how to support learning. Knowledge about our ability to "know what we know" and "think about our thinking" (metacognition)

and the different ways we learn and process information were informed by information-processing theories. This knowledge provides perspectives on understanding how to support the diverse learners in our classrooms.

Information Processing: Capturing the Complexity of Human Learning

During the 1950s and 1960s, a number of technological changes and advances occurred in society. The most notable were the beginning of the space age with the launch of *Sputnik* in the late 1950s and the introduction of the microprocessor and subsequent computer advances. The launch of *Sputnik* caused governments to look more closely at education and to question the learning processes of their citizens.

Artificial Intelligence

Scientists began to be interested in *artificial intelligence* (AI), that is, intelligent performance by computers and other machines, such as robots. They turned to descriptions of human learning to help them design "intelligent machines" (Newell, Shaw, & Simon, 1958). However, it quickly became apparent that explanations of learning developed in the first half of the 20th century were too simplistic. Human learning and thinking are very complex, especially when used to solve problems.

While educators have always been interested in solving problems, problem solving became more of a research focus with the advent of computers and research into AI. To design machines that could duplicate human thought, we had to first understand how humans manipulated information. If a person is given a problem such as 2 + 2, what process is used to arrive at the answer of 4? Obviously, the process depends on whether the individual is a novice or an expert within the subject area. The information-processing model was used as a framework for understanding novice and expert performance (Bransford, Brown, & Cocking, 2000).

Information-Processing Model

In 1972, Newell and Simon introduced the information-processing model of cognition and learning. It was a descriptive outline of the human cognitive process. It abstractly represented the process of knowledge selection, acquisition, and utilization:

> Information-processing analyses are clearly distinguished from behaviorist ones . . . by their explicit attempts to describe *internal* processing. They differ from the cognitivist Gestalt and Piagetian positions in their attempts to describe the actual flow of performance—to translate "restructuring" or "logical operations" into temporally organized sequences of actions. (Resnick, 1976, p. 64)

The Gestalt and Piagetian positions emphasized that we understand concepts best as structured wholes rather than as a collection of pieces (Sternberg, 1999b).

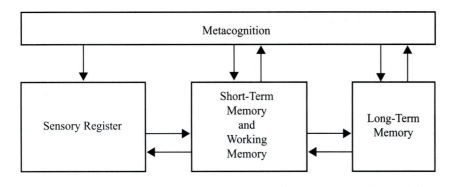

Sensory memory: Collects incoming information from the senses. Passes along to short-

term memory and working memory the information selected as important or

needing attention.

Short-term and working memory: Assembles and constructs information either for future

storage in long-term memory or combines with information obtained from long-

term memory to problem solve. Rehearsal is one method of keeping information

in short-term memory longer.

Long-term memory: Holds large amounts of information for future use. There is a

constant storage and retrieval of information from short-term and working

memory.

Metacognition: Controls all aspects of the cognitive process: Attention, perception,

encoding, storage, retrieval, and so on.

FIGURE 5.1

Information-Processing Model

Information-processing theorists focused on the logic and timing of the various pieces, believing that articulating thinking processes in this way helped us understand steps in thinking. The information-processing model provided a basis for the logic involved in thinking, as well as a language that allowed description of the complex process of thought and, as an extension, problem solving.

In this chapter we introduce a basic description of the information-processing model (Figure 5.1). Research has added to this basic model by introducing many of the complexities associated with human thinking. In general, the information-processing system consists of three stages (Newell & Simon, 1972):

- Sensory register
- Short-term memory
- Long-term memory

Sensory Register

The *sensory register* picks up stimuli from the environment in the form of sight, sound, touch, and other inputs and then determines the relative importance of each. This processing of knowledge is demonstrated by an interface between the individual and the environment. Our senses connect us to the environment. The sensory register is the basic, visible source of all incoming and outgoing activity of the individual.

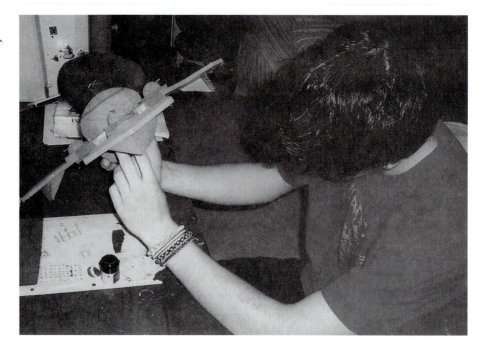

PHOTO 5.1
Students' ability to focus influences their performance in the classroom.

The process of *perception*, which is the meaning we give to information we receive through our senses, influences the sensory register. We engage in a complex process of sorting sensory information, one that involves both perception (interpreting the stimuli) and also *attention* (deciding to focus on it).

Stimuli that are not important are eliminated and decay without conscious awareness that they ever existed (Photo 5.1). For example, a student in your class might be so engrossed in writing an essay that he doesn't hear the additional instructions you give regarding editing. Information considered important by a student, however, may trigger her attention. Hearing that something will be on a test may rouse a student from daydreaming.

Short-Term Memory

When information is passed along from the sensory register it enters short-term memory. *Short-term memory* provides an elementary information-sorting system. Here decisions are made as to whether incoming information has importance or an association with the knowledge base of the individual. Unimportant items, like the ticking of a clock in the background, are selectively forgotten or ignored, while other items are processed for storage with previous information or as separate units of new information (Figure 5.1). This process is considered *conscious thinking*, or consciousness. It deals with the immediate thinking a person does: handling input from the senses, pulling out stored information needed at this time, and sorting and storing information for future use.

Multitasking   All of us have tried to do several things at once, only to realize that we have limits. There is a capacity limit on short-term memory. Only 7 ± 2 pieces of information (or fewer, depending on the age of the individual) can be held and manipulated at any one time (Loftus & Loftus, 1976; Miller, 1994).

Chunking   Information can be held in discrete pieces, such as a new 7-digit phone number, or it can be grouped into logical *chunks*, thereby freeing the remaining short-term memory to deal with other items. For example, the phone number might be chunked into the prefix (321), the next two digits (55), and the last two (44), making three, rather than seven, pieces of information. As persons become more expert in a field, they are able to hold more in short-term memory than a novice (Chase & Simon, 1973).

Time Limitations   Not only is short-term memory limited in terms of space, but it also must move information through to keep up with conscious thought and sensory input. The average amount of time a chunk of information remains within the system is approximately 20 seconds (Atkinson & Shiffrin, 1968). After this time, the information is either sent to *long-term memory* for filing and storage or it is allowed to decay, or be forgotten. Information can be actively kept in short-term memory by constantly replacing it; for example, repeating a phone number while dialing provides constant information input. This is called *rehearsal*.

The limitations of the short-term memory system explain why the sensory register has to be selective about what is passed along. While the senses are constantly registering information, we cannot handle all this information at once; thus our brain sets priorities. This is why we have problems paying attention to several things at one time, particularly if they are new to us. Too much of our short-term memory is taken up, leaving nothing for additional items. Within a very short period of time, then, we choose items of importance, sort and classify, reduce information into concentrated units for storage (*chunking*), and then label it for retrieval, all in processes called *encoding* and *labeling*.

Long-Term Memory

All stored information resides in long-term memory. Long-term memory stores many kinds of sensory information in a variety of complex units. It stores and retains symbolic structures or encoded information until it is retrieved by short-term memory for immediate use. Key words or stimuli can cue these information units and draw up subsidiary units, allowing for a large range and variety of information pieces to be accessed (Photo 5.2).

Access to long-term memory can occur by something as discrete as an odor or a word. We all have had experiences in which the smell of a certain food cooking brings back memories from childhood or when the memory of an emotional experience causes one to feel those same emotions again. What appears to be the key to the retrieval of long-term memory is a specific trigger in the form of a word, phrase, or sensory cue. Since the information must be accessible for future use, it must be properly stored. Thus all associated information needs to be stored and properly labeled with an appropriate key word or cue that allows it to be accessed when needed. The storing of information can be deliberate, such as when we study for a test. All the details are combined in such a way that if a question is about photosynthesis, for example, we can generate knowledge of this topic. We also have the ability to store details without deliberately concentrating on the process, such as when we relay details of an incident that occurred during work or relate a conversation we had with a friend.

Working Memory

An information-processing concept that is not part of Newell and Simon's (1972) model, but that is also relevant to understanding thinking and learning, is *working memory*. Working memory involves keeping information in memory while processing additional information (Case, 1985; Hitch & Towse, 1995).

PHOTO 5.2

Security codes used by banks and credit cards rely on people's long-term memory.

Whenever we need to process and recall multiple units of information, we use our working memory capacity. Teachers are required to do this on a daily basis as students make requests, ask questions, and give information. They process each request, question, and unit of information as it occurs and need to be able to recall the results of this processing. This is like recalling what is in desktop files without being able to look in the files. While similar to short-term memory, working memory is more *dynamic* because of its continuous processing demands.

Working memory capacity increases as children mature, allowing them to solve more complex problems. For example, 6-year-olds can remember the results of two consecutive counting operations, but have difficulty remembering more than that. By the time they are 10, they can remember the results of four consecutive counting operations (Case, 1985, 1995). This improvement is believed to be due to the development of their neurological system and increased efficiency in processing information (Case, 1985).

As children enter adolescence, they can operate on and remember more sophisticated concepts, such as ratio. As in childhood, adolescents remember increasingly greater numbers of results of the operations they have conducted. Similar growth takes place in their ability to remember the results of operations in other subject areas. Because of these marked developmental changes, working memory is an important concept in understanding how cognitive skills develop from simple to complex.

Applying Information-Processing Theory in the Classroom

Information-processing theory provides a model of how information is received from the environment, stored, and then retrieved at appropriate times. This model provides teachers with an understanding of why certain procedural steps are important to learning, such as the importance of having students' attention before giving instructions and of not overloading students with information.

Information-processing theory also provides a framework for helping teachers understand when students have difficulty processing information. Students with learning disabilities, attention deficit disorder (ADD), or attention deficit disorder with hyperactivity (ADHD) all experience difficulties of one sort or another in processing the huge amount of information that comes at them every school day. They may have problems remembering what is heard or in retrieving information from long-term memory. Children with learning disabilities have smaller working memory capacity than others of the same age (Crammond, 1992), resulting in difficulty holding the results of information processing in memory as they solve problems.

Children with learning disabilities may have trouble with perception; that is, they may not interpret auditory or visual stimuli completely or accurately. They may also experience difficulty with attention, taking others' perspectives into account, and spatial orientation. Children with ADD or ADHD, in particular, have considerable difficulty focusing, because so many stimuli compete for their attention. Similarly, these students need considerable support in reflecting on their own thinking and learning and in using appropriate learning strategies. They can be helped through the instructional applications discussed next.

Conceptual Mnemonics One instructional method that addresses the limitations on children's working memory capacity uses *conceptual mnemonics* to help children overcome these limitations. Anne McKeough (1992; McKeough & Sanderson, 1996) teaches children to tell stories with well-articulated plots and grammatical structure by drawing children's stories for them and indicating characters' feelings and thoughts through the use of icons such as happy faces and "thought clouds."

Because "knowing what we know facilitates further learning" (McKeough & Sanderson, 1996, p. 163), mnemonics make children's existing knowledge explicit and provide effective traces of their thinking (McKeough, 1992; Meichenbaum & Biemiller, 1998; Scruggs & Mastropieri, 1990). This teaching strategy helps learners to remember previous story components. If they rely on their working memory alone, children may forget what they have already done.

Documentation Other instructional strategies, such as having students show their work or record their impressions in a learning log, accomplish the same goal. Teachers can also *document* students' learning in written or visual form. This documentation provides a visible trace of the students' thinking that allows them to reflect on what they have learned and their ways of learning (Rinaldi, 2001). Documentation "makes learning visible" (Giudici, Rinaldi, & Krechevsky, 2001), allowing students to reflect on their thinking and learning.

Surfing Terms 5.1

Learning disability

Specific learning disability

Reading disability

Math disability

Dyslexia

Dysgraphia

Written output disorder

Visual–spatial learners

Attention deficit disorder

Attention deficit disorder with hyperactivity

Strategic learning

Strategy instruction

Curriculum adaptation

Curriculum modification

Metacognition

Awareness of what we know and how we think contributes to effective learning and academic achievement. This awareness is known as *metacognition*. Because metacognition involves reflecting on and monitoring one's own thinking (Donovan et al., 1999), it is important in facilitating learning (Photo 5.3). Several determinations are made when one thinks metacognitively:

- What is important
- What will happen to information (stored or forgotten)
- Whether rehearsal is necessary to keep information active in short-term memory
- What system works best for inputting information into long-term memory

Metacognition acts as a general monitor of the thinking process. For example, you use metacognition to decide whether you have studied enough for a test or if you really understand a topic in depth. Often it is referred to as "thinking about thinking." While this phrase may be valid, it is somewhat confusing in that it does not explain exactly what metacognition does within an information-processing framework.

There are two main aspects to metacognition:

1. *Metacognitive knowledge* involves monitoring factual knowledge, ranging from knowledge of specific topics or items to self-knowledge, such as whether you are capable of hitting a fast ball in baseball (Flavell, Miller, & Miller, 1993).
2. *Metacognitive activity* monitors thinking and purposely adapts to a variety of thinking strategies, such as using an analogy to problem solve (Ferrari & Sternberg, 1998).

Using Metacognition to Enhance Learning

Students often use inappropriate or ineffective strategies for learning, even at the university level. Studies have shown, however, that students learn better when they have been taught specific strategies for learning (Diekhoff, Brown, & Dansereau, 1985). For example, when a teacher gives out a list of topics to review prior to a test, students' ability to access their knowledge allows them to determine what they already know and what they need to study.

As teachers, we can enhance student performance by emphasizing the processes of metacognition—teaching our students how both to think effectively and to monitor their own thought processes. Donovan et al. (1999) emphasized that metacognitive strategies must be incorporated into the teaching of specific subject matter. Metacognitive strategies are not generic for all disciplines; that is, metacognitive activity in physics is not the same as monitoring one's own thinking about creative writing. When students have been taught subject-specific metacognitive strategies, their understanding of the subject increases (Donovan et al.).

Metacognition and Knowledge Acquisition

Metacognition is our ability to understand not only the content of our thinking, but also to know that we have the ability to manipulate or control the process of knowledge acquisition. Understanding the controls means we can be more efficient in acquiring knowledge and become more effective problem solvers. Three broad categories of cognitive activity are involved in controlling the knowledge process. Each category has associated general questions we can ask about our learning (Sternberg, 1986) (Table 5.1).

Sternberg (1985) added detail to the three broad categories presented in Table 5.1 by considering the information processing components involved in metacognitive activity. He termed these more detailed strategies *metacomponents*. The questions associated with metacomponents help students become more knowledgeable about how they think and assist them to be better problem solvers (Table 5.2).

Self-Regulated Learning

Metacognition is a component of self-regulated learning (SRL). Perry (2002) defines *self-regulated learning* as "independent, academically effective forms of learning that involve metacognition, intrinsic motivation, and strategic action" (p. 1). More specifically, SRL involves both using metacognition and being motivated to do so. Perry offers the following example: "A student expresses, 'Wow, this is hard,' while working on a math problem" (student engages in SRL) and then

TABLE 5.1

Examples of Metacognitive Activity

Cognitive Activity	Metacognitive Self-Questions
Encoding of knowledge	What is relevant in this information? Is there something I can leave out?
Finding combinations	Where can I fit this in with what I already know?
Comparing with other knowledge	Is this the same as another piece of knowledge? Is it related in some way?

TABLE 5.2

Questions Associated with Metacomponents

Defining the problem	What are the main and subordinate issues here? What is important?
Selecting a strategy	What is the best or most effective way to handle this information?
Sequencing strategies	What part should I do first? Is there a right way to order the strategies?
Selecting ways to represent the information	What is the best way to think about this? For example, could I use a road map to represent the problem? Words, pictures, etc.
Determining time spent on problem sections	How much time is it taking to do one aspect of the problem? Is it too much?
Monitoring the process	How am I doing? Is the time reasonable? Am I making progress? What do I still need to do?
Evaluating the process	How good a job is it so far? Being aware of what others think of me as I problem solve.
Solving the problem	Did it work? If not, why? Is it correct or reasonable?

"takes out a piece of paper to make a table that reflects aspects of the problem" (student exercises SRL) (p. 1).

Students become more thoughtful, interpretive, and metacognitive about their learning when they are taught strategies to help them take control of their own learning (Duffy, 1993). For example, a second-grader who learned the strategy of prediction in reading reported, "Before I read, I think about the story and predict, and if I get stuck, I stop, go back, read it over again, and try to make sense of it" (Duffy, pp. 110–111). In Chapter 10, ways to foster SRL in your classrooms are discussed, and in Chapter 11 assessment strategies that encourage self-reflection are presented.

Problem-Based Scenario 5.1 gives you the opportunity to think about how you might apply information-processing theory to help two students cope with the demands of school.

Thinking and Learning Styles

Cognition and intelligence are influenced and enhanced by genetics, culture, and environment. For most of history, when a student could not perform within a learning situation, it was thought that there was something wrong with his or her intelligence; that is, failure to perform was due to some inherent lack of ability on the part of the learner. Over the past century, our knowledge of how people learn has expanded our understanding of this complex process. We have identified components of personality and learning called *thinking and learning styles*. These styles are not inherent abilities, but rather personal preferences for gathering, retaining, and manipulating information.

Generally, our learning preferences do not mean that we cannot function in another mode, but rather that we have certain preferences for learning

Problem-Based Scenario 5.1

Students: *Joey and Monique*
Teacher: *Donna*

It was 3:30 on a stormy November afternoon. Donna Tremblay needed some breathing space and time to think, so she retreated to the staff room and poured herself a mug of coffee. Donna was particularly concerned about two children in her grade 3 class, Joey and Monique. Each had experienced a particularly difficult day.

First Joey. Reflecting on the day, Donna realized that most of the activities she had planned involved some written work, not Joey's strong point. He usually did almost anything to avoid it—talking (preferably to her about his latest invention), taking an exceptionally long time to get organized, or "spacing out." Today was a day when, in addition to *all* those strategies, he got involved in a fight with another child—not his usual pattern, but it did happen from time to time. Nobody seemed to know how it got started. What a contrast to his "success stories"! Donna thought about his enthusiasm and commitment to the school science fair.

When Joey was involved in science projects, he was focused and cooperative. Donna also noticed that he tried to write more if science was the focus of the writing assignment—but with a lot of difficulty. She really should have let him tape-record some work today. His taped stories were always better than his written ones. (See Figure 5.2, page 134.)

Strange, though—he could really handle felt pens and paint brushes. Along with his knowledge of science, Joey's claim to fame among his classmates was his amazing artwork.

In a lot of ways, Monique was just the opposite of Joey. Her artwork was quite immature. Today Donna tried to help her organize a title page for science. Monique's first attempt was two tiny stick figures and a sun in one corner of the page. After Donna showed her the covers of some books and drew an example of how a title and a picture can be organized on a page, Monique crumpled up her new attempt, put her head down on her desk, and cried. Then there was gym.

Donna had six stations organized in the gym. The children "numbered off" so they knew where to start. Monique should have started at Station Four, but somehow got confused. The other children teased her, calling her "dummy." Donna got that straightened out, but soon heard Monique scream in frustration. Donna could hear the children at her station calling, "No. Monique! You're supposed to start *behind* the red line, *Pay attention.*" What was up? Did she really not get it? (See Figure 5.3, page 135.)

Donna felt as if she'd been torn in different directions all day. She needed some guidance about how to help Joey and Monique as soon as possible.

Source: Jordan, Porath, and Jamieson (2000). *Problem-Based Learning in Inclusive Education.* Pearson Canada. Reprinted with permission of the publisher.

(Photo 5.4). Some individuals can study with CD headphones on, for example, while others need complete silence. Another example is the student who shines when given an essay assignment, but has difficulty with more artistic endeavors.

Types of Learning

Most preservice teacher education programs emphasize the need to teach in a particular style—discovery learning, for example. In an attempt to follow this dictum, preservice teachers often overlook or fail to see value in other formats. Remembering that very few things in our world are black and white, positive or negative, or the like can alleviate this. The following three examples illustrate the range of different teaching–learning styles.

Intentional versus Incidental Learning   *Intentional learning* can be described as consciously goal directed learning. A person might deliberately set

out to learn something, for example, by reading the directions in a repair manual. *Incidental learning*, on the other hand, occurs without deliberate intent. For example, middle school students pick up a great deal of knowledge about the high school culture simply by listening to and observing older adolescents.

Rote versus Meaningful Learning   In *rote learning,* the intent is to memorize something without necessarily tying it to any existing knowledge base. In contrast, *meaningful learning* ties new material together with known concepts to make sense of the new material.

Of course, teaching from either of these extremes would actually hinder a student's learning. Throughout much of history, however, education meant rote learning: teachers instructed students to memorize large quantities of information and rarely asked them to apply the information in any useful manner. The pedagogical backlash to employing this extreme was that educators abandoned memorization in an attempt to make everything meaningful for the student.

With this movement between extremes, educators failed to realize the need for students to have certain amounts of information at their disposal, even if it does not initially hold much meaning for them. An ideal example of this is learning the alphabet or the multiplication tables, both by rote memorization. At the time, we took the importance of this information on faith; our parents and teachers simply told us that we needed to learn it. Bringing these learning styles into balance, then, teachers should use memorization as a tool when needed, but also make every effort to connect the information to meaningful knowledge.

Reception Learning versus Discovery Learning   *Reception learning* is knowledge presented in its final form—the statement that "Earth is round," for example. Information is stated as factual and is usually supplemented with examples, as it would be in a lecture. *Discovery learning* exposes the learner to experiences and guides the design of the learning situation to lead the student

to find target concepts on his or her own (Photo 5.5). For example, students might observe a sailboat over several hours, watching it diminish in size until it disappears. This observation would then lead to a discussion of the curvature of Earth.

Using Learning Styles in the Classroom

With our attempts to describe the complex structure of learning, we must also consider how these styles apply to classroom learning. Specifically, what do thinking and learning styles mean to a classroom teacher? The results of two research studies in particular give some direction to teachers:

1. When an instructional practice matches a learning style, there is an increase in achievement. The match between a student who prefers lectures and an instructor who teaches predominantly by lecture means the student will outperform classmates with other style preferences (Onwuegbuzie & Daley, 1998).
2. No particular type of learning style is associated with high, average, or low achievers (Burns, Johnson, & Gable, 1998).

Given this information, then, teachers should provide students with a variety of teaching methodologies (e.g., lecture, group work, essays, portfolios, and audiovisual assignments). Students will tend to excel more in their preferred style of learning, thereby increasing achievement overall.

Developing a Teaching Style

Effective classroom teachers know and understand the concept of learning styles, and tests are available to determine learning styles, such as the Myers–Briggs Type Indicator (Myers, 1962). But when a teacher automatically uses variety in his or her teaching, there is no need to test students to identify

TABLE 5.3

Teaching Strategies

Lecture Based	Skills Based	Inquiry Based	Individual vs. Group	Technology Enhanced
Oral: Lesson is delivered orally	*Isolated drill and practice:* Not connected to concepts being studied (e.g., learning random spelling words, learning times tables by rote)	*Cases:* A case is presented, followed by prepared questions for inquiry and discussion	*Self-study:* Student undertakes a project on his or her own	*Simulations:* Film or computer- enhanced replications of experiences relevant to learning (e.g., flight simulator)
Written: Lesson is supplemented with notes on the blackboard or projector	*Contextualized practice:* Practice connected to meaningful concepts and material (e.g., learning to spell words needed to convey meaning in an essay; learning timestables as an adjunct to understanding the concept of multiplication and as tools to solve mathematical problems)	*Problems:* Students must find and articulate the problem, then decide how to solve it (problem-based learning)	*Cooperative learning:* Learning groups work cooperatively toward a learning goal	*Electronic tools:* Computer-assisted drafting, Internet searches
Narrative videos: Similar to an oral lesson, but given via video	*Modeling:* Teacher models behaviors or skills; students copy the teacher	*Projects:* Students engage in projects that develop their knowledge e.g., preparing a guidebook on the local community's history)	*Jigsaw learning:* Group members undertake tasks (related to a learning goal independently, then pool their knowledge	*Assessment opportunities:* Self-checking drill and practice (computer- or electronic calculator-based); student-produced PowerPoint presentations
		Learning by design: Teachers design learning environments that encourage student learning (e.g., science centers with books, artifacts, magnifying glasses, CDs, and a computer)		*Communication environments:* Computer networks, Web-based courses, blackboard discussions

Source: Headings from Donovan et al., 1999, p. 18.

learning styles. The results of a variety of assignments and testing situations will show where individual students perform the best. Most teachers develop a particularly comfortable method of teaching, known as a *teaching style*. Thus, it takes a deliberate effort in planning to make sure variety is incorporated both in teaching methodology and assignments.

Teaching styles are influenced by more than just the unique personality of the teacher. The subject or content being taught and the context of the classroom also influence the choices teachers make. The pedagogy of language arts, for example, is different from that of physical education. Often, teachers must make allowances for the structure of a given topic. Although you might like to have a hands-on type of science class, many topics may be too complex and/or dangerous to approach in any other way than by direct teaching or by lecture. This choice may cause you to question whether you are doing the right thing when giving a lecture, rather than using a hands-on approach. This leads us into a discussion of the types of learning that you might select.

Choosing a Particular Teaching Strategy

Donovan, Bransford, and Pellegrino (1999) effectively illustrated the many strategies from which teachers can choose. Using our knowledge of how people learn, current categories range from lecture-based teaching to technology-enhanced teaching. These strategies are summarized in Table 5.3.

Donovan et al. (1999) steer readers away from asking which of these is the best technique for their students. Rather, they suggest that a teacher choose strategies based on their specific *learning goal* (e.g., books and/or lectures to transmit new information and projects to enhance the level of understanding). Donovan et al. wisely state, "There is no universal best teaching practice" (p. 19).

The most effective teachers work back and forth along a continuum between two extremes, making decisions about the most appropriate content for each learning goal. Factors such as time, available supplies and materials, and students' cognitive and skill levels must be taken into consideration to determine the most effective teaching practices for the learning goals in each subject area. Problem-Based Scenarios 5.2 and 5.3 present two teachers who are struggling with how to match their teaching styles with the needs and learning styles of their students.

Problem-Based Scenario 5.2

Students: All
Teacher: Emma

After putting a great deal of thought into how Sammy understood math, Emma was experiencing mixed emotions. She felt more confident about offering children different opportunities to demonstrate their knowledge and about her ability to analyze how they processed information. But, at the same time, she was daunted by the possibility that there may be other children who were just as constrained by her instructional approaches as Sammy had been. In fact, maybe this was a factor in Charlie's reluctance to work. Emma felt she had developed more competence in formative assessment of her students' progress. Marking now was more than just determining level of mastery; she was much more analytic about how children might have been thinking when they answered questions. She had also begun to get a handle on how to observe her students as they worked individually and together. But there were times when she simply got overwhelmed by constant analysis and the potential range of knowledge and thinking styles in her class. Were there strategies she could use to help her in a more proactive way? Could she plan lessons differently to allow the children to "find their own way" more readily? Maybe it was more than lesson planning. Should she be thinking about how she structured the classroom? More group work? Change desks in rows to learning centers? Who could she talk to about all this?

Problem-Based Scenario 5.3

Students: All
Teacher: Elaine

The eleventh-grade history class ended in the usual flurry of chatter, banging of chairs, and shuffling toward the door. The class had gone well. They had been given a PBL historically based scenario, so there had been a lot of group work during the hour. Elaine had met with each group to make sure they were on track when the bell rang. Since it was the final block of the day before a weekend, Elaine quickly did a bit of clean-up before she left. Elaine had been introduced to the technique of Problem-Based Learning in one of her preservice teacher education classes. She had a great time with the problems and had worked with a group of her friends. In fact, she liked it so much she had brought the methodology to the eleventh-grade class she now taught. But it was not her only technique. Elaine was careful to provide variety and offer several options on assignments that tapped into the learning styles and multiple intelligences of her students. Elaine felt things were going quite well until she picked up the note from the floor.

> How come she doesn't just tell us the answers.
> She likes to see us work.
> No, she doesn't like to do the work herself. It's easier for us to do all of the research.
> I like her but she doesn't teach anything. What happens next year when I want to get into college?

> I'm sick of listening to everyone give speeches and show posters.
> Why doesn't she . . . .

FIGURE 5.4

Summary

In this chapter you supplemented your knowledge of developmental and behavioral theories with theories on how we process information. Because the processing of information is so complex, students have individual preferences for learning. Information-processing theories help teachers plan for these preferences by suggesting different ways of teaching that can accommodate diverse ways of learning.

■ Thinking involves complex information processing. Different types of memory, problem-solving, selective attention, sensory input, and decision-making processes are involved in thinking. Higher-order thinking is helped by our abilities to monitor our own thinking and regulate the strategies we use to learn.

- We can monitor and think about our own thinking through a process called metacognition. Students' capability is enhanced if they are able to think effectively and strategically by utilizing metacognitive processes.
- Effective teaching includes consideration of students' preferred ways of learning and the use of teaching styles that accommodate students' learning styles and are appropriate to the subject matter being taught. You will be most effective as a teacher if you offer students opportunities to express their knowledge in different ways and include a variety of teaching strategies in your instruction.

A Metacognitive Challenge

You should now be able to reflect on the following questions:

- What do I know about how information is processed?
- What do I know about learning and teaching styles?
- What do I know about how thinking and learning are monitored by students?
- How do my knowledge of influences on behavior and learning and regulation of learning help me to teach the learners in my classroom?

Surfing Terms 5.2

Implicit learning
Explicit learning
Rule-based learning
Instance-based learning
Strategy instruction
Authentic pedagogy
Authentic reading
Authentic mathematics
Instructional discourse
Thinking style
Learning style
Teaching style
Teaching methods

Artifacts for Problem-Based Scenarios

FIGURE 5.2 ■ **Joey's Writing Samples**

> I Just finished space acadamy and I'm
> going on a trip to mars. I can see shooting
> Stars, planets and other space ships to. When I
> reach mars I emidieatly start diging. I reach
> 3 feet when I hit something.
>
> by Joey

Joey's Prehistoric Story (Tape Recorded October 17, 1998)

Once there was this guy and, um, he was this old guy and he was really wise. And he told—he kept on telling everybody that there was a beast—that there were beasts that were coming to the land. And that they were going to charge everybody and stomp on them and crush them and kill everybody. But nobody believed him. So the guy knew that it was going to happen, so rather than just waste his time telling the people that this monster was coming 'cause he knew that—'cause they weren't believing him, he just went up to the mountain . . . um . . . to save his own life. So he climbed up the mountain and found a magic jewel and it said on it, "He who holds this jewel will defeat anyone—can defeat anyone." So he thought, "Hmm, maybe I can use this to defeat the beasts and save our land." So—but he didn't see the small print that said, "But—um—the beast—but . . . ."

And it said, "But if the beasts find the jewel, they will take it." But he didn't see the its . . . the printing. So he put it down. He climbed down the mountain, went back to his village, and he said, "Hey everybody, I've got the magic jewel that can kill the beasts!" But nobody . . . still nobody believed him. And the next morning the beasts came and everybody was scared frozen. And nobody could do anything because they were so scared. So—ah—so the guy threw—thought—thought that if he threw the jewel at the beast then it would go into his stomach and kill it and kill the beasts. But when he threw the jewels, it didn't do anything. Instead, the beast ate the jewels and the jewels were lost forever. And so—um, the people—um, well, the people were all killed and . . . the beasts ate themselves all up. So everyone was dead. The end.

FIGURE 5.3 ■ Monique's Math Assessment

Lynnwood Elementary

Math assessment: Review of addition skills

Name: Monique   Date: Sept. 10/98

Basic facts to 10: Oral recall	Couldn't do in her head or by using the number line.
Basic facts to 20: Oral recall	Not done.

$$2 \atop +8 \atop \overline{10}$$ $$5 \atop +4 \atop \overline{9}$$ $$7 \atop +1 \atop \overline{8}$$ $$4 \atop +1 \atop \overline{2}$$

$6 + 3 = 7$ $3 + 7 = 5$ $2 + 5 = 8$

Understanding Our Learners: Social and Emotional Development

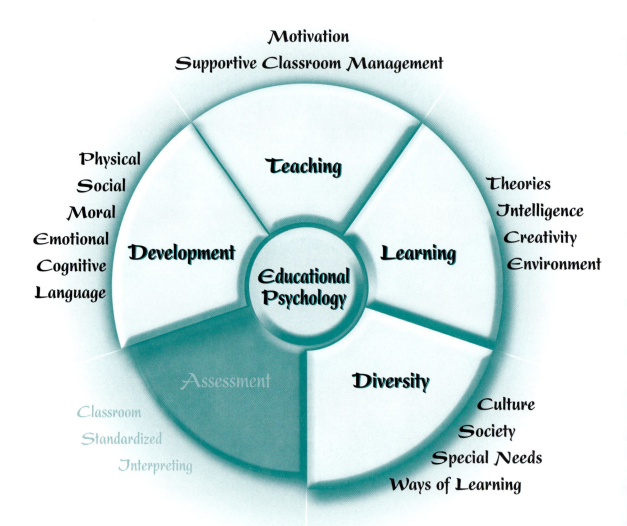

Motivation

Supportive Classroom Management

Physical
Social
Moral
Emotional
Cognitive
Language

Teaching

Development

Educational Psychology

Learning

Theories
Intelligence
Creativity
Environment

Assessment

Diversity

Classroom

Standardized

Interpreting

Culture
Society
Special Needs
Ways of Learning

The topics presented in this chapter concern the social and emotional lives of students. We are highly social beings. We are also emotional beings. A well-rounded education must therefore address the social and emotional lives of students. Every day you will come face to face with the social and emotional influences on the lives of your students. The importance of social and emotional factors for the well-being and academic progress of students will also become evident as you work through this chapter (Photo 6.1).

Teachers have what Goleman (1997) called "on-the-ground experience" (p. xv); that is, they come to know the realities of their students' lives and how these realities affect their learning. This experience acknowledges the critical role of social and emotional, or *affective*, factors in healthy development. In this chapter, topics are presented that will help you build on your understanding of social and emotional issues and then integrate this information with theoretical perspectives on social development and your own classroom experience.

Theoretical background on and current issues in moral development also are presented. Education is a moral undertaking, strongly influenced by societal values. Curricular, instructional, and administrative decisions are all underpinned by our values. As we will show, moral development parallels cognitive development in certain ways. It also relates to a child's social and emotional development. Another significant influence on these aspects of development is the school environment itself. The theoretical perspectives of social, emotional, and moral development are expanded by discussing their implications for education. The broader influence of the school environment is discussed in Chapter 7.

PHOTO 6.1

Social and emotional factors influence the academic progress of students.

Social Development

From the moment we are born, we are part of society. Our social world is at first limited, but it is highly social nonetheless. As infants, we are introduced to the conventions of social interaction with our caregivers and our families. We begin to form close relationships that are central to our lives. These close and intensely personal relationships lay the groundwork for subsequent, more extensive social relationships. By the time we enter school, we have had social experiences in our homes, neighborhoods, and preschools. The nature and quality of these relationships will influence how well we adjust to our entry into school.

Formal schooling introduces children to a new and complex social environment with particular rules for conduct and routines, new expectations, and a variety of new roles and relationships. Children need to be supported and guided through this important transition. The socialization experiences and social knowledge they bring with them to school interact with the social environment of schools, classrooms, and academic demands. This interaction greatly influences children's success in school.

Social Developmental Competencies

Competencies: Skills; areas in which a person is competent.

A set of *competencies* common to many families, communities, and cultures comprise the social developmental tasks of childhood (Masten & Coatsworth, 1998). These competencies include three overall goals (Masten & Coatsworth):

- School adjustment
- Getting along with peers
- Rule-governed conduct

The degree of mastery of these tasks is, in turn, related to academic success. Because social development and academic development are closely related, children do better academically if they arrive at school able to interact effectively with their peers and teachers. They also do better academically if they adjust to school quickly and follow school routines and procedures for conduct. These children are socially responsible, a characteristic that contributes to academic success (Wentzel, 1993). They also have a better chance of acquiring *prosocial behaviors*, which are believed to be necessary for effective adjustment to our increasingly complex world (Eisenberg, 1992).

Prosocial Behavior   Prosocial behavior is defined as "voluntary behavior intended to benefit another, such as helping, donating, sharing, and comforting" (Eisenberg, Losoya, & Guthrie, 1997, p. 329). Children who are prosocial tend to be viewed as socially able and are popular (Eisenberg et al.). Prosocial behavior, together with mastery of the developmental tasks just described, contributes to a healthy relationship between social development and school success (Photo 6.2).

Theory of mind: The ability to understand our own and others' thoughts, emotions, and intentions.

Perspective taking: The ability to comprehend a situation from another's point of view.

Intersubjectivity   Bruner (1996) argued that day-to-day life requires that everybody be a psychologist. This argument certainly applies to understanding what happens in school. We need to be able to form explanations for why others act the way they do in order to live our lives effectively and, more specifically, to adjust to school. Children who understand their teachers' intentions and those of their peers cope better at school. Bruner termed this critical capability *intersubjectivity*—"how people come to know what others have in mind and how they adjust accordingly" (p. 161). This ability to understand others' intentions has been described by others as a *theory of mind* (e.g., see Astington, 1993) or as *perspective taking* (e.g., Eisenberg et al., 1997).

PHOTO 6.2
Prosocial behavior contributes to success in school.

Intersubjectivity is also important for you as a teacher. It allows you to interact effectively with students, parents, other teachers, administrators, and school district personnel. To make sense of our experiences, it is critical that we be able to link thought and action, to understand that we, and others, act as we do because we are motivated in a certain way or influenced by certain feelings. This understanding is central to effective and meaningful social relationships; it provides a foundation for *social cognition*, or knowledge about the social world (Case, 1992; Case & Okamoto, 1996).

Development of Social Cognition

As with cognitive development, one's *social cognition*, or how one understands social situations, is highly relevant. The nature of young children's social cognition is very different from that of adolescents. (Recall the discussion of children's knowledge of intentions and social roles in Chapter 3.) This difference is reflected in school and classroom environments.

Young children need guidance and approval from teachers. They are just beginning to learn the territory of peer relationships and to discover that there is a "system" of school life. If classmates reject a first-grader, concrete discussion about the link between his feelings and the act of rejection is more appropriate than an abstract discussion of friendship. He likely interprets the act in a straightforward way: I feel _____ because _____. For example, "I feel sad because they won't play with me."

Adolescents, in contrast, are much more independent and usually have mastered peer relationships. Their peer group is very important and influential, often more so than the significant adults in their worlds (Harris, 1998). They also have figured out the rules of the game of schooling (Harter, 1981). Adolescents are capable of interpreting motives in light of others' personalities (Marini & Case, 1994) and are more able to take part in an abstract discussion. An adolescent might state, for example, "She might not have invited me because she's a bit unstable. She can't really commit to a friendship."

> **Social cognition:** Knowledge and understanding of social situations. Cognition, in general, refers to how we perceive, remember, represent, and problem solve. Social cognition is cognition directed to social events and issues.

Case's Stages of Social Cognitive Development

It is helpful for you as teachers to know the general developmental characteristics of social cognition. These characteristics help in understanding how children and adolescents may interpret social situations. They also help you think about how to respond when social issues arise. Case (1992) and his colleagues (Case, Okamoto, Henderson, McKeough, & Bleiker, 1996; McKeough, 1992) articulated stages in the development of social cognition. These stages, described here, provide general guidelines for understanding how learners view their social world.

Early Childhood   Action-based descriptions of social events reveal children's understanding of their social world. For example, from about age 3, young children can usually describe in detail the sequence of events that take place when they go to a fast-food restaurant or a birthday party. Young children also know about familiar feelings (e.g., happy, sad, mad), and they understand that feelings are influenced by actions and events.

Generally, though, young children don't coordinate their knowledge of events and feelings. They can explain and predict events in familiar action sequences, but generally do not explain these actions in terms of the thoughts or feelings that motivate them. For example, a 4-year-old might say that "happy" is going to a birthday party (Griffin, 1992) and proceed to tell you in detail about the events of the party. Bruner (1986) described this sort of explanation as the *landscape of action* in which feelings and intentions are explained in terms of external events and actions. For young children, "actions speak louder than words" (Astington, 1993, p. 73).

Age 5 or 6   Children go through a major transition in social cognition at about this age. They start to be able to think of another person's actions in terms of the thoughts or feelings that underlie or cause their actions. They become able to coordinate actions and the intentions that motivate them in their thinking about others' behavior. The internal component of this thinking is termed the *landscape of consciousness* (Bruner, 1986). This landscape is characterized by the explanation of actions or events in terms of internal states (feelings, thoughts). At this point in development, a child might say, "I *feel* happy because I'm going to a birthday party." There is an *explicit link* between the two landscapes described by Bruner: *action and consciousness.*

Middle Childhood   During middle childhood, children become more adept at coordinating their knowledge of mental states with events and actions. By around the age of 8, they can explain someone's behavior by considering two mental states. For example, "Danny hit him because he was feeling angry and frustrated." Then, by age 10, they include higher-order concepts, such as care, responsibility, and affection in explanations of behavior. For example, when asked what a girl's mother would do if there were a fire in the girl's bedroom, a child replied, "The mother probably puts out the fire and asks her daughter if she's OK, because she wants to know. She loves her daughter and doesn't want her hurt" (Goldberg-Reitman, 1992, p. 144).

Adolescence   During adolescence, another major transition in development takes place. Social cognition becomes more abstract. Adolescents link mental states and actions, but also *interpret* behavior in light of the type of person being evaluated (Marini & Case, 1994). They understand that someone may act as they do because he or she is concerned with justice, is patient and kind, or is temperamental. Adolescents also may use a broader lens for their interpretation, by including references to social and/or ethical issues, for example (Photo 6.3).

PHOTO 6.3
Social activities help develop social cognition.

Social Skills: Cultural Conventions for Behavior

The descriptions of social cognition just given represent important *concepts* for understanding social experiences. There is also a set of social *skills* important for functioning effectively in school and in society. These skills are the conventions for appropriate behavior in one's own culture and include the following competencies (Gresham & Elliott, 1990):

- Turn taking
- Sharing
- Completing one's work
- Standing up for one's self appropriately
- Giving compliments
- Following rules

Other social skills are also critical to success in school (De Falco, 1997):

- Impulse control
- Anger management
- Empathy
- Self-regulation
- Communicating effectively
- Evaluating risks
- Decision making
- Goal setting
- Resisting peer pressure

These skills are fundamental to social relationships throughout one's life. They also are related to emotional well-being, a topic discussed later in the chapter.

Developing Social Expertise

An individual's social skills *and* his or her conceptual knowledge of social situations are important contributors to social development (Hatch, 1997). A goal of education is to develop expertise. *Social expertise* can be defined as a level of competence in

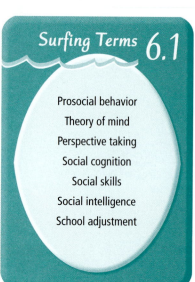

the social skills that are required to function effectively in social, academic, and work situations *and* to understand our own and other's reasons for acting as we do.

Having social expertise as an educational objective is equally important to academic expertise. This means linking social skill development to underlying concepts, such as perspective taking. Think back to the models of mind (Bruner, 1996) described in Chapter 2. If, as teachers, we focus on imparting sets of social skills only, we run the risk of children behaving without understanding their reasons for doing so. In social cognition, as well as academic cognition, there is a need to link skills to understanding at a deep level, akin to the expert (vs. novice) level of understanding discussed in Chapter 3.

Forming Healthy Peer Relationships

Social understanding and social skills are very important in making and sustaining relationships with peers. If children master certain social skills such as turn taking, giving compliments, sharing, impulse control, and empathy, among others, they have a better chance of being accepted by peers and forming positive relationships. As we pointed out, these skills are important for both healthy social development and academic achievement. Equally important is a conceptual understanding of one's own and others' intentions, thoughts, and feelings—*mental states*—and how these relate to actions. (See Info Byte 6.1 for categories and examples of mental state terms.)

Socially skilled children who effectively understand others tend to adjust well to school. They generally are well accepted and liked by their peers. On the other hand, having a limited ability to understand others' mental states has been linked to antisocial behavior and rejection by peers (Ladd, Buhs, & Troop, 2002). One of the authors remembers a child, Thomas, who repeatedly poked and pinched other children in his class.

"These children understandably got quite irritated and some eventually retaliated. Thomas got very upset and complained to me on a number of occasions. When I asked him to describe what had taken place, he invariably talked only about what had happened to him. Even when I had observed what had happened and described it to him, Thomas was unable to take other children's perspectives into account. Despite being a very likable child in many ways, Thomas was rejected by his peers."

Problems with Peer Relationships: Bullies and Victims

When children experience repeated peer rejection, it can lead to externalizing behavior problems (or disorders) that persist into adolescence (Laird, Jordan, Dodge, Pettit, & Bates, 2001). Common difficulties surrounding peer relationships include

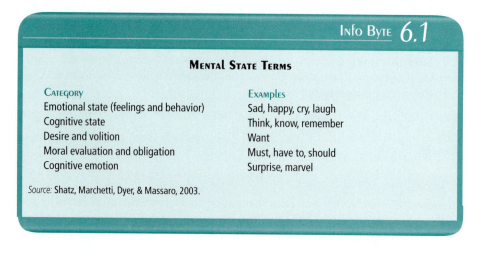

INFO BYTE 6.1

MENTAL STATE TERMS

Category	Examples
Emotional state (feelings and behavior)	Sad, happy, cry, laugh
Cognitive state	Think, know, remember
Desire and volition	Want
Moral evaluation and obligation	Must, have to, should
Cognitive emotion	Surprise, marvel

Source: Shatz, Marchetti, Dyer, & Massaro, 2003.

externalizing disorders, internalizing disorders, rejected children, bullying and relational aggression, and neglected children.

Externalizing Disorders   Children with *externalizing disorders* display aggression and noncompliance. The various disorders are characterized by hostility, high reactivity, having negative emotions, and lacking adaptability (Eisenberg, Fabes, & Losoya, 1997). Externalizing behavior problems are associated with involvement with antisocial peers (Laird et al., 2001). One of the authors taught a child who, new to the author's fourth-grade classroom, brought with him a reputation for aggression directed at both teachers and peers.

> *"Tim lacked the skills to interact appropriately with others and had suffered a good deal of trauma in his young life. His classmates shunned him. The school staff was very supportive and accepting of him but despite these adult models, his classmates rejected him. There were just too many punches thrown and disruptions to classroom life. By seventh grade, he had found a peer group, but not the one any of us had hoped for. His antisocial, aggressive behavior continued into adolescence, complicated by academic challenges."*

Internalizing Disorders   Another set of behavior problems that impairs social development is termed *internalizing disorders*. Children and youth who are anxious and/or depressed report negative emotions (e.g., sadness, shame, guilt), unhappiness, and distractibility (Eisenberg et al., 1997). Girls tend to demonstrate overcontrolled behavior. That is, they tend to hide negative emotions or mask them with more socially acceptable behaviors, such as being helpful or polite.

Eisenberg et al. (1997) also reported that extreme shyness and inhibition may indicate an internalizing disorder. A girl in one of the authors' classes was believed to be very bright yet internalized in her interactions with peers:

> *"When Sonja was 'on,' she did very well. These were rare occasions, though. Many assignments went unfinished while she curled up in a corner with a book. It was very hard to engage her in conversation; one-word responses were the norm. Her appearance was unkempt, and she projected unhappiness. She participated little in class activities, often distancing herself physically from others. She was diagnosed with depression. Cooperation between school, home, and the school psychologist resulted in appropriate support for her."*

Rejected Children   Rejected children are disliked. Their aggression and tendency to disrupt classroom and social activities result in rejection by their peers (Santrock & Yussen, 1992). These behaviors are seen in Problem-Based Scenarios 6.1 and 6.2, in which one student is an aggressor and the other, a victim. Beth and Tanis, elementary teachers who team-teach a group of 7- and 8-year-olds, are concerned about a little boy, Darren, who is aggressive in and out of class. Beth and Tanis are struggling to find a way to provide support and appropriate consequences for Darren. Dan is a middle school teacher who is very concerned about Luis, who is the victim of physical and verbal aggression.

Bullying and Relational Aggression   We tend to think of fighting and threats as characteristic of aggressive behavior, what many of us describe as *bullying*. Such behavior tends to be more typical of boys. While they sometimes do engage in physical aggression, girls who aggress tend to take part in indirect aggression, also referred to as *relational or social aggression* (Underwood, 2002). Verbal insults, attempts to ruin another's reputation, and social exclusion typify relational aggression. It is a more covert form of aggression than physical aggression, but equally upsetting to the recipient.

Surfing Terms 6.2

Bullies

Victims and victimization

Bully and victim

Relational aggression

Dominance

Antisocial behavior

Reactive aggression

Proactive aggression

Indirect bullying

Social aggression

Conduct disorders

Antibullying programs

Bullying prevention

Shared concern

Problem-Based Scenario 6.1

Student: *Darren*

Teachers: *Beth and Tanis*

Beth Littler and Tanis Cevic retreated to the staff room for a cup of coffee. It had been one of those days! Both were experienced teachers, but this year had started off with several challenges that really tested their beliefs and their strategies. Beth and Tanis team-taught a multiage grouping of 7- and 8-year-olds. They had teamed for 4 years and loved it. Each year they greeted a new group of about twenty 7-year-olds that joined their "veterans," the twenty-five or so 8-year-olds who spent a second year with them.

This year their new students presented a few challenges, but Darren was the one who seemed to cause them to seek frequent solace over coffee. Such a cute little kid—sandy hair that went in several directions at once and blue eyes that lit up when learning excited him. Tanis recalled the time he watched her demonstrate block printing. As she pulled the print and showed it to the class, Darren gasped, "It's magic!"

But—every recess was full of conflict. Darren came back to class red-faced and crying, screaming that others always picked on him. Both Tanis and Beth had spent time watching his play when their turns came up for recess playground supervision, but had found it hard to tell for sure what might be contributing to Darren's difficulties. There was some teasing on the part of older boys, but Darren seemed to hold his own. In fact, Darren could hardly wait to get out the door at recess. Tanis described him as a

"little power package ready for launching" (Figure 6.1 on page 174).

Darren's relationships and behavior in class were troubling to Beth and Tanis too. He had trouble making and maintaining friendships and often disrupted class activities. "Darren hit me" or "Darren's bugging me" were heard all too frequently. Beth and Tanis used cool-off periods as a strategy, giving Darren time in a quiet corner of the class and encouraging him to take the initiative of returning when he felt more composed.

It was now mid-October, and that strategy seemed all wrong. The cool-offs increased and Beth and Tanis decided a more meaningful consequence may be necessary. Because the class Halloween party was fast approaching, they talked to Darren and told him he would miss 5 minutes of party time for each occasion when his behavior interfered with the class. Now they began to wonder about their decision. Each stared at the note Darren had delivered after lunch. It lay on the staff room coffee table and seemed to stare back at them (Figure 6.2 on page 175).

Apply

- How can theories of social–emotional development help you understand Darren?
- How would you respond to the note from Darren's mother?

Neglected Children   Children and adolescents may not be overtly rejected by peers, but may be neglected. Obvious rejection (e.g., "You're not invited to my party!" or "I'm going to beat you up") is easy to spot. Teachers may take longer to realize that a child is being ignored.

Neglected children are not necessarily disliked; but they get little peer attention (Santrock & Yussen, 1992). Neglected children, unlike rejected children, do possess social skills. They may be shy or prefer to pursue solitary activities. They have not been found to be at risk for mental health problems, although extremely withdrawn children may be rejected by their peers when they get older (i.e., in middle childhood) (Berk, 1991; Ladd et al., 2002).

Factors Affecting the Formation of Peer Relationships

A variety of factors affect patterns of behavior with one's peers. Negative situations at home may affect peer relationships. For example, children who are

Problem-Based Scenario 6.2

Student: Luis
Teacher: Dan

When Dan Gill was offered a position teaching senior English and Drama at Kennedy High School, he jumped at the chance. After teaching in middle school for 11 years, he felt like he needed a new challenge. He loved his work at West Hill Middle, but felt a high school position would add to his experience. Besides, he was a poet, and the chance to work with more mature writers might give him the inspiration he felt he lacked lately. He had always promised himself that he would publish one day. This would get him back on track.

So far, so good—until now. The first term went well, both at school and with his own writing. Concern about one of his students clouded his enthusiasm, though. Dan had been so pleased to see Luis in his Creative Writing class. Dan had taught Luis at West Hill Middle. He was an astoundingly sensitive writer at 13, and his work now showed even more style and maturity. Luis was a very talented writer. This talent didn't show up in his social life though. Luis hadn't been "one of the boys" at West Hill, and that appeared to be even more the case now.

At West Hill, Luis once had come to class with a black eye, and Dan had seen him walking home alone on another occasion, jacket torn and shoulders shaking. He assumed Luis had been crying. Dan's students

trusted him and often came to him for advice. He also felt he could approach them to offer support when he thought it might be needed. Luis had refused to talk about either incident, though. He'd always seemed somewhat removed from other students and the life of the school. After each incident, he retreated further into himself. Now, 4 years later, Luis's withdrawal appeared complete. His writing reflected alienation and loneliness. He seldom spoke.

Dan stared at the two pieces of paper on his desk. He had found one rumpled up under Luis's desk as he tidied the classroom after school. The other was Luis's in-class writing assignment for the day (Figures 6.3 and 6.4 on page 176). Both disturbed him profoundly, but nothing prepared him for finding Luis curled up in a fetal position by his locker. Red spray point dripped menacingly from the locker door—FAG CREEP.

Apply

- How might research on peer relationships help you to understand what is happening to Luis?
- What would you do upon finding Luis curled up by his locker? What are your short- and long-term plans for helping Luis?

exposed to family violence suffer difficulties with peer relationships. They also report feeling lonely and either have no best friend or have a lot of conflict with close friends (McCloskey & Stuewig, 2001). Transience and/or time spent in shelters can complicate the maintenance of peer relationships (McCloskey & Stuewig). Similarly, children whose parents are incarcerated may experience shame or depression or may be angry and aggressive (De Angelis, 2001). As with other topics we have discussed, however, children's responses to their circumstances are complex and unpredictable.

Resilience to stress and adversity can help children form positive relationships. Children show a great deal of variability in how they respond to stress and adversity (Rutter, 2001). A cheerful, outgoing personality; high intelligence; support from at least one adult in the child's life; well-developed social cognition; ability to regulate emotions; and ability to cope are all factors that help children to deal positively with stress and adversity.

Children who cope well with stress have been termed *resilient* (Rutter, 2001; Werner & Smith, 2001). Resilient children may handle significant responsibility for care of younger siblings, tension between parents, financial adversity, and/or addiction in the family with maturity and keep their own sense of self intact. As adults, these children report the support of an adult (grandparent, aunt or

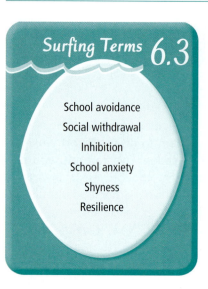

uncle, teacher, or friend) as critical in helping them maintain self-confidence and a positive outlook. Researchers have found that, in addition, the children's intelligence, engaging personalities, and social–emotional maturity contributed to adults' positive responses (Werner & Smith). Problem-Based Scenarios 6.3 and 6.4 describe students who appear to be resilient in their classrooms. Even if they are resilient, however, all children still need support in dealing with adverse circumstances. Protective factors such as understanding adults and successful academic and social experiences are important in maintaining positive developmental outcomes (Rutter; Werner & Smith).

Understanding Friendship

Healthy peer relationships are important in ensuring positive academic and social experiences. In the following section we discuss the importance of friendship in school adjustment and social development and present an outline of the development of children's perceptions of friendship. One of the most important sources of support for children in their adjustment to school is their relationship with friends (Ladd, 1990). Positive, stable relationships with classmates help children manage the increasingly complex demands of schooling and also adjust to transitions like entrance to junior high school (Berndt, Hawkins, & Jiao, 1999).

Problem-Based Scenario 6.3

K-5   6-8   9-12   SpEd

Student: Neil
Teacher: Dave

Dave Harris decided to focus on something positive. He had had "one of those days" and he needed to take his mind off it for awhile. He went to the staff room to get a snack and take a break before tackling the next day's planning. His mind wandered to Neil.

Neil was a straight-A student, a natural leader, and well liked by his classmates. In fact, everyone in the school seemed to like to be with Neil. He was one of those extremely personable kids who attract positive attention. Dave thought about how impressed he had been by Neil's way of relating to his parents at the fall Meet the Teacher night last week. Mr. and Mrs. Cameron arrived at the event clearly in the midst of an argument, and a fierce one at that. They managed to conduct themselves appropriately, but you could feel the tension between them. Dave thought Neil's mom had been drinking.

Neil guided his parents around the classroom, keeping the conversation pleasant and upbeat. He focused their attention on displays of work, filling

them in on what the class had studied so far. He introduced them to his friends and to Dave. Dave thought, "Wow. What a kid to keep it so together under those circumstances." He mentioned how impressed he was to a colleague in the staff room. She had taught Neil the year before.

"Yes," said Maureen. "That kid is really beating the odds. How he does it, I don't know. He must be really resilient."

Dave thought further about Neil being resilient. What did that mean, anyhow? And how could he be of help to Neil?

Apply

- Consider the two questions Dave asked himself about Neil. Does Neil appear to be resilient? Why?
- Can knowing if Neil may or may not be resilient inform what you do as a teacher?

Problem-Based Scenario 6.4

Student: *Cathy*
Teachers: *Beth and Tanis*

Beth and Tanis responded to the knock on their classroom door to find Joe Kipling there with a worried look on his face. They invited him in, and the three settled around one of the round worktables to talk. Joe was always so upbeat. Beth and Tanis shot worried glances of their own at each other as they sat down. Joe's daughter Cathy had joined their classroom two months ago. She was a friendly, happy child who was doing very well in school. Beth and Tanis loved teaching her, and they always enjoyed their relaxed chats with Joe when he came to pick Cathy up from school. Often he had Vicky, Cathy's little sister, with him. She was in kindergarten and was just as engaging as Cathy.

Joe spoke first. "I'm sorry to just drop in at the end of the day, but Cathy's so upset. I left Cathy and Vicky with a neighbor and just headed up here. The kids have been teasing Cathy about her mom the last few weeks, and it's just got too much for her."

Beth responded, "What are the kids saying?"

Joe looked surprised. "Her mom's in jail. Didn't you know?"

Tanis said, "No we didn't, Joe. And we had no idea that Cathy was being teased in this way. We're so sorry. Leave this with us. We'll look into it and do everything we can to support Cathy. Could you drop by in a couple of days so we can talk again?"

Joe agreed and thanked them for their understanding. He shared that his wife was convicted of selling marijuana. He, Cathy, and Vicky visited his wife every week, and they were doing everything they could as a family to work through the experience.

After Joe left, Beth and Tanis sat quietly for a few minutes, shocked by Joe's news. Beth broke the silence. "Wow. Do you have any experience with this sort of thing?" Tanis didn't, and together they wondered out loud about how to support Cathy and to ensure that the teasing stopped.

Apply

■ As a teacher, what could you do to support Cathy? How would you justify your method of support to your principal?

Aspects of Friendship

Pellegrini and Blatchford (2000) emphasize that friendship should not be confused with popularity. One's degree of popularity does not necessarily equate with his or her quality of friendships. In fact, popularity is more a reflection of social power than friendship (Vaillancourt, 2001). Bukowski, Newcomb, and Hartup (1996) emphasize that one must distinguish between *having friends* (related to self-esteem and success in relationships), *the identity of one's friends* (e.g., antisocial friends are related to antisocial tendencies), and *friendship quality,* or friendships that are based on understanding and loyalty.

The kind of friendship a child has in elementary school predicts his or her adjustment to secondary school. For example, an adolescent's friendships may be stable, but negative. If children with behavior problems have stable friendships with others who have behavior problems, their own behavior problems increase in junior high school. Sensitive, isolated students with friends who are also sensitive and isolated experience more isolation in junior high. High-quality friendships, on the other hand, predict sociability and leadership (Berndt et al., 1999) (Photo 6.4).

Early Theories on Friendship

Two early theorists contributed to our understanding of friendship. Piaget described children's friendships within his theory of moral development (discussed later in the chapter). He believed that children developed morality

PHOTO 6.4

Sensitive, isolated students with friends who are also sensitive and isolated experience more isolation in junior high.

Reciprocity: A balance in the relationship between two actions.

through their relationships with peers. He reasoned that children must cooperate with each other to reach their goals. Cooperation requires mutual respect, which, in turn, depends on *reciprocity norms* (Berndt, 1996). For example, "I can do to you what you do to me"; "I evaluate your actions, you evaluate mine"; and "we did the same work, we get the same reward" (Damon, 1977). Piaget's description of features of peer relationships is still relevant today (Berndt). It is central to educational approaches like cooperative learning and moral education.

Harry Stack Sullivan, a psychiatrist, emphasized intimacy and collaboration as defining characteristics of friendship. Sullivan tied his work on friendship to personality development, believing that too much competition between friends has a negative impact on personality (Berndt, 1996). There is general agreement that children's and adolescents' friendships are defined by the following actions (Bukowski et al., 1996):

- Reciprocities in regard, cooperation, conflict management
- Liking
- Affection and having fun

Development of the Nature of Friendship

By age 4, most children have the word *friend* in their vocabulary (Bukowski et al., 1996) and enjoy mutual friendships (Hartup & Abecassis, 2002). The *meaning* of friendship stays constant throughout childhood and adolescence, but friendship *expectations* and *relationships* change with age (Hartup & Abecassis; Pellegrini & Blatchford, 2000). A summary of the development of the nature and meaning of friendship is described here.

Early Childhood   In early childhood (preschool and early elementary), thinking about friendship is egocentric, with the result that there is low commitment to the relationship (Pellegrini & Blatchford, 2000). Playmate activities and acceptance by the group define ideas about friendship (Buhrmester, 1990). Notions about what makes a friend are concrete: "We play" (Hartup & Abecassis, 2002, p. 286). Friendship is easily begun (Damon, as cited in Berk, 1991), as described by a six-year-old girl to one of the authors: "Once I had a problem because I didn't have a friend to play with at recess. And then I asked Molly if she would be my friend and then she said, 'Yes.' So we played together and we were friends."

Friendships at this stage are just as easily ended. They also can be easily recovered, as revealed in the "and then we said sorry and played again" ending to stories told to one of the authors by six-year-olds.

Middle Childhood   Shared activities and group acceptance also are focal points of friendship in middle childhood (ages 8 to 12) (Buhrmester, 1990). By this point in development, however, children are more aware of their friends as persons with their own characteristics and points of view (Pellegrini & Blatchford, 2000).

At this stage, friendships involve more understanding of each other's needs and feelings. Trust is important (Hartup & Abecassis, 2002), and friends are counted on to help each other and spend time together. Breaches of trust, such as not helping, breaking promises, or talking about a friend behind his or her back, are viewed seriously. Friendships are not recovered as easily as they were a few years before. Apologies are necessary, but they need to be more serious and committed than they were in early childhood (Damon, 1977).

Adolescence   During adolescence, friendships involve more loyalty and commitment than they did in childhood. Others' points of view and values are taken into account (Pellegrini & Blatchford, 2000). More intimacy is demonstrated (e.g., self-disclosure); in fact, friends are believed to satisfy the need for interpersonal intimacy that emerges in adolescence (Newcomb & Bagwell, 1996). Adolescent friends recognize the time it takes to truly get to know someone and respect each other as individuals (Hartup & Abecassis, 2002). Friends at this stage count on each other to see them through difficult periods. Lack of loyalty or insincerity is viewed as a serious threat to friendship (Damon, 1977).

There is a stronger relationship among the ability to forge a close personal relationship, adjustment, and social competence in adolescence than in childhood (Buhrmester, 1990), revealing the unique importance of peer relationships to adolescent development. This is not to say that friendship is unimportant in childhood; it plays a critical role in adjustment. However, the importance of one's friendships is heightened in adolescence. They become deeper because they are understood at a more abstract level.

Friendship and Diversity

Many of today's classrooms are culturally diverse. James Deegan (1996) studied friendship in a culturally diverse elementary classroom in Atlanta. He described friendships as continually negotiated by children in unique situations. Some of the characteristics of friendship and forms of dissonance in friendship observed by Deegan are common to all children, while others are particularly relevant in classrooms where a variety of cultures is represented.

Characteristics of Friendship   The following characteristics of friendship were identified by the majority of the class:

- *Encounter,* or "going up to them" (Deegan, p. 44). Encounter involves getting to know others by asking names or inviting them to play. It was evident across the cultures in the classroom Deegan studied.
- *Togetherness,* or being present for a friend (sharing conversation, play, and work). Togetherness was demonstrated across racial, ethnic, and socioeconomic lines.
- *Niceness,* or sharing and respect.
- *Fighting.* Despite adult conceptions of fighting as negative, the children in Deegan's study saw fighting as part of making and breaking friendships.

Surfing Terms 6.4

Social network
Friendship quality
Peer support
Friendship features
Friendship stability

Surfing Terms 6.5

Virtues
Moral culture
Ethical mentor (Lickona, 1997)
Moral discipline
Sibling relationships
Birth order
Moral disengagement
Ethics curriculum
Values clarification
Ethic of care
Caring community
Social justice

The effects of fighting are generally short-lived. The children also saw fighting in defense of a friend as legitimate.

Dissonance in Friendship   Deegan (1996) described two forms of dissonance in friendship: *immigrant dissonance* due to misconceptions about culture and "acculturation, assimilation, and accommodation concerns and issues" (p. 47) and *life-situational dissonance*. Life-situational dissonance is the more significant problem. It stems from serious issues in children's lives, such as a drug-addicted parent or transience, and affects their school lives in ways that make it difficult to sustain friendships.

Children in today's classrooms also are diverse in terms of having varied academic and social needs. Many school districts follow the philosophy of inclusion (see Info Byte 6.2), meaning that children and adolescents with learning disabilities, developmental disabilities, advanced intellectual development, and physical and/or sensory handicaps receive much of their education in regular classrooms. We still don't have a solid research base on the ways in which inclusion affects friendship. The research that has been done suggests that elementary schoolchildren are more tolerant of physical disability than intellectual disability (Nowicki & Sandieson, 2002). Understanding children's attitudes toward differences among their peers is essential in helping educators plan effective interventions.

Social Development and Education

A number of educational approaches and programs exist to support healthy social development. However, they often are conceived of as add-ons to the academic curriculum. Several studies and programs have identified ways in which schools can promote healthy social development.

Adding Social Development to the Curriculum   De Falco (1997) made an important point about teaching skills and understanding related to the development of social competence. He advised schools to think about the ways in which they teach other important areas of the curriculum—systematically and sequentially—whereas social competence tends to be taught in a fragmented way, often in response to a problem. Without having a soundly conceived, developmental

---

INFO BYTE 6.2

Historically, in North America any student who was handicapped or disabled in any way was segregated to special schools or institutions. At the time it was felt students would learn better when specialists taught groups of children all with the same or similar difficulties. However, in the 1960s, movements arose that sought to have these students moved into a more "normalized" environment. As children were moved from specialized situations (often residential programs) into the local schools, there were resultant philosophical changes for teachers and the public in general. The term *mainstreaming* reflected the program shift as these students were made part of the local education program. At first students were segregated into classrooms with special teachers, but within the local school. This amounted to only a geographic shift from special institutions or schools to the local school. Students were taught separately and not incorporated into the community life of the school. By the 1970s, a further change occurred. Students were now incorporated into regular classrooms and taught by the regular classroom teacher, with a special education support system. Students were fully included in the school community. This education philosophy, known as *inclusion*, allows all students the opportunity to become independent, self-directed individuals.

program for teaching social skills, we are unlikely to make a significant difference in supporting social development. Bruner (1996) argued that, given the importance that one's understanding of others has in life, social development should have a prominent place in the school curriculum.

Social Skills Programs   Zins, Travis, and Freppon (1997) examined Second Step: A Violence Prevention Curriculum (Committee on Youth, 1995), a developmental program designed to teach prosocial skills in grades K to 8. They emphasized that no single program can address all the factors that may contribute to behavior problems. They also identified important complements to social skills programs, such as peer tutoring, school and community projects, parent involvement and support, and family literacy (Zins et al.).

A school that can provide an effective, caring community can also be a key component in supporting healthy social development (Photo 6.5). Mulvey and Cauffman (2001) emphasized that "promoting healthy relationships and environments is more effective in reducing school misconduct than instituting punitive penalties" (p. 800).

Positive support was similarly found to be effective in dealing with bullying in schools. Olweus (2003) described the importance of nonpunitive consequences for bullying; positive interest, involvement, and support from adults; firm limits on inappropriate behavior; and communication between and among students, teachers, and parents. Cooper and Snell (2003) suggested a preventive approach that includes clear guidelines and policy for behavior, helping adults recognize bullying and take action when it occurs, and taking a whole-school approach to supporting positive interactions.

Addressing Teachers' Preconceptions   Other important considerations in translating research and theory on social development to classrooms are our own perspectives. For example, Deegan (1996) discussed a study by Grant (1984) that found that teachers view white girls as cognitively mature and black girls as socially mature. It is important to examine our own notions of race, culture, and socioeconomic status and our own understandings of friendship and community and how these notions may contribute to the sorts of communities we create in classrooms. This examination of our own perspectives applies to children with special needs as well. We will discuss school communities further in Chapter 7.

PHOTO 6.5

Community projects complement social skills programs.

Development of Self

Underlying our development as social and emotional beings is our conception of who we are as individuals—our *self*. In this section, theoretical background on how the self develops is presented. As teachers, it is important for us to know how children and adolescents understand who they are and the nature of the developmental tasks they undertake in achieving mature self-concepts.

Psychosocial Development

The term *psychosocial* captures the strong relationship between who we are, that is, how we develop as psychological beings, and how we function in our social worlds. Erik Erikson (1950, 1968) was a psychoanalyst who articulated eight stages of psychosocial development. He has been described as "identity's architect" (Reis & Youniss, 2004). Erikson viewed psychological development in terms of an individual's resolution of certain challenges, or the developmental crises we face across our life-span (see Table 6.1). He used the term *crisis* to identify a turning point in an individual's life. Each stage is described in terms of the positive and negative outcomes that result if the crisis is more or less effectively resolved. If we progress through each of these stages successfully, we develop in a healthy fashion.

Theories of Self-Concept and Erikson's Crises

Contemporary work that applies Erikson's theory to adolescence recognizes that most adolescents are stable in their development of identity (contrary to popular opinion that adolescence is a time of turmoil) (Reis & Youniss, 2004). However, some adolescents actually regress to the previous stage of self-development, and about one-quarter of late adolescents still don't have a clear identity. Currently, Erikson's theory is seen by some as focusing on individuals out of context; it fails to recognize the influences of exploration, commitment, and contemporary culture on identity. Current work moves away from the idea of static stages. Instead, Erikson's stages are used as guidelines only, as general reference points for the variety of influences on the development of self (e.g., different social relationships) (Reis & Youniss). Other contemporary theorists recognized Erickson's theory for its emphasis on an individual's adaptation to the social context (Peterson, Marcia, & Carpendale, 2004) and extended his work to describe ways in which late adolescents may deal with identity issues.

Marcia (1966; as cited in Peterson et al., 2004, p. 114) developed four identity statuses.

1. *Identity achievements*: Individuals who have undergone, or are undergoing, exploration and made commitments to occupation, values about relationships, and religious and political beliefs.
2. *Identity crisis*: Individuals who are exploring issues and have made only vague commitments.
3. *Foreclosures*: Individuals who are committed without having undergone any exploration. They usually have taken on others' directions for themselves.
4. *Diffusions*: Individuals who have not undertaken any exploration and have not committed to any life directions.

Self-Conceptions in Childhood

Besides knowing about the developmental challenges we face across our life-span, it also is useful for teachers to understand how children's and adolescents'

TABLE 6.1

Erikson's Eight Psychosocial Stages

Stage	Developmental Task
Trust vs. **Mistrust** (Infancy–first year)	A sense of trust depends on physical comfort and minimal fear and apprehension.
Autonomy vs. **Shame and Doubt** (1–3 years)	Assertion of independence and autonomy. Too much restriction or punishment results in shame and doubt.
Initiative vs. **Guilt** (3–5 years)	Developing a sense of responsibility helps young children achieve a sense of initiative. Guilt can result from too many demands for self-control (child can become over-controlled and anxious)
Industry vs. **Inferiority** (6 years–puberty)	Children develop a capacity for productive work, cooperation with others, and pride in doing things well. Inferiority results when feelings of competence and mastery are not fostered.
Identity vs. **Identity Confusion** (adolescence)	Individuals are faced with finding out who they are, what they are all about, and where they are going in life. Need exploration of different roles and paths to form a positive identity.
Intimacy vs. **Isolation** (early adulthood–20s, 30s)	Developmental task is the formation of intimate relationships with others.
Generativity vs. **Stagnation** (middle–40s, 50s)	A chief concern is to assist the younger adulthood generation in developing and leading useful lives (generativity). The feeling of having done nothing to help is stagnation.
Integrity vs. **Despair** (late adulthood–60s on)	Retrospective look at one's life can be either positive or negative.

self-concepts develop. The plural, *self-concepts*, is used deliberately. We do hold a general opinion of our worth as individuals (usually known as our *self-esteem* or *self-worth*), but we also hold a variety of different conceptions of ourselves that affect our overall self-esteem (Harter, 1986; Marsh, 1993). (See Info Byte 6.3.) Self-perceptions in specific areas such as academic competence and social acceptance are important in understanding school performance (Harter, 1982, 1986; Strein, 1993). Personal images of school success and acceptance by peers affect achievement.

The Changing Academic Self-Concept Susan Harter (1982; Harter & Pike, 1984) described how, in the early school years, children's perceptions of themselves are relatively undifferentiated. They have a sense of their cognitive competence (e.g., "good at numbers," "can write words"), their physical competence (e.g., "good at running"), and their acceptance by peers (e.g., "have friends to play games with") (Harter & Pike, 1983) (see Figure 6.5 on page 154).

By about third grade, children's self-concept becomes more differentiated. They have conceptions of their scholastic competence (e.g., "feeling of being smart"), social acceptance (e.g., "feeling that most kids like them"), athletic competence (e.g., "do well at sports"), physical appearance (e.g., "happy with the way they look"), behavioral conduct (e.g., "doing the right thing"), and global self-worth (e.g., "like themselves as a person") (Harter, 1985). Physical appearance, as described by Harter, becomes particularly important to children around fifth grade and grows in importance as they enter adolescence.

INFO BYTE 6.3

DIFFERENCES BETWEEN SELF-CONCEPT AND SELF-ESTEEM

Self-concept: A *descriptive* term for the images we hold of ourselves in academics, the social arena, sports, and the like. (Brinthaupt & Erwin, 1992; Hoge & Renzulli, 1993). For example, I can solve complex math problems, but I have some trouble interpreting English literature.

Self-esteem: An *evaluative* term (Brinthaupt & Erwin) for how we feel about ourselves as persons. For example, I feel good about myself or I feel like I'm not a worthwhile person. Self-esteem is sometimes referred to as *self-worth*.

FIGURE 6.5

Who Am I?

Marsh (1992) found that academic self-concept is more specific than Harter (1985) suggested. For example, we can hold different perceptions of our competence in specific school subjects like reading, math, and social studies.

Increasing Complexity in Self-Concept As we mature, our understanding of the world not only widens but also deepens. We start to understand that most subjects or topics we encounter are often more complex than at first glance. We know that there may be several levels of understanding or several perspectives that are relevant. For example, if we wanted to play cards with friends on Saturday night, we might find the date doesn't work due to a spouse's previous plans or children's sports activities. Thus, the world widens beyond the initial interaction. We also need to understand the social implications of friendships and the realities of schedules and timing. Now, the interaction has depth in understanding.

Until a child reaches the point of thinking beyond the concrete world, the ramifications of being turned down for a play date are difficult to understand. While we can tell a child that the date is canceled, they really don't fully grasp the "whys." By adolescence, thinking matures to the point where the depth and expansion of understanding allow manipulation of topics in the abstract. Along with this is the ability to place oneself in this abstract understanding and to evaluate abilities and talents against the wider and deeper world. At this point we start to add to our concept of who we are (self-concept) and how valuable we are (self-esteem).

Self-Conceptions in Adolescence

Because of their ability to think in abstract terms, you will find that many adolescents describe themselves in terms of values and beliefs. For example, you may hear a student say he or she is a realist, or a pacifist, or a reliable person. They will describe themselves in terms of internal qualities rather than concrete, visible characteristics (Byrne, 1996). They also describe others in these terms, as is evident in the concept map that Bruce, an eighth-grader, did to capture the character in a story his class had read (see Figure 6.6). Add to that the expansion of the adolescent's life to include work, cars, money, additional peer groups (e.g., people they work with), a variety of interests, and new clubs or groups. Adolescents form self-perceptions in relation to specific contexts (e.g., school, home, job, skating rink) (Byrne). Now self-esteem becomes complex.

Not only are students' actual capabilities important, but their knowledge of themselves and how they react in different contexts also influences their self-esteem. Students' perceptions of their own competence also influence their moti-

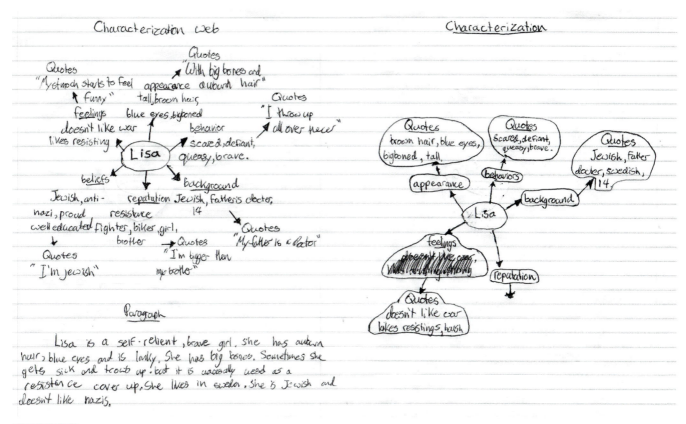

FIGURE 6.6

Characterization Concept Map

vation (Harter, 1999). Motivation, in turn, affects their choices and the challenges they are willing to accept. Starting at about the middle school years, the complexity of self-esteem starts to influence achievement (Marsh & Yeung, 1997).

Adolescents analyze all aspects of their lives to determine importance. One person may be influenced by his or her ability to use words skillfully, so the student may join the debating team. If, on the other hand, the person doesn't attach importance to being good with words, he or she may not be interested in joining the debating team, despite having the talent. One of the authors remembers a high school coach who was thrilled when a tenth-grade student transferred into the school. The young man was almost 6 feet tall, ideal for basketball. Unfortunately, even though the student was a good player, he was more interested in music and joined the band. With equal talent in both music and basketball, the music held a more prominent position in his world. Self-esteem is not only complex, but stratified according to a personal value system. This is why programs designed to build self-esteem are hard to organize. Everyone has a different system, personalized by experience.

Self-Conceptions, Values, and Gender across Childhood and Adolescence

In a study of how children and adolescents (grades 1 to 12) view their competence in mathematics, language arts, and sports, Jacobs, Lanza, Osgood, Eccles, and Wigfield (2002) looked at how beliefs about competence develop and whether there are gender differences. They found the following:

- Boys start out with stronger beliefs in their mathematics competence than girls. However, by grade 9 boys' and girls' scores were equal.
- Both boys' and girls' beliefs in their mathematics competence declined over time, but the boys' competence beliefs decreased at a faster rate.
- In language arts, boys and girls start at the same point. By grade 6 there is a significant gender difference favoring girls.
- Boys decline rapidly in their feelings of competence in language arts. This decline slows down in middle school. Girls' feelings of competence also decline, but more slowly than boys. Their decline slows down through middle and high school, but girls remain more confident in their ability in language arts than boys do.
- In sports, boys start out more confident and remain that way despite declines in both boys' and girls' perceptions of competence.

Jacobs et al. (2002) found that changes in perceptions of competence are related to changes in the values students hold for mathematics, language arts, and sports. Overall, values for all three subjects declined over time. However, students who felt competent in particular subjects were more likely to value these subjects.

The following two conclusions in Jacobs et al.'s (2002) study need to be emphasized:

- The declines in boys' beliefs in their competence indicate that they are not feeling successful in school.
- The study was done in urban schools with middle- to upper-middle-class European American populations. The pattern of findings in this study may be different in diverse populations of children and/or different educational contexts (Jacobs et al.).

Perspectives on Self-Esteem

Harter (1985) incorporated two classic perspectives on self-esteem, or self-worth, in describing how children and adolescents see themselves. One is that of William James (1892; as cited in Harter, 1985), who believed that our overall sense of worth is determined by our aspirations to be competent in different areas. For example, if we believe academic success is important, aspire to be successful in school, and achieve that success, our perception of our academic competence is positive. This positive conception contributes to high self-esteem. Conversely, if we aspire to academic success but are not successful, low self-esteem may result. Some of us may not be academically successful but, because we don't deem academic success important, our self-esteem is not negatively affected.

Harter (1985) also incorporated Cooley's (1902, as cited in Harter, 1985), view of the self as a social construction. That is, it is not only our own perceptions of competence and acceptance in various areas and the importance we ascribe to these areas that determine our self-esteem, but also the perceptions that we believe that others have of us. So, if you believe your teacher does not view you as academically competent, this perception affects your self-esteem negatively. We will have more to say on the topic of teacher expectations in Chapters 9 and 10.

Montemayor and Eisen's (1977) work on self-conceptions also is interesting to consider from the point of view of understanding learners in classrooms. Montemayor and Eisen studied children in grades 4 to 12. They found that children's descriptions of themselves changed from concrete to abstract over the period of development. Fourth-graders described themselves in concrete terms like physical appearance, address, likes and dislikes, and school attended (e.g., "My name is John. I have blue eyes."). By sixth grade, there were indications of psychological and abstract terms (e.g., "I'm a kind person" or "I try to be helpful.")

mixed with concrete descriptors. By twelfth grade, the use of abstract and psychological terms had increased significantly, as indicated in the use of terms like indecisive, ambitious, conservative, and moody. (See InfoByte 6.4.)

In Problem-Based Scenario 6.5, a first-grade teacher uses a "Who Am I?" activity to try to understand a child whose developmental profile is a mix of behaviors and thinking typical of both early and middle childhood.

Self-Conceptions and Diversity

Much of the research on children's and adolescents' conceptions of themselves and their abilities has been done on children of Caucasian background. The research is limited by the lack of representation of different cultures. Marsh and Hau (2003) took culture into account when they studied the academic self-concepts of students in 26 countries. They found that children in different cultures respond to questions about their abilities in a similar fashion, suggesting that children of all cultures understand these concepts in the same way. Still, we need to keep in mind that culture may be relevant in understanding how children and adolescents view themselves. What a culture deems important can influence children's self-perceptions. Different cultures may, for example, place differential values on mathematical and language competence or value physical competence more highly than academic ability.

INFO BYTE 6.4

Montemayor and Eisen (1977) looked at the development of self-concept from childhood to adolescence by analyzing the response to this question: "Who Am I?" In these samples taken from this study, you can see not only a shift in cognition from concrete to abstract, but the deepening of personal understanding by each unique individual.

GRADE 4 BOY, 9 YEARS OLD (MISSPELLINGS IN THE ORIGINAL)

My name is Bruce C. I have brown eyes. I have brown hair. I have brown eyebrows. I'm nine years old. I LOVE! Sports. I have seven people in my family. I have great! eye site. I have lots! of friends. I live on 1923 Pinecrest Dr. I'm going on 10 in September. I'm a boy. I have a uncle that is almost 7 feet tall. My school is Pinecrest. My teacher is Mrs. V. I play Hockey! I'am almost the smartest boy in the class. I LOVE! food. I love freash air. I LOVE School. (p. 317)

GRADE 6 GIRL, 11 YEARS OLD

My name is A. I'm a human being. I'm a girl. I'm a truthful person. I'm not pretty. I do so-so in my studies. I'm a very good cellist. I'm a very good pianist. I'm a little bit tall for my age. I like several boys. I like several girls. I'm old-fashioned. I play tennis. I am a *very* good swimmer. I try to be helpful. I'm always ready to be friends with anybody. Mostly I'm good, but I lose my temper. I'm not well-liked by some girls and boys. I don't know if I'm liked by boys or not. (pp. 317–318)

GRADE 12 GIRL, AGE 17 YEARS OLD

I am a human being. I am a girl. I am an individual. I don't know who I am. I am a Pisces. I am a moody person. I am an indecisive person. I am an ambitious person. I am a very curious person. I am not an individual. I am a loner. I am an American (God help me). I am a Democrat. I am a liberal person. I am a radical. I am a conservative. I am a pseudoliberal. I am an atheist. I am not a classifiable person (i.e., I don't want to be). (p. 318)

Problem-Based Scenario 6.5

Student: Dylan
Teacher: Shelly

As a way of getting to know her students better, Shelley Lim always had her first-graders write four sentences about themselves and draw a self-portrait. She provided four sentence stems, and the children discussed how they might complete each. She thought that this activity might provide some insight that would help her understand her students' perspectives.

There were a few children she was particularly interested in. She looked through the stack of papers to find Dylan's. After watching him on the playground at recess, she really needed to figure out what was going on. From a distance, she saw him running enthusiastically toward the fifth-grade boys who were choosing teams for baseball. The next time she saw him was a few minutes later when she spotted him walking away. Then there was the outburst of tears and protests about the unfairness of the older boys as the class gathered after recess

Figure 6.7 appears on page 177.

Apply

- What might peer relationship researchers say about Dylan? How would you connect their observations to practice?

We also don't have a very good idea of whether children with exceptional learning needs view themselves in the same way as typically developing children. Familiar norms do not apply to these children, and significant adaptations need to be made in the academic and social aspects of their schooling (Robinson, Zigler, & Gallagher, 2000). Their academic and social developmental profiles vary significantly from those of typically developing children (Keating, 1991; Liddle & Porath, 2002; Matthews, 1997; Robinson et al.; Yewchuk & Lupart, 2000). We also need to keep in mind that special learning needs may influence children's views of themselves.

Learners' Self-Knowledge: Implications for the Classroom

Knowing that there are different types of self-perception is important to teachers. The different ways in which children perceive themselves (e.g., academic, social, behavioral) influence how good they feel about themselves overall. Educational approaches to developing overall self-esteem have been sharply criticized (e.g., Katz, 1993; Kohn, 1994). These approaches aim to help learners "feel good about themselves." They focus on global self-esteem with activities that have been described as "all about me" (Katz, 1993a). Katz suggested that many of the activities designed to promote self-esteem in classrooms, while well intentioned, "may instead inadvertently develop narcissism in the form of excessive preoccupation with oneself" (p. 200). Kohn concurs: "Merely being told (or asked to repeat) that one is worthwhile isn't likely to change anyone's underlying self-image" (p. 277).

Instead, Katz (1993a) advocated emphases on challenge, effort, and acquisition of skills, knowledge, and appropriate behavior. In this way, children build the specific competencies outlined by Susan Harter and Herbert Marsh, competencies that contribute to their self-esteem in genuine ways. Adults and peers convey esteem to children when they "treat them with respect, ask them for their views and preferences . . . and provide opportunities for real decisions and choices about those things that matter to the children" (Katz, p. 201). Perceived competence derives from successful experiences (Kohn, 1994). The likelihood of successful educational experiences can be enhanced by linking practice to theory in well-informed ways and considering children's and adolescents' points of view and experiential backgrounds in our educational planning.

Emotional Development

The value of including consideration of emotions in the study of cognitive and social development is gaining recognition. There is a constant interplay between cognition and emotion (Suizzo, 2000); how we feel determines our actions, which are, in turn, reacted to by others and reflected on by ourselves. Children who are well supported in their learning demonstrate higher levels of cognitive functioning (Fischer, Knight, & Van Parys, 1993). Antonio Damasio (1994), a neurologist, argues that emotions are essential to reasoning. Daniel Goleman (1995), whose work on emotional intelligence has been particularly influential in education, goes even farther and argues that healthy emotional development may be more important than cognitive development.

As you read this discussion on emotional development, you will notice similarities to the topics discussed under social development. This is because there is a close relationship between social and emotional development. If you go back to our earlier discussion of Erikson (Table 6.1), you can see that while the crises he describes are social, they also are "emotionally charged." You will also see a connection between social-emotional development and society and culture in the next chapter.

Emotional Intelligence

Based on work in psychology and neuroscience, *emotional intelligence* has been identified as a distinct capability (Damasio, 1994; Mayer, Caruso, & Salovey, 2000). Mayer and Salovey (1997) define emotional intelligence as involving

> The ability to perceive accurately, appraise, and express emotion; the ability to access and/or generate feelings when they facilitate thought; the ability to understand emotion and emotional knowledge; and the ability to regulate emotions to promote emotional and intellectual growth. (p. 10)

Mayer and Salovey (1997) stress that their definition makes an essential connection between emotion and intelligence. "Emotion makes thinking more intelligent and . . . one thinks intelligently about emotions" (p. 5). Mayer and Salovey see emotions as contributing to thought by highlighting what is important for us to think about. However, they do recognize that there are instances where emotions can "hijack" (p. 9) thought because of their intensity (Photo 6.6).

This point has been picked up by De Falco (1997), an educator who describes children and youth who, because of their life circumstances, cannot attend to the business of school. Some children find school a place of safety that helps them to cope; for others, however, life stressors make success in school very difficult. One of our colleagues once commented, "How can I interest a child in the long *a* sound when his mother has been beaten up?" As discussed earlier in the chapter, this sort of "life-situational dissonance" (Deegan, 1996) can have a significant negative effect on academic and social development. In Problem-Based Scenario 6.6, you will see how a whole school can be "hijacked" emotionally.

Emotional Adjustment

Raver, Izard, and Kopp (2002) emphasized the importance of healthy emotional adjustment for success in school. As with social adjustment, children who are well

PHOTO 6.6
There are instances where emotions can "hijack" thought because of their intensity.

adjusted emotionally have a better chance of succeeding in school. Raver et al. state that "emotions matter" (p. 3). Emotional skills can protect children from stress.

Mayer and Salovey (1997, p. 10) identified four components of emotional intelligence and a developmental continuum within each component. These are summarized next. The abilities that appear early in development are listed first in each category; those that are mature accomplishments are listed last.

Problem-Based Scenario *6.6*

Teacher: *Ruth*

As Ruth pulled her car into the teacher's parking lot, she noticed a small group of very upset grade 9 students. From their reaction as she turned the car off, they were obviously waiting for her. They all started talking and crying at once. "Ms. Moore, did you hear about Mike killing Charlie last night?" "How could he do that to his best friend?" "Charlie was the greatest soccer player this school ever saw."

As Ruth tried to settle them down, the story unfolded. While driving home from soccer practice the car somehow swerved and went into a ditch. Charlie was dead instantly (no one was wearing seatbelts), and Mike came out without a scratch. Since Mike was driving and he wasn't hurt, he was being held responsible for the death of his closest friend.

Because both boys were so popular, everyone knew who they were and the students were taking this very hard.

The whole school seemed stunned. The district had sent grief counselors. But Ruth thought, in "true adolescent tradition," it would become common knowledge among the students that these strangers couldn't help because they didn't know Mike or Charlie. Sure enough, the counselors sat alone while the students turned to each other for comfort.

As Ruth set up her room for class, she needed to think about what was going on in the halls. Was it worthwhile teaching her lessons as planned? If not, then what?

Perception, Appraisal, and Expression of Emotion

- Identification of one's own emotions
- Identification of others' emotions and emotions in art, language, sound, appearance, and behavior
- Accurate expression of emotions and related needs
- Discrimination of accurate–inaccurate and honest–dishonest emotions

Facilitation of Thinking through Emotions

- Emotions direct our thoughts to important information.
- Emotions can be accessed to aid in judgment and memory.
- Different moods help in understanding different points of view.
- Emotions are associated with different problem-solving approaches (e.g., happiness facilitates creativity).

Understanding and Analyzing Emotions

- Accurately labeling emotions and recognizing relationships between emotional terms (e.g., mad and angry)
- Interpreting relationships between emotions and events (e.g., pride and winning a scholarship)
- Ability to understand multiple emotions that co-occur (e.g., anger and grief)
- Recognition of transitions between emotions (e.g., anger to shame)

Regulation of Emotions

- Openness to feelings
- Ability to engage or detach from a feeling, depending on whether it is helpful or harmful
- Reflective monitoring of one's own and others' emotions (e.g., are the emotions typical or reasonable?)
- Managing unpleasant emotions and enhancing positive ones

The developmental continua articulated by Mayer and Salovey provide guidelines as to which emotional competencies teachers might expect at given landmark ages during the school years and a roadmap of the building blocks of emotional development. Carolyn Saarni (1999) charted the relationship between emotional development and social interaction, providing another helpful guideline for teachers (see Table 6.2).

Culture Influences Parameters of Emotion   Another important factor in understanding your students' emotional development is the influence of culture on children's understanding and display of emotions. The ways in which children appraise, communicate, and act on emotions are influenced by their cultural backgrounds (Cole, Bruschi, & Tamang, 2002). For example, a culture that prizes a high degree of self-control may believe that anger should not be communicated. A culture that values societal harmony may emphasize selflessness and freedom from emotional wants (Cole et al.).

Educational Implications for Fostering Emotional Intelligence

The development of emotional intelligence in schools has received increased attention since the publication of Daniel Goleman's book, "Emotional Intelligence: Why It Can Matter More Than IQ" in 1995.

TABLE 6.2

Relationships between Emotional and Social Development

Developmental Period	Regulation of Emotions and Coping Strategies	Mode of Expression	Nature of Social Relationships
5 to 7 years old	Regulation of self-conscious emotions like embarrassment	Showing a "cool emotional front" with peers	Increasing ability to coordinate emotions (own and others') with social skills
7 to 10 years old	Problem solving or distancing if child lacks control	Understands norms for expression of emotion	Awareness of multiple emotions; uses personal knowledge about others to forge friendships
10 to 13 years old	Understands the degree of control he/she has; develops more strategies for dealing with stressful situations	Distinguishes genuine and "managed" emotions	Development of social sensitivity and knowledge of the relationship between social roles and expected emotions
13 years and over	Awareness of the range of one's own emotions; emergence of personal approaches to coping	Development of "self-presentation strategies"	Understanding that communication of emotions influences relationships

Curriculum-Based Emotional Learning   Mayer and Salovey (1997) offered suggestions for building opportunities for emotional development into the standard curriculum. In the language arts, for example, analyses of story characters' feelings, thoughts, motivations, and coping strategies offer the chance for "natural emotional teaching" (Mayer & Salovey, p. 19). Matthews, Zeidner, and Roberts (2002) state that "curriculum based emotional learning comes naturally with many of the liberal arts (e.g., literature, theatre, poetry, etc.)" (p. 443).

Literature becomes increasingly complex as learners progress through the school system, in concert with their emotional development. Art, music, and drama also offer opportunities to develop emotional intelligence (Mayer & Salovey, 1997). Often the value of art, drama, and music is overlooked in budgetary decisions, allowing programs to be "cut." The emotional learning that occurs in these programs is not as tangible an outcome as reading and math.

Concerns with Emotion-Based Curricula   Mayer and Salovey (1997) express a concern about programs that purport to teach emotional intelligence similar to that expressed by Katz (1993) and Kohn (1994) about "self-esteem programs." Some of these programs adopt an "emotions are good" (Mayer & Salovey, p. 21) philosophy in a superficial manner. Others aim to increase emotional intelligence. However, there are programs that target other social and emotional competencies that are effective in teaching about emotions. For example, the Promoting Alternative Thinking Strategies (PATHS) program emphasizes readiness and self-control, feelings and relationships, and interpersonal cognitive problem solving. It is also effective in building emotional competence (Greenberg, Kusche, Cook, & Quamma, 1995; Matthews et al., 2002).

Mayer and Salovey (1997) offered the following reflection on educational programming, with reference to a conflict resolution program.

Conflict resolution is based on learning the skills of an emotionally intelligent person . . . how to identify the feelings of your adversary, your own feelings, and the feelings of others involved . . . . It is more concrete and easier to agree upon implementing a conflict resolution curriculum (from our perspective) than a program devoted to increasing emotional intelligence (should such be possible) per se. The more focused goals of such a program also prevent it from being misinterpreted as teaching the "right" (or "best") way to feel. (p. 21)

The above discussion of programs that have among their objectives the development of emotional competence highlights that a number of factors influence emotional intelligence. Children's own emotional experiences, the affective environment in school and community, the interactions between teachers and students, and the media all influence emotional competence. Table 6.3 summarizes the desired features of programs structured to build emotional intelligence recommended by Matthews et al., (2002).

Moral Development

Every once in a while, teachers are faced with this question: "Should we teach morality in our schools?" This is actually an interesting question. Can we teach morality? Whose morality do we teach, especially if you live in a multicultural community? If we start to contemplate the definition of morality, we find it is a complex combination of knowing "right" from "wrong," social customs and mores, and religious beliefs and customs, all within an age-related set of conditions and understandings. It is the ethical underpinning of acceptable human behavior.

TABLE 6.3

Desired Features of Programs Designed to Build Emotional Intelligence

1. Intervention should be based on a conceptual framework.

2. Goals should focus specifically on emotional intelligence—"awareness, understanding, expression, and regulation of emotions in self and others" (Matthews, Zeidner, & Roberts, 2002, p. 461).

3. The whole school and the community need to value emotional intelligence, and should be consulted and involved in the program.

4. Consider culture, gender, and socioeconomic standing of staff and students.

5. The program should include a variety of related variables such as social problem solving, social understanding, social and emotional skills, and learning climate.

6. Staff should prepare adequately.

7. The program should be integrated into the curriculum, not "added on."

8. The program should be developmentally appropriate.

9. There should be opportunities for practice and application of skills in and beyond school.

Stages of Moral Development

Until the 20th century, the issues associated with moral understanding and development were relegated to theologians. Theologians postulated the idea that children developed a sense of right and wrong at about the age of 7 years, when they entered the *age of reason*. Interestingly, this age of reason coincides with the onset of the concrete stage within the Piagetian framework. Until this point, children were not considered capable of being held accountable for their actions. While not every religion agrees with this, generally the age of 7 appeared to be a "magic time" when enlightenment suddenly occurred in a person.

Piaget's Stages of Moral Development

Piaget (1932) was one of the first theorists to question young children in an effort to understand their conceptions of right and wrong. He outlined two general stages of moral development: heteronomy and autonomy.

Heteronomy   The initial stage of moral development is called *heteronomy*. For very young children, right and wrong are based on personal consequences. If the consequence will be unpleasant, such as getting yelled at, then the action is wrong. The child is responding to an outside authority that controls rewards and punishments. As the child grows and develops his understanding of the world, he learns to internalize judgments of good and bad.

Autonomy   The next stage internalizes judgments of good and bad. This process leads to *autonomy* in decisions where the volition or free will of the child takes over from the previous outside authority. The importance of Piaget's theory was in its recognition of the role of cognition in moral development.

> **Heteronomy:** Subjection to an external law. "Don't do that because it's against the rules!"

> **Autonomy:** Personal freedom; free will. "I won't do that because I know it's wrong."

Kohlberg's Theory of Moral Development

Lawrence Kohlberg (1964) expanded on Piaget's work on a stage theory of moral development. Kohlberg's work consisted of presenting people with stories of different moral dilemmas and asking them how they would react in the same situation and why. From this research he developed a theory of moral development that contained three levels, with two stages within each level. The three levels are similar to the two stages of heteronomy and autonomy. Kohlberg's levels show the expansion from an outside, controlling authority to an internal personal will or self-control.

Level 1: Preconventional   Children at this level react to what is right or wrong according to an accompanying reaction from an authority figure.

Stage 1: They comply with rules solely to avoid punishment and receive praise.

Stage 2: While primarily concerned with themselves, they will accommodate other people as long as it results in something for them ("you scratch my back and I'll scratch yours").

Level 2: Conventional   As children grow, they become aware of the necessity of maintaining social order.

Stage 3: To have good social relations with peers and others, it is necessary to be seen as complying with the group rules.

Stage 4: Group rules or laws become very important, and following them exactly is seen as a way to become a good person.

Level 3: Postconventional   At this point, individuals start to develop a more abstract understanding of moral concepts and social conventions. Flexibility in administering laws becomes more important that an automatic rule imposition.

Stage 5: The understanding that laws need to reflect such things as society and culture, individual rights, and circumstances of the individual lead to a realization that laws can be changed.

Stage 6: In this final stage, there is a clear conception of the abstraction of principles. Human dignity, fairness, and justice start to become more important than the law. For those people who reach this stage and find themselves in situations where laws do not match society, it becomes necessary to change laws in an orderly manner. Kohlberg believed that very few people reach this final stage. He felt only certain individuals in history were able to stand up and suffer for their beliefs, such as Socrates, Jesus, Gandhi, and Martin Luther King, Jr.

Responses to Kohlberg's Theory

Kohlberg provided a general outline of moral development. However, there have been a number of criticisms of his theory. The manner of using levels and stages implies that the higher the stage or level, the more advanced the thinking. Many people can give examples where as an adult you follow rules just to avoid an unpleasant reaction, for example, obeying speed limits so you won't get a traffic ticket. Does that mean this person is at a lower level or stage in development? Or does it demonstrate that moral decisions are often situation specific? Can someone who obeys the speed limit so they don't get a ticket think on a higher level, for example, by arguing a position on a Supreme Court case with his or her friends?

Gilligan's Stages of Women's Moral Decision Making   One of the more interesting criticisms of Kohlberg's theory was Carol Gilligan's (1982). She pointed out that all of Kohlberg's research subjects were men. This would lead to a one-sided and perhaps misleading picture of moral development.

Gilligan's research involved interviews with a sample of pregnant women who were being counseled and were struggling with the issue of abortion. Some of the women decided to have an abortion, some carried their babies to term; one had a miscarriage; and some never actually made decisions about the abortion. In her work, Gilligan found that the reason for the decision was much more important than the actual decision in determining the underlying level of moral development. She identified the following three stages in women's moral decision making.

Stage 1: The decision is determined by what is good for the woman herself: "I want."

Stage 2: There is a move toward greater responsibility for society, beyond oneself.

Stage 3, the Morality of Nonviolence: The individual contemplates all parties involved in the decision and tries to select the result that will have the greatest benefit or least impact on everyone involved.

Gilligan has pointed out a woman's perspective. However, if you look at Kohlberg and Gilligan carefully you will see a similarity as the individual progresses from a self-centered stage, to more awareness of others, and finally to an understanding that we are all part of a larger and more complicated community.

Problem-Based Scenario 6.7

Student's Parent: *Mrs. Nardi*
Teacher: *David*

K-5   6-8   9-12   SpEd

David sat in the staff room waiting for Anne and Chris, the other two teachers who organized and ran the lunchtime dances. It had started off as a great idea—at least that's what the three of them thought several months ago. Since this was a middle school in a rural farming community, the teachers felt it would be good to provide the students with some opportunities to develop social skills. The school covered a large regional district, so most students had little chance to interact outside of school time or on the school bus.

David, Anne, and Chris had approached the principal with the idea of condensing lunch time by a few minutes per day and then holding a 45-minute dance in the gym once a month in the winter when the weather got too bad for students to go outside. This idea had been well received by the principal and the superintendent, who thought it was a great idea. Most of the teachers participated and the activity ran smoothly. It consisted primarily of a lot of noise, groups sitting and chatting, and very little actual dancing. The entry "fee" was either a quarter or a "Teacher's Free Pass" given for good work, prizes, or if a teacher knew a student didn't have a quarter. The money generated alternated between the "Wish List" for the library and the sports teams. Everyone had a great time. Even the feedback from some of the parents had been positive.

The problem David needed to talk to Anne and Chris about was the phone call he got that morning from Mrs. Nardi. While David and the other teachers knew several students had religious prohibitions on dancing, they thought it had been taken care of when these students volunteered to sell tickets, make posters, and set up the gym. The students were active socially with their peers, but not attending the dance. Mrs. Nardi was actually very nice on the phone, but it seems she was speaking for several members of her church and their concern about the moral implications of dances. They felt that even the peripheral help with the dances was unacceptable. They wanted all of their children removed from any association with the dances.

Now David, Anne, and Chris needed to figure out what to do next.

This does not imply that there aren't differences between the male and female perspective. In very general terms, women tend to be more responsive to social relationships and less interested in hypothetical situations, while men tend to be more concerned with social justice and abstractions. It would be misleading to think that all men have one perspective while women have another.

Cultural Morality and the Limits of Kohlberg's Morality   Similarly, cross-cultural research on moral development has found that global views of societies (e.g., Western societies as individualistic; non-Western societies as group-oriented) are insufficient to explain differences in moral reasoning. There is considerable variability within cultures, pointing to the "complexity, diversity, situational specificity, and critical nature of individuals' social judgments at all ages" (Neff & Helwig, 2002, p. 1431).

Another criticism of Kohlberg's view of the development of moral reasoning is that his view of morality was restricted. Walker, Pitts, Hennig, and Matsuba (1999) found that adolescents and adults focused more on relationships when recalling real-life moral dilemmas, rather than the issues of justice, rights, and duties emphasized by Kohlberg. Walker et al. emphasized that real-life concerns and religious beliefs also are important to consider when thinking about morality.

Problem-Based Scenario 6.8

Student: Lisa
Teacher: Dave

Dave Harris was really enjoying this Open House. It was a tradition at Lincoln Heights Elementary, always done just before the spring break. After weeks of preparation, he was proud of the way his classroom looked, and so were his students. They were doing such a good job of showing their parents around, describing the work contained in folders and exercise books, and answering questions. Dave also felt good about the conversations he was having with parents. They were supportive and positive about their children's education in his fifth-grade class.

Suddenly, the spell was broken. Mrs. Davis stormed up to him, holding her daughter Lisa by the hand. "Why is Lisa getting such poor marks in spelling?" she screamed. Waving Lisa's spelling book at him, she said, "Look at this—6, 7, 6 . . . . What kind of marks are those? I expect 10 out of 10 every time."

Dave explained that class time was devoted to a pretest every Wednesday and that his students were given the opportunity to practice spelling with a partner. He really tried to emphasize individual responsibility for learning, in addition to helping his students acquire strategies to monitor their own learning. He also encouraged studying the weekly word list at home before the final test on Friday. Mrs. Davis seemed unconvinced.

Dave thought about this incident often over the next couple of weeks, wondering if some changes in the way he approached spelling were necessary. At the same time, though, Lisa earned perfect marks on two spelling tests. Her mother arrived to pick her up for a dental appointment early one afternoon. Dave mentioned the improvement and congratulated Lisa. "Well, I hope so," said Mrs. Davis. "After the Open House, I gave Lisa the belt. Then we prayed together. I don't think we'll be seeing any more of those low marks in spelling."

Dave felt sick as he watched Mrs. Davis and Lisa leave the classroom. How on earth should he deal with this?

Figures 6.8 and 6.9 apear on pages 178–180.

Educational Implications of Theories of Moral Development

As future teachers you are probably wondering how this discussion applies to the classroom. Can morality be taught? What if you, as an adult, feel strongly about an issue that your community disagrees with? How are you going to handle that? Students often hold the opinion of a teacher in high esteem, so you have a tremendous influence on their thinking. What is *your* moral obligation toward the students and their families? What about students within one class who have different religions and different moral views on a situation? This is a very wide open debate, and the issue of moral education often leads communities to some heated arguments.

Consider Problem-Based Scenarios 6.7 and 6.8 in which religious beliefs have an impact on school activities. In the first, high school teachers must respond to parental feedback about their children's participation in school dances; in the second, an elementary teacher grapples with a point of view on discipline that is very different from his own.

Day-to-day moral dilemmas, such as cheating and lying, also confront teachers. Problem-Based Scenarios 6.9 and 6.10 concern students who were caught cheating by their teachers and peers. Teachers in both narratives are challenged by how to handle their situations in ways that are fair to all concerned.

Problem-Based Scenario 6.9

Student: Darren

Teachers: Beth and Tanis

Beth took the chance to do some marking while Tanis gave the weekly spelling test to the younger children. The older students were in the library, and there was just enough time to finish up some Math marking. "What a civilized way to start the day!" thought Beth.

Because the classroom was a large carpeted area, the children had the option of working on the carpet rather than at a table or group of desks if they wished. Darren often worked on the carpet, especially for spelling tests. It seemed to suit his energy level to be able to stretch out. Beth noticed a distinct pause in Tanis's delivery of the spelling test and looked up to see Tanis approaching Darren. Beth could see that Darren had a small piece of paper in his hand. As Tanis came closer, he slipped it under his stomach and lay down flat. Tanis asked to see the paper, but Darren refused to budge. In fact, he seemed to be glued to the floor, and his face showed that he had no intention of getting up.

Beth went over and together she and Tanis tried to reason with Darren. Finally, they convinced him that he would have to get up eventually, so it might as well be now. Sure enough, when he did the piece of paper revealed a scribbled list of the week's spelling list. They sent him to what had become known as "Darren's corner." They told him to read quietly and that they would talk to him later. His expression had changed from defiant to distinctly upset.

At recess, Beth and Tanis stayed in their empty classroom to talk. They so rarely had to deal with cheating that they had to discuss what to do. Obviously there had to be a consequence, but what was appropriate for a 7-year-old?

Approaches to Teaching Morality

Sometimes schools do take it upon themselves to actively teach morality. Curricula can address values education, character education, as well as various models of moral decision making.

Values Education   This may be done through values education or values clarification, where it is not so much the function to teach individual, specific values as it is to clarify the student's own value system. Values education includes foci on both moral and nonmoral values (Leming, 1997).

Values clarification programs provide opportunities for students to discuss and think through dilemmas to come to some understanding of their own set of values. Usually, these dilemmas are designed to demonstrate good behavior and citizenship. When carefully presented, they can provide the student with an opportunity to encounter new and challenging differences of opinion. However, teachers must take considerable care to respect differences of opinion, especially in our multicultural society.

One of the authors remembers a neighbor whose child brought home a notice from school. It notified the parents that the school was a Values School (meaning that the teachers were going to take an active role in values and moral education). This child's mother sent back a note saying that she "thought all schools were Values Schools, so what had they been doing up to now?" This is an interesting point: Can you have a school that doesn't teach values and morality? If you understand that the classroom is a reflection of the community and society then the answer is no. The values and moral understanding held by society allow us to work as a community.

Problem-Based Scenario 6.10

Student: Larry

Teacher: John

John thought that the day had gone really well. The weather was perfect for the cross-country race, partly cloudy and not too hot. The eighth-graders had been getting ready for this event in particular. It was usually the highlight of the June Sports Day, when everyone lined up along the soccer field and started together.

Parents lined up around the field as students started the paced run through the groomed wooded paths into the trees. John was standing beside Mrs. Nelson. They had been through a lot that year together so they knew each other pretty well. Larry was in John's homeroom and, because the school worked on a system by which each homeroom was considered a community, John had become very involved with his students.

Larry had gotten into trouble with everything from fighting in the lunchroom to destroying a girl's homework. The incident when Larry locked another boy in his locker had resulted in a 3-day suspension from school. But in the past 2 months, Larry had really turned things around. Everyone was pleased to see him running with the rest of the group, although pretty much at the end of the pack.

The cheering subsided when the students entered the wooded section of the race. It would take about 10 to 15 minutes before they reentered the soccer field area. As students began to appear from the trees, there was great excitement when Larry was in the top dozen students. He turned on extra speed, and with arms raised, came in third! Mrs. Nelson was jumping up and down screaming. John offered to take pictures of the award ceremony and even got a few shots of Mrs. Nelson and Larry with his hard fought prize. This year they gave out ornate ribbons for the top three runners. What a great ending to a very troubled year.

About an hour after the event, Janice, the principal, asked for a couple of minutes to discuss something. It seems that quite a few students were upset with Larry. Apparently, he had taken a shortcut and then reentered the race toward the front of the group. This only became evident when students started to compare notes about who saw him pass them during the race. The spotters along the track didn't really know all the students, so they couldn't verify the story.

This was an issue that had to be dealt with, but it had extra complications. It was the end of the year, so the ribbons and awards had already been given out, and most people (including Mrs. Nelson and Larry) had already left the school grounds. If something wasn't done—and done quickly—the students might escalate the situation.

FIGURE 6.10

INFO BYTE 6.5

CRITICISMS OF CHARACTER EDUCATION

- There is no theoretical base, common set of practices, agreement on what is meant by "character," or research on outcomes (Leming, 1997; Molnar, 1997).
- There is a strong political component in the objectives of character education that privileges the powerful and advantaged (Purpel, 1997).
- It is assumed that there are universally agreed upon values when conservative values often are emphasized (Kohn, 1997).
- Rather than focusing on individuals as part of communities and societies, it focuses on individuals alone. Much of human behavior is attributable to the social environment; therefore it is preferable to transform the classroom or school rather than "remake" the students (Kohn, 1997).

Character Education   Another approach to teaching moral development is character education. The focus of *character education* is the development of virtues (Noddings, 1997). As with values clarification, the approach is controversial, often focusing on "reinforcing 'good' behaviors and censoring 'bad' ones" (Molnar, 1997, p. ix), rather than on genuine understanding of what makes a good person and a civil society. (See Info Byte 6.5 for a summary of the criticisms of character education.)

Also, as with values clarification, one can raise the question of how to educate without addressing character. Can educational strategies and outcomes be completely rational and neutral (Noddings, 1997)? As Purpel (1997) emphasized, "To talk of education is inevitably to talk of personal character and a moral community . . ." (p. 151).

A follow-up question, then, is this: "How do we educate for character in an appropriate, well-informed way?" Noddings emphasized that for character education to be meaningful it must reflect the values of "well-ordered communities" that stand for something (p. 1).

Lickona's Model of Moral Education   Thomas Lickona (1991, 1997) detailed how teachers could promote the moral development of children within classrooms. His work is based on the concept of the classroom and school as a form of community life. He urged "the teacher to view the child as a moral thinker, to try to see things from the child's viewpoint, and to recruit the child as a partner in creating a just and caring community in the classroom" (p. 146).

Through the following interconnected set of four processes, Lickona developed a model of moral education:

1. Building moral community and self-esteem
2. Cooperative learning
3. Moral reflection
4. Participatory decision making

The model is a combination of understanding the rationale for moral behavior and the actual demonstration of moral actions within a caring, supportive classroom environment.

Once the appropriate environment is developed, teachers utilize incidents within their classrooms as opportunities to promote moral understanding and decision making. This may have more importance for students since personal issues and understandings are at stake. In Piagetian terms, these incidents put students into a state of disequilibrium that causes them to question the incident and the possible, or probable, outcomes. The personal quality of moral understanding and behavior makes this process an effective technique for promoting moral development (Leming, 1997).

Educating for Morality and Character: The Importance of the School Community

The previous discussion emphasized the importance of the school community in conveying moral messages. Beverly Cross (1997) conducted an interesting study in which she asked children and adolescents in inner-city schools about the characteristics of good and bad people and what they had learned about good character at home and at school. Although the children had no formal character education, they had learned a great deal about character just from being in school; their responses matched the sorts of things said by teachers and researchers interested in character education.

Cross (1997) raised the following questions central to informing thinking about character education:

- *"What opportunities are there for character education programs to move children beyond mere recitation to a genuine critique of social, political, and economic forces that shape how we live our lives?"* (pp. 124–125). This question was prompted by the finding that, "inner-city children say the 'right things' about character" (p. 123) and they do so "uncritically."
- *"What is the degree to which children are controlled versus engaged in learning?"* This question stems from the finding that the values cited by the children are largely designed to control their behaviors, to change those behaviors, and to create "miniature adults" (Cross, p. 125).
- *"Whose voices are represented in the children's understanding of character?"* This was prompted by the finding that "the students' perspectives on character were rooted in negative views of urban communities, of families, and of the experiences of children" (Cross, p. 125).

Problem-Based Scenario 6.11

Student: Darren

Teachers: Beth and Tanis

Beth and Tanis got to the classroom early to hide Easter eggs and then prepared a few last-minute things before the children arrived. The children knew that they would start the day in a special way today, and there was a high level of excitement as coats were hung up and homework handed in. After the children had assembled in the group meeting area, Beth and Tanis told them that there were two eggs for each of them hidden around the classroom. All were within their reach. As soon as Beth said to start, the hunt would begin.

This was a favorite activity of Beth's and Tanis's. The Easter egg hunt was one of their traditions. They enjoyed it as much as the children. They watched as, one by one, the children found their eggs, put them in the small paper bags they had decorated for the occasion, and returned to the meeting area. Josette and Lily were still searching and had begun to look frantic. Beth and Tanis assured them that there were enough eggs for all. Still, after they themselves joined in the hunt, they began to understand Josette's and Lily's frustration and disappointment. They checked all the hiding places, but nothing. Just as they were reassuring the now tearful Josette and Lily, one of the children called out, "Mrs. Littler! Darren has a whole bunch of eggs in his bag." Beth and Tanis looked at each other in despair. Would this never end?

Problem-Based Scenario 6.12

Students: *John's homeroom class*
Teacher: *John*

John had requested the sophomore homeroom this year. He had worked with so many of the eighth-graders last year that he felt many of them could benefit from the stability of having the same homeroom teacher again. This was a bit of an experiment for the school, since it was policy to change groups each year. The main goal of these homeroom classes was building self-esteem, and John felt that the more he knew about his students, the greater his chances of success.

John smiled as he looked down the list. He had seen Larry Nelson over the summer. Larry had a small scar on his right check where some of the boys from the cross-country race had taken things into their own hands. The entire episode had ended up involving the police and a total of 12 stitches among the "combatants." The class also listed Dominic Bartollo, a tall young man with the beginnings of a mustache. Dominic struggled with school and with reading in particular. There had been an unfortunate incident in elementary school where he had been called "stupid"

by an adult. No one could get him to tell who it was, but the hidden scar was still there. It was interesting to see such a large boy try to hide at a desk.

The list also had three girls who were known by some of his wife's friends as "Barbies"—very pretty, very made-up, and very boy-oriented. Then there was Fred. Fred had mild cerebral palsy and used a laptop computer to write. His problem lately was that he had finally noticed girls. John was guessing that the CP was a barrier to gaining the necessary social skills to talk to girls. The rest of the homeroom was made up of students from several ethnic backgrounds and represented a nice cross section of academic and sports abilities.

John had his work cut out for him. He wondered if there were any programs for bolstering self-esteem. What if he had to set up a program for himself? The school was using their Professional Development time for this project, but the first day wasn't until October. What could he do in the meantime?

The questions raised by Cross's research are similar to the points made by Kohn (1997), who advocates a constructivist approach to character education. Kohn states

> The process of learning . . . requires that meaning, ethical or otherwise, be actively invented and reinvented, from the inside out. It requires that children be given the opportunity to construct meaning around concepts such as fairness or courage, regardless of how long the concepts themselves have been around. Children must be invited to reflect on complex issues, to recast them in light of their own experiences and questions, to figure out for themselves—and with each other—what kind of person one ought to be, which traditions are worth keeping, and how to proceed when two basic values seem to conflict. (p. 160)

The chapter ends with two classroom narratives, one from elementary school and the other from middle school (see Problem-Based Scenarios 6.11 and 6.12). In both cases, the teachers are faced with issues pertaining to moral and social development and the development of self-esteem.

Summary

Social development is tied to the cognitive development of children and adolescents. Acquisition of social skills is critical for appropriate peer relationships and friendships, as well as for influencing academic achievement.

By understanding "who we are," individuals build self-concepts and self-esteem. Our understanding of our own strengths and weaknesses affects the way in which we approach challenges in life. A teacher who grasps the importance of this for a student's future can provide a variety of opportunities for students to develop positive self-concepts.

As with other forms of development, emotional development progresses in stages. Certain educational activities, such as art, music, drama, and literature, play a major role in the development of emotional intelligence.

Several theorists have outlined the growth of moral development in the individual. When deciding whether an action is moral or not, a person bases the final decision on the rationale, or the "why," behind an action. Through programs such as values clarification, attempts are made to provide opportunities for students to consider and clarify their methods for thinking through dilemmas.

A Metacognitive Challenge

You should now be able to reflect on the following questions:

- What are the main features of social development?

- How do these social aspects influence students in an educational setting?

- Could I discuss theories of social development around issues such as bullying?

- How are psychosocial development and self-concept related? What implications do these have for understanding students in a school setting?

- How are emotional intelligence and social development related?

- Can I discuss theories of moral development? What is the importance of understanding students' moral development to working in a school community?

Artifacts for Problem-Based Scenarios

FIGURE 6.1 ■ **E-Mail from a Teacher in Darren's School**

```
Date:    Monday, October 16, 2000
Subject: Hallway Incident
To:      Beth Littler blittler@sd83.clearlake.nd.us,
         Tanis Cevic tcevic@sd83.clearlake.nd.us
From:    rwong@sd83.clearlake.nd.us (Rosalind Wong)




Hi Beth & Tanis,

     Sorry to have to send this sort of message but
I thought you'd want to know.  Darren Upton was
pelting my window with gravel at about 4:30. Luckily
there's no damage.  I called him to come into my
classroom but he ran off.  I've seen him outside my
room after school several times now but this is the
first time he's done anything like this.
Ros



Rosalind Wong
5th grade teacher
Jefferson Elementary
```

FIGURE 6.2 ■ Letter from Darren's Mother

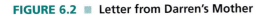

Oct. 15/00

Dear Beth & Janis,

I understand how challenging Darren can be at times, and I do want him to learn to be responsible for his actions. I wonder if there's some other way besides having him miss part of the Halloween party. He's so upset about it that he's not sleeping. Please let me know what you think.

Sincerely,

Linda Upton

FIGURE 6.3 ■ Note to Luis

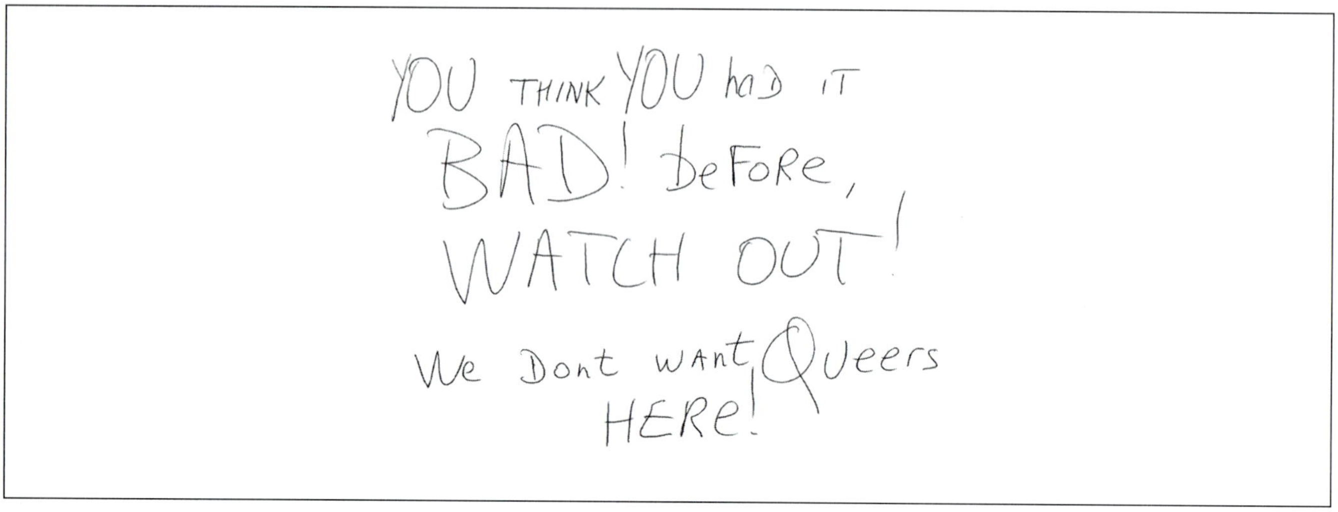

FIGURE 6.4 ■ Luis's In-Class Writing Assignment

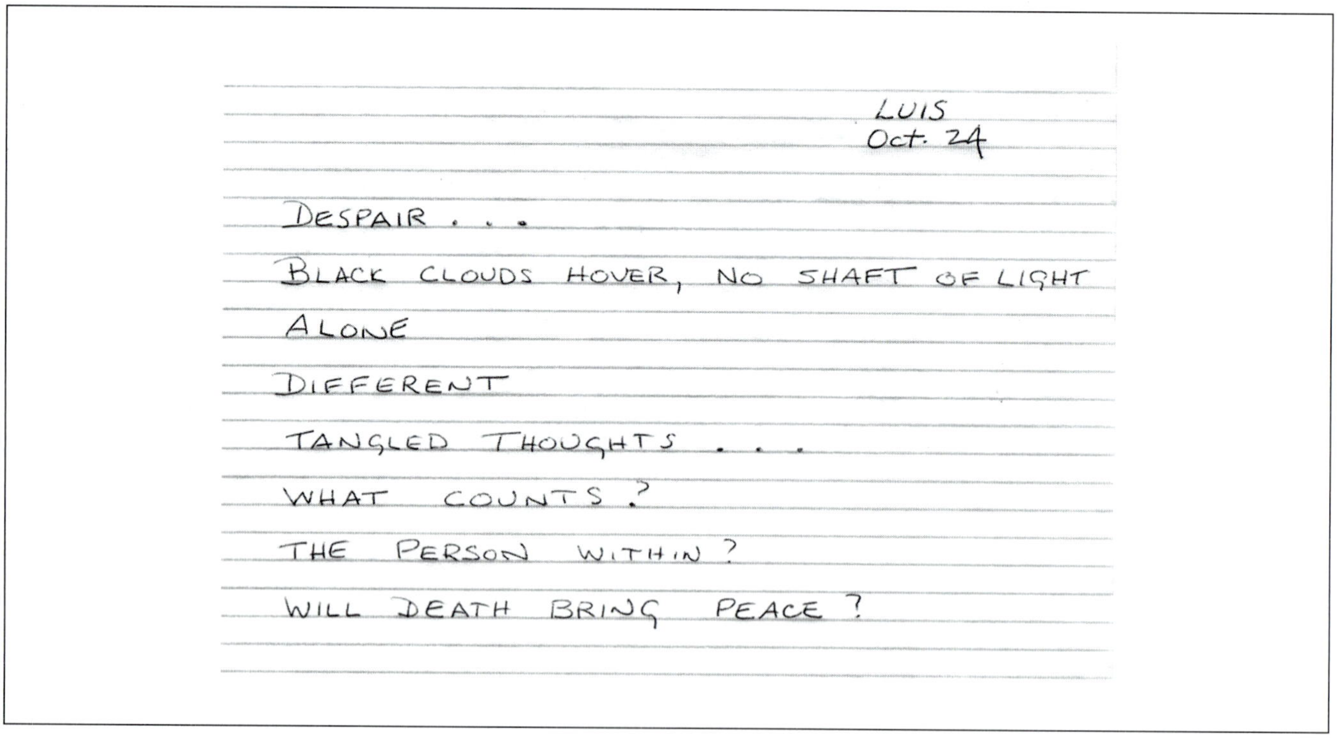

FIGURE 6.7 ▦ Dylan's Who Am I? Activity

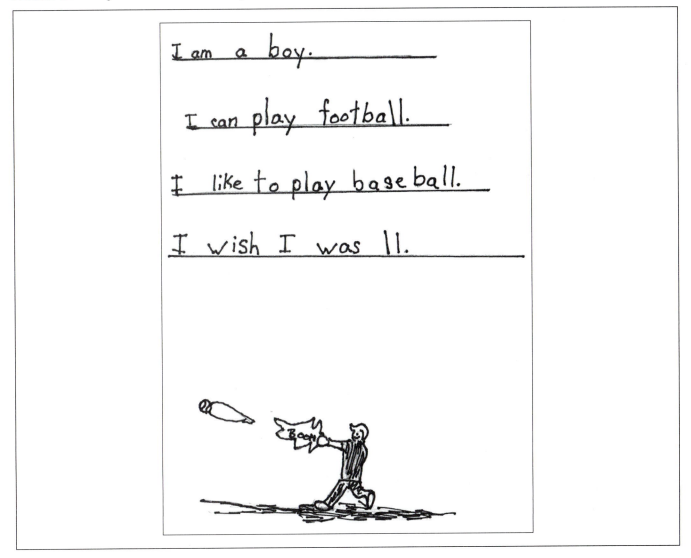

FIGURE 6.8 ■ Lisa's Report Card

REPORT CARD

LINCOLN HEIGHTS ELEMENTARY

NAME: Lisa Davis   **GRADE:** Five   **REPORTING PERIOD:** Fall 2001

ACADEMIC PROGRESS

Subject	Letter Grade	Effort and Work Habits*
Mathematics	B	S
Reading	B	S
Written Expression	C+	N
Spelling	C+	N
Social Studies	A	S
Science	B	S
Art	A	S
Physical Education	C+	I
Computer Skills	C+	I

*N = Needs improvement; I = Improving; S = Satisfactory

FIGURE 6.8 ■ Lisa's Report Card (continued)

COMMENTS:

It is a pleasure having Lisa in my class. Across the subjects we study in fifth grade, she is making average to above average progress. Her strengths are in Math, Reading, Social Studies, Science, and Art. In particular, she shows great interest and talent in art and her depth of knowledge in Social Studies is advanced for her age. Lisa demonstrates inconsistent effort in creative writing and spelling. She has the potential to do better in both areas but needs to apply herself more consistently. Her grade in Spelling reflects an average of marks ranging from average to perfect on our weekly spelling tests. We have an in-class study program for spelling. It may be helpful for Lisa to study at home as well.

Lisa's participation in P.E. and computer classes is improving steadily. Well done, Lisa!

SOCIAL DEVELOPMENT:

As we discussed, Lisa is experiencing some difficulties getting along with her classmates. She can be very helpful. She did a wonderful job of helping others remember the schedule of rehearsals for the class play. We are working on supporting her in using positive interpersonal skills more consistently.

Teacher: D. Harris   Date: November 27, 2001

FIGURE 6.9 ▪ Conference Notes–Lisa

Conference Notes — Lisa

<u>October 26, 2001</u> Mentioned Lisa's difficulty in working with others, unwill-ingness to consider others' opinions; some hurtful comments to other girls. Mrs. Davis promised to look into it.

<u>February 20, 2002</u> Discussed concerns about introversion. Lisa often appears withdrawn and hesitant to contribute to discussions in class. This seems to be getting worse. Mrs. Davis has noticed it as well. She put it down to puberty. I'll continue to observe when/where this happens so I can be more specific next time we talk.

Understanding Our Learners: Society and Culture

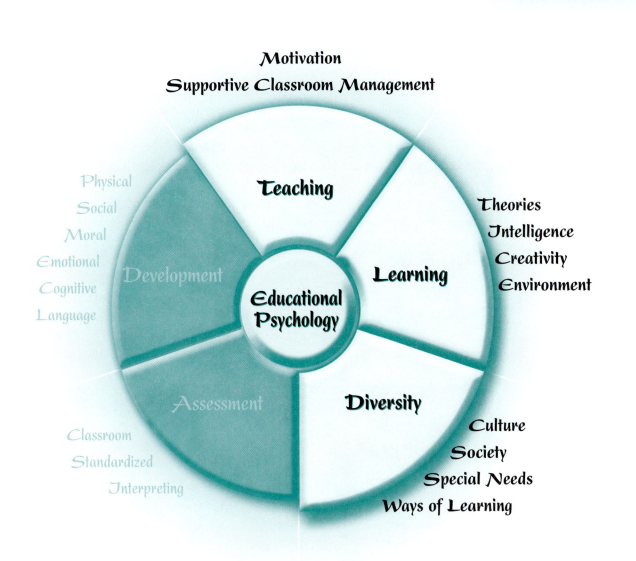

Motivation

Supportive Classroom Management

Teaching

Theories
Intelligence
Creativity
Environment

Physical
Social
Moral
Emotional
Cognitive
Language

Development

Learning

Educational
Psychology

Assessment

Diversity

Classroom
Standardized
Interpreting

Culture
Society
Special Needs
Ways of Learning

Humans are social beings, living and learning in communities. These communities, in turn, are defined by their *culture*—the accomplishments such as art, knowledge, beliefs, morals, laws, and customs that are inherited and practiced by members of a society (Cole, 1999). In this chapter, society and culture are discussed as media in which development takes place.

Earlier we emphasized that development results from the interaction between genetics and environment (or *nature* and *nurture*). Now you are introduced to culture, an influence that mediates the effects of genetics and environment on human development. In essence, our biology and environment act through the medium of culture, as practiced by the society in which we live, to influence our development (Cole, 1999). School forms a significant part of this mediating cultural influence. For example, in China, where there is a strong artistic tradition, children learn from a very early age the steps to drawing a variety of forms. These steps are modeled by teachers, resulting in childhood competence in drawing (Golomb, 2002). In contrast, North American early childhood educators, reflecting a cultural delight in spontaneous child art, tend to take a hands-off approach to early artistic education, thinking that instruction will stifle children's creativity (Golomb, 2002) (Photo 7.1).

In this chapter the social and cultural backgrounds learners bring to the classroom as well as how school itself serves as a social–cultural conduit and influence on development and education are discussed. Because society and culture are so closely related, they are often blended into one term, *sociocultural,* when both influences need to be considered.

In all discussions concerning education, there exists an underlying background of experiences that all people bring to a classroom. This background consists of the influences of family, culture, community, personal experiences, and general influences of the world around us. An example of this would be the changes to the world as the result of the events of September 11, 2001, when terrorists destroyed the World Trade Towers in New York City. The changes our society underwent as the result of this event range from overt, such as travel delays, to more subtle, such as a deepening sense of nationalism. These same events have changed students and education. For example, we are becoming more proactive

PHOTO 7.1

In North America, spontaneous child art is valued.

about the issues of violence and bullying in our schools (Olweus, 2003; Sullivan, 2000). The old rules were that these behaviors were not tolerated. But, in reality, unless the situation spilled over into the community or exceeded some undefined line of acceptability, most adults felt bullying was a normal part of growing up.

These examples highlight the changing world, national, community, school, and classroom situations that influence students and their learning. Bring in students' social, cultural, socioeconomic, religious, and ethnic backgrounds, and you can see why the classroom should be considered as a community of individuals or a *learning community* (Beins, 2002).

The number of factors affecting students is too varied for a comprehensive discussion here. Instead, several of the most evident factors are selected for discussion. It is hard to isolate any one aspect of a person's life due to the interconnectedness of various factors or influences. Therefore, we would like you to think of all the influences mentioned as squares put together to form a quilt. We can pull out one square, examine it, and then replace it to reconnect with all the others in the quilt. In this way we can examine one square, or influence, while still maintaining our knowledge of the interwoven nature of all influences that contribute to the unique quality of one particular quilt.

As a teacher, it is important for you to identify the aspects of students' lives that have the greatest influence over their learning and to gather some background information on these topics. This means you need to understand the community and the cultural influences students bring to school. This will provide you with an understanding of the perspective students are using to grasp the curricular materials you are presenting. No matter whether you are working in an inner-city school, private school, West Coast, East Coast, rural community, or suburb, your effectiveness as a teacher depends on your understanding of the students and the perspectives they bring to their learning.

> **Learning community:** A community that understands how people learn and provides the rich environments for learning to occur across the life-span.

Development in a Cultural Context

Two theories are introduced here to try to give you some sense of the complexity of the influences just mentioned. These theories are Bronfenbrenner's ecological theory and Erikson's life-span development. While not all-inclusive, they do provide a framework within which other interactions can readily be understood.

Bronfenbrenner's Ecological Theory

Urie Bronfenbrenner (1986) developed an ecological model of social influences. The model, which combines work done in both social and anthropological fields, places the development and growth of an individual within the constraints of the social environment. Bronfenbrenner proposed a series of "progressively more sophisticated scientific paradigms for investigating the impact of environment on development" (p. 723). Two dimensions are proposed in this series. These consist of "the external systems that affect the family and the manner in which they exert their influence . . . and the degree of explicitness and differentiation accorded to intrafamilial processes that are influenced

Surfing Terms 7.1

Culture and mind
Culture and cognition
Community of learners
Learning communities
Vygotsky
Luria
Michael Cole
Sylvia Scribner

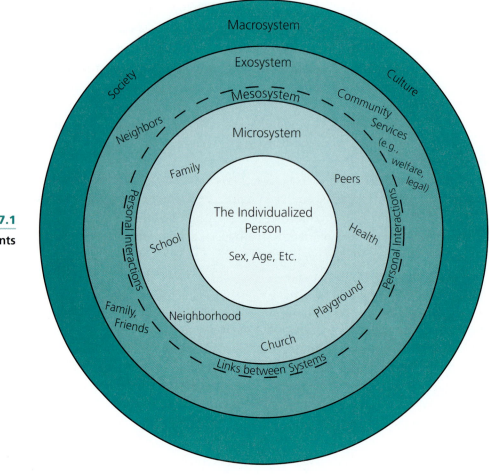

FIGURE 7.1

Bronfenbrenner's Environments

by the external environment" (p. 723). The model includes five environments that shift in influence as a child grows (Figure 7.1).

The Microsystem   This is the environment in which individuals deal directly with family, friends, and schools. It consists of the immediate neighborhood in a child's life. This should not be considered as a strict geographic area, but rather an environment where a child spends a considerable amount of time. For example, a grandparent may be a very active participant in the child's life and yet not live in the immediate area.

The Mesosystem   This system links the various microsystems. It provides the overlap that occurs in our lives when one area of our experience connects or intertwines with others. As an example, grandparents may tell a child a story that connects with what the child learned in school that week. This is an overlap of two different environments.

The Exosystem   This is the external environment that influences our lives. We usually have very little control over this environment. For children in particular, there is usually no control over any of these systems. For example, the Parks Department may close a school field to reseed turf and force a cancellation of a planned T-ball game.

The Macrosystem   This is the overarching culture in which the child lives. It consists of the social values, customs, and mores of the group of people who make up the child's world. With the broad ethnic diversity of our culture, it becomes apparent that any teacher must be aware of and sensitive to the effects of this environmental influence.

The Chronosystem   This system includes the sequence of sociohistorical developments that occur during a child's life. Going back to one of our first examples, the events of September 11, 2001 have far-reaching influences. There were numerous reports in our community about children who were afraid to go to sleep at night. While these children overcame this problem, the continued changes to our society have given this event a historic permanence in the child's life.

Erikson's Theory of Life-Span Development

Within the complex community described by Bronfenbrenner, we would like to embed the eight stages of human development proposed by Erik Erikson (1968) (see Chapter 6). In Erikson's model, an individual is confronted by a task during certain stages of development. How the person handles the task and decisions made as the result of the task influence the person and future tasks. While Erikson used the term *crisis* for these tasks, they are meant to be thought of as turning points in a person's life. For example, for an infant the first crisis or task is developing a level of trust versus mistrust (see Table 6.1). If a baby's experience is with a loving, nurturing environment, then the baby will learn to trust. If, on the other hand, a baby encounters an environment of neglect and inconsistency, then the child will learn to mistrust the environment. As a person grows, the turning points or decisions made about the environment influence who this person becomes.

> **Niche:** One's unique "place" in life; one's personal developmental space.

Integrating the Two Theories

By combining the work of Bronfenbrenner and Erikson, you can start to understand the huge number of influences that have made you who you are today. These influences form the *developmental niche* (Super & Harkness, 1986, 1997; cited in Cole, 1999) in which you grew up.

As you combine these two theories, you can start to see not only the numerous effects of various aspects of community life (Bronfenbrenner's theory), but the resulting effects on an individual over time, as a person grows (Erikson's theory). For both theories, the intent is to show a lively interaction between an individual and the sociocultural community. In the following sections, different aspects of developmental context are discussed in more detail.

> **Developmental niche:** The sociocultural context in which we develop—family, community, church, school, cultural traditions, national identity.

The Social Context of Development

In this section, we present influences on development that are social in nature. Our families, neighborhoods, cultural and ethnic backgrounds, and friends all represent powerful influences on our development. This is certainly not an all-inclusive list, but rather the primary contexts in which children grow, starting with the most basic social influence, the family.

The Influence of Family on Development

Today's children and adolescents come from families that are perhaps more diverse than at any other time in history. There is a range of characteristics from economic to marital status, nuclear or extended families, single-parent and same-sex parent families, all of which differ in economic, cultural, religious, and

PHOTO 7.2

Family structure and dynamics have become more diverse than ever before.

ethnic characteristics and in their commitment to education (Photo 7.2). These characteristics are important to understanding and supporting the overall development and achievement of the child or adolescent.

It is vital for you as a teacher to understand the influence families have on children's development. For example, one of the authors had a long talk with a secondary student who wanted to transfer out of an academic program that was designed for university entrance. It was hard for the student to think in terms of going to university in 2 years because her father had just been laid off from his job and the family was in a financial crisis. The student had trouble seeing that, in 2 years, the family's financial circumstances would probably be different. Changing her program of studies due to a current family situation would have major repercussions for this student's future. By being sensitive to family situations, teachers can often be a stabilizing influence for students.

Parenting Styles

One aspect of family influence is parenting style. Baumrind (1971, 1991) identified the following four main parenting styles.

Authoritarian   The parenting includes very firm rules for the children. Children are expected to be "seen but not heard." Children whose parents are authoritarian often have poor communication skills and tend to lack initiative. They often lack essential social skills.

Authoritative   The parents expect children to behave by the rules, but also allow children an opportunity to discuss controls or actions. This tends to be supportive in nature. Children whose parents are authoritative tend to have good social skills and get along well with peers. They also tend toward self-reliance and show good self-esteem.

Neglectful   The parents are not involved in the child's life. Often these parents have no idea what the child or adolescent is doing in school or in the community. Children whose parents are neglectful tend to lack motivation to achieve. They are not independent and often lack social skills.

Indulgent   There are very few limits put on the child or adolescent. It does not necessarily mean that the parents aren't caring, but rather that they give the child or adolescent too much control. Children whose parents are indulgent tend to lack self-restraint. They are used to having the world bend to their wants and needs. They lack the behaviors necessary for personal achievement.

Cultural Differences in Parenting Styles

Miller (2004) pointed out that Baumrind's categories of parenting style do not fully take cultural variations into account. While all cultures distinguish between good and poor parenting, there are differences in perceptions of what constitutes good parenting relative to cultural values. For example, in poor and/or dangerous neighborhoods, restrictive (or authoritarian) parenting may be important to healthy, positive development. Korean adolescents equate parental control with warmth, and Chinese families hold a similar view. Control on the part of Chinese parents is seen as preserving family integrity and results in high academic achievement (Miller).

As a teacher, it is important to be in contact with parents. In general, the parents and/or guardians of elementary children are more known to teachers than they are at the high school level. This may be due to parents often being available when they pick up children from school. As a high school teacher, it was a common saying that "You really only see the parents you don't need to see. The parents you really want to talk to are never available." While this statement isn't always accurate, it does exemplify some of the frustrations teachers often feel when they can't talk to a parent or only see them at a Parent Night at school.

However, as you can see from Problem-Based Scenarios 7.1 and 7.2 that follow, the influence of parenting styles is complex. As mentioned before, when we take a square out of a quilt and focus on just this square, it can appear fairly straightforward, such as Baumrind's (1971, 1991) parenting theory. But complexity becomes apparent when a real situation is viewed within an overall sociocultural context.

Socioeconomic Status

Socioeconomic status (SES) is complex. It refers to the social class or categorization of an individual according to several factors. Many governments use indicators such as annual income, education, and occupation to place people into categories (i.e., low, middle, or high SES). In addition, society adds other more personal factors onto this categorization, such as the neighborhood in which one lives and one's ethnic background, and cultural heritage. This provides a category or group with which a person is thereafter associated, whether the person resembles any of the generic characteristics of the group or not. For example,

Problem-Based Scenario 7.1

Student: Trevor
Teacher: Katy

It was Katy's first day as a junior high school teacher. She was nervous but excited. She really enjoyed working with young adolescents and she thought she was pretty good at it. She was teaching grade 8 and 9 English and Drama and had a grade 9 homeroom class. Katy spent a lot of time organizing the physical environment of the classroom at the end of August, trying to make it feel comfortable and welcoming. She was on her way to the library to get a few last-minute additions for her bookshelf when she met her vice-principal. Larry welcomed her and then told her he had some bad news.

"Trevor's back," said Larry. "I'm sorry, but I have to place him in your homeroom and English 9 class. There's no room anywhere else. He really should be in a treatment facility, in my opinion, but his grandmother won't hear of anything other than a regular class placement."

Katy's heart sank. "What do you mean?"

"Well, Trevor's been in and out of schools in the community since kindergarten. Poor kid. His family's a mess. There's been some long and drawn out custody

battle started by his grandmother. I think she's fighting his dad for custody. His dad's her son, would you believe. Anyhow, Trevor can be violent. He threatened his grade 2 teacher with a knife and it's gone downhill since then. Be careful."

Half an hour later Katy called the roll in her own classroom for the first time. Trevor responded pleasantly. She looked up to see a nicely groomed, well dressed adolescent. "What did I expect?" she chided herself. Later that day, in English 9, she was shocked to see how much difficulty he had with an introductory writing assignment. He could barely spell and his handwriting was very immature. It was the drawings around the edges of the page that really upset her, though (see Figures 7.2 through 7.4 on pages 209–211).

Apply

- Does parenting theory help you in planning support for Trevor?
- How might Katy proceed with academic planning for Trevor?

there is a historical pattern in which minorities tend to leave school earlier than the general population and therefore secure lower-paying jobs conferring a lower social status. This certainly doesn't mean all people in a minority follow this pattern. But, in general, this is considered to be the case for governmental intervention and the funding of programs. SES aids governmental agencies in understanding problems and issues when dealing with large groups of people.

The demographics of an area often provide insights into the specific needs of a population. One of the authors describes an elementary school in which she supervised student teachers.

"I was told that most of the children in this school came from low-income, single-parent families. The school was beside a large government-subsidized apartment complex with a large number of single mothers and children. One student teacher, a young man in his mid-twenties, was the center of most of the attention for this whole school. All of the teachers and the principal were female.

This young man became a role model for many of the boys very quickly. He set up soccer games at lunch, baseball games after school, and before-school help sessions. The teachers were thrilled, since he was involving many of the children who were having trouble academically.

Within a short period of time it became apparent to the principal that this particular elementary school was in need of more male teachers. While the demographics of the

Problem-Based Scenario 7.2

Student: Franco
Teacher: Della

Della had only been teaching for 2 years. So when she got the note from the principal about the meeting with Franco's father she felt apprehensive.

Della taught an eleventh-grade home economics course that was very popular with a number of the boys. While it was a general cooking class, she had tailored it to the tastes of the largely Italian neighborhood of the school. One of her rules for working in the kitchen was there was to be no trash left in the sinks; everything must be kept clean. During a lecture period last week, Franco had thrown a wad of paper in the sink near his desk. Della saw this, stopped what she was doing, and asked Franco to remove it. She started to remind everyone of the kitchen rules when Franco told her "No." Della paused, and then repeated the request. Again, Franco told her, "No. Do it yourself if you want it taken out." Della told Franco to remove himself from the class and go to the office. This was when Franco told her to "Fuck off." Della had never expected to be spoken to this way, and there was a huge pause in the room while the rest of the class looked at her to see what she was going to say. It was then that Don stood up and told Franco that they should go down to the office now before it got any worse. After they left, Della somehow gave some directions to the class, asked Nathan across the hall to watch her class, and followed the two boys to the office.

Mr. Sarni, the principal, called and set up a meeting with Franco's parents to discuss the attitude and the language problem. Della thought that things would be fine and that the parents would back her up—until she got Mr. Sarni's note (see Figure 7.5 on page 212). Now what could she say at the meeting?

Apply

- How might Della prepare for the meeting with Franco's father?
- Is there a strategy she could use to establish guidelines for appropriate behavior with Franco?

neighborhood were well known to the principal, it didn't become apparent how influential a male role model could be to the academic achievement of her students until that young student teacher was assigned to her school. I think this was a case of not wanting to stereotype a group based on SES. I can understand that, but at the same time, we should be more sensitive to the characteristics based on SES to provide support if necessary."

Poverty

Poverty is one of the primary issues concerning socioeconomic status. In general, there is a connection between a low income, or poverty, and education. The ramifications of poverty on a child are so great that it is considered a risk factor for social, behavioral, and academic outcomes. Students who are at risk have the potential for failing academically, dropping out of school, getting into trouble with the law, and having drug problems (Photo 7.3).

While poverty actually includes a number of issues, the most obvious one is financial stress for the family. Mistry, Vanderwater, Huston, and McLoyd (2002) found that economic stress produced parental psychological stressors that "take their toll on their mental health, in turn, diminishing their capacity to be sensitive and supportive parents" (p. 935). Poverty contributed to parents' lowered feelings of efficacy and increased feelings of depression. Teachers judged the children from economically stressed families to be less socially competent and to display more problem behaviors (p. 947).

These results held for both boys and girls and different ethnic groups. While researchers had for a long time used intelligence as a key predictor of success in

PHOTO 7.3

Poverty is a major predictor of academic difficulties for children of all ages.

school, Blair (2002) found that "Whether defined as the regulation of emotion in appropriate social responding or the regulation of attention and selective strategy use in the execution of cognitive tasks, self-regulatory skills underlie many of the behaviors and attributes that are associated with successful school adjustment" (p. 112). He went on to point out that these abilities for self-regulation may be "equally powerful predictors of school adjustment" (Blair, p. 112).

The Link between Family Income and Vulnerability

Children from financially stressed families tend not only to start school with behaviors that put them at risk, but often are also the targets of negative responses from those who are not poor.

Distancing   Lott (2002) found that the dominant response to poor people and poverty was that of *distancing*. This is seen in activities such as "separation, exclusion, devaluation, discounting and designation as 'other' . . . in both institutional and interpersonal contexts" (p. 100). Cognitive distancing (interpersonal contexts) occurs when poor people are seen in a negative stereotype, such as lazy, unpleasant, uneducated, unmotivated, stupid, criminal, and so on. This is carried into institutional distancing, which consists of public education, housing, health care and legal assistance, and politics and public policy. For example, schools receiving federal funding were viewed as academically inferior to those of middle-class schools. It was not of concern that dropout rates were high in poorer communities since it tended to reinforce the negative academic stereotype.

As a teacher, it is imperative that you are aware of this natural tendency to stereotype and distance ourselves from poor people and poverty. Teachers can only make a difference if they truly believe that the student is a worthwhile, talented individual with future potential.

The Environment of Poverty   So far, we have only touched on one aspect of poverty—a lack of money. As Evans (2004) notes, there is an entire physical and social aspect to poverty that he calls the "environment of poverty." In an article summarizing numerous studies on poverty, Evans points out that, as the result of finances, poor families often live in situations that add to the individual risk factor of lack of money. For example, a single mother may have such a limited income that she lives in an apartment in a neighborhood known for high crime, drugs, fewer municipal services, and so on. This accumulation of multiple risks adversely affects the healthy development of children. "Adverse socioemotional and cognitive developmental outcomes are accelerated by exposure to multiple risks relative to singular risk exposure" (p. 86). Evans makes several points about poor children in comparison to their economically advantaged counterparts.

Poor children:

- are "exposed to more family turmoil, violence, separation from their families, instability, and chaotic households"
- "experience less social support"
- have parents who "are less responsive and more authoritarian"
- are "read to relatively infrequently, watch more TV, and have less access to books and computers"
- have parents who "are less involved in their children's school activities"
- live in environments where "the air and water . . . consume[d] are more polluted"
- live in homes that "are more crowded, noisier, and of lower quality"
- live in neighborhoods that "are more dangerous, offer poorer municipal services, and suffer greater physical deterioration"
- attend "predominantly low-income schools and day care that are inferior" (p. 77)

All this points out how important it is to understand not only the SES of your community, but also the other potential risk factors. It is also possible that even with poverty students attain a high level of school involvement and achievement. Unfortunately, for many students, the statistics do not support positive outcomes, instead identifying children of poverty for potential academic problems. Vulnerability, or risk, is not limited to students growing up in poverty, though (see Info Byte 7.1).

Culture and Ethnicity

Culture is the sum of the beliefs, customs, achievements, history, and literature of a group of people, while *ethnicity* refers to a membership in a group based on race, culture, or language. Both of these terms have shared meanings and often people use these two words interchangeably. Most people don't think much about culture or ethnicity since it generally consists of the social organization of how we live our daily lives. The time it becomes important is when we encounter another cultural or ethnic group. It often forces us to think about who we are and why we do things the way we have in the past.

Presently, in North America we have come to accept that our society is not really one culture, but rather is made up of many cultures, forming a pluralistic society. In the United States it is referred to as a melting pot society in which many people from different nationalities bring the best of their cultures to form America. In Canada it is referred to as multiculturalism or, as some people note, it is like a giant stir-fry where everyone retains his or her own uniqueness but blend together to form Canada. In other terms, the macrocultures of Americans

Surfing Terms 7.2

Homework
Safe schools
Family involvement
Latchkey children
School breakfast programs
Children at risk
Vulnerable children

> **INFO BYTE 7.1**
>
> ### POVERTY AND CHILDHOOD VULNERABILITY
>
> The relationship between family income and childhood vulnerability (children who are vulnerable to poor cognitive, social, behavioral, and motor development) is relatively weak. Willms (1999) found that 37% of Canadian children whose family income was in the lowest quartile (lowest 25%) were considered vulnerable. Of those from families with income in the lower-middle and upper-middle quartiles, 28.6% and 25.4%, respectively, were considered vulnerable. Twenty-four percent of children from high-income families were vulnerable to poor developmental outcomes. These findings indicate that the stereotype that children who have problems at school are from poor families needs to be reexamined (Willms). It also is important to note that these statistics do not mean that poverty does not matter (Willms). Clearly, it matters a great deal.
>
> Another important finding regarding children growing up in poverty is that schools make a difference. Hertzman (2004) has mapped the developmental outcomes of kindergarten children in British Columbia, Canada, by neighborhood. His findings regarding family income and vulnerabilities were similar to Willms's. He also found that in all neighborhoods there are schools where children's academic and social development meets or exceeds expectations for their age and that the numbers of these schools in poor neighborhoods is greater than might be expected. Hertzman concluded that schools need to think of themselves as developmental agents—they can and do make a difference in children's lives.

and Canadians are made up of distinct microcultures, that is, identifiable groups with backgrounds unique to each group.

Culturally Relevant Teaching

It is important for you as a teacher to understand the cultural and ethnic backgrounds of the students in your school and community. Failure to recognize the importance of culture and ethnicity can result in a great deal of frustration for you as a teacher, but especially for your students. It also means that your understanding must go beyond just collecting the demographics, or basic descriptive statistics, of a community. It is important to walk through the community, meet people, talk to them, and get to know what is important in their lives and what they expect of you as a teacher.

Immigration   New immigrants to North America bring their culture and values with them. Sometimes there is a clash between value systems. For example, some cultures place a higher value on male education, while girls are relegated to more subservient roles. One author relates a conversation she had with a teacher who taught in a school where many of the students were from another country and just learning English. She described how hard it was to have the boys clean up after an activity. The boys sat back and waited while the girls frantically cleaned up around the boys' desks before cleaning their own. This teacher worked an entire school term on personal responsibility and the introduction of a new and different set of expectations. However, she was realistic enough to know these activities were strictly school related.

An Example of a Culturally Relevant Approach   Tatum (2000) described a successful culturally relevant approach to teaching reading to African American youth in a poor, ghettoized neighborhood in Chicago.

> A culturally relevant approach involves talking to black students about the personal value, the collective power, and the political consequences of choosing academic achievement. In such an approach, activities

based on African American norms are incorporated into the classroom, cooperation is emphasized over competition, and learning is structured as a social activity. (p. 53)

Guidelines   Ladson-Billings (1995; cited in Tatum, 2000) offered additional guidelines for culturally relevant teaching that are consistent with the constructivist approach advocated by Tatum and emphasized in this book. The following guidelines also are consistent with the characteristics of positive school and classroom climate discussed later in the chapter:

- Students must experience academic success, develop and maintain cultural competence, and develop a critical consciousness to challenge the status quo.
- Teachers should attend to students' academic needs, not merely make them feel good.
- Students' culture should be made a vehicle for learning.
- Students need help to develop a broader sociopolitical consciousness that allows them to critique the cultural norms, values, mores, and institutions that produce and maintain social inequities. (p. 53)

Problem-Based Scenarios 7.3 through 7.6 highlight the complexity of sociocultural influences on students' development and teachers' decision making.

Problem-Based Scenario 7.3

K-5   6-8   9-12   SpEd

Student: *Malcolm*
Teacher: *Greg*

Greg Norris felt pretty proud of himself. This year he had decided to *do* something about Halloween. While he knew that fourth-graders wouldn't really understand the origins of the event or the symbolism associated with it, he thought he could at least use some good literature as a way of getting the kids to think beyond candy and fireworks. He did a dramatic reading of the witches' scene in Macbeth as a stimulus for the writing and illustration of poems that captured some of the Halloween drama. The class really enjoyed the activity and produced some very good work. However, Greg's positive feelings were short-lived. He returned to his classroom after school shaken by the telephone conversation he just had.

Mrs. Fredericks talked to Greg calmly but, to him, her voice seemed to drip with threats. Her son, Malcolm, was in Greg's class. He hadn't done a very good job of poetry writing that day, but Greg had put it down to his difficulties with written language. Mrs. Fredericks started by telling Greg how upset Malcolm was to hear reference to witches in the classroom. She pointed out how evil the whole idea was and that no child should be subjected to such material.

Greg tried to explain that he had wanted to expose the children to good literature and that Shakespeare certainly met the criterion. Mrs. Fredericks wasn't convinced. In fact, it was at that point that she questioned his integrity and values, noting that no honest Christian would think of doing this with children.

Greg was floored; he hadn't even thought of a religious argument against this portion of a classic drama. He apologized to Mrs. Fredericks. She thanked him and ended by saying that she was confident there would be no more references to devil worship in her son's classroom. Otherwise, she said, she was sure he understood that she would have to file a formal complaint with the superintendent.

Now Greg wondered how he could get past his feelings to finish his planning for the following day. But he also questioned what else he might do inadvertently that would offend the Fredericks. He really needed to think about this.

Apply

- How could Greg account for different religious beliefs in his class? Should he?

Problem-Based Scenario 7.4

Student: *Jon*

Teacher: *Marilyn*

Marilyn had always given Jon a bit more leeway than she had some of the other ninth-graders in the science class. Even though he wasn't a student with any identified special needs, Marilyn had mentally grouped him in with other students who had various learning difficulties. She knew the family had significant money problems, and that academics were often of secondary importance when families struggled to put food on the table. Marilyn realized all of this when she got the letter this morning from Jon's mother. The topic they were covering in class was some introductory, basic genetics. Jon told the class the story of his mother's cousin who had been scared by a bear when she was pregnant, and the baby was born with a bear paw instead of a hand. The class thought this was a great story, especially when Jon verified the hand looked exactly like the claw of a bear. Marilyn had worked hard to explain in as nice a way as possible why this couldn't possibly happen, referring back to the basic genetics they had just learned. She thought it was clarified, until the letter came.

Now, looking back, Marilyn found that there was very little she knew about Jon's home life. The principal, Ted, had commented that since the family lived on the outskirts of this rural community near the landfill, the mother made her living by picking through the dump and selling salvage to recyclers.

There was only Jon and his mother, Mrs. Webb. Marilyn had met Mrs. Webb on a parent night once. The only thing Marilyn remembered was that Mrs. Webb was extremely quiet and said very little during the meeting and that her glasses were held together in the center with white bandage tape. On the first Wednesday of the month, Jon would miss school to help his mother bring home their monthly allotment of food from the state food program. Jon was always well groomed and an exceptionally polite young man. He had a couple of friends at school, but basically was a loner in classes. Beyond that, Marilyn felt she knew nothing about him.

Marilyn started to have doubts about whether she had lowered her expectations of Jon based on the small amount she knew about him and the at-risk nature of children raised in poverty. The extremely well written letter (Figure 7.6 on page 213) in her hands made her think about reassessing Jon. And now, what was she going to say to Jon and the class since they all seemed to know about the letter?

Apply

- How might Marilyn discuss the letter from Jon's mother with her class?
- What might Marilyn consider in rethinking her expectations for Jon?

Each teacher struggles with building positive home–school connections and with understanding their own and their students' perspectives on learning and the curriculum. It is valuable to read through these scenarios even if they refer to a different age group than your studies focus on. They show not only where students "come from" developmentally, but the challenges they may meet in the future. Culture can cross ethnicities. In Info Byte 7.2, we present culture as viewed by individuals who are deaf.

Peers

Think back to Chapter 6 where we discussed the importance of healthy peer relationships and the negative outcomes of poor peer relationships. Good peer relations are important for normal development in both childhood and adolescence (Hightower, 1990; Howes & Tonyan, 2000). In any person's life, peers are one of the most important and powerful influences (Photo 7.4). Peers are people of about the same age and maturity who work, study, and play together.

Problem-Based Scenario 7.5

Student: *Kamaljit*

Teacher: *Greg*

Greg Norris came to the last report card template on his computer. He had deliberately left this one to the end, mainly because he had turned over and over in his mind how to communicate his concerns about Kamaljit's development. She had joined his fourth-grade class at the beginning of January. Her family had recently immigrated from India. She spoke very little English, and the school's ESL teacher became involved immediately. Kamaljit was getting intensive help, but her progress was very slow. Now, at the spring reporting period, Greg wrestled with a number of issues.

Kamaljit was hemiplegic. She had suffered some brain damage at birth. She was often sick with colds and looked very tired. Greg had met with her parents, and they passed on medical information to him. They brought an interpreter with them who was adamant that it was the school's responsibility to foster Kamaljit's development. He said that her parents were much too busy with getting settled and caring for a large family. Greg was proud of the supportive parent network he had established, and he really believed in close communication with families, so this was a shock to him.

Kamaljit was well supported socially, despite her extreme passivity. The kids in Greg's class loved her and did a lot to help her with her work and school routines. Greg was worried that they did too much and that Kamaljit wasn't learning to be independent. She was significantly below grade level in academic skills, more like a grade 1 student in her mastery of basic math skills. It was hard to determine her language level. Even Sara, the school's ESL teacher, was having trouble disentangling if it was primarily Kamaljit's lack of English or her developmental delay that accounted for her very slow progress.

Kamaljit's parents hadn't responded to the notices about conferences that were sent home. The school had a large immigrant population, and notices were translated into several languages. Greg really wanted to talk to them further. He was worried that a written report card wouldn't be well understood, even if it were translated. He called a colleague and shared his worries before continuing with his efforts to write comments on Kamaljit's development.

Now he felt even worse. Joan had said, "Well, of course her parents aren't involved. They probably don't think education is important for her. It's a cultural thing. Why do you think she's home so often? She has younger brothers and she baby sits them."

How much truth was there in what Joan said? Greg now felt concerned on more than one level.

Apply

- Greg has a number of concerns about Kamaljit's development. What would be a reasonable first step in addressing these concerns?

They provide information beyond that given within a family unit. It is very often our peers who clue us in on the workings of the world beyond our home. This is one reason why a multicultural grouping provides such a rich knowledge base for a child or adolescent. Multicultural schools and classrooms have the potential to support *cultural competence* (Lonner & Hayes, 2004).

Students' competence in self-control, cooperation, and understanding and responding to others is related to cultural competence (Lonner & Hayes, 2004). When respectful interactions with others are modeled at school and students are given supportive opportunities to discuss cultural perspectives with their peers, the school climate is positive. This in turn leads to increased cultural competence. It is important to recognize that respectful interactions and opportunities for discussion must take account of cultural variation in perspective. In Chapter 6, Gilligan's theory of moral development was discussed. It reflects a Western view

Cultural competence: The ability to function competently in another culture and/or with people from other cultures; respect for and the ability and desire to learn about other cultures (Lonner & Hayes, 2004).

Problem-Based Scenario 7.6

Students: David and Sung-So
Teacher: John

As the grade 9's left the lab, John thought it was ironic that the district had been spending so much time and money working on awareness of multicultural issues for teachers. Here was a perfect example of the problems students brought with them from their original countries.

After giving directions for the short lab he had planned, John assigned students into pairs. He had changed some of the students around for this lab because the nonworking students had somehow chosen each other to work with last time. Everyone started right away except for David and Sung-So, both excellent students. John had approached them to ask why they weren't working. It took a bit to get either one to explain why they were just sitting there with their arms folded. David announced that he wouldn't work with a Korean, and Sung-So responded that his parents would be furious if they thought he had worked with someone from Japan. John didn't know what to say about this situation, so he told them they had to work as a pair because everyone else was well into the lab already. When neither boy responded, John explained that if they didn't get to work they would end up with an F on this lab. Both boys agreed to the F rather than work with each other and noted that their parents would back them up on the decision. John saw that everyone in the class was watching this exchange. He told them they were old enough to make that decision and left them sitting at the lab bench. Neither one did anything or spoke to anyone for the rest of the period. Since nothing was handed in, both boys got an F on that lab.

John wasn't sure what he could or should do about this situation.

Apply

- Would you have handled this situation in the same way John did? Why or why not? Think about having a strong rationale for justifying your approach to your principal.

FIGURE 7.7

INFO BYTE 7.2

One of the strongest links among any cultural group is shared language and experience. For people who are deaf, this linkage is through American Sign Language (ASL) and the experiences shared in successfully adapting to living in a hearing world. Known as Deaf (with a capital D) Culture, this community has developed a tremendous sense of pride and accomplishment, with a fierce group loyalty and mastery in areas such as skillful storytelling. It is felt that hearing individuals, even if fluent in ASL, could never truly become members of this group since a person needs to be deaf to experience a true Deaf identity. This sense of a Deaf identity is so highly valued that many people within the Deaf community react negatively to the speech and thinking of the hearing community. As with many other cultural communities, parents who want their child to develop the same values, experiences, and language select schools that emphasize these characteristics. For this reason, there are numerous schools specifically for children and adults who are deaf or hard of hearing. One of the most famous and influential is Gallaudet University in Washington, D.C. Founded in 1864, it provides undergraduate and graduate programs for students who are deaf, hard of hearing, or hearing imparied.

that combines emphases on individual development and care for others (Miller, 2004). Japanese communities view care as a communal responsibility, and Hindu Indians view it as part of their role and a moral requirement to meet the needs of friends and family. In North America, we tend to take into account the degree of closeness to others and our own financial and time-related commitments when considering how, or even if, we will help (Miller).

Multicultural Classrooms and Cultural Competence

All the influences on children's and adolescents' development that vary in societies and cultures are reflected in the social–cultural contexts of schools and classrooms. As previously discussed, there are many ways in which students can differ. They may also share many characteristics, such as their cognitive developmental level (as discussed in Chapter 2), their social developmental level (as discussed in Chapter 6), and gaining mastery of an identity (as discussed in this

PHOTO 7.4

The importance of peers in adolescents' growth and development is hard to overestimate.

chapter and Chapter 6). These shared characteristics are what lead people to say things like "That's typical of a preschooler" or "Just like an adolescent!" Like the students who attend them, schools are similar to each other in some ways and distinct in others. And, within each school, individual classrooms are both similar and different. They may look alike, but they are inhabited by groups whose social dynamics may differ significantly. Like parents, teachers can be authoritarian or authoritative; in some cases, they may be neglectful or indulgent. Their personal style, combined with their instructional strategies, interacts with the diverse characteristics of the students in their classrooms.

Schools and Classrooms

School Culture

Schools are *minicultures*. Like cultures more broadly defined, they share certain beliefs, have histories and achievements, and practice certain customs. Think, for example, of graduation photos that line school hallways, the cups and plaques on display in glass-fronted cases, the senior prom, and the dedication to the school's founder that appears at the school entrance. Much of what defines school culture reflects the culture in which the school is situated but, in addition, some aspects of school culture are uniquely schoollike. Consider the administrative system, the physical layout of school buildings and surrounding play areas, displays of student work, and school routines and events like recess, school photos, bells, and cheerleading practice that define North American schools. If you grew up in Canada or the United States, you have particular memories of the time you spent in your school culture. If you grew up in a different culture, your memories may be different.

Schools also are *minisocieties* in which adults with different roles and responsibilities function more or less successfully and students with different backgrounds learn and get along more or less successfully. The degree of success is influenced by many factors. Again, not all possible factors are discussed in this chapter, but directions that will allow you to consider the complexity of the sociocultural world of schools are pointed out.

Drawing on Past School Experience   As you begin a career in teaching, you may draw on the memories of your own schooling to a significant degree. Because schools are so central to our lives, the experiences we had in school shape our understanding of education. Now is the time to reflect on what worked for you, the teachers that stood out and the reasons they did, and the positive and negative aspects of your education. As you learn more about the theories underpinning education and educational research, some of the following questions may help you to reflect on your experiences:

- Were the school cultures that I experienced nurturing, supportive places? Did I feel like I was part of a community? What made them that way (or what didn't)?
- Were there times when I truly felt excited by learning? When did this happen?
- What is my image of an excellent teacher?
- Is there a part of my education that stands out for its excellence? Think about what contributed to this excellence.
- What contribution do I wish to make to promoting a healthy school culture?

Assessing School Culture   As you start to visit various schools as a beginning teacher, have a careful look around before you enter the building. Note what is happening on the playground or athletic field. Look for where students congregate before school and at lunch. See how students arrive at school and how they're expected to enter the building. When you go inside, see if you can pick up the *tone* of the school. Is it welcoming? Are children and adults respectful of each other? These observations can serve as hypotheses about the social–cultural milieu of the school.

Schools That Make a Difference

Douglas Willms's (1999) research shows that schools do make a significant difference in children's lives. When the effects of family background and ability are accounted for, schools differ in the "added value" (Willms, p. 83) they contribute to children's development. Schools that encourage parental involvement, expect that all students are capable of mastering the curriculum (i.e., schools with high *academic press* or high expectations for all students), and foster positive interactions between and among school personnel and students have a positive influence on student achievement. Schools that add value to children's development contribute to competence, mastery, cooperation with others, and the development of healthy identity.

Capability versus Ability   It is important to note that academic press does not involve a focus on ability but is, rather, a focus on all students' capability to learn. Eccles and Roeser (1999) reported on a series of studies that they did with middle school students. When students believed their school was focused on ability, this belief was associated with

> declines in their educational values, achievement, and self-esteem, and increases in their anger, depressive symptoms, and school truancy from seventh to eighth grade. . . . In contrast, schools that emphasize effort, improvement, task mastery, and the expectation that all students can learn appear to enfranchise more children in the learning process, promote adaptive attributions (e.g., achievement is based on effort and is therefore malleable), reduce depression, and decrease the frustration and anxiety that can be generated in achievement settings. (p. 526)

Reggio Emilia   A similar focus on competence prevails in the early childhood classrooms of Reggio Emilia, Italy (Katz, 1993b; see Info Byte 7.3). These classrooms are internationally recognized for their outstanding work with young children. The children are viewed as competent, their ideas are taken seriously, and their teachers, parents, and community have high expectations for them (Katz). Teachers, students, and parents work together with mutual respect. The result is highly engaged learners who think deeply.

Part of the success of this approach, replicated elsewhere in Italy and adapted in Canada and the United States (e.g., see Project Zero and Reggio Children, 2001), stems from a conception of children as full members of society and a responsiveness to regional beliefs and priorities (New, 2001). Central to the educational success stories described in this chapter is the image of the child–adolescent as strong and competent. Excellence is promoted in particular social and cultural settings; it is the result both of individual competence and "smart contexts" (Barab & Plucker, 2002). Ferrari (2002) suggests that the important question to ask is this: "What sort of social and personal conditions promote excellence, and what sort of actions can educators take to assure that students will learn to become excellent in ways that both they and society value?" (p. viii).

Surfing Terms 7.3

School culture
Academic press
Home schooling
Reggio Emilia
Reggio Children
Project Zero
Gender roles
Deaf culture
Cultural incompatibilities
Learning society
Academic self-concept
After-school programs
Ethic of care
Effective schools
School size
Gender differences

INFO BYTE 7.3

The Reggio Emilia Approach to Education

In 2001, one of the authors was privileged to visit the early childhood classrooms of Reggio Emilia in northern Italy. Reggio Emilia is part of a region that has a long-standing commitment to socialist principles. Their approach to preschool education began in 1945. The citizens of Reggio Emilia believed fascism had taken hold because of blind obedience. They were determined that their children would learn to think for themselves. Mothers began building a school with bricks pulled from the rubble of war. They were joined in their endeavor by Loris Malaguzzi, who became the first teacher and founder of the approach that has gained international attention.

The education of young children is supported by the municipality of Reggio Emilia. This education is not viewed as "preschool"; this term is viewed as demeaning because it implies an introductory experience (Gambetti, 2001). *School* is taken seriously from infancy onward because of the powerful learning that takes place from the time children are born. Parents and members of the community are respected collaborators in children's learning.

Children are viewed as having many possible "languages" through which they express their understanding—drawings, sculptures, symbols, words, constructions, and drama, to name a few. They are aided in the representation of their understanding by an *atelierista*, or resident artist. These representations are then revisited by the children as a way to help them build their knowledge. For example, a painting may be "re-represented" verbally or by sculpting another version of the initial representation. The children are viewed as capable of using adult tools to represent their knowledge. Knives, wire, and pens with nibs are used to full potential by the children and without harm to themselves.

Respect for young children as full participants in their society permeates the early childhood classrooms of Reggio Emilia. Children eat at tables covered with white linen cloths and floral centerpieces. Curriculum begins with their questions and interests. Panels of photographs and accompanying narratives document the children's learning and are displayed in the foyers of the schools. The children are fully engaged in their learning. Their teachers, parents, and members of the community follow every step of this learning with genuine interest and curiosity, offering questions, comments, and supporting activities to extend and enhance the children's knowledge.

Teacher–Student Relationships

Part of a "smart" school context is healthy relationships between teachers and students. Positive relationships are related to students' competence with peers, academic achievement, social development, concept development, and behavioral competence (Davis, 2003). A sociocultural perspective on these relationships recognizes that they cannot be separated from the classrooms and schools in which students and teachers spend much of their time. Davis describes how relationships are embedded within classrooms. Classrooms are, in turn, embedded in schools and schools in an "academic culture dictated by local and societal norms" (p. 218). As teachers, you will need to reflect on how each of these factors may influence your practice and how you need to be responsive to the backgrounds and experiences of your students. With these considerations as a backdrop, the following are indicators of good teacher–student relationships:

- Teacher support in helping students to label, express, and manage their emotions
- Teacher respect for students' minds and their ways of understanding
- Providing opportunities for autonomy and recognition
- Providing opportunities for self-evaluation, including helping students to understand what counts as good work
- Teacher emphasis on doing things well and understanding (learning), rather than simply getting it done and getting it right (performance)

- A positive affective climate in the classroom, including teacher efforts to foster social responsibility and support prosocial behavior
- Teacher organization and preparation
- Teacher modeling of effective strategies for learning (Davis, 2003).

Cultural Differences in Schools

In this section, we refer to differences between the school cultures of elementary, middle, and secondary schools. Generally, there are marked differences between elementary and secondary school cultures.

Elementary, Middle, and High School Cultures

Secondary classrooms are larger and more teacher centered (regarding control, discipline, and choice) (Eccles et al., 1993) and tend to focus on coverage of the curriculum, rather than individual student learning. Relationships between teachers and students also tend to be less positive than they were in elementary school. Elementary schools are generally smaller; small schools usually are more effective in supporting academic engagement and achievement (Anderman, 2002). Elementary schools also tend to have more parental involvement and demonstrate more focus on learners than on the curriculum. Elementary teachers also are, in general, able to establish closer bonds with their students because they simply see more of them than they would in a secondary school. The changes in school culture from elementary to secondary can result in decreased motivation to learn, a topic we discuss in more detail in Chapter 9.

Grade Configuration

Some school districts have instituted middle schools as a way of ensuring a developmental match between school structure and the needs of learners that allows a smoother transition from elementary to high school. Successful middle school programs result in positive motivational and achievement outcomes and meaningful school attachment (Eccles et al., 1993). However, simply moving the middle grades (generally sixth to eighth grade) to a separate school building does not guarantee better student adjustment during this important school transition. When the transition is discontinuous and students experience a loss of status, students' adjustment suffers (Davis, 2003). If the student–teacher ratio also increases, with a corresponding decrease in student–teacher support, students may feel increased anonymity and depression and decreased self-esteem (Davis; Reddy, Rhodes, & Mulhall, 2003).

Anderman (2002) emphasizes that it is not the grade configuration that is important but, rather, the actual practices used within the school. Small school and class size, extended time with a homeroom teacher, and support in negotiating increased curricular demands all help to support adolescents in their transition from elementary to middle or high schools. Teacher support is particularly critical, resulting in positive values, self-confidence, and self-esteem (Reddy et al., 2003).

School culture does not exist in a vacuum. It needs to consider the broader social context and be responsive to this context. The conceptualization of current societal trends should provide the framework for education.

A Learning Society

As discussed earlier, the type of society we now live in has been described as a "learning society" (Keating & Hertzman, 1999). As with previous major shifts in human history (the agricultural revolution, the industrial revolution), we live in a time when social, political, and cultural structures are undergoing significant changes. However, current changes are occurring at a more rapid rate than ever before, requiring high levels of adaptability (Keating, 1999). We need to think about how development can be optimized in families, communities, schools, workplaces, and society, with *developmental health* (Keating) as our goal. Developmental health includes "physical and mental health, competence, and the ability to cope with stress and novelty" (Keating, p. 338). A learning society is one "that commits to understanding and then acting on these core dynamics of human development" (Keating, pp. 338–339).

Learning Adaptability, Innovation, and Collaboration

We need to learn in ways that are compatible with managing change productively. The necessary academic skills in a learning society are not restricted to mastery of existing knowledge [recall Bruner's (1996) models of mind, discussed in Chapter 2]. Academic preparation must also include developing the capacity for innovation and generation of knowledge in a collaborative way (Keating, 1999; Scardamalia & Bereiter, 1999). Collaboration, in turn, requires interpersonal skills. *Interpersonal competence* also needs to be a focus of learning (e.g., Bruner; Hymel, Comfort, Schonert-Reichl, & McDougall, 1996) since we need citizens who can function effectively in a global community.

A Caring School Community

Schools need to be aware of the society and culture in which they are situated and respond to the local and wider communities in sensitive ways, making education appropriate and meaningful. Schools also can be proactive, providing their communities with leadership in effective teaching and learning strategies and models of caring communities. Nel Noddings of Stanford University argues that, without a caring school community, effective learning is difficult. A violent school environment, for example, does not provide the optimal conditions for learning. The kind of care Noddings (1995) describes is infused into the curriculum and structures of schooling. It means addressing questions of ethical and moral concern in all subjects and offering learners a real "school home" where trust and meaningful connections are forged. The sort of school environment Noddings envisions may help to contribute to a learning society. "Caring implies a continuous search for competence" (Noddings, p. 675)—one of the core components of healthy human development.

Classroom Culture

Imagine two grade 6 classrooms about 15 minutes before school starts for the day. In one, the teacher is working at his desk, but looks up to greet a few arriving students. Most of the students have already settled into their desks and are working quietly on the math assignment that is posted on the board. In the classroom next door, chaos reigns as students arrive, push each other, and shout insults. The teacher arrives just before the final bell rings at 9:00 A.M., shouts at the students, and slams the door. The learning environments described have significant effects on the learning that takes place within them. They are, in effect, the culture in which students spend a significant part of their day, the mediating influence on their development. Another term that is often used is *classroom climate*.

Establishing a Positive Classroom Climate

Educational researchers Walberg and Greenberg (1997) found that the social environment in the classroom is one of the primary determinants of learning.

Interpersonal competence: The ability to understand others' points of view and to respond accordingly.

Using the learning environment inventory they designed, they found that students rated the following aspects of classrooms highly:

- Enjoyment of work
- Challenge
- Class cohesiveness
- Good physical environment (books, equipment, space, light)
- Shared decision making
- Clear goals
- Formal rules to guide behavior
- Speed with which work is covered
- Student diversity
- The extent to which diversity is taken into account

Students found the following to have a negative impact on their learning:

- Apathy
- Favoritism
- Cliquishness
- Disorganization
- Friction

The Social World of Classrooms

As discussed earlier, teacher–child relationships also are extremely important in ensuring academic and behavioral success in school. Early positive relationships with teachers are particularly important for students' long-term success in school. One author notes that, in her experience with secondary students, those who had positive relationships with previous teachers were confident about their education and comfortable with their teachers. Hamre and Pianta (2001) followed children from kindergarten to grade 8 and found that positive teacher–child relationships in kindergarten predicted positive school outcomes. Positive relationships are, in turn, related to the student-teacher ratio (Pianta; cited in Anderman, 2002). When classes have lower student-teacher ratios, teachers can know their students better and practice the constructivist principles we outlined in the beginning chapters of the book more effectively.

Culture and ethnicity are relevant to teacher–student relationships. Quiocho and Rios (2000) argue that teachers from different cultural backgrounds bring a "power of presence" and "cultural mediation abilities" to their work (p. 523). Quiocho and Rios discuss the effectiveness of teachers from minority group backgrounds with students from the same backgrounds, but emphasize that they also bring something very valuable to Euro-American students (and, we would argue, teachers): "positive images of people of color, a realistic understanding of our growing multicultural society (Shaw, 1996), and the sheer understanding of learning from people of different backgrounds" (p. 488).

The Importance of a Sense of Belonging

As discussed above, a sense of belonging is important to students. Anderman (2002) found it to be related to psychological outcomes in adolescence. Adolescents who believe they do not belong in school tend to feel more depressed, to be socially rejected, and to experience more school problems. We have known elementary students who have experienced the same issues as a result of not feeling that they are a part of their classrooms. Overall, students benefit from feeling acceptance and belonging by achieving better, being more motivated to learn, and being engaged and committed to learning (Osterman, 2000). Possessing a sense of belonging is related to the cultures of school and classroom, but peer relationships also play a significant role, as discussed in Chapter 6. As we mentioned in Chapter 6 as well, children and adolescents who are victims of bullying (physical or relational) and/or who are rejected or neglected by their peers do not find school a safe and satisfying place.

In Problem-Based Scenario 7.7, it is evident that too much teacher control may be as difficult an educational situation as too little classroom control, leading to an unhealthy classroom climate in which students do not feel a sense of belonging.

Gender and Schooling

Boys and girls experience school differently in a number of ways, so it is important to consider how gender plays a role in the social–cultural milieu of schools and classrooms. Some general findings will be presented, but it should be noted that culture is a mediating factor in gender effects (Liben & Bigler, 2002). The roles males and females assume in different cultural groups should be considered. It also is important to recognize that there are differences *within* gender. For example, males are generally recognized to be better than females in spatial ability, but some women are superior to some men. Liben and Bigler also note that individuals may differ in how they are gendered in different domains (e.g., personality vs. work).

Gender Differences in the School Experience

In Hamre and Pianta's (2001) study of teacher–child relationships, they suggested that the benefits of early relationships vary for boys and girls. Boys who were less dependent on their kindergarten teachers did better long-term,

Problem-Based Scenario 7.7

K-5   6-8   9-12   SpEd

Students: *Social Studies 8 Class*
Teacher: *Alice*

As the new vice-principal, Alice sometimes felt overwhelmed with all the issues that crop up in such a large high school. With over a thousand students covering grades 8 to 12, it was always a pretty active place. Alice liked wandering through the staff room at intervals throughout the day. It kept her in touch with teachers on a more informal basis, and it also was the source of a lot of information that wasn't available if she sat in her office.

She had wandered into the staff room just after period 3. The laughing was what she heard first. Apparently, there was a substitute teacher in for Mr. Jablonsky who taught social studies. The substitute teacher was commenting on how incredibly quiet and good the grade 8's were last period. Not one word was whispered. They all put their heads down and did the sheets Mr. Jablonsky left for them. After about half an hour, the substitute asked what was going on since she had never encountered a class like this one. It took a fair amount of encouragement to

have anyone speak at all. Finally, one boy at the back stood up (which amazed the substitute) and explained that they knew Mr. Jablonsky was not really away that day but was sitting in the office listening to them over the intercom. They wanted Mr. Jablonsky to know they were working very hard and were being good.

This is what everyone was laughing at. But Alice had a number of other concerns. As she left the staff room she tried to figure out what was going on and how to handle it tactfully.

Apply

- As a substitute teacher, what would you do in this situation? Why?
- What might Alice do first? Consider that Alice may need time to figure out this situation and will need to think carefully about tactful strategies.

whereas, for girls, close relationships with their kindergarten teachers related to positive behavioral adjustment long term. Negative teacher–boy relationships also were related to disciplinary problems more strongly than to academic outcomes. Hamre and Pianta suggested that future research needs to take account of the child's point of view, however, something that was missing from their research.

Females tend to have different *ways of knowing* than males, preferring relational, intuitive, and subjective approaches to learning, whereas males prefer more objective methods (Belenky, Clinchy, Goldberger, & Tarule, 1986; Brown & Gilligan, 1992; Porath, 1998). Teachers react differently to boys and girls. Boys receive more teacher attention, interact with their teachers more frequently, receive detailed feedback, and engage in independent problem solving. Girls, in general, are rewarded for good behavior and "neat work" (Sadker & Sadker, 1994). This form of reward, however, is not supportive of girls. Girls receive less attention and support from their teachers than boys and tend to have low levels of engagement with teachers (Sadker & Sadker). This means that the teacher support identified as important to successful adjustment to middle or high school may not exist for girls. Some studies have identified close relationships between girls and their teachers, however (Reddy et al., 2003). What is important to your practice is to ensure that *all* students are supported in their academic and social–emotional development.

Gender and Expectations for Academic Success

Teachers rated profiles of girls who demonstrated average creativity as more creative than boys with similar levels of creativity (Scott, 1999; as cited in Cropley, 2003), but rated both highly creative boys and girls the same. We will discuss creativity in more detail in Chapter 8. This study result is presented here to highlight how perceptions of gender may affect our thinking. As teachers, it will be important to examine your own thoughts about gender, the texts and materials you use in your classroom for explicit and implicit messages about gender, and your practice for possible differential gender effects (Photo 7.5).

Different approaches to learning, along with parent, teacher, and societal expectations and classroom and school environments, are factors in expectations

PHOTO 7.5

Teacher feedback is often related to gender.

Problem-Based Scenario 7.8

Student: *Sally*

Teacher: *Joan*

Joan Whitworth collected the papers from her grade 8 English class. As she usually did in September, Joan had asked her students to write about what they expected from high school and what their first impressions were. The students had discussed these topics before beginning to write. Joan was somewhat disturbed by Sally Johnson's responses. Sally seemed so unclear about what she expected from her secondary school experience, and she seemed withdrawn from her classmates. Now, as Joan glanced down at Sally's paper, she saw that very little had been written.

What was up? Sally's reputation preceded her. During her grade 6 year, her poetry appeared in the local paper. Laura Johnson, her mother, had dropped off a portfolio of writing at the school last June. Joan was impressed with the contents—Sally expressed herself creatively. There was some need to refine the mechanics of writing, but Joan felt this was developmental. In her experience, this wasn't unusual. Some elementary schools emphasized the creative aspects of writing over skills. The other thing that troubled Joan was that, in checking with Sally's other teachers, she found that Sally appeared similarly disengaged in their classes. Was there something she had overlooked? Or was there something else going on that she needed to think about?

Apply

- What might Joan do to support Sally?
- Are there developmental and/or cultural factors that she should consider?

for success in different subjects (Lupart & Pyryt, 2001). Lorenz and Lupart (2001) found significant gender differences in Canadian students' expectations for success in mathematics, language arts-English, and science, with females demonstrating higher expectations for success than males in advanced language arts-English courses and in careers involving writing and speaking ability. Despite equivalent achievement levels, males had higher expectations than females for success in advanced math and science courses and in careers requiring these abilities. Gender, then, becomes one of the important considerations in creating good *person–environment fit* (Eccles & Roeser, 1999) in schools.

In Problem-Based Scenario 7.8, consider Sally's development in terms of fit with a new school environment.

Learning Beyond the Walls of School

Our learning takes place both outside and inside educational institutions. Parents are often described as their child's first teacher; some broaden that description by choosing to home-school their children. In either case, learning takes place at home as well as in extended families, peer relationships, and communities. In this mesosystem, children and adolescents also approach the tasks of mastery, competence, and self-identity. Close links between home, school, and community help children and adolescents to be successful at these tasks and may be especially important in high-risk communities (Eccles & Roeser, 1999).

Involvement in extracurricular activities is related to educational attainment, lower rates of school dropout, lower rates of substance use, and school engagement (Eccles & Roeser, 1999). Constructive, organized activities are more beneficial than leisure activities like watching television or "hanging out" because of their requirement of effort and commitment (Carpenter, 2001; Eccles & Roeser)

PHOTO 7.6

Involvement in extracurricular activities leads to positive developmental outcome.

(Photo 7.6). As with good school programs, youth organizations put "youth at the center," involving them in decision making, emphasizing responsibility and accountability, and valuing the diverse perspectives and talents they bring to the organizations (Heath & McLaughlin, 1994).

There is still a great deal to know about extracurricular activities, however. For example, characteristics of children and adolescents enter into the mix. Bright, well-adjusted children, for example, are more likely to seek out after-school activities (McHale, Crouter, & Tucker, 2001). Encouragement by peers and family also may be important factors. We also need to think about our own perceptions about activities. Computer game play is considered unhealthy by some, but recent research shows it to be related to positive outcomes like school engagement, mental health, and self-concept (Durkin & Barber, 2002), possibly due to the challenging nature of the activity.

Summary

In this chapter, you saw how society and culture shape development. This shaping includes the influences of the society and families in which we grow up, the cultural beliefs we learn in our families and through social practices, our gender, the experiences we have in school, and our relationships with our peers and teachers. We considered the characteristics of a supportive learning community—a community that includes teachers, students, families, and the wider community in meaningful ways that respect sociocultural background.

- Ecological and life-span developmental theories can help you to understand how each of us has a personal "developmental space" or "developmental niche."
- Including parents in the education of their children can bring valuable perspectives on cultural, religious, parenting, economic, and family variables that help you to understand the learners in your classroom.
- Poverty may result in vulnerability to poor academic and social outcomes, but vulnerability is evident across all income levels. Schools can reduce vulnerability in significant ways.

Schools and classrooms are social and cultural in nature. Positive school and classroom environments enhance achievement and sense of belonging.

A Metacognitive Challenge

You should now be able to reflect on the following questions:

- What do I know about the influence of culture on development?
- What do I know about school as a culture?
- What do I know about the characteristics of a positive learning environment?
- How does my knowledge of culture, social context, socioeconomic status, gender, and classroom climate help me to teach the learners in my classroom?

Artifacts for Problem-Based Scenarios

FIGURE 7.2 ■ Trevor's Drawing

FIGURE 7.3 ■ Artifact for Problem-Based Scenario 7.1

```
Date:     Wednesday, September 9, 2002    19:05:13
Subject: Questions
To:       Danielle Langer danielle.langer@sd91.lakehuron.ca
From:     katy.moss@sd91.lakehuron.ca (Katy Moss)


Dear Danielle,
I'm new at Huron Junior Secondary this semester.  I
have Trevor Hall in my homeroom and English 9. I
know it's only the beginning of the year but I'm
really worried about him.  What really scares me are
his drawings. He draws knives dripping with blood
all over his work and men hanging from gallows on
the covers of all his books.


I just had a look through his confidential file and
I have a lot of questions.  Would it be possible for
us to meet soon and talk over my concerns?
Thanks very much, Danielle.


Katy
```

FIGURE 7.4 ■ Artifact for Problem-Based Scenario 7.1

```
Date:     Monday, October 7, 2002          9:00:03
Subject: Meeting
To:       Katy Moss katy.moss@sd91.lakehuron.ca
From:     danielle.langer@sd91.lakehuron.ca (Danielle Langer)


Dear Katy,
I'd be happy to meet with you. I assessed Trevor two
years ago.  Could we meet in a couple of weeks?  I
should be finished with the elementary assessments
by then. How about after school on Oct. 21, in my
office?


Danielle



Danielle Langer, M.A.
School Psychologist
Lake Huron School District
```

FIGURE 7.5 ■ **Artifact for Problem-Based Scenario 7.2**

CONFIDENTIAL MEMO
From the desk of

JULIO D. SARNI

Della,

I spoke to Franco's father on the phone. I just wanted to forewarn you. His father uses the "F" word as a regular part of his vocabulary, so I'm not sure he will be that supportive of our concern. Also, the counseling office supplied a file. This problem has come up before anytime Franco has had a female teacher. After speaking to Franco's father I think we may have some problems here beyond just defiance and inappropriate language concerns.

I will support you but you should know it will only be us, Franco and his father at the meeting. His mother does not come to the school I have been told.

FIGURE 7.6 ■ Artifact for Problem-Based Scenario 7.4

October 12, 2001

Dear Mrs. Collins,

What Jon told you about Benjamin (Bear Paw) Webb was correct. His mother had been frightened by a bear when she was pregnant. The bear tried to break into her home through the kitchen door. Her husband, who was in the barn, heard the noise, and ran it off with a shotgun. When Benjamin was born he had black fur covering his shoulder, and down his left arm. His hand wasn't like a normal hand but rather was shaped in the form of claws, much like a bear paw. He had great strength in that arm and was able to lift more with that one arm than other men could with both hands. I grew up with Benjamin and know this is true.

We had a neighbor several years ago who had the mark of a snake head between her breasts. She got it because someone threw a snake at her when she was pregnant and it landed around her neck. (Please do not tell that to Jon since it is inappropriate for him at this age, perhaps when he is older. I have seen the snakehead so I know it is true.)

I think science often tries too hard to explain these phenomena by discounting other theories. If I hadn't been a witness to these things I would be skeptical as well. If you would like further details on any of this please send a message home with Jon.

Sincerely yours,

Esther Webb

Understanding Our Learners: Intelligence and Creativity

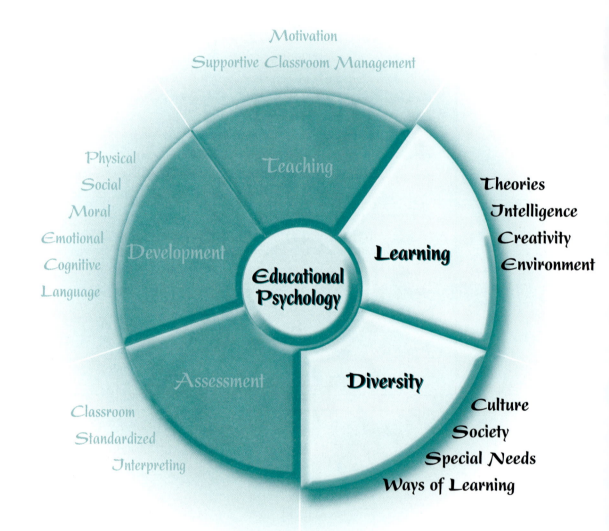

Motivation

Supportive Classroom Management

Teaching

Physical
Social
Moral
Emotional
Cognitive
Language

Development

Learning

Educational
Psychology

Theories
Intelligence
Creativity
Environment

Assessment

Diversity

Classroom
Standardized
Interpreting

Culture
Society
Special Needs
Ways of Learning

Humans have been interested in intelligence and the measurement of cognitive abilities for centuries. The Chinese developed a civil service testing program over 4000 years ago, based on their definition of intelligence, to measure items such as knowledge of ceremonies and horsemanship (Thorndike, 1997). Plato, in *The Republic,* suggested that individuals of different levels of intelligence might be suited to different ranks in society. In more recent times, scientists and others in

Europe and North America attempted various methods for measuring intelligence, reaching some untenable conclusions about intelligence and instituting questionable practices based on intelligence tests (Gould, 1981). We also have debated whether intelligence is unitary (i.e., a general ability that predicts level of learning and problem solving across different disciplines) or occurs in multiple forms (i.e., one could be highly mathematically and musically intelligent and average in learning and using language) (Photo 8.1).

Think about what intelligence means to you. What sorts of abilities do you consider as contributing to intelligence? If you think someone is smart, what do they do that makes you consider them smart? Do you think intelligence can be measured? If so, how do you think it should be measured? For what purposes should intelligence be measured?

We also have been interested in creativity for centuries, celebrating the accomplishments of writers, artists, musicians, scientists, and political and religious figures that changed the way we think about things. Think about the questions above, substituting creativity for intelligence. This will give you a framework for this chapter, in which we present background on different theories of intelligence and creativity, current thinking on what constitutes intelligent and creative behaviors, and the meaning of intelligence and creativity for education.

PHOTO 8.1

Children can be extraordinarily gifted in only one area, possessing an intelligence that is often missed in standardized tests.

Intelligence

One Intelligence or Many?

Is there one intelligence or are there many? This question has occupied psychologists for at least a century. Those who favor the unitary model of intelligence argue that, although there may be numerous specific abilities (like language and mathematics), these specific abilities are all related to a general, overarching intelligence, or "g" (see Thorndike, 1997). Those who favor the existence of more than one intelligence note that different "intelligences" are valued by different cultures (Gardner, 1983). For example, in Western cultures verbal and logical abilities are valued, whereas tribal cultures may value the exceptional spatial ability needed for navigation or for identifying one's cattle.

Other intelligences include reasoning, knowledge acquired from the culture, and a variety of memory and information-processing components (Horn & Noll, 1997). Theorists also note that mental activity, experience, and adaptation to the environment (Sternberg, 1997) combine to define intelligent behavior.

Intelligence Quotient or IQ

In North America, one conception of intelligence has dominated our thinking and educational practice for almost a century. After Lewis Terman published the Stanford–Binet Intelligence Scale in 1916 and shortly thereafter advocated that every child be given a mental test, IQ testing in schools became widespread (Thorndike, 1997) (Photo 8.2). The Stanford–Binet Intelligence Scale is now in its fifth edition. It and the other individual intelligence test, the Weschler Intelligence Scale for Children (now in its fourth edition), and related preschool and adult scales are the most commonly used tests of intellectual ability. Both yield scores that are derived by comparing an individual's score to those of others of the same age. The tests are thus *norm-referenced*. This concept is discussed in more detail in Chapter 12.

Both the Stanford–Binet and Wechsler Intelligence Scales emphasize verbal intelligence (the capacity to understand and reason with language) and performance, or abstract–visual, intelligence (the capacity to understand and apply visual–spatial relationships). The Stanford–Binet adds quantitative ability (competence in understanding and using numerical concepts) and short-term memory (the ability to retain in memory verbal and visual–spatial information presented just before recall is attempted). Both tests are premised on the notion of *general intelligence*. Each component of each test (verbal, performance, etc.) is believed to reflect a general intellectual ability. Separate scores on the components of each test are combined to yield an intelligence quotient (IQ). This is called a composite score on the Stanford–Binet and a full-scale IQ on the Wechsler scales.

Norm-referenced: Tests that compare an individual's performance to a large group of individuals of the same age who also took the test. The larger group is called the *norm* group.

General intelligence: A general ability to reason and solve problems believed to underlie all human thinking; sometimes referred to as g.

PHOTO 8.2

Group IQ tests are given widely in North America.

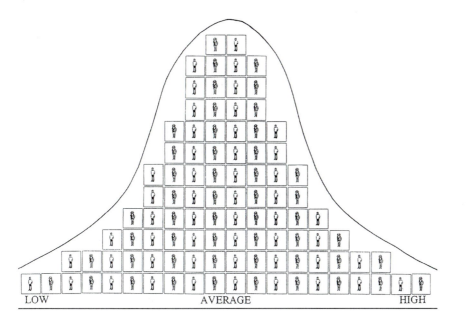

LOW   AVERAGE   HIGH

FIGURE 8.1

The Bell Curve
Source: Reprinted with permission of Dr. William McKee, The University of British Columbia.

IQ is related to academic achievement; students with high IQs do well in school, in general, and those with low IQ scores tend to do poorly. Both intelligence and academic achievement tests measure aptitude, learning, and achievement, thus the relationship between scores (Sattler, 1992). However, intelligence tests are broader in their coverage, and test the ability to solve novel problems.

The Bell Curve

Intelligence is believed to have a normal distribution in the population (see Info Byte 8.1). That is, scores on an intelligence test form a bell curve (or *normal curve*) with a mean, or average score, of 100. Scores tend to be distributed as follows (Figure 8.1):

- Approximately 68% of the population score between 85 and 115 (average intelligence).
- Approximately 14% score between 70 and 84 (below-average intelligence).
- Another 14% score between 115 and 129 (above-average intelligence).
- About 4% score between 55 and 69 or between 130 and 144 (developmental delay or very superior intelligence).
- Very few individuals score below 55 or above 144 (severe developmental delay and extremely gifted).

People with IQs of 69 or below are considered mentally retarded (U.S. terminology) or developmentally delayed, disabled, or challenged (Canadian terminology). People with IQs of 130 and above are considered gifted. The numbers attached to degree of intelligence and the resulting labels have permeated thinking about intelligence until relatively recently. Based on this information, try interpreting the assessment report in Problem-Based Scenario 8.1.

In Problem-Based Scenario 8.1 your objective was to interpret assessment data that suggest high overall ability and academic achievement. As teachers, you may receive assessment data that show average or above-average (perhaps even superior) intelligence and below-average achievement. In some school districts, this discrepancy may define a learning disability. Although many jurisdictions have moved away from defining learning disabilities in this way because the definition is not helpful in planning educational programs, you may still need to interpret a report that is suggestive of a learning disability. As an example, a student may have an IQ of 120 (above average) and standard scores of 70 in reading achievement and 60 in written language. You probably already have curriculum-based data that tell you that the student has problems with reading and writing. We will discuss curriculum-based assessment in more detail in Chapter 11. In the mean-

Problem-Based Scenario 8.1

Student: *Sally*
Teacher: *Joan*

Joan was still struggling to understand Sally's disengagement from school. Sally continued to write very little in Joan's English 8 class, despite the obvious love for writing she had demonstrated in elementary school. Sally's other teachers had also noticed Sally's lack of participation in class and the confusion she expressed about expectations in secondary school. Joan's conversations with these teachers had been limited to short exchanges over coffee, so she decided to follow up on her concerns by asking to meet with Sally's other teachers. The meeting was scheduled in 10 days.

Two days after she had arranged the meeting, Sally's mother, Laura Johnson, came in to see Joan and brought a report on the assessment done with Sally the year before. Laura also was concerned with Sally's adjustment to secondary school. Joan told her of the upcoming meeting and invited her to join in. In the meantime, Joan said, she would read the report and bring any thoughts and questions to the meeting.

After reading the report (see Figure 8.3 on pages 236–239), Joan was even more baffled. What could have made the enthusiastic, bright girl portrayed in the report become so withdrawn and uninterested in school?

FIGURE 8.2

INFO BYTE *8.1*

BELL CURVE

The *bell curve*, or *normal curve*, in Figure 8.1 on page 217 is provided to give you a pictorial sense of how a characteristic is distributed throughout a large population. The characteristic can be anything from intelligence to shoe size.

With any characteristic, most people cluster in the middle; that is, most of us tend to be average. For example, most people in your class or community are probably of average height and therefore would have an average foot size. However, we do know that there are basketball players who are incredibly tall, and with incredibly large feet compared to the average foot size. Some players are so large that their shoes are specially made. Manufacturers often use these shoes for advertisements. The reason the advertisement is so noticeable and effective is that very few people have such large feet. If the bell curve represented shoe size, the basketball player would be graphically represented in the upper area ("high" in Figure 8.1), indicated by only one or two people. If we overlay numbers on the curve, we could narrow down the percentage of people with shoe sizes similar to, or greater than, the basketball player. Most curves you find will indicate percentages and divisions that mathematically cluster in similar groups (e.g., all people with size 8 shoes). This makes the curves easier to use. Instead of saying only one or two people in the population have the same shoe size, you can be more specific and say, "Only 2% of the population has the same size shoe."

Figure 8.1 is designed to provide you with a mental image of how the bell or normal curve represents a population *in general*. By identifying a characteristic, and then finding where it sits within the population, teachers are provided with information that can be useful as an additional component for educational planning. No one characteristic or result should be used by itself. It must be seen as one more piece of information to be used for planning. This will be discussed further in Chapter 12.

time, consider the definition of learning disabilities used in the authors' educational jurisdiction:

> Learning disabilities refer to a number of disorders that may affect the acquisition, organization, retention, understanding or use of verbal or nonverbal information. These disorders affect learning in individuals who otherwise demonstrate at least average abilities essential for thinking and/or reasoning. As such, learning disabilities are distinct from global intellectual disabilities.
>
> Learning disabilities result from impairments in one or more processes related to perceiving, thinking, remembering or learning. These include, but are not limited to: language processing, phonological processing, visual–spatial processing, processing speed, memory and attention, and executive functions (e.g., planning and decision making).
>
> Learning disabilities range in severity and may interfere with the acquisition and use of one or more of the following:

- Oral language (e.g., listening, speaking, understanding)
- Reading (e.g., decoding, phonetic knowledge, word recognition, comprehension)
- Written language (e.g., spelling and written expression)
- Mathematics (e.g., computation, problem solving)

> Learning disabilities may also involve difficulties with organizational skills, social perception, social interaction and perspective taking. (British Columbia Ministry of Education, 2002)

Working with a definition of learning disabilities that includes details of possible information-processing difficulties (see Chapter 5) can help teachers understand how a child can demonstrate average or superior intelligence in many situations, but have significant difficulties in some academic areas.

Criticisms of IQ

The use of IQ to determine educational placement was called into question during the 1960s when it was discovered that certain cultural groups, particularly African Americans and Hispanics, were overrepresented in special education classes designed for persons with mental retardation in the United States. These groups protested against the white, middle-class bias of IQ tests. Certainly, one is advantaged by high socioeconomic status and socialization in white Western or Anglo-Saxon-dominant American or Canadian cultures when taking an intelligence test (Helms, 1997; Valencia & Suzuki, 2001). The tests fail to measure indicators of intelligent behavior in other cultures (Ceci, 1996; Gardner, 1983; Suizzo, 2000).

Another criticism of IQ is that it is not the whole story as far as intelligent behaviors are concerned. One of the authors relates this story.

> *"I have taught students whose measured IQs were about 70. This is considered 'borderline' mentally retarded (Sattler, 1992). However, these students were in my "regular" Grade Four classroom, earning grades of C or C– in the Grade Four curriculum, in part because of their hard work and interest. It is doubtful that they would have continued to manage grade level curriculum into high school. However, they had other characteristics that predict life success—commitment to task, responsibility, pleasant personalities, good self-image, and social skills."*

Adaptive behavior:
Age-appropriate social skills (e.g., being able to dress oneself; personal care; simple money management; communication).

The students described above demonstrate *adaptive behavior.* Students like these and those having what is called "5-hour retardation" prompted calls for a change in the definition of mental retardation. Students displaying 5-hour retardation have significantly below average academic performance in the 5 hours they attend school, but have the ability to cope well outside school (adaptive behavior). In 1983, the American Association on Mental Deficiency (AAMD) proposed the definition currently in use, which includes significantly below average intellectual functioning as well as deficits in adaptive behavior (Sattler, 1992).

IQ Is Not Enough

Stephen Ceci (1996) discussed what he terms "mismatches between intelligent performance and IQ" (p. 29). Ceci described a number of studies of "everyday" problem solving where individuals do impressively complex thinking (like using multiple variables to predict which horse will win a race) but have measured IQs in the average range or lower. Ceci pointed to context, culture, motivational level, and sex-role expectations as important variables in demonstrating intelligent behaviors (Photo 8.3). Daniel Goleman (1995) emphasized emotional variables such as the ability to delay gratification and a strong sense of personal identity as more important than IQ in predicting life success. These variables describe *emotional intelligence,* discussed in Chapter 6.

Even when IQ is high, it alone does not guarantee the demonstration of gifted-level abilities. Ellen Winner (1996) argues that, in addition to their *precocity,* gifted children show "an insistence on marching to their own drummer" and "a rage to master" (p. 3), characteristics that allow them to think in novel ways and make deep sense of what they undertake. Gifted children also need educational opportunities that allow them enough scope to demonstrate their abilities and classroom environments that support them in thinking

Precocity: Developmental advancement (e.g., the ability to read several grade levels above one's age peers).

PHOTO 8.3

A number of important variables contribute to intelligent behavior.

broadly and deeply. In Problem-Based Scenario 8.2, you meet Jessica, a gifted third-grader. Her teachers are trying to deal with their own beliefs about giftedness and what constitutes an appropriate education for a gifted child. (By using the normal curve in Info Byte 8.1, you can find out how Jessica's test results compare with the larger group of third-graders.)

IQ and Educational Planning

Another criticism of IQ is that it is of little relevance in educational planning (Keating, 1991). Results of intelligence testing give only global indicators of level of ability. They do not translate into specific guidelines about a student's reading or math ability, for example. They do not help with what teachers call the "Monday morning question"—what to plan specifically for the individual learners in their classrooms. Bruer (1994) concurs: "Test results tell teachers where students rank but are mute about where individual children are on domain-specific learning trajectories" (p. 284). That is, IQ gives teachers an indicator of how students compare to others their age in general problem-solving ability. This can be useful, but it is also limited. We need other information, such as classroom- or curriculum-based assessment and teacher observations (discussed in Chapter 11) to help us know where a student is on the path to becoming a competent reader, writer, mathematician, or scientist.

In Problem-Based Scenario 8.3 you meet two teachers who have different attitudes about student intelligence, learning, and teaching. Teachers' preconceptions about what different levels of intelligence mean for classroom learning may obstruct appropriate educational planning. These preconceptions may also unconsciously interfere with opportunities for student success.

A Place for IQ

Despite the criticisms, there can be a place for intelligence testing in education. Knowing a student's IQ can draw attention to educational need, particularly at either tail of the normal curve (Keating, 1991; Robinson, Zigler, & Gallagher, 2000). A high or low score can alert educators to the need to investigate further by doing curriculum-based assessment to determine appropriate levels of instruction (see Chapters 11 and 12 for further discussion of assessment strategies).

Surfing Terms 8.1

Multiple intelligences

IQ

General intelligence (g)

Gifted

Learning disabilities

Mental retardation

Developmental disabilities

Emotional intelligence (EQ)

G/LD

Twice exceptional

Bell curve or normal curve

Francis Galton

Charles Darwin

Lewis Terman

Alfred Binet

Acceleration

Enrichment

Individual differences

Genius

Mentorship

Curriculum compacting

Problem-Based Scenario 8.2

Teachers: *Beth and Tanis*
Student: *Jessica*

Beth Littler had a vague feeling of unease that her relationship with her teaching partner, Tanis Cevic, might be tested. It started when Jessica joined their class. Jessica McCoy was a third-grader who had been in a gifted program in her previous school. Jessica's mother expressed concern about the program that would be provided for her in her new school. Mrs. McCoy told Beth and Tanis that Jessica's IQ was 145 and that she really wants and needs challenge in her curriculum. Mrs. McCoy handed Beth and Tanis the report on Jessica's psychoeducational assessment done the previous year (see Figure 8.4 on pages 240–243). Beth told Mrs. McCoy she was interested in trying to meet Jessica's needs. After taking a summer course on gifted learners, Beth was keen to apply her new knowledge, and she promised that she would make every effort to make Jessica's education challenging and rewarding.

Jessica settled in well. Beth and Tanis already had a great deal of individualization in place in their grade 2/3 classroom, so it was fairly straightforward to start the process of accommodating Jessica's advanced understandings and skills. Today, though, Tanis looked up from marking Math assignments and commented, "Look at this work of Jessica's! I thought she was supposed to be gifted. There's no evidence of that here." Beth felt a small alarm bell go off. She examined the work. It was accurate. Jessica had done what was expected. She asked Tanis what made her comment as she had. "Well," said Tanis, "I just think she could have done a lot more with this set of problems."

"How?" asked Beth, pointing out that Jessica's mathematical ability wasn't as strong as her other abilities. "How can that be?" asked Tanis. "She's supposed to be such a genius. Let's see some evidence of it."

This comment really unsettled Beth. She and Tanis got along so well, and Beth had always been impressed with Tanis's sensitivity to children's learning profiles. Beth's professor had really emphasized that gifted children most typically have variable academic profiles. Their achievement can vary across subjects, and there can be different reasons for this. Beth saw Jessica as a budding scholar. She was thoughtful and asked the most probing questions Beth had ever encountered. Beth loved this about her. Usually, she and Tanis agreed on their perceptions of children. Why was this not the case with Jessica?

Beth's mind became even more tangled up in questions after having a meeting with Mrs. McCoy. Mrs. McCoy asked if IQ changed over one's lifetime. Did school experiences affect IQ? Did Beth think Jessica was challenged adequately? How did she know? Was there any chance a program might be started in the district?

Beth had occasionally thought about starting a program for gifted children. Could she pull it off? She didn't really have adequate answers for Mrs. McCoy's questions. She would need more background for sure. What next? Beth thought she'd better sort out all of these questions and think first about what to do in the immediate future.

Children who obtain high scores on an intelligence test in spite of having a first language other than English and/or spending their formative years in another culture demonstrate that they have exceptional abilities in acquiring languages and adapting to a new environment. The latter is one of the essential qualities of intelligence (Sternberg, 1997).

Intelligence testing can be part of a tool kit for understanding children's general learning and ability profiles. Like most tools, however, it needs to be used appropriately and should be supplemented with tools that are specialized. Many educators turn to multiple intelligences to help them understand students' specific abilities.

Multiple Intelligences

In 1983, Howard Gardner of Harvard University published his book, *Frames of Mind: The Theory of Multiple Intelligences.* Based on his work in neuropsychology and developmental psychology, findings from experimental psychology, studies

Problem-Based Scenario 8.3

Teachers: *Tim and George*

Tim Roland was pretty concerned about George working on the School-Based Team. George had confided in him about how annoyed he was to get this memo (see Figure 8.5 on page 244) from the principal. As Tim drove home he replayed the conversation from the staff room. Tim became more worried about some of his students. Would George do a good job of the planning?

George had pointed out that he would have to give up his after-school prep time to serve on a School-Based Team. Tim said everyone did that. George knew that the entire science department had taken turns working on this committee and that it was probably his turn. But he was far too busy to listen to all of that jargon. He had a great group of twelfth-grade physics students, and he was getting them ready for the regional physics challenge. They had a wonderful chance to win this year.

Besides, even at university when he had to take that special education course for his teaching certification, he had little patience with all the allowances teachers had to make for these kids. He taught grades

11 and 12 physics and worked with the brightest kids in the school. He felt he shouldn't have to spend time on this committee. He agreed that gifted kids were also part of the special group, so why not let him work with them alone? Instead, he was stuck on this committee figuring out what to do with kids who "couldn't even read! They should be put in special classes and learn how to fix cars or something." (Tim couldn't believe that one!) Now it seems they expected things from him—he had hoped to just sit there and maybe do some mental planning for the physics challenge. That was when George showed Tim the memo.

Tim was concerned; he had a lot invested in several of those kids. Tim argued with himself. Should he speak to the principal? No, bad political move. Should he walk George through it? But when would he have time to do it right? Where did George's attitude come from? Should he take over the position from George? No, he had already done his year on the team and had been looking forward to a bit of a break. But now what?

of other cultures, and logical analysis, Gardner originally presented candidates for seven intelligences. The first two are those most valued in North America: linguistic and logical–mathematical. The others are musical, bodily-kinesthetic, spatial, interpersonal, and intrapersonal intelligence. Gardner (1999) has since added three new candidates: naturalist, spiritual, and existential intelligence. The intelligences are viewed as independent; students, therefore, are likely to be stronger in some intelligences than in others.

Gardner's theory seems particularly attractive to teachers, possibly because teachers recognize and value the different ways their learners think and express themselves (Krechevsky & Seidel, 1998). The theory also provides indicators of abilities in the various intelligences (see Info Byte 8.2). Educational applications of the theory abound, including approaches to assessment (see Chapter 11) and teaching via the different intelligences. Teachers often use Gardner's list of intelligences as a basis for planning but making an attempt to reach all students by providing a variety of different activities (see Info Byte 8.3). Gardner views intelligences as educable (Krechevsky & Seidel), a view that is compatible with the philosophy and mission of teachers.

In Chapter 7, we introduced Bronfenbrenner's (1998) ecological theory of development. One element of that theory that is relevant to this discussion is the chronosystem, or sociohistorical context in which a person develops. Gardner (1999), like Keating (1999), characterizes the present sociohistorical context as one of significant change. He argues that conceptualizing intelligence as "a range of capacities and potentials—multiple intelligences—that, both individually and

INFO BYTE 8.2

Indicators of Ability in Multiple Intelligences

- *Linguistic intelligence:* Sensitivity to language, both spoken and written; ability to learn languages; and the ability to use language to meet objectives. The following demonstrate high linguistic intelligence: lawyers, writers, poets.
- *Logical–mathematical intelligence:* The abilities to analyze problems in a logical way, execute mathematical operations, and use a scientific approach to investigate problems. Scientists and mathematicians demonstrate this form of intelligence.
- *Musical intelligence:* Sensitivity to and appreciation of musical patterns; ability to perform and compose music.
- *Bodily–kinesthetic intelligence:* The use of the body to solve problems or create products or performances. Bodily–kinesthetic intelligence is seen in athletes, dancers, actors, craftspersons, surgeons, and mechanics.
- *Spatial intelligence:* Recognition and manipulation of spatial patterns in wide space (e.g., pilots and navigators) and confined space (e.g., chess players, sculptors, architects).
- *Interpersonal intelligence:* The ability to understand the intentions, desires, and feelings of others and to work effectively with others (e.g., teachers, salespeople, actors, psychologists).
- *Intrapersonal intelligence:* Understanding of oneself (abilities, feelings, desires) and the ability to act effectively on this understanding.
- *Naturalist intelligence:* The ability to recognize and distinguish among species; the capacity to articulate relations among species.
- *Spiritual intelligence:* Interest and concern with the deep questions of existence (e.g., Who are we? Why do we exist?).
- *Existential intelligence:* "The capacity to locate oneself with respect to the furthest reaches of the cosmos . . . and the related capacity to locate oneself with respect to such existential features of the human condition as the significance of life, the meaning of death, the ultimate fate of the physical and psychological worlds, and such profound experiences as love of another person or total immersion in a work of art" (Gardner, 1999, p. 60).

Source: Based on Gardner, 1999, pp. 42–43, 48–60.

INFO BYTE 8.3

Educational Applications of the Theory of Multiple Intelligences

- Take individual differences in abilities seriously.
- Value other intelligences in addition to the linguistic and logical–mathematical intelligences that represent the primary emphases in most schools.
- Create a rich classroom environment that includes materials that "activate the different intelligences" (Gardner, 1999, p. 136) (e.g., musical instruments, a variety of art materials, science displays, math puzzles, building materials).
- Observe students as they interact with the different materials in the classroom to determine where their abilities lie.
- Be flexible and creative in offering a variety of curricular options linked to well-defined outcomes (Gardner, 1999).
- Provide opportunities for students to demonstrate their knowledge in ways that are consistent with their abilities (e.g., paint their interpretation of a short story, act out a scientific concept).
- Have an *assessment repertoire*, rather than rely on a single form of assessment (see Chapter 11 for suggestions).
- Support students in understanding their own ability profiles.

in consort, can be put to many productive uses" (p. 4) is a better match to the developmental tasks we face as a global community than a static, unidimensional notion of intelligence.

Criticisms of Multiple Intelligences

Gardner's (1993, 1999) theory of multiple intelligences is not universally accepted. Klein (1997) summarized reactions to the theory and did an extensive critique of Gardner's perspective on intelligence. The following are criticisms that have the most relevance for teachers.

- There are few systematic evaluations of the theory.
- Most things we do involve several intelligences (e.g., dance is bodily–kinesthetic and musical; conversation is linguistic and interpersonal). Pairs of intelligences may overlap or be related.
- Exceptional abilities may not be based in a specific intelligence. For example, Gardner cites skill in chess as an indicator of spatial ability. However, chess masters do not have high spatial intelligence except in the recognition of strategic board arrangements.
- It is unclear what the role of language (linguistic intelligence) is "in moving information within and among other 'intelligences'" (Klein, 1997, p. 381).
- School need not be the institution responsible for developing all the intelligences.
- Students may avoid activities in "weak" intelligences when they might learn from doing these activities.
- Students may attribute success to their "high" intelligences, leading them to interpret failure as lack of ability (see our discussion of motivation in Chapter 9).
- Not all educational applications of Gardner's view of intelligence are related to theory or are good practice (Klein, 1998).

Another Alternative to IQ

Robert Sternberg (Sternberg & Grigorenko, 2000) is another theorist who has challenged the traditional view of intelligence represented by IQ. He argues that IQ matters somewhat for life success, but that other abilities are more important (compare the arguments made by Stephen Ceci discussed earlier in this chapter and by Daniel Goleman discussed in Chapter 6 under emotional Intelligence). This is not to say that the abilities measured by intelligence tests are unimportant; rather, they are not the whole story when it comes to success in life.

Sternberg and Grigorenko (2000) argue for the importance of *successful intelligence*. The following three abilities make up their concept of successful intelligence:

1. *Analytical ability:* Analysis, evaluation, comparison, and contrast
2. *Creative ability:* Creation, invention, or discovery
3. *Practical ability:* Put into practice, apply, or use what has been learned

The ability to analyze is stressed in school, whereas creative and practical abilities may be more important in the real world (Sternberg & Grigorenko). They have identified the following as the major elements of successful intelligence:

- The set of abilities needed to attain success in a person's life, however the person defines it.
- Success is defined only in terms of a *sociocultural context*. It does not occur in the abstract, but rather with respect to standards or expectations either held personally or by others.

- A person's ability to recognize and make the most of his or her *strengths*. Almost everyone is good at something.
- A person's ability to recognize and compensate for or correct his or her *weaknesses*. No one is good at everything.
- A person's ability to *adapt to, shape*, and *select environments* by adjusting thinking or behavior to fit better into the environment in which the person is functioning or by choosing a new environment. (Sternberg & Grigorenko, 2000, p. 6)

Children's Conceptions of Intelligence

In keeping with a prominent theme of this book, that of understanding the learner's point of view, it is fitting to include information on how children understand intelligence. Knowing how our students conceive of intelligence can inform how we motivate students and promote self-confidence in their academic endeavors (Stipek & MacIver, 1989).

There is a developmental progression in children's understanding of intellectual competence. Yussen and Kane (1985) asked elementary school children in grades 1, 3, and 6 a number of questions about the meaning of "intelligent" and "smart." The developmental progression in understanding they identified is consistent with that summarized by Stipek and MacIver (1989) and with work done by one of the authors (Porath, 1997). Examples from the latter study are included to illustrate children's thinking about intelligence.

To young children in the first years of school, intelligence is undifferentiated. They see themselves as either "all smart" or "all dumb" (Harter, 1982; Stipek & MacIver, 1989); they don't take into account any differences they might have in school achievement. Moreover, young children rely on mastery standards to judge their work. "Getting it right" equates with ability, for example, "being a good reader." Good work habits and good conduct also figure in their conceptions of intelligence (Stipek & MacIver). People who work hard and behave themselves are considered intelligent. The younger children in Yussen and Kane's study identified social skills as "smartness."

By the third to sixth grades, children begin to take performance in different academic subjects into account (e.g., "drawing better; being stronger than other kids"), while work habits and behavior assume less importance. Third-graders in Porath's (1997) study also showed the beginnings of a social comparative process, found to be typical of children at this age (Stipek & MacIver, 1989) (e.g., "To be good at things that others aren't good at"). Older children in this grade range demonstrated a rudimentary understanding of a differentiated notion of intelligence (e.g., "Do good in school and in all subjects and sports, an all-around good person").

Junior high school students fully differentiate among academic subjects and recognize differences in ability and achievement in themselves and others (Stipek & MacIver, 1989; Thorkildsen, 1993) (e.g., "You can answer a lot of things. You will be a better person in life. You will be more successful; more people will be happy for you. Maybe you will graduate sooner or something.")

Intelligence and Culture

Not all cultures share North American perspectives on intelligence, which tend to emphasize cognitive achievements. Sternberg and Grigorenko (2004) found that different cultures include interpersonal intelligence, or social competence, intrapersonal intelligence, practical problem-solving, nonverbal reasoning skills, determination, mental effort, ability to adapt to new events, facilitation of harmonious social relationships, and memory for facts in their definitions of intelligence. They also emphasized that there are important *within-culture* differences. For example, Taiwanese Chinese value general ability, interpersonal competence, intrapersonal competence, intellectual self-assertion, and intellectual self-effacement, whereas Hong Kong Chinese value nonverbal reasoning, verbal reasoning, and social skills (p. 210). In the United States, Latino parents value social competence, in contrast to the cognitive skills emphasized at school where most teachers are Anglo. Parental views of intelligence informed by culture are important for teachers to consider.

Think again about the questions at the beginning of this chapter. Does your definition of intelligence differ from that of someone whose definition may be informed by cultural perspectives different from your own?

Creativity

One of the authors always relates the following story whenever the topic of creativity is introduced.

> *"I think the first time I ever really started to think about the actual definition of creativity was once when I was driving my 10-year-old son and three of his friends to a scout meeting. We picked up the last boy, Ricky, on our way to the meeting. During the drive, Ricky announced to his friends that he had forgotten to do the picture he needed to fulfill the final part of a badge on arts or crafts. I originally wasn't paying that much attention to the conversation since it was a dark, rainy night and I was concentrating on the road. To my embarrassment, the boys produced some paper and a broken crayon with which Ricky proceeded to draw a picture on his lap. I walked into the meeting with this group of boys and watched as Ricky gave his drawing, done in a dark moving car with one crayon, to his scoutmaster. The scoutmaster proceeded to praise Ricky for his work and announced how 'creative it was.' At this point I became more aware of the flexible concept of creativity."*

Certainly these boys were being given the message that anything they did was creative, even something that required very little effort. Is that what creativity truly consists of? Or do we overuse a word we are not quite able to define? And yet, at the same time, creativity is a valued commodity. We attempt to encourage it in schools, at our work, and in the community. Glover, Ronning, and Reynolds (1989) proposed that we know creativity when we encounter it but, at the same time, it is difficult to define and measure.

What Is Creativity?

Our society recognizes that many people are creative in certain areas and not in others; for example, a person may be an exceptional artist, but be fairly average in terms of physical ability in sports. This definitely ties in nicely with Gardner's (1983) theory of multiple intelligences and the idea that we tend to be stronger in some areas than in others. Runco (1987) found that gifted children tended to be seen as creative in specific domains, thereby supporting Gardner's notion of domain specificity. Creativity tends to be tied to intelligence, but IQ tests do not measure creativity (Sternberg, 1985). People who have high IQ scores are not necessarily more creative than the average person. However, to be creative requires a fairly high level of intelligence (whether it shows up on a test or not). A certain amount of knowledge in an area is necessary for creativity to occur (Keating, 1980; Runco & Nemiro, 1994). For example, rarely does an artist emerge as new and creative without extensive background knowledge of a specific art medium and/or spatial construction.

Creativity research has been conducted for over 50 years, yet creativity maintains a certain mystery. As with intelligence, there are multiple definitions of creativity, emphasizing the cognitive aspects of creativity, personality, social factors, behavioral factors, and developmental evolution (Runco & Dess, 2001; Sternberg, 2004). Does your definition of creativity include any of these factors?

Sternberg (2001) pointed out that, despite their variability, definitions of creativity have in common high-quality, novel products. There are degrees of novelty, however. Some creative work "forward increments" (Sternberg, p. 361) current ideas; other creative work truly redefines a discipline—it "redirects" or "reinitiates" a field (Sternberg, p. 361). For example, Einstein reconceptualized physics and Picasso revolutionized art.

Convergent and Divergent Thinking

A number of theorists have attempted to define creativity and by extension to measure it in some way. Guilford (1959; as cited in Cropley, 2003) incorporated two components of mental operations, *convergent* and *divergent* production, in his model of the structure of intelligence. He theorized that when information was retrieved from memory, it could involve manipulation that could produce direct answers (such as adding up a cash register tape) or it could produce a variety of ideas (such as what will I buy Mom for her birthday?).

- *Convergent thinking* tends to be more linear; it requires the person to come to a defined, identifiable point.
- *Divergent thinking* tends to be more flexible, fluid, and original, often requiring perhaps one idea to be selected as more plausible than others that are generated. Divergent thinking is more closely associated with creativity than most other characteristics (Keating, 1980).

Neither convergent thinking nor divergent thinking is more important than the other; it is more a question of *when* to apply convergent and divergent thinking to a problem. For example, one of the authors had a student who produced a résumé as part of a portfolio. This was a very artistic person who put great effort and much of her emotional self into her work. The résumé was put in a bound booklet form, with graphics and poetry. While it was an exceptional piece of work, it would not have satisfied the requirements of a résumé for an employer. A résumé, by definition, is a succinct listing of qualifications and strengths; it is not a place where creativity is valued. On the other hand, the portfolio itself exemplified her interpretation of the world as she conveyed a perspective on the topic that was unique and insightful.

In classrooms, if we think teaching creativity is an important goal, then we should also include some direction for students as to *when* divergent thinking is appropriate. This suggestion is not meant to limit divergent thinking, but rather to make students aware of the variety of mental operations at their disposal. This awareness of matching tasks to mental operations or thinking ties in nicely with the concept of metacognition. Students need to be exposed to opportunities to select and practice different forms of thinking skills. Divergent thinking is only one type, but it is not always valued in education. For many teachers and students, getting the right answer is what school is all about. Even when students are given opportunities to generate their own ideas, teachers often put tight limits on the boundaries of the lesson, such as the teacher who would only accept certain mathematical proofs, even though a student could generate valid alternative proofs (these were marked as wrong). This teaches students that divergent thinking is not appropriate for school, when in fact it forms the basis for creative thought.

Can We All Be Creative? Cultural and Personal Creativity

Often people use the term *creative* as synonymous with *gifted*. This leads us into a discussion of what we mean by gifted or talented. Certainly, creativity is one of a group of criteria often used to identify gifted students, along with higher than average intellectual ability. But what about those individuals who make up the majority of the population? Can they be creative? Renzulli (1973) observed that creativity is common in small children, but rare in adults. What happens? Theorists have offered a number of ideas, but generally it appears to be the need we have in society for conformity. This influence of conformity leads to sayings like "think outside the box" or "expand your horizons."

Cultural Creativity   While most people can be and are creative in their personal life, there is often a difference when it comes to being creative on a community level. This is what Gowan (1981) termed the difference between personal creativity and cultural creativity. It is cultural creativity that provides the world with new ideas and discoveries (Photo 8.4). In an article on Linus Pauling, a Nobel Prize winner in chemistry, Nakamura and Csikszentmihalyi (2001) discuss the necessity for the context within which innovations are created to be accepting of these changes. This cultural creativity requires the field to be willing to accept and be changed by new ideas. Kuhn (1970) discussed this in depth

PHOTO 8.4

Bill Gates's ideas changed the way we use computers.

INFO BYTE 8.4

Wisdom

One natural extension of the discussion on intelligence and creativity is this question: What is *wisdom?* Throughout time, people have valued those individuals who were considered *wise*. Today there is considerable debate over the characteristics of a "wise person" and even difficulty defining the word *wisdom*. It seems to be agreed that, while a person needs a certain level of intelligence to be wise, there is no need to have a very high IQ. Wisdom is often explained or defined in terms of characteristics an individual possesses, beyond that of intelligence. In *Wisdom: Its Nature, Origins, and Development,* edited by Sternberg (1990), a number of characteristics are identified, reflecting several theorists' notions of wisdom. Individuals are rich in knowledge; culturally attuned; able to have exceptional insights into human development and life matters; good at planning and management; virtuous; able to grasp the breadth and depth of knowledge; able to redefine the limits of change; reflective; exceptional in their ability to formulate judgments; preoccupied with questions rather than answers; exceptional in their understanding; exceptional in their communication skills; and generally competent. As you can see, even the theorists have difficulty defining and explaining this particular construct. If you were to try to describe a *wise teacher,* what characteristics, or attributes, would you look for?

when he explained how paradigms in science shift with the introduction of new knowledge. For example, at one time scientists believed the continents on Earth were static. Not until new knowledge and proof of the drifting of the continents was introduced did they began to "see" the results of the drifting. Now entire theories of mountain building and earthquake activity are based on this knowledge.

Sternberg (2001) carefully points out the differences between intelligence, creativity, and wisdom. Wisdom consists of a balance between intelligence and creativity. Info Byte 8.4 is introduced here to make you aware that intelligence, creativity, and wisdom are all interconnected.

Personal Creativity   In many respects, we perhaps are limiting ourselves if we develop a definition limited to cultural creativity. Once we expand the concept of creativity to include personal creativity, we start to see evidence of it in a number of places. This means the average person has an aspect of his or her nature that encompasses creativity; it is not limited to people with high IQs.

Interestingly, people find outlets for their creative nature if it is not provided them at school or work. Outlets come under headings like hobbies and arts or crafts. When asked, many will explain that they derive pleasure in making something that appeals to some inner drive. Milgram and Hong (1993) found in an 18-year longitudinal study that out-of-school activities were additional predictors, along with intelligence and school grades, of adult life accomplishments. These leisure activities often provide opportunities for creative thinking and performance that may not be available elsewhere. There is an emotional quality to the creative endeavor that taps into the affective, sensing, and cognitive nature of humans. Thus some aspects of creativity are integral components of what it means to be human. In 1985, Robert Sternberg introduced the idea of creativity as an aspect of intelligence that is necessary for humans to interact with and adapt to their environment. Since then he has encouraged teachers to try to incorporate opportunities for students to learn to utilize their naturally occurring creative ability (Sternberg & Lubart, 1991).

Assessing Creativity: The Torrance Test

Using Guilford's (1959) model of intelligence, Torrance (1966, 1974) developed tests based on fluency, flexibility, and originality to try to determine creative ability. The Torrance Test has been used for a number of years and has been part of numerous screening programs for school districts who have Gifted or Challenge Programs. Other tests are now available, but the Torrance Test is perhaps the best known by teachers. The test taps into a person's thinking in terms of *flexibility, fluency,* and *originality,* or as Guilford's model theorizes, divergent thinking.

As with many constructs we encounter in education, creativity is very hard to define. We know when we encounter it, but have difficulties delineating the boundaries of what it is and is not. Going back to the story about Ricky and the drawing, was that a creative piece of art? It really wasn't. How could the scout-master have identified this as the thrown-together drawing that it was? Perhaps he could have identified it by the wrinkled paper or the way it was presented to him. Since most creative endeavors are the result of a holistic combination of human functions, such as intellect, emotions, perceptions, and skills, there is an ownership and pride that goes along with the product. If the scoutmaster was in doubt, he could have asked about the drawing.

Ownership and pride in creativity usually show themselves in how the individual speaks of his or her product. It would have been fairly evident in this instance that this drawing was not the "creative work" that was expected for the badge. It may not be as obvious in other circumstances so teachers should be cautious.

Creativity is such a personal thing that constructive criticism, real or perceived, is often deeply felt. The student who did her résumé in booklet form is an example. When the discussion got around to the need for a résumé to be in a different format, the student had trouble not crying. It was a very difficult conversation. The discussion needed to strike a balance between praise for her divergent approach to a mundane task and the need for conformity (convergent thinking) in some situations.

Teaching Creativity

As mentioned above, conformity tends to stifle creativity. However, we need conformity, especially if we are trying to deal with large numbers of people. Schools in particular need to have set rules and procedures; otherwise there would be general chaos. But our society values creativity. It allows human abilities to progress, resulting in a better life-style with each successive generation. Thus, we need a balance between conformity and creativity. In Problem-Based Scenario 8.4, an elementary teacher grapples with finding this balance.

Brainstorming   Too often schools overlook creativity as an extension of cognition, often restricting creative activity to brainstorming. While this is a valid divergent thinking activity, many teachers fail to realize there are rules for brainstorming. For example, all ideas must be recorded regardless of validity, correctness, or plausibility. When students do not respond, the technique is often abandoned, or schools import a specialized program to teach creativity.

Numerous curricula are available for teaching brainstorming and creativity. When schools use these curricula, they do not see creativity as part of the overall intellect of the individual, but relegate it to an isolated place in the timetable (Photo 8.5). It should be a regular component of teaching, rather than an add-on to the curriculum. It should be an expected part of a student's development. Teachers have no problem understanding learning styles, so there should be little problem in understanding preferences for styles in creativity. Not everyone will be good at drawing, or creative writing, or mechanical tasks. Teachers need to adapt to the range of strengths in creative ability in the same way that they adapt to differences in intellectual ability or learning styles. But, in the end, all

Flexibility: The ability to adapt to a situation.

Fluency: The ability to understand abstract and novel relationships.

Originality: The ability to produce something that is new or that is not copied.

Problem-Based Scenario 8.4

Student: *Josh*

Teacher: *Greg*

Greg really felt like he was experiencing some sort of crisis. In the course of a week, he'd received the phone call from Mrs. Fredericks about his choice of literature. Now he anticipated another call from an upset parent. That day over the noon hour the teacher responsible for lunch supervision had summoned Greg out of the staff room. Josh had hung crepe paper and fabric all over the windows of his class and now was perched on a ladder hanging paper streamers from the ceiling. Had Mr. Norris given permission for this? Josh claimed he had, but the supervisor was skeptical. Could Greg please just come and check out the situation?

Josh was the class clown and mostly appreciated for his comments and actions by Greg and the rest of the children. He occasionally crossed the line, but seemed to understand when it was explained to him that his humor wasn't always appreciated in ways he might have anticipated. Josh could be counted on to question the directions for every assignment. He always had an alternative in mind, and Greg had to admit that the alternatives were often quite good. Josh doodled on everything, usually creating set designs and novel stage curtains. He also organized class plays, and the other children responded well to

these projects. Greg enjoyed having Josh in his class. He liked his unique perspective on things.

Greg arrived at the classroom to find it transformed into a swirl of color, Josh teetering on the top of the ladder as he tried to accomplish the finishing touches. "What on earth, Josh?" Greg blurted out.

"Oh, Mr. Norris, I just had to get this ready. We have a big production to surprise you with this afternoon."

"But Josh. You really should have checked this with me first, especially since you're using a ladder. There's a safety concern there. Also, we have a guest speaker this afternoon. It's on your planner. Now, please come down and put the ladder away."

Josh's face fell. As he came down the ladder, Greg assured him that they would discuss when the production could be done. Josh bolted through the door without replying and wasn't there when class resumed for the afternoon. Greg asked the school secretary, Louise, to call his parents. After she completed the call, Louise came to Greg's classroom to tell him that Josh's mother was on her way home from her office to comfort Josh. She would be in after school to discuss the situation with him. Louise commented on how angry she sounded.

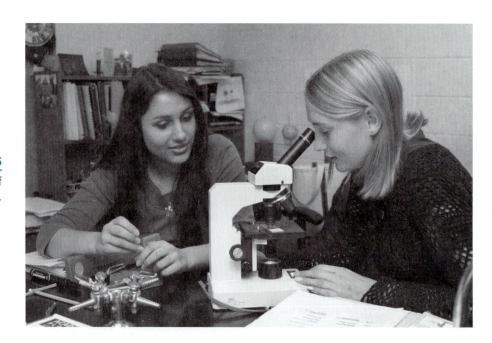

PHOTO 8.5

Creativity should be part of instruction in all subjects.

students should be encouraged and challenged to respond creatively (Simplicio, 2000). In Problem-Based Scenario 8.5, a high school teacher considers just how he will encourage creativity in his classroom.

Keating's (1980) view of creativity is still relevant today, especially because it has direct implications for education. Keating described four aspects of creativity:

1. *Content mastery:* Knowledge and skills are needed before one can be creative.
2. *Divergent thinking:* Many ideas or possible solutions to a problem are generated.
3. *Critical thinking:* Ideas generated must be analyzed critically to determine which are most useful and/or important.
4. *Effective communication:* Ideas that redirect a field must be clearly communicated to be influential. Students need to learn that communication of ideas is just as important as generating and evaluating them. Each discipline has conventions for communication (e.g., scientific papers, art exhibits, literary publications); students can learn to communicate their ideas in appropriate ways.

Creativity: Natural or Learned? Given all the above information, we should ask this question: Are children naturally creative? An interesting article by Feldman (1991) discounts natural childhood creativity by emphasizing the qualities necessary for true creativity to emerge (what we have referred to as cultural creativity). These elements, as previously discussed, include the following:

- Thorough mastery of an existing body of knowledge
- Mastery of appropriate technologies or techniques
- Valued contribution to the field

Problem-Based Scenario 8.5

Teacher: David

In general, for a Professional Day, it went fairly well. David had particularly liked the workshop on students who are gifted and talented presented by a professor from the local university. He thought the overall presentation was practical, but questioned whether many of the ideas could be implemented in his classroom. It was one thing to talk about challenging these students, but it was another thing altogether to try to put some of the ideas into practice with a class of 28 to 32 students.

In the past, David had given extra projects and variations on assignments. It was pretty hard in a ninth-grade science class to encourage students to be creative. He had even tried brainstorming as the professor suggested, but often only small groups of students responded. From the workshop he knew that brainstorming was supposed to be fun. What usually started off as an exercise in divergent thinking often ended up in what David called "extreme teenage foolishness." Maybe he was doing something wrong.

At the same time he knew quite a few students who had hidden "talents" but who would never be considered for the school's Challenge Program. As he thought about it, he realized that there were a number of students in his classes who really fell into the category of creative. He knew this, not from his class, but rather when they talked to him during hallway duty or in the cafeteria. Even some of the students who were barely passing had interesting hobbies and activities outside school.

So, if they could be creative outside class, how could he get them to be creative in his class? And, if he wanted to start encouraging creativity, should he give grades for it? How would you do that? Maybe instead of targeting the higher-ability students he needed to think about how he could include an entire class. This would make creativity part of his regular class, rather than an add-on for a few kids, making it much easier. But how?

Feldman further states that we identify creativity in a child when he or she is open to experience and also observes and experiences the world without preconceived ideas. This openness is foundational to adult creativity and needs to be nurtured.

If teachers adhere to strict definitions of creativity, they will fail to help students gain the tools for solving problems creatively. Why bother with teaching or encouraging creative problem-solving strategies if children cannot be creative? We need to recognize the limitations of a strict definition of creativity while acknowledging the importance of encouraging creative learning strategies in our students. Our knowledge of Piaget's cognitive theory encourages teachers to not only teach strategies, but also to provide opportunities that challenge children's thinking for cognitive growth to occur. This applies to creative problem solving too. If we don't challenge students to think creatively or provide some direction in terms of strategies, we leave it to chance that they develop into creative adults.

Creative Problem Solving

Almost all curricular guides have as a goal fostering students' ability to solve problems. This goal is especially important given our present technological capabilities. Students who solve problems creatively can do the following (Fatt, 2000):

- Think critically
- Judge the relevance of information
- Detect bias
- Generate plausible alternatives
- Predict outcomes

Thus, we are trying to teach students not merely to apply an algorithm or set rule to all problems, but rather to identify those times when several plausible solutions to a problem should be generated (Photo 8.6). Some topics do need algorithms, such as finding the area of a surface. These are considered structured problems. Here we refer to the ill-structured problems that require the student to gather knowledge, generate ideas, and test hypotheses.

Runco and Nemiro (1994) caution against concentrating on teaching divergent thinking activities, such as brainstorming. They point out that creativity is much more than just generating a list of solutions; it requires thought and reflection as well. From our discussion above it is evident that the creative aspect to

PHOTO 8.6

Science fair projects can offer opportunities for students to sort through and solve messy, real-world problems.

solving any problem is fairly complex. As a teacher, what could you incorporate into your classes that would encourage and stimulate creative thinking? To begin with, Runco and Nemiro suggest emphasizing the aspect of *problem finding*.

Too often teachers present problems in fairly clear terms. We organize the problem in a way that allows students to head in a certain direction for solutions. But in the real world, problems are generally messy, without clear direction and often only partially revealed. When students are challenged to sort through a problem, generate questions, identify knowledge gaps, list components of the problem that are given and missing, and design a solution strategy, they start to learn how to discover and solve problems. These are the skills that open the way for creativity. Encouraging risk taking, allowing a variety of solutions to a problem where appropriate, and providing rewards for answers that are different and yet appropriate or correct are other ways to support creative problem solving (Simplicio, 2000; Sternberg & Lubart, 1991).

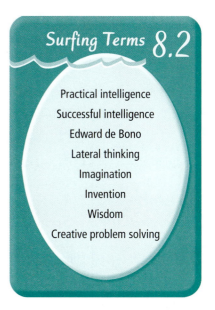

Surfing Terms 8.2

Practical intelligence
Successful intelligence
Edward de Bono
Lateral thinking
Imagination
Invention
Wisdom
Creative problem solving

Summary

In this chapter, you learned about different views of intelligence and the educational implications of different perspectives on intelligent behavior. It is important to make explicit your own understanding of intelligence. It also is important to understand how children conceive of intelligence. We also discussed definitions of creativity, examined different components of creative behavior, and related both to classroom practice. Here, too, it is important to be aware of how you understand creativity and compare your understanding to that of different theorists.

- The definition of intelligence is complex, encompassing a number of valued human characteristics as they relate to culture and society.
- An understanding of intelligence as it relates to students and academic activities is necessary to be an effective teacher. It will have direct impact on students in terms of who they are as individuals, how they fit into the community, and their talents as scholars.
- Creativity is much more than divergent thinking. Teachers need to know about creativity, value it in children, encourage risk taking, make creative thinking skills an integral part of the curriculum, and provide appropriate rewards.

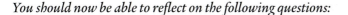

A Metacognitive Challenge

You should now be able to reflect on the following questions:

- How does my understanding and definition of intelligence compare to that of the cognitive theorists?

- What does my understanding of intelligence mean for me as a teacher and my planning?

- What would I say to a parent who asks about IQ and any testing my school district does for intelligence and creativity?

- How can I plan and implement a curriculum that enhances and rewards creativity?

Artifacts for Problem-Based Scenarios

FIGURE 8.3 ■ Artifact for Problem-Based Scenario 8.1

CONFIDENTIAL PSYCHOEDUCATIONAL REPORT

Lynn McKay, Ph.D.
Registered Psychologist

MacDonald Building
North Ashford, Ontario

Personal information

NAME:	Sally Johnson
BIRTH DATE:	April 2, 1989
AGE:	13 years, 3 months
GRADE:	7 (completed, going into 8)
PARENT(S):	Laura and Ted Johnson
ADDRESS:	13 Montclair Blvd., North Ashford, ON
HOME PHONE:	555-7888
ASSESSMENT DATES:	July 4 and 6, 2002

Background information

Sally's mother described her as having had a very healthy childhood. She reached all developmental milestones at age-appropriate times, and no behavioral problems were reported. Sally is an only child who has a good relationship with her parents. She demonstrates exceptional ability in writing as well as in reading. She also enjoys music, art, collecting stamps and hockey cards, and exploring books. Sally has a very good sense of humor and is good at sports. She always tries to do her best when working on projects and is known to redo her work until it meets her high expectations, often working until 1 or 2 in the morning.

Sally completed grade 7 in her neighborhood school and received awards for student excellence in grades 5, 6, and 7. Mr. and Mrs. Johnson would like Sally to work on skills and techniques to enhance her writing ability. Away from school, Sally takes piano lessons, theory lessons, and swimming. She has numerous friends of both genders at school as well as outside of school. She has maintained a small number of very close school friends since kindergarten. Mrs. Johnson described Sally as having average self-confidence and as maintaining high personal standards in her schoolwork.

Sally presented as a very personable young woman. She approached each assessment session with enthusiasm. She expressed the wish to know more about her abilities so that she can think about whether her goal of being a doctor is realistic. She wanted to know about admissions to medical school and whether there were volunteer opportunities in hospitals.

FIGURE 8.3 ■ **Artifact for Problem-Based Scenario 8.1 (continued)**

Tests Given
Wechsler Intelligence Scale for Children Third Edition (WISC-III)

This test of general cognitive ability compares children's performance over a broad variety of tasks with the performance of other children their age. The WISC-III, like other IQ tests, measures only a portion of the competencies involved in human intelligence. The results of IQ tests are best seen as predicting current performance in school and reflecting the degree to which children have mastered the middle-class symbols and values. This is useful, but it is also limited. IQ tests do not measure innate genetic capacity and scores are not fixed. Some persons do exhibit significant increases or decreases in the measured IQ.

Performance on the WISC-III is interpreted in terms of Full Scale, Verbal Scale, and Performance Scale scores. The Full Scale IQ is a summary score reflecting overall test performance and is usually considered to be the best measure of cognitive ability, general intelligence, scholastic aptitude, and readiness to master a school curriculum. Children's Full Scale IQ may be affected by their motivation, interests, cultural opportunities, natural endowment, neurological integrity, attention span, ability to process verbal information (particularly on the verbal subtests), ability to process visual information (particularly on the performance subtests), and conditions under which testing occurs. The Verbal Scale IQ is a measure of verbal comprehension that includes the application of verbal skills and information to the solution of new problems, ability to process verbal information, and ability to think with words. The Performance Scale IQ is a measure of perceptual organization that includes the ability to think in visual images and to manipulate these visual images with fluency and relative speed, to reason without the use of words (in some cases), and to interpret visual material quickly. The average range for general scores is 90 to 109.

General Score	Interval	Percentile*	Classification
Verbal IQ	121–134	97	Superior
Performance IQ	107–123	87	High Average
Full Scale IQ	119–131	96	Superior

*A percentile score indicates that the examinee's score is equivalent to or superior to the given percentage of the population of individuals of that age.

Sally obtained a Verbal IQ of 129, a Performance IQ of 117, and a Full Scale IQ of 126. Her Verbal Comprehension at the 96th percentile is better developed than her Perceptual Organization skills at the 73rd percentile. The difference may be a result of various factors, such as learning style, preference in modes of expression, or general interest in the task. The chances that the range of scores described in the intervals above includes her true IQ are about 95 out of 100.

FIGURE 8.3 ■ **Artifact for Problem-Based Scenario 8.1 (continued)**

Observations of Performance

Sally's overall performance as indicated by the Full Scale IQ score falls into the superior range. This level of performance is attained by only 4% percent of the population.

Sally's performance in the verbal domain falls into the superior range. In the performance domain, Sally's score is in the high average range. Performance on this set of tasks may be influenced by the degree of experience with similar tasks. Sally met the session with confidence and enthusiasm. It was not until she realized that she was being timed for selected subtests that she appeared a little uneasy. Upon being encouraged to perform her very best and ignore the fact that she was being timed, she paid little attention, if any, to the timing factor. Good rapport was established and, given the optimal conditions under which the WISC-III was administered, it is believed that the data from this intellectual assessment are valid.

WOODCOCK-JOHNSON PSYCHO-EDUCATIONAL BATTERY - REVISED (WJ-R): TESTS OF ACHIEVEMENT - STANDARD BATTERY

This battery of individually administered academic achievement tests measures various aspects of scholastic achievement in basic academic skills, reading, mathematics, written language, and general knowledge in the area of Sciences, Social Studies, and Humanities. Test items on this measure do not necessarily measure achievement within any specific school curriculum, but rather reflect more general academic achievement and development of skills across the assessed domains.

Individual performance on the battery of achievement tests is interpreted in terms of each of five achievement cluster scores. The Broad Reading score reflects the ability to identify letters and words and to use vocabulary and comprehension skills. This is a broad measure of reading achievement, including performance of both oral reading and passage comprehension tasks. The Broad Mathematics score reflects performance in mathematical calculation and the analysis and solution of practical mathematical problems. The Broad Written Language score indicates achievement in written language, including both single-word responses and production of sentences embedded in context. This cluster score reflects achievement in the application of skills in spelling, punctuation, capitalization, and word usage, as well as the overall quality of expression in written form.

The Broad Knowledge cluster score provides a measure of the extent to which the child has achieved a general knowledge of concepts and vocabulary in various areas of sciences, social studies, and art, music, and literature. The Skills cluster score is an index of general achievement in prerequisite academic skills, including language and mathematics performance. Achievement cluster scores in the range of 90 to 110 are representative of average performance.

FIGURE 8.3 ■ Artifact for Problem-Based Scenario 8.1 (continued)

Achievement Cluster	Cluster Score	Percentile
Broad Reading	111	77
Letter–Word Identification	108	71
Passage Comprehension	111	77
Broad Mathematics	134	99
Calculation	127	96
Applied Problems	127	96
Broad Written Language	116	86
Dictation	109	72
Writing Samples	123	93
Broad Knowledge	116	86
Science	111	76
Social Studies	109	72
Humanities	122	93
Skills	116	86

Sally's test results indicate a very academically competent young woman. In particular, her abilities in mathematics, creative writing, and humanities are exceptional, and she will need to be challenged in these areas of the curriculum.

Lynne McKay Ph.D.

Lynne McKay, Ph.D., R. Psych.

FIGURE 8.4 ■ **Artifact for Problem-Based Scenario 8.2**

DR. FRANK LEFKOWITZ,
REGISTERED PSYCHOLOGIST
612-3976 SECOND STREET
PRINCEVILLE, ON
519-555-1163

DATE:	August 11, 2001
NAME:	Jessica McCoy
BIRTH DATE:	July 26, 1993
AGE:	8 years
GRADE:	Beginning Grade 2
PARENT(S):	Bonnie and Ron McCoy
ADDRESS:	1125 Maple Street, Princeville, ON M64 8N8
HOME PHONE:	519-555-7678
ASSESSMENT DATES:	July 31 and August 2, 2001

BACKGROUND

Jessica is the older of two children; she has a 4-year-old brother. Her mother is a school teacher and her father is a research scientist. Both parents have graduate degrees. Her mother described Jessica as having a close relationship with her family.

Jessica's health has always been good. She began to speak at 7 months, and her mother described her as showing a fondness for long, difficult words. Gross motor skills developed at an average rate, according to Mrs. McCoy, and fine motor skills early. Jessica began to read at age 3; by 4 she was reading juvenile paperbacks. At age 4 1/2, she began writing chapter stories. Jessica has an excellent memory, a keen sense of humor, and an interest in art. She learns very quickly.

Jessica takes piano, swimming, and gymnastics lessons. She reported that she enjoys playing with her friends, doing crafts with her mother, and sitting and talking with her family.

Jessica was in a regular grade 1 classroom last year and she found the work very easy. Mr. and Mrs. McCoy requested an assessment to inform educational planning. Their concern is that Jessica be sufficiently challenged in school.

FIGURE 8.4 ■ Artifact for Problem-Based Scenario 8.2 (continued)

TESTS ADMINISTERED
WECHSLER INTELLIGENCE SCALE FOR CHILDREN - THIRD EDITION
(WISC-III)

Performance on the WISC-III is interpreted in terms of Full Scale, Verbal Scale, and Performance Scale scores. The Full Scale IQ is a summary score reflecting overall test performance and is usually considered to be the best measure of cognitive ability, general intelligence, scholastic aptitude, and readiness to master a school curriculum. The Verbal Scale provides information about a child's ability to process and reason with language, to attend to language-based problems, and to learn and remember verbal information. The Performance Scale provides information about a child's ability to process visual–spatial material, to plan and organize, to attend to problems that involve visual–spatial material, and to learn and remember nonverbal information. Spatial abilities are important in mathematics, science, and the arts. The Full Scale provides information about a child's general intellectual ability, aptitude to learn, and ability to achieve in school. There is a strong relationship between Full Scale IQ and school achievement.

On the WISC-III, the average range for general scores is 90 to 109.

GENERAL SCORE	SCORE INTERVAL	PERCENTILE*	CLASSIFICATION
Verbal IQ	133 – 145	99.7	Very superior
Performance IQ	113 – 129	94	Superior

Jessica obtained a verbal IQ of 141 and a performance IQ of 123. Because the difference between the two scores is statistically significant, a full scale IQ is not reported. The chances that the range of scores described in the intervals above include Jessica's true IQ are about 95 out of 100.

Observations of Performance

Jessica's overall verbal performance as indicated by the Verbal IQ score falls into the very superior range. This level of performance is attained by only a fraction of 1% of the population. In the performance domain, Jessica's scores fall into the superior range. This level of performance is achieved by only 6% of the population. Performance on this set of tasks may be influenced by the degree of experience with similar tasks.

Jessica worked well throughout the testing and was enthusiastic about beginning new tasks. She often expressed the desire to do more challenging items; however, once items became difficult, she often would not persevere with the task.

The results of this intellectual assessment appear to be valid.

FIGURE 8.4 ■ Artifact for Problem-Based Scenario 8.2 (continued)

WOODCOCK-JOHNSON PSYCHO-EDUCATIONAL BATTERY - REVISED (WJ-R): TESTS OF ACHIEVEMENT - STANDARD BATTERY

Performance on this battery of achievement tests is interpreted in terms of each of five achievement cluster scores. The Broad Reading score reflects ability to identify letters and words and use of vocabulary and comprehension skills. This is a broad measure of reading achievement, including performance of both oral reading and passage comprehension tasks. The Broad Mathematics score reflects performance in mathematical calculation and the analysis and solution of practical mathematical problems. The Broad Written Language score indicates achievement in written language, including both single-word responses and production of sentences embedded in context. This cluster score reflects achievement in the application of skills in spelling, punctuation, capitalization, and word usage, as well as overall quality of expression in written form. The Broad Knowledge cluster score provides a measure of the extent to which the child has achieved a general knowledge of concepts and vocabulary in various areas of sciences, social studies, and art, music, and literature. The Skills cluster score is an index of general achievement in prerequisite academic skills including language and mathematics performance. Achievement cluster scores in the range of 90 to 110 are representative of average performance. Percentile scores for each academic cluster are also reported. Percentile scores can provide a means to compare the child's performance with the performance of other children of the same age who have completed this battery. A percentile score represents the percent of the population who achieved at the same or lower level of performance on this cluster of academic skills. For example, a percentile score of 95 for a cluster indicates that the child's performance is most like the top 5% of children of the same age who completed this cluster in the battery of tests. This would be a superior level of performance in this area of academic achievement.

FIGURE 8.4 ■ Artifact for Problem-Based Scenario 8.2 (continued)

The following table presents the results of the current administration of the WJ-R Standard Achievement Battery:

Achievement Cluster	Score	Percentile
Broad Reading	152	99.9
Letter–Word Identification	153	99.9
Passage Comprehension	149	99.9
Broad Mathematics	140	99.6
Calculation	133	99
Applied problems	144	99.9
Broad Written Language	133	99
Dictation	146	99.9
Writing Samples	124	95
Broad Knowledge	148	99.9
Science	163	99.9
Social Studies	151	99.9
Humanities	144	99.8
Skills*	153	99.9

*(This comprises letter-word identification, calculation, and dictation.)

Jessica's performance on this battery of academic achievement tests was uniformly very superior. Her scores in all the achievement clusters are in the top 1% of children her age. Jessica demonstrated consistently strong performance across the skills and reasoning components of the tests. On the Writing Samples subtest, Jessica lost some credit on higher items because she did not respond in complete sentences. Her responses, however, demonstrated sophisticated language use.

SUMMARY

Jessica shows exceptional potential and achievement. Her abilities will require appropriate curricular matches in all subject areas to ensure that she is sufficiently challenged. As evidenced during the assessment sessions, she is very interested in her learning and is highly curious. She desires challenge; however, she may need support and guidance in the initial stages of learning new things. This is especially important in the primary grades as children learn the skills of independent problem solving and gain confidence in their own judgments.

Frank Lefkowitz, Ph.D., R. Psych.

FIGURE 8.5 ▨ **Artifact for Problem-Based Scenario 8.3**

COUNSELING DEPARTMENT MEMO

TO: George Sherman
FROM: Lana Drury, Head of Learning Assistance
RE: SBT Meeting in Room 24243
TIME: Tuesday, September 17, 2002, 3:45 to 5:30 pm

I'm including the names of 4 students we hope to plan for during this meeting. The files are available in the Main Office; ask Julie or Martha for them. Please read them there. DO NOT REMOVE THEM FROM THE OFFICE. Please also note the limited time we have for this planning. Make sure you come totally prepared. If we can work through these students and keep to a reasonable schedule, we will be able to have all of them done in a few weeks. I'll get the names of the next 4 students to you in time for the Thursday meeting.

Students:

Howard Walters (newly identified)

Ellen Steeves

Larry Ng

Marc Pantini

Understanding Our Learners: Motivation

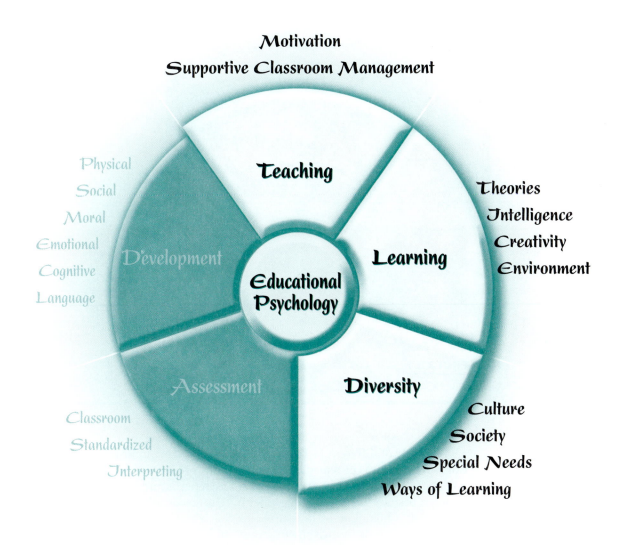

Motivation

Supportive Classroom Management

Teaching

Theories
Intelligence
Creativity
Environment

Physical
Social
Moral
Emotional
Cognitive
Language

Development

Learning

Educational
Psychology

Assessment

Diversity

Classroom
Standardized
Interpreting

Culture
Society
Special Needs
Ways of Learning

In this chapter we introduce you to theories of motivation and their educational implications. Like the other concepts discussed in this book, children and adolescents have certain personal characteristics that influence their motivation to learn. We can attribute their willingness to take risks and their excitement about challenges, in part, to their nature. Home and school environments also play a part in how motivated students are (Photo 9.1). In this chapter, we introduce you to some of the key concepts of motivation. We follow this with a discussion in Chapter 10 of the sort of environment that energizes a student's motivation to learn.

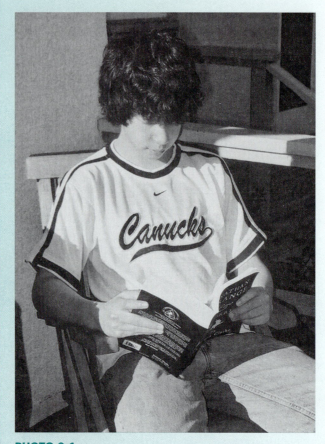

PHOTO 9.1
Interest motivates learning.

A number of different factors are relevant to understanding student motivation. An overview is provided in Table 9.1.

Understanding who we are, our learning strengths and weaknesses, and how we learn best are actually higher-order human needs. Abraham Maslow (1970) articulated a hierarchy of human needs that emphasized that only when our basic human needs (nourishment, safety, and love) are met can we develop the sort of self-understanding discussed in this chapter. Think of the following list as a triangle with physiological needs at its base. You may teach children whose basic human needs are not met. Children who come to school hungry and tired, are homeless, or do not experience a stable home environment may find it very hard to think about their learning and their own development. They need considerable support in achieving a level of safety and belongingness before they can fully develop as learners.

- *Self-actualization:* becoming all one can be (self-fulfillment)
- *Esteem:* self-esteem and positive recognition by others
- *Love and belongingness*
- *Safety*
- *Physiological:* water, food, air, sleep

TABLE 9.1

Influences on Motivation

Personal	Environmental
Personal needs	School environment
Identity	Classroom environment
Self-concept	Degree of match between learner and environment
Self-esteem	
Gender	Learning goals (performance; mastery)
Self-efficacy	Teachers' theories of intelligence
Attributions for success or failure	Rewards
Self-regulation	
Theory of intelligence	
Enjoyment of learning	

Components of Motivation

If we recall Erikson's Stages of Man Theory and Marcia's contemporary interpretation of Erikson (Chapters 6 and 7), we can start to see where the knowledge of who we are begins to take shape. As we encounter new situations and experience the world, we build a knowledge base about who we are in relation to the events we experience. We soon know whether we are competent at a task by our success when we attempt it or by others' reactions to our efforts. Building on that understanding, we develop a *self-concept,* an understanding of our strengths and weaknesses.

The reactions of others provide us with a judgment on which to base our *self-worth.* Often the terms *self-concept* and *self-worth* are used interchangeably since they do overlap (Marsh & Craven, 1997). There are differences, however. Self-*concept* is associated with beliefs about oneself (I'm good at math; I swim well; I don't write very well), while *self-worth* is an affective or emotional reference (I'm a good person) (as discussed in Chapter 6). See Info Byte 9.1 for definitions of different "self" terms.

Learners' Self-Images: Understanding What It Means to Learn

In Chapter 6, we discussed how children's perceptions of themselves develop from a simple, concrete understanding to a differentiated and abstract concept. In Chapter 8, we presented a complementary discussion of children's conceptions of intelligence. Taken together, these discussions help us understand children's images of themselves as learners.

The Developing Sense of Self

When they enter school, children have a sense of their academic competence, describing it in terms such as "good at numbers" (Harter & Pike, 1984). They express their images of themselves as learners as generic judgments, such as "all smart" or "all dumb" (Harter, 1982; Stipek & MacIver, 1989).

INFO BYTE *9.1*

DEFINITIONS OF "SELF" TERMS

Self-esteem: A student's *personal judgment and belief about his or her general value and worth*. What are my strengths and weaknesses? Am I a worthwhile or valuable person in a specific situation (e.g., as a baseball outfielder, as an actor in a school play, as an entrant in a math competition)? Similar to self-worth.

Self-worth: A student's *personal belief about his or her ability to deal with his or her environment*. People's reactions to another person's strengths and weaknesses send specific messages about his or her ability. For example, one author overheard a father telling his 8-year-old son after a hockey game, "You rot as a goalie." Granted, while the child wasn't particularly good as a goalie, the person giving the evaluation and the words chosen conveyed considerable meaning to the child. The child now knows about his lack of ability to play goal; he is not a good goalie.

Self-concept: A student's *conceptions of himself or herself in various areas*. Self-concept is developed as the result of experience. Am I a good student, artist, friend, and so on? Am I physically attractive, athletic, strong? Am I reliable, moody, intelligent)?

Self-efficacy: A student's *personal belief in his or her own capability to attain certain goals*. By knowing one's own strengths and weaknesses, a person can judge the probability of achieving certain goals. For example, if one has limited talent as an artist and needs a poster made for an event, he or she would ask someone who has far better creative talents to make the poster.

By the time they reach the third grade, children are beginning to understand that their abilities are differentiated (e.g., good reader; not so good at math), and they begin to compare themselves to others. A similar progression can be seen in children's understanding of what learning means (see Info Byte 9.2).

INFO BYTE *9.2*

CHILDREN'S CONCEPTIONS OF LEARNING

Gillian Bickerton (1994) asked children what learning means and what happens when they learn. She found that a child's understanding of the meaning of learning develops in the following manner:

- Four-year-olds think of learning as behavioral events (e.g., playing, going to school, building a tower). They also think of learning as involving the presence of a learning agent, such as Mom or Dad.
- Six-year-olds define learning as a relationship between a *behavioral event* and an *internal state*. For example, "If I *do good work*, I get *happy*." "Sometimes learning gets me frustrated because I make so many mistakes" (Bickerton, 1994, pp. 6–7).
- Eight-year-olds are able to relate a *behavioral event* to two *internal states* when defining learning. "You get *better* at it if *you try your hardest*" (Bickerton, p. 7).
- Ten-year-olds add a personal element to their definitions of learning. "*To me*, learning means knowing how to do something without having any problems doing it (Bickerton, p. 7).
- Twelve-year-olds' responses are more psychological in nature, recognizing *states of mind* as important in learning. "Learning is developing a smarter mind." "Learning is knowing and understanding things you didn't know before" (Bickerton, p. 8).

PHOTO 9.2
Adolescents develop particular talents and confidence.

Adolescence

By the time a student reaches adolescence, his or her experiences have become more complex than they were in childhood. The student's personal understanding of others' reactions during those experiences has greater depth. We would expect this because, cognitively, the development from concrete understanding to formal understanding occurs at about this time.

Adolescents begin to analyze situations in more abstract ways. With the introduction of more interpersonal relationships, greater autonomy and independence, and more personal responsibilities, adolescents come to a greater realization of themselves as individuals with talents, weaknesses, and aspirations (Photo 9.2). Their belief systems expand to include knowledge within domains—the knowledge that one is a good swimmer, for example, without considering oneself an athlete.

Intrinsic versus Extrinsic Motivation There is also the possibility of change from intrinsic (or internal) to extrinsic (or externally influenced) motivation depending on one's self-concept within a specific subject area (Harter & Jackson, 1992). The nature of an adolescent's motivation to learn can also be influenced by the secondary school environment (Eccles, Wigfield, & Schiefele, 1998; Harter, 1985). (The nature of intrinsic and extrinsic motivation and the influence of school environment on motivation are discussed in more detail later in the chapter.)

PHOTO 9.3

Adolescent boys often show confidence in their ability in math and science.

Gender and Beliefs about Learning   Gender also plays a role in self-concept. As girls go into the intermediate grades in elementary school (and into high school), there is a drop in intrinsic motivation in math and science, whereas there is a maintenance or increase in language arts and social studies (see our discussion in Chapter 7). This drop in intrinsic motivation has been attributed to a variety of influences, such as sociocultural factors that present stereotypes for males and females and their related career goals (Photo 9.3) (Harter & Jackson, 1992).

Adolescence is an important time because it is at this juncture that students make choices in life and school that will affect them later. A student may select an elective by saying, "I don't want to sign up for that art class. I can't draw." This reflects an analysis of the student's own capabilities and the prediction of an outcome. What the student means is, "If I take that class I will not do well, because I don't have artistic talent." The result of this self-evaluation is called *self-efficacy*.

Self-Efficacy: Our Sense of Our Own Competence

Bandura (1997) discusses self-referent thought. Self-referent thought is considered to be an aspect of metacognition, by which a person makes a personal estimate of his or her own competency. *Self-efficacy* consists of two components: the actual skills required for the performance and an estimate of personal competency.

These two components influence not only what a student will do, but also the amount of time he or she will put into a performance and how persistent the student will be. Zimmerman (1989) described learners who used strategies such as self-observation (self-monitoring), self-judgment (comparison to peers), and self-reaction (how well one succeeds) as *self-regulated learners*.

Self-Regulated Learners   Self-regulated learners both learn effectively and feel effective as students; they are *effective learners*.

Bandura (1997) outlines the following four influences on a person's judgment of self-efficacy.

1. Actual experiences
2. Vicarious experiences

PHOTO 9.4
Students with high levels of self-efficacy are more likely to complete a task, despite its difficulty.

3. Verbal persuasion
4. Influence of emotional states

Bandura also feels that the individual's expectation of achievement is a major determinant in his or her willingness to join activities, expend effort, and follow through with an activity (Photo 9.4). Bandura (1981) argues that we make the most important judgments when comparing ourselves with our peers.

Influences on Achievement   Research studies have found higher self-efficacy and self-esteem (or positive self-evaluations) to have positive influences on achievement. For example, students with high self-efficacy tended to use more effective learning strategies and were more persistent in their work than those with lower self-efficacy (Eccles et al., 1998; Pintrich & Schunk, 1996; Zimmerman & Bandura, 1994). In Problem-Based Scenario 9.1, you again meet Emma. As a teacher, she is concerned about another of her third-graders, Rafael. Rafael experiences a number of academic difficulties and has a very low opinion of his ability as a learner.

Attribution Theory: Beliefs about Why We Succeed or Fail

Attributions are the explanations we provide for our successes or failures (Dweck, 1986; Weiner, 1986). Attributions are attempts to provide rationales for certain results. For example, "I didn't do very well on that test because my teacher doesn't like me" or "I did really well because I studied hard." Attributions are important for everyone to understand, but even more so for students because so many classroom successes and failures are public knowledge.

Problem-Based Scenario 9.1

Student: *Rafael*

Teacher: *Emma*

Emma thought back to her "crisis"—the day she had felt so overwhelmed by the individual needs of the children in her classroom and her lack of knowledge and direction about how to help them that she had actually thought about leaving teaching. She remembered how the questions spun in her head and she was simply too tired to make sense of them. Then, thank goodness, she had talked to Suzette. Suzette said immediately, "You can't do it all at once and you certainly can't do it all yourself. How about letting the kids do more of the work?"

Emma thought Suzette must be crazy. What did she mean? Emma had had visions of all her work being wasted as the class ran riot. Were third-graders capable of this? Suzette interpreted the look on Emma's face correctly. "No, no!" she said. "What I mean is, give more responsibility for their own learning to the children. They're quite capable of it, you know. They know how they learn best. Talk to them about it. Let them talk to each other about it; let them write and draw about it. I'll bet you'll be very pleasantly surprised."

So it began. Emma worked her way slowly by finding out what the children's questions were about and using those to help her plan lessons and units. She had the children talk, write, and draw about their learning. Gradually, she and the children became more engaged in learning together. The teaching profession was looking better!

Emma thought back to how she had wondered if there might be other children like Sammy in her class, children who processed information very differently from most other children. She had vague intuitions that Rafael might be one of those children. He was a puzzle—so bright in so many ways but struggling with reading, writing, and math. Now she began to see how things looked from his perspective. On her desk were the answers Rafael had given to the questions on writing she had done with the class that day (see Figure 9.1 on page 268). He had completed the survey on the class computer. Emma thought, "I really need to talk to Rafael's mom. And I probably need to have another chat with Suzette to see if she has any suggestions about strategies that I can use to help Rafael and make him feel more a part of the class."

Dimensions of the Rationales for Success or Failure

Students have been found to have four rationales for success or failure: personal ability, effort, good or bad luck, and difficulty of the task. These rationales vary along the three dimensions described next (Weiner, 1984).

Internal versus External Causes of Learning Outcomes (Locus of Control)

Does the control of an outcome exist inside or outside the individual? If an individual believes a result is due to luck, then he or she judges that there is no control over the situation (external cause).

In this instance, it is probably not worth expending any more effort because it will not change the outcome. If, on the other hand, the individual believes that luck has less to do with the result than the effort he or she has expended, the person will work toward the goal (internal cause).

Controlled versus Uncontrolled
Is there some aspect of the situation the individual can control? A student might reason, "While I know I can't control my abilities in math, I know I can control how much effort I put into studying. Even if I don't do well on a quiz, I controlled the outcome as much as possible because I tried to do my best. If I feel that there are other factors, beyond my control (uncontrolled), involved in the outcome, then I probably shouldn't even try."

This aspect of attributions also involves the degree of personal responsibility one takes for one's actions.

Stable versus Unstable Effects on Learning   Will the factor influencing the results change over time or will it stay the same? A student might reason, "If I know I won due to beginner's luck, then I certainly can't expect the same results next time (unstable, uncontrolled, external). The factor is unstable and only gives that result once. If, however, I know I am pretty good at math then I have a certain expectation that I should do well on the next quiz, if I make an effort to study (stable, controlled, internal)." When a student says, "I just can't do this stuff," he or she is attributing the failure to a lack of ability that is unlikely to change. This is an internal, stable trait that is out of his or her control.

It is important for a teacher to be able to analyze these statements to help the student make a change. It does no good simply to tell a student convinced of failure that he or she can, in fact, do it. Experience is a powerful tool on its own. It is up to the teacher to provide situations in which the student can encounter success. Students need to prove to themselves that they are capable individuals. Individual autonomy is a very important factor. Children who come from homes and schools that support individual, personal control over situations become more competent people who are motivated to become involved in school activities (Connell, Spencer, & Aber, 1994; Connell & Wellborn, 1991). See Info Byte 9.3 for examples.

Self-Worth

People like to present a positive image to their peers. This is why we go to such lengths as adults to find out what everyone is wearing to an event, if it isn't self-evident. We like to be seen as competent individuals in the eyes of others. Covington (1984) referred to this sense of competence as *self-worth*, or the positive self-image we present to others (Photo 9.5).

Self-worth theory explains that to maintain a competent image with others we will find ways to avoid failure. For example, a student may simply not participate to avoid failure ("If I don't raise my hand I won't get called on"). This is called a *performance avoidance goal* (Church, Elliot, & Gable, 2001). A student might also blame other factors for the failure ("I just didn't have time to do it")

> ### INFO BYTE 9.3
>
> **ATTRIBUTION THEORY**
>
> When people try to discover the motivation for their behavior, they may attribute results to everything from luck to hard work. Researchers in *attribution theory* identify several aspects of motivations underlying actions. They often display these in the graphical format used in Table 9.2. By listening to students' comments after a test, you can determine how each student views his or her abilities and talents in relation to the academic task.

TABLE 9.2

Examples of Internal and External Loci of Control

	Internal Locus of Control		External Locus of Control	
	Stable (factor remains relatively the same over time) (e.g., previous success)	Unstable (factor differs over time) (e.g., mood)	Stable (factor remains relatively the same over time) (e.g., easy task)	Unstable (factor differs over time) (e.g., luck)
Controllable (e.g., I studied hard)	"I've never studied and I always get A's on tests."	"I usually study but I just couldn't study for this test."	"That was an easy test."	"Nobody would help me."
Uncontrollable (e.g., I can't draw)	"I just can't do math."	"I wasn't feeling good that day."	"It depends on the teacher you get."	"Just wasn't my lucky day."

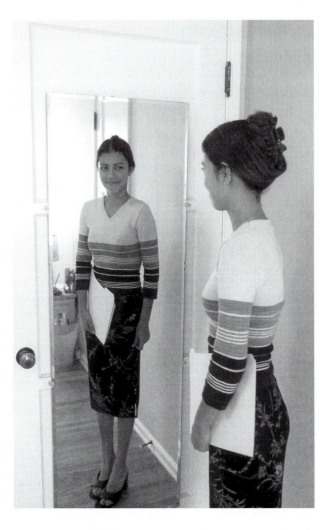

PHOTO 9.5

Self-worth. Adults also go to great lengths to project a sense of competence to their peers.

or set low goals ("If I can just pass, I'll be happy"). One outcome of avoidance of failure is the *self-fulfilling prophecy*, by which repeated failure and excuses result in lower self-esteem (Covington & Omelich, 1984).

Intrinsic and Extrinsic Motivation: Why We Learn

Intrinsic and extrinsic motivation (as with the internal versus external locus of control discussed under attribution theory) refers to an individual's motivation to learn (or do other things.) On one hand, this motivation may result from the pleasure the individual obtains from learning *(intrinsic motivation)*. Alternatively, he or she may be motivated by external rewards, such as marks *(extrinsic motivation)*.

Learning for Enjoyment versus Learning to Perform   Gottfried, Fleming, and Gottfried (2001), drawing on the work of several motivation theorists, define intrinsic motivation as "the performance of activities for their own sake, in which pleasure is inherent in the activity itself" (p. 3). As it applies specifically to the school setting, "*Academic intrinsic motivation* concerns enjoyment of school learning characterized by a *mastery orientation*; curiosity; persistence; . . . and the learning of challenging, difficult, and novel tasks" (Gottfried et al., p. 3.) As you might expect, learners who are intrinsically motivated achieve more, perceive themselves to be more competent, and experience less academic anxiety than those who are extrinsically motivated (Gottfried et al.; Harter, 1981).

Mastery orientation: An orientation to learning that involves learning for learning's sake, rather than for the sake of performance (e.g., high marks on a test).

TABLE 9.3

Motivation to Learn

Dimension	Intrinsic Motivation	Extrinsic Motivation
Motivational dimension	Likes challenging tasks	Likes easy assignments
	Curious learner	Needs to satisfy the teacher
	Interested in learning for its own sake	Interested in learning for grades
	Likes to figure out problems independently	Depends on the teacher for guidance
	Feels capable of making own judgments about school	Relies on teacher's opinion and feedback and/or marks to make decisions about own learning
Cognitive informational dimension	Can judge own success or failure in school	Relies on teacher's opinion and feedback and/or marks to judge own success or failure in school

Source: Categories based on Harter, 1981.

Dimensions of Motivation   Susan Harter (1981) divides motivation to learn into two dimensions, *motivational* and *cognitive informational*. The motivational dimension includes challenge, interest, and mastery. The cognitive informational dimension focuses on what children know about school and the basis on which they make decisions about school. See Table 9.3 for a summary of the characteristics of intrinsically and extrinsically motivated students on each dimension.

Awareness of Personal Motivation

Another important concept in motivation is that of *self-regulation of extrinsic motivation* (Ryan & Deci, 2000) or, as Wilson and Corpus (2001) call it, *internalized extrinsic motivation*. This refers to a *personal decision* about working toward a goal that involves extrinsic motivation. The critical element here is choice, as Ryan and Deci point out: Students who do their homework because they personally grasp its value for their chosen career are extrinsically motivated, as are those who do the work only because they are adhering to their parents' control. Both examples involve *instrumentalities*, rather than enjoyment of the work itself, yet the former case of extrinsic motivation entails personal endorsement and a feeling of choice, whereas the latter involves compliance with an external regulation (Wilson & Corpus, p. 71, italics added).

Developmental Patterns in Motivation

A number of researchers have found that academic intrinsic motivation (the motivational dimension) declines as students enter and progress through middle and secondary schools (e.g., Eccles & Roeser, 1999; Gottfried et al., 2001; Harter, 1981). Harter raised the important question about whether this decline is real or a result of school environments that become increasingly performance

Surfing Terms 9.1

Intrinsic motivation

Extrinsic motivation

Academic intrinsic motivation

Interest

Goal orientation theories

Self-fulfilling prophecy

Self-determination

Intentional behavior

Self-regulation

Self-directed learning

Learned helplessness

Abraham Maslow

Hierarchy of needs

Instrumentality: A factor that helps one reach a goal (e.g., "I have to spend a long time working on these proofs because I really want to be a math teacher, and I need to understand math concepts very well").

oriented. (See also our discussion of school culture in Chapter 6 regarding the nature of middle and secondary schools.)

Influence of School Environment on Motivation

Steinberg (1993) explains the challenges faced by early adolescents in school, sometimes called the "grade 7/8 slump." He suggests that this slump is the result of a mismatch between developmental needs and the structure of education. As early adolescents make the transition to middle school or junior high school, they face an increase in anxiety, in the number of teachers instructing them, and in the frequency of social comparison. They also experience a decrease in confidence, motivation, and the grades that they receive.

Stage–Environment Fit

Eccles et al. (1993) suggest that "some types of changes in the educational environment may be developmentally regressive" (p. 92). They question the degree of *stage–environment fit* as early adolescents, who are beginning to think in complex and abstract ways, enter an environment that is often regimented and does not encourage complex thinking. Gottfried et al. (2001) also found that the decline in motivation is differentiated by subject in the high school years, with students showing declines in motivation in mathematics, but not in social studies.

Bruer (1994) spoke forcefully on the topic of the fit of school environment to learners:

> School culture tends to define intelligence as success at school tasks. . . . Yet we have seen repeatedly that many students perceive school tasks as meaningless and next to useless outside the culture of school. Worse, students can succeed at these tasks with little understanding of a subject domain's basic principles. . . . Should we be surprised, then, that many students adopt strategies to get by or to please the teacher and fail to see the purpose of school in terms of developing the knowledge, skills, and intelligence useful in the larger world? (p. 284)

Bruer's (1994) comments highlight another of Harter's (1981) findings. She found that the informational dimension of motivation increases over the school years. Students learn the *rules of the game* at school. This is not necessarily a good thing. As Bruer suggested, students may learn rules that help them play a game focused on performance rather than true understanding. Our discussions in Chapters 1 and 2 about conceptual learning and in Chapter 7 about what it means to be part of a learning society are relevant to this discussion.

Theories of Intelligence and Students' Motivation to Learn: What These Mean in School

Now that you know some of the constructs involved in motivation theory, the question of how you, as a teacher, can motivate students remains. How can you encourage those students who have decided that they are incompetent to risk trying something? What does research show us works for teachers and students alike?

Teaching Characteristics and Motivation

We know that certain teaching characteristics are most effective in encouraging and motivating students. It must always be remembered that students have very different motivations, comprised of a range of rationales, experiences, and cognitive frameworks. Thus, when we discuss teaching and instruction we, by necessity, have to generalize. This is where the art of teaching is applied. How do you reach each student within a class?

Avoid Undermining Motivation

When teachers use organizational techniques such as ability groupings and public displays of achievement, students are provided with obvious comparisons, which encourage negative reactions (Ames, 1992; Rosenholtz & Rosenholtz, 1981). Classrooms in which these techniques are used actually undermine achievement and reduce student risk-taking. This is evident when students are hesitant to attempt an activity and when they ask the teacher if what they are doing is "right." In other words they are seeking only the right answer, not the learning experience. They are anxious about "getting it right."

Inconsistency

Teachers need to be very clear about their goals. One of the authors explains:

> "During a parent–teacher night, the math teacher told parents she was concerned with the process of mathematics, rather than the exact product (although that was obviously important). Since this emphasis was part of a movement within the schools, it was not a new policy to parents.
> "When my son came home with his first test, it became obvious that this wasn't exactly accurate. The test sheet was set up with work done in the left column and the final answer written on a line to the right. My son had gotten the problem correct but had transposed two numbers on the answer line to the right. The entire problem was marked wrong. The teacher did not give partial credit for any work and could not understand why students were upset when this occurred. She very quickly set up a classroom in which the students focused only on the 'right' answer, rather than the mathematical process that she had said was her goal. She also was upset that they were not willing to 'try' different types of problems or risk attempting challenging questions."

Performance Goals

The teacher just described had inadvertently shifted students' thinking and motivation toward achievement of *performance goals*, or achieving for the sake of performing well, rather than toward mastering the subject. According to Dweck (1986), students oriented toward performance goals require a great deal of self-confidence to accept challenges.

Entity Theory of Intelligence

One of the authors saw how this emphasis on performance goals affected elementary students:

> "I worked with two other teachers in a team that taught grades 3 and 4. We emphasized creativity and problem solving and would often pose the question 'Why do you think so?' to our students and encourage them to think of new and different ways of representing their knowledge. Students who had previously experienced an environment where the right answer was of prime importance were extremely stressed by our approach. We had to lead these students slowly and carefully to a point where they understood that their ideas were as important to us as right answers."

INFO BYTE 9.4

PERFORMANCE GOALS CAN COMPLEMENT MASTERY GOALS IN LEARNING

- A performance goal that involves competing with others to demonstrate high performance can motivate students to use self-regulated learning strategies that result in mastery (Ablard & Lipschultz, 1998).
- If students have high performance goals, they may be motivated to demonstrate both good performance and competence (mastery) (Ablard & Lipschultz).

Practical implications include the following:

- Skills and reasoning are important in all academic areas. For example, computational skills and problem-solving ability are important in mathematics. Having the *performance goal* of knowing high-level mathematical facts complements the *mastery goal* of understanding the relevant mathematical concepts.
- Self-regulated learning (organizing information, transforming information, reviewing notes, seeking assistance) that furthers a student's mastery goals (Ablard & Lipschultz), requires skill sets that the student can acquire by achieving his or her performance goals (e.g., learning multiplication tables perfectly, using punctuation correctly, spelling correctly, knowing relevant historical dates).

Students with little confidence find that failure is inevitable and directly related to their ability. They attribute failure to a stable, fixed intelligence. The level of intelligence they attribute to themselves is not necessarily realistic. These types of students hold an *entity theory of intelligence*. Highly intelligent students may even have an entity theory of intelligence and thus not be confident of their abilities. They may also hold the belief that they do not have to work because they are intelligent.

Increasing Competence through Effort

Performance goals are not always a bad thing. Some skills may be acquired through performance goals (e.g., learning the multiplication tables or musical scales). It is when *all* learning is directed at performance that students suffer lack of confidence. Info Byte 9.4 provides examples of how performance goals can be useful within an approach to learning that focuses on increasing competence through effort. Throughout the book we have mentioned that there is a continuum involved in many educational concepts. Learning goals also are on a continuum. We use different combinations of performance and mastery goals when we learn.

Mastery Goals and the Incremental Theory of Intelligence

If teachers emphasize *mastery goals* directed at increasing individual personal competence in the subject, students will strive for increased competence through effort. Here, intelligence is seen as changeable, or malleable, through personal effort. This is called an *incremental theory of intelligence*. No matter how bright the student, personal competence can be developed through effort. See Table 9.4 for examples of entity and incremental theories of intelligence as they relate to school. In Chapter 11, we discuss assessment strategies that encourage reflection on learning and self-evaluation. Both strategies are important in developing personal competence.

TABLE 9.4

Entity and Incremental Theories of Intelligence in Classrooms

Theory of Intelligence		Classroom Examples
Entity	Student:	I'm too dumb to do this math.
	Teacher:	Let's work through some problems together.
	Student:	I just don't get it. Nothing's going to help.
	Teacher:	You need to finish this problem set.
	Student:	I already know this stuff. Why should I waste my time working on this?
Incremental	Student:	There's one part of this essay on the Louisiana Purchase that really needs more work. Do you know where I can find more information on Napoleon's reasons for selling Louisiana?
	Student:	I knew if I kept trying, I'd make the finals!

Teachers' Theories of Intelligence: Their Influence on Practice

Teachers certainly must understand the theories of intelligence that their students hold, but they must also reflect on how they as teachers view intelligence. In Chapter 2, we discussed how a teacher's model of mind (Bruner, 1996) influences his or her practice. The same is true of the theory of intelligence a teacher holds. Instructional practices that support an entity theory of intelligence seriously diminish motivation for learning (Bruer, 1994). These practices can stem from a teacher's beliefs in the nature of intelligence. Like students, teachers hold either an entity or incremental theory of intelligence. Think about your theory of intelligence. Do you think that your achievement is due to your ability only or your ability in combination with your effort? Has this theory influenced your teaching practice? If so, how?

Ability–Goal Orientation   Teachers who hold an entity theory of intelligence have an *ability–goal orientation*. They emphasize relative ability, social comparison, and competition in their classrooms (Eccles & Roeser, 1999). In these classrooms, children expend their energy on making themselves "look smart" and on low-level learning strategies (Eccles & Roeser).

Task–Goal Orientation   Teachers who hold an incremental theory of intelligence have a *task–goal orientation* that stresses self-improvement and effort. Learners in these classrooms are engaged learners with images of themselves as competent students.

Influencing Motivation in the Classroom

Classroom environment is a powerful influence on motivation. In this chapter we discuss the components of classroom environment that have been emphasized in research on motivation. Other aspects of classroom environment also are important in engaging learners and in ensuring that their educational experiences are satisfying. These are discussed in Chapter 10.

Mastery Goals

Mastery goals are linked to engagement with learning and to the absence of an evaluation focus that places a high degree of emphasis on grades and performance evaluation. Classrooms focused on mastery make criteria for excellence clear, support students in achieving their potential, and help students reflect on their own development as learners. Teachers in these classrooms model their own engagement with learning for the students.

Creating Anxiety over Performance

Performance goals, on the other hand, are linked to harsh evaluation practices (a difficult grading structure that makes success unlikely). The latter environment is also likely to produce anxiety in students and lead to performance-avoidance goals (Church et al., 2001). In classrooms focused on performance, you might see public displays of marks, such as charts showing results of spelling tests. Students in these classrooms might hear things like "The marks on this test were too high so I'm scaling the marks down." They also are likely to experience confusion about the standards for excellence because the standards either are not transparent or change without reason.

Creating Engagement with Learning

Ames (1992) used the acronym TARGET to describe the following classroom influences that effect mastery goal orientation (Photo 9.6).

- *Tasks.* Use diverse and interesting tasks that students have a reasonable chance to finish successfully.
- *Authority.* Students have some autonomy in decision making and are responsible for their own learning.
- *Recognition.* All students have an opportunity to be recognized for their work, not just the best students.
- *Grouping.* Students have opportunities to work with heterogeneous groups of students.

PHOTO 9.6

Diverse and interesting tasks that students have a reasonable chance to finish successfully will engage students and enhance their sense of mastery.

- *Evaluate.* Students recognize that evaluation includes mastery, progress, and improvement, rather than only the right answer.
- *Time.* Pacing within a class is adjusted to accommodate variations in work tasks and abilities.

In a classroom where everyone has the opportunity to be successful, where emphasis is on improvement, and where competition is controlled, there is an increase in self-esteem among students (Ames, 1992). Educators can help ease the challenge of school transitions when they understand this dynamic. Teachers can also ease transitions when they work toward providing experiences across elementary, middle, and secondary schools that emphasize the following:

- Highlighting mastery goals and the increase of intelligence through learning
- Using multisensory learning strategies
- Improving self-esteem

Teaching is a social enterprise in which the teacher and students interact and react to overt and subtle messages. In the author's example of rewards in mathematics above, students reacted to what the teacher did, rather than what she said. When teachers are aware of concepts in motivational theory, they tend to be more responsive to the individual needs of students. They demonstrate creativity in designing lessons that spark interest in students, encourage risk taking among students, are cautious of the nonverbal cues or messages they may deliver, and generally have a more humanistic approach to education (Alderman, 1999).

Reward Systems in Education

While reading this chapter, you may have wondered about the place of rewards in education. Did you receive gold stars for your work in elementary school? One of the authors recently gave a workshop on educational psychology to senior secondary students.

"I asked them what motivated them to learn, and the reply from many was 'Candy. We love teachers who give us candy!' A few described classrooms where they could have cared less about candy because the learning environment was so exciting."

External Rewards and Intrinsic Motivation

The debate about whether to reward or not has gone on for some time in education. Deci's (1971; cited in Deci, Koestner, & Ryan, 2001) finding that extrinsic rewards like gold stars, pizzas, and honor rolls undermine intrinsic motivation was not viewed as tenable by educators. Educators use external rewards often. Recent research, however, supports that external rewards do not enhance motivation to learn (Deci, Koestner, & Ryan; Deci, Ryan, & Koestner, 2001). Edward Deci and his colleagues assert that "underlying intrinsic motivation are the innate psychological needs for competence and self-determination" (Deci, Koestner, & Ryan, p. 3). If rewards convey *information* that contributes to one's sense of self-determined competence, they enhance intrinsic motivation. If a reward is perceived as *controlling* (e.g., someone else decides that you will take part in a competition), it will diminish intrinsic motivation. Table 9.5 summarizes the results of Deci, Koestner, and Ryan's analyses of the effects of different kinds of rewards on intrinsic motivation.

Kohn (1993) presented a compelling challenge to rewards in his book, *Punished by Rewards: The Trouble with Gold Stars, Incentive Plans, A's, Praise, and other Bribes.* These findings support those of Deci, Koestner, and Ryan (2001) and

TABLE 9.5

Effects of Rewards on Intrinsic Motivation

Type of Reward	Message Conveyed	Effect on Intrinsic Motivation
Verbal rewards (positive feedback)	Information "This was a very powerful paper. The opening paragraph really grabbed me, and your use of language throughout was evocative."	Enhanced when given in an informational style. Student knows what was done well.
Verbal rewards (positive feedback)	Control: "Your science project was exactly what I wanted. Good work!"	Undermined when given in a controlling style. Feedback is positive, but is given in relation to the teacher's idea of what an assignment or project should cover.
Tangible rewards (money, prizes, trophies)	Information and respect: "You'll be awarded the scholarship for the student who has improved the most this year. It is so well-deserved. You have worked very hard."	Enhanced when given in the context of respect for effort. Feedback emphasizes recognition of effort in a respectful manner.
Tangible rewards (money, prizes, trophies)	Control: "If you get straight As, I'll take you to Disneyland."	Undermined. The student has not chosen the reward; no recognition of or respect for interests, strengths, and weaknesses is conveyed.
Unexpected rewards	Information: "You all did such a creative job on the class play and put in so much extra work that I think we should celebrate. Tomorrow we'll have a pizza party for lunch."	Not detrimental to intrinsic motivation. The class put in effort because of their interest and engagement, not because they expected a reward. The celebration honors their creativity and work after the event.
Engagement-contingent rewards (e.g., award for working on an art activity)	Control: "I have a new felt pen for those of you who work quietly on their art today."	Undermined. Reward is for work habits; it is unrelated to art.
Completion-contingent rewards (award for completion of a task)	Control: "Those of you who finish your math assignment before 3:00 will earn bonus points for your class team."	Undermined. Reward is for completion, not accuracy or understanding of math. It especially undermines the motivation of those who have difficulty with math or who need time to reflect on their work.
Performance-contingent rewards (reward for doing well at a task or performing to a standard)	Information: "Several of you reached our class's standard of excellence in poetry. The state poetry journal is looking for outstanding poems to publish. Would you be interested in submitting yours?"	Enhanced when students interpret the feedback as information on their accomplishments.
Performance-contingent rewards (reward for doing well at a task or performing to a standard)	Control: "Several of you reached our class's standard of excellence in poetry. You will be reading your poems at the school assembly tomorrow."	Undermined when interpreted as controlling. Students have no choice in the "reward"; some may not interpret this as a reward at all.

Source: Based on Deci, Koestner, and Ryan, 2001, pp. 9–13.

Deci, Ryan, and Koestner (2001). Kohn summarizes the following three primary findings on rewards:

1. "Young children don't need to be rewarded to learn" (Kohn, p. 145). They arrive at school intrinsically motivated to learn.
2. "At any age, rewards are less effective than intrinsic motivation for promoting effective learning" (Kohn, p. 145). Students who are interested in what they are learning achieve better; extrinsic motivation interferes with learning.
3. "Rewards for learning undermine intrinsic motivation" (Kohn, p. 148). Rewards have the effect of diluting the satisfaction that comes from interest in what one is learning and success in learning itself. (This result connects to the research findings on operant conditioning discussed in Chapter 4.)

Another important finding in research on motivation is that rewards may influence immediate behavior positively (behaviorist model, as discussed in Chapter 4), but they will have a negative influence in the long term (Wilson & Corpus, 2001).

Rewards versus Celebrations

Wilson and Corpus (2001) note that it is possible to control low-level, physical behaviors through rewards, but that a behaviorist model is not appropriate for encouraging intrinsic academic motivation.

Implications for teachers include the following:

- Distinguish between *rewards* and *celebrations*. Rewards are offered before an activity is undertaken, so students' motivation is undermined because they work toward the reward. Celebrations, on the other hand, occur after a desired outcome is achieved and may be unexpected (Wilson & Corpus).
- Provide a social context in the classroom that includes choice, relevant feedback on learning, interpersonal involvement, and real-life models (Wilson & Corpus).
- Ensure that learning tasks are meaningful to students.

In Problem-Based Scenarios 9.2 through 9.4, you meet Krista, an eighth-grade teacher who is challenged to find ways to motivate two of her students. Each student appears to have different underlying reasons for his and her lack of motivation in school. You also meet Dave, a fifth-grade teacher. One of his students has a number of special needs. Dave is searching for ways to support and motivate both academic and behavioral development.

Problem-Based Scenario 9.2

K-5   6-8   9-12   SpEd

Student: Jim
Teacher: Krista

Krista had been teaching for 6 years and the first day of school was still exciting. She had been setting up the science classroom since last week. Over the summer, Krista had visited the Kennedy Space Center in Florida and had bought some wonderful pictures of the space station, Earth, and the space shuttle for the room. She remembered thinking how every student needed to have images like these as goals to dream about. Even though these had been her dreams too, she still felt that the pictures could give her students a "charge" about the possibilities of the

future. At least that was what she had thought until the grade 8-C block had come for their first class.

Krista stood at the door, monitoring the hallway, as the students filed in. Most were excited and knew their way around already. The counseling department worked hard to bring all grade 7s into the school several times in the spring for orientations. Students knew where their classes were and what supplies they would need for each class.

When everyone was in the room and had selected a seat, Krista took her place at the front of the class,

Problem-Based Scenario *9.2* (continued)

hugging the sheets with the class list and safety directions for the science classroom. Directly in front of her was a blond-haired boy with a scowl on his face. He folded his arms, slid down in his seat and announced to Krista, "You might as well give me my F now. I always get Fs."

The whole class went silent. The only thing Krista could think of was to ask him his name. It turns out this was Jim Walker and, by his statements, he always failed in school. He was quite adamant that she, as he put it, "cut to the chase" and "give the F now." Krista had been at a loss for words and so told him that she would speak to him later. For the rest of the subdued class, they went over orientation in the science lab and safety issues.

After class, Jim stayed behind. He was pleasant but quite firm about his chances in the class. Krista then checked with the counselor at lunch. Yes, Jim usually failed. No, there was no obvious reason for it. No, there was nothing on intelligence testing to suggest any reason for it. Yes, the parents were cooperative and he came from a good home. Now Krista had to figure out what to do with him.

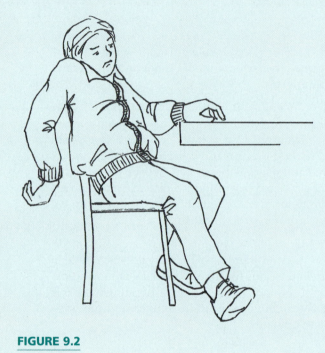

FIGURE 9.2

Problem-Based Scenario *9.3*

Student: *Cathy*
Teacher: *Krista*

After about 2 months, Krista felt she was finally getting somewhere with her grade 8-C block group. She was still working on Jim Walker, but now Cathy had become a problem.

Cathy was a popular girl with a number of friends in the class. She wore her hair in the beaded-cornrow-style she had acquired during a trip to the Caribbean with her family. She was an average (C) student in class—polite and cooperative most of the time.

After talking with the counselor, Krista found out that Cathy's mother had died from breast cancer 2 years earlier. Cathy was born when the next youngest in the family of four children was 19 years old. All her brothers were married with children almost as old as Cathy. That left Mr. Schell to raise Cathy on his own. The counselor told Krista that because he was a bit older than most parents raising a teenager, he seemed to have limited patience with her antics. Krista thought, "and antics they are." Also, the counselor was a neighbor and knew Mr. Schell. According to the counselor, things were actually going quite well for the family.

Mr. Schell was coming in for a parent conference after school today, so Krista was organizing her thoughts to make sure she outlined her concerns as clearly and carefully as possible. Within the past 3 weeks, Cathy had started to "turn off" after about 10 minutes in class, no matter what the assignment or activity. Sometimes she just sat there staring into space. But it was the other times that disrupted everyone. She would crawl under her desk, everyone would start laughing, and then Cathy would start to sing the cat food commercial, "meow, meow, meow, meow." If Krista weren't careful, Cathy would be in "full voice" by the time she found her under the desk.

At first Krista used her normal teacher voice to control things, then after-school detentions with a friendly talk. Nothing seemed to get through to Cathy, even though she was cooperative during the talk. Krista was hoping Mr. Schell could offer some ideas about how to get Cathy interested and involved in the current group projects the class was doing. If not, Krista would need to develop some ideas of her own.

Problem-Based Scenario *9.4*

Student: *Chip*
Teacher: *Dave*

Dave Harris was lazily staring out the staff room window after lunch, gathering energy for the big afternoon event, the Valentine's Day party, when he saw Chip Lawson proudly carrying in a cake that was almost as big as he was. Several classmates ran to greet him, obviously overjoyed at the sight of the beautifully decorated cake. Dave's thoughts went back to last June and the conversation he'd had with his principal, Maria Fortunato.

Maria had asked Dave to take Chip into his fifth-grade class. "You'd be good for Chip," Maria pleaded.

Knowing how difficult Chip's school history had been, Dave was hesitant but, at the same time, flattered that Maria thought he could make a difference for Chip. Maria had clearly reached the point where something had to be done. Chip spent most days sitting in the hallway outside the school office, balancing an exercise book and a large box of pencils and crayons on his lap. It seemed as if spilling the contents of the box was an attention-getting strategy. Dave watched Chip do this with apparent glee every time someone passed by.

Problem-Based Scenario *9.4* *(continued)*

The most telling incident, Dave thought, was at Sports Day last year. Dave had watched in horror as a teacher put Chip in a large plastic garbage bag, feet first, and proceeded to run around the field with the bag over his shoulder. Chip's head protruded from the otherwise tightly held bag and he and other children screamed with glee. Chip was a school joke. Dave hated the way Chip was viewed by staff and students and he hoped he could change that.

Chip had so many strikes against him. He was 2 years older than his classmates and a foot shorter. He had a physical condition that resulted in limited growth. He lived in foster care with a retired couple that doted on him and their other foster son. Both boys had physical and cognitive limitations. Chip also was prone to tantrums and "tall tales"; the school bus driver reported that Chip told him he'd been to Australia where he had met Prince Philip. Chip's school file was several inches thick. It contained the results of several psychoeducational assessments and special educational interventions over the 7 years Chip had been in school. Chip spent 2 years in kindergarten because he required a great deal of behavioral support. The same thing happened in first grade.

Dave thought things had settled down considerably this year. Chip spent his days in class, not at the office. Dave told him in the first week of school, after Chip shouted out loudly in class, that when you're in grade 5 you behave like a fifth-grader! Chip worked on a modified curriculum and took classroom responsibilities seriously. There were occasional outbursts, like the time Dave returned from recess to find Chip with a thick wad of wet paper towels around his thumb, rocking back and forth and moaning loudly. Reassured that there was no injury, Chip quickly regained his composure. This sort of behavior didn't go over well with his classmates, though. They were civil to him, but he was essentially neglected—never invited to join activities or work groups. He also was the cause of complaints in collaborative activities. The kids described him as "too goofy"; they were accommodating of academic weaknesses, but Chip's behavior struck them as exceptionally immature.

Dave noted the look on Chip's face as he brought the cake into the classroom. He was overjoyed to be making this contribution to the party. Dave thought this was an excellent opportunity to involve Chip in the class community on a positive note. Still, it was a short-term solution. "Well," thought Dave, "It's a start. Once I get through the excitement of Valentine's Day, I'll think about some long-term strategies."

See Figures 9.3 to 9.7 on pages 269–278

Summary

In this chapter, you saw that theories of motivation can impact school achievement. Certain personal characteristics influence our motivation to learn. However, the nature of the classroom environment is central to the enhancement of this motivation. Teachers who emphasize mastery, effort, and self-improvement, who allow for autonomous decision making, and who respect their students' abilities to learn will enhance intrinsic motivation. We also presented information on the ways in which students' sense of their own competence and their beliefs about intelligence influence their achievement and how, in many cases, rewards can inhibit learning.

- Attribution theory can help you to understand your students' beliefs about why they do or don't do well in school.
- Examining your own beliefs about intelligence will help you to understand the relationship between your beliefs and your practice and give you a foundation for development.
- School and classroom environments have significant influences on students' motivation to learn.
- Rewards can undermine motivation. In the long term, learning for its own sake is the best motivator for continued engagement with learning.

A Metacognitive Challenge

You should now be able to reflect on the following questions:

- What do I know about the influence of motivation on learning?

- What do I know about how the school environment influences motivation to learn?

- What do I know about the characteristics of a teacher who supports intrinsic academic motivation?

- How does my knowledge of personal theories of intelligence help me understand the learners in my classroom?

- How does my knowledge of performance goals and mastery goals help me plan learning activities?

Artifacts for Problem-Based Scenarios

FIGURE 9.1 ■ **Artifact for Problem-Based Scenario 9.1**

STUDENT WRITING SURVEY[1]

NAME: *Rafael*

DATE: *Oct 2*

1. Do you think of yourself as a writer? Why do you think this way?

No. I can't write. I can't spell. My wurk is so mesy.

2. Does your teacher think you're a writer?

No. She think I dum.

3. What does your teacher think is good writing?

Good wurk no mes

4. Where do you get your ideas for writing?

I got no ideas.

5. Do you like to write alone or with a friend?

I hat writing.

$$62 + 36 = 98$$

$$31 + 82 = 119$$

$$33 + 44 = 34834$$

$$61 + 10 = 611$$

$$92 + 11 = 9211$$

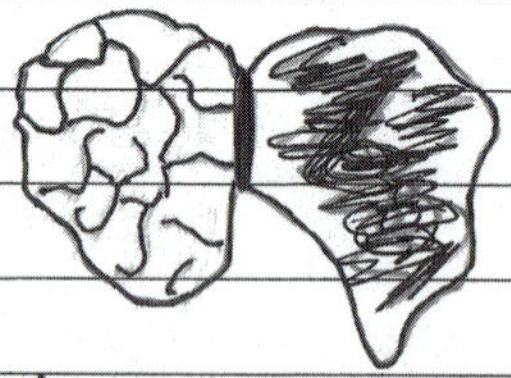

My brane on Math

Source: Questions based on the work of Paris & Ayres, 1994.

FIGURE 9.3 ■ Artifact for Problem-Based Scenario 9.4

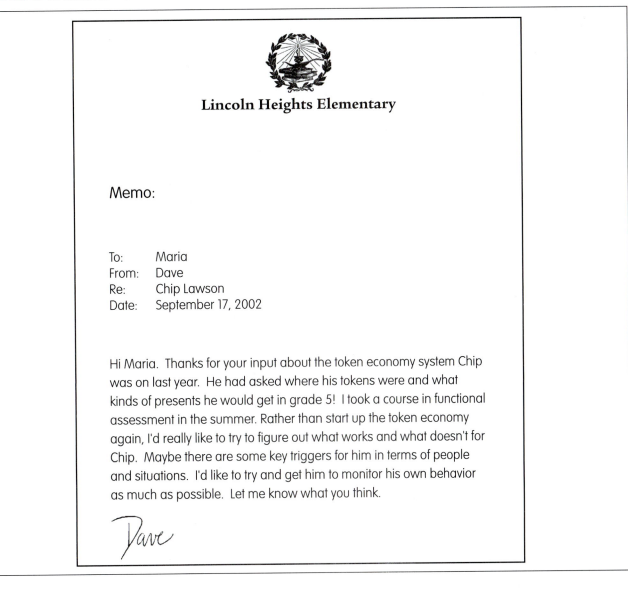

Lincoln Heights Elementary

Memo:

To: Maria
From: Dave
Re: Chip Lawson
Date: September 17, 2002

Hi Maria. Thanks for your input about the token economy system Chip was on last year. He had asked where his tokens were and what kinds of presents he would get in grade 5! I took a course in functional assessment in the summer. Rather than start up the token economy again, I'd really like to try to figure out what works and what doesn't for Chip. Maybe there are some key triggers for him in terms of people and situations. I'd like to try and get him to monitor his own behavior as much as possible. Let me know what you think.

Dave

FIGURE 9.4 ■ Artifact for Problem-Based Scenario 9.4

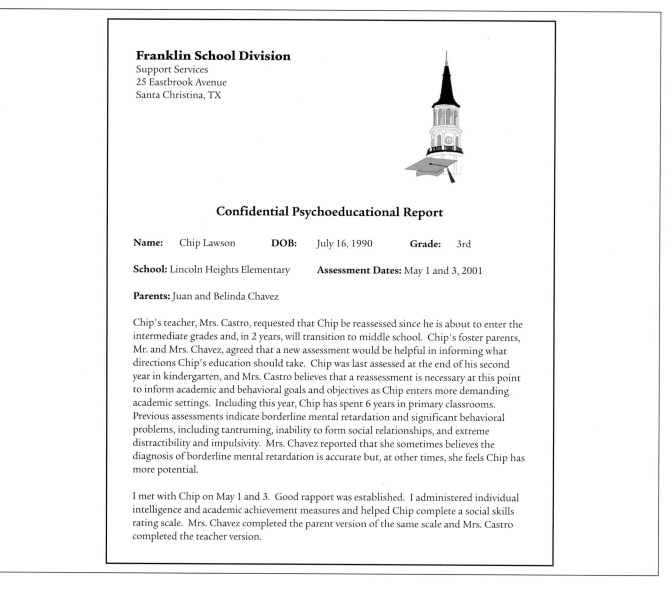

Franklin School Division
Support Services
25 Eastbrook Avenue
Santa Christina, TX

Confidential Psychoeducational Report

Name: Chip Lawson   **DOB:**   July 16, 1990   **Grade:**   3rd

School: Lincoln Heights Elementary   **Assessment Dates:** May 1 and 3, 2001

Parents: Juan and Belinda Chavez

Chip's teacher, Mrs. Castro, requested that Chip be reassessed since he is about to enter the intermediate grades and, in 2 years, will transition to middle school. Chip's foster parents, Mr. and Mrs. Chavez, agreed that a new assessment would be helpful in informing what directions Chip's education should take. Chip was last assessed at the end of his second year in kindergarten, and Mrs. Castro believes that a reassessment is necessary at this point to inform academic and behavioral goals and objectives as Chip enters more demanding academic settings. Including this year, Chip has spent 6 years in primary classrooms. Previous assessments indicate borderline mental retardation and significant behavioral problems, including tantruming, inability to form social relationships, and extreme distractibility and impulsivity. Mrs. Chavez reported that she sometimes believes the diagnosis of borderline mental retardation is accurate but, at other times, she feels Chip has more potential.

I met with Chip on May 1 and 3. Good rapport was established. I administered individual intelligence and academic achievement measures and helped Chip complete a social skills rating scale. Mrs. Chavez completed the parent version of the same scale and Mrs. Castro completed the teacher version.

FIGURE 9.4 ■ Artifact for Problem-Based Scenario 9.4 (continued)

Wechsler Intelligence Scale for Children - Third Edition

Verbal Scale	Mild mental retardation
Performance Scale	Low average
Full Scale IQ	Borderline

Overall, Chip's performance is in the borderline classification. This means that approximately 95% of other children his age would score better, overall, on this test. However, it is useful to examine the two areas of this test. Chip's verbal ability is in the mild mental retardation range, indicating adult potential for processing and using language at about the sixth-grade level. Chip's ability to plan and organize and learn and remember nonverbal information (performance scale) is in the low average range. Spatial abilities are important in mathematics, science, and the arts. Chip's adult potential in this area is relatively stronger than in the verbal area.

Wechsler Individual Achievement Test (WIAT)

Reading	Standard score 70	Percentile 2nd
Writing	Standard score 73	Percentile 4th
Mathematics	Standard score 90	Percentile 25th

Chip's scores on the WIAT are consistent with his verbal and performance scores on the WISC-III. His academic progress is also consistent with his obtained scores on the WIAT.

Observations of Performance

Chip was cooperative and interested in the testing. He attended well during the sessions, except when material became too hard for him. Despite reassurance, he became aggressive and threw materials on the floor several times.

Chip will continue to need special educational support throughout elementary, middle, and high school, including modified curricula that allow him to develop functional academics.

FIGURE 9.4 ■ Artifact for Problem-Based Scenario 9.4 (continued)

Social Skills Rating System (Gresham & Elliot, 1990)

The Social Skills Rating System provides a measure of social behaviors that can influence the development of social competence and adaptive functioning at school and at home. There are three rating forms: student, teacher, and parent. Ratings include social skills, academic competence, and problem behaviors as perceived by the student, the parent, and the teacher.*

Student ratings
Social skills: 119, Percentile rank 90th
Parent ratings
Social skills: 90, Percentile rank 25th
Problem behaviors: 121, Percentile rank 92nd. Externalizing and hyperactivity: More than average
Internalizing: Average
Teacher ratings
Social skills: 82, Percentile rank 12th
Problem behaviors: 136, Percentile rank 99th. Externalizing and hyperactivity: More than average
Internalizing: Average
Academic competence: 90, Percentile rank 25th
Both parent and teacher ratings of social skills differ significantly from Chip's. Mrs. Chavez and Mrs. Castro agree that Chip demonstrates aggressive and hyperactive behaviors. Focused discussion of social skills using concrete demonstrations may be helpful in assisting Chip to reflect on and improve his behavior.

Melissa Santana MA

Melissa Santana, M.A.
School Psychologist

Social skills include cooperation, assertion, responsibility, empathy, and self-control. Problem behaviors include externalizing, internalizing, and hyperactivity. Academic competence includes teacher ratings of reading and mathematics ability, overall ability, motivation, and parental support (Gresham & Elliott, 1990).

FIGURE 9.5 ■ Chip's Individual Education Plan

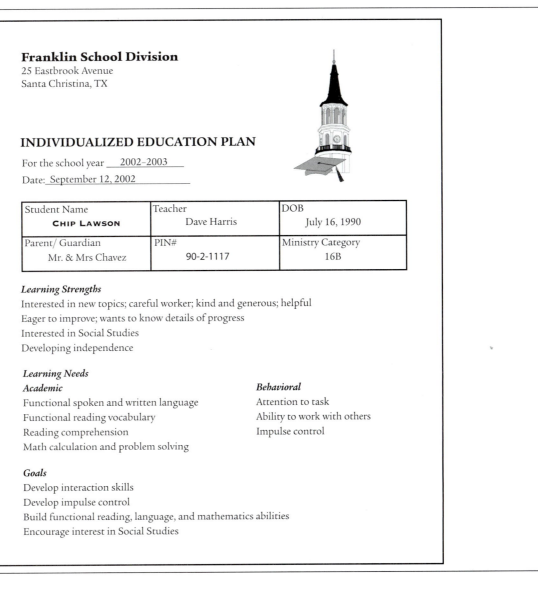

Franklin School Division
25 Eastbrook Avenue
Santa Christina, TX

INDIVIDUALIZED EDUCATION PLAN

For the school year ___2002–2003___
Date:_ September 12, 2002 _____

Student Name	Teacher	DOB
CHIP LAWSON	Dave Harris	July 16, 1990
Parent/ Guardian	PIN#	Ministry Category
Mr. & Mrs Chavez	90-2-1117	16B

Learning Strengths
Interested in new topics; careful worker; kind and generous; helpful
Eager to improve; wants to know details of progress
Interested in Social Studies
Developing independence

Learning Needs

Academic
Functional spoken and written language
Functional reading vocabulary
Reading comprehension
Math calculation and problem solving

Behavioral
Attention to task
Ability to work with others
Impulse control

Goals
Develop interaction skills
Develop impulse control
Build functional reading, language, and mathematics abilities
Encourage interest in Social Studies

FIGURE 9.5 ■ Chip's Individual Education Plan (continued)

Strategies/Methods

Academic

High-interest/low-vocabulary reading series; individual novel study with focus on comprehension; phonemic awareness exercises

Spelling: combine Dolch word list and Chip's choices

Tape record creative writing assignments; parent volunteer will transcribe and edit with Chip

Review addition with carrying (2 digits), subtraction with borrowing (2 digits), and times tables to 10 in context of functional math; computer drill and practice

Applied problems: time, money

Resource room 3X per week

Collect hot dog money each week; count, check, and deliver to office

Buddy with partner for help with reading Socials text and volunteer to tape record sections of the text

Behavioral

Social skills training (approach and respond appropriately)

Reward sustained attention (record time on task on own chart; reward with homework coupons)

Conduct functional assessment of attention, group work

Join Circle of Friends group with school counselor? Dave will follow up.

Evaluation/Review period

Review progress at next meeting

Invite Mr. Knowles: discuss progress in Science

Invite Mrs. Pereira: discuss Chip's participation in Circle of Friends

Next meeting November 30, 2002, 3:30 PM

Student Name CHIP LAWSON	Parent/ Guardian Juan Chavez	Teacher Dave Harris
Counselor	LAT/RR John Tanaka	Other

FIGURE 9.6 ■ **Artifact for Problem-Based Scenario 9.4**

Name Chip Lawson

Teacher Mr. Harris

Grade 5

Lincoln Heights Elementary
Report Card

Date Nov. 16, 2002

Semester 1

Subject	Semester 1	Semester 2	Semester 3
Language Arts			
Reading			
Spelling			
Language Skills			
Written Language			
Mathematics			
Science	D B.K.		
Social Studies			
Computers			
Spanish			
Art			
Music			
Physical Education			

Semester Comments:

Work Habits:

Chip is an interested learner, but often finds it difficult to sustain attention. I am observing him regularly to determine how and when he is able to keep his attention focused. I'll discuss this with you when we meet. Chip is learning to work independently; his need for constant feedback on his work is slowly diminishing. Chip always makes an effort to produce neat work.

Social Relationships and Responsibility:

Chip is a kind and generous member of our classroom. He takes responsibility for classroom tasks well and I value his help. He is developing more maturity in classroom interactions. Chip still needs considerable support in working with groups for a sustained period of time. I am observing these interactions carefully to see what can be done to help him. I would appreciate your perspectives on this when we meet.

FIGURE 9.6 ■ **Artifact for Problem-Based Scenario 9.4 (continued)**

Chip has an Individual Education Plan (IEP) to address his learning needs. Because it is district policy in the Franklin School Division to provide only written comments for students on an IEP, I have reported on Chip's academic and social progress relative to the learning goals set out in his IEP.

Chip currently reads at a mid-second-grade level. Like all the students in my class, he has a reading program designed specifically for him. He is reading books that are appealing to his age group, but have a reading level that matches his. He enjoys reading, and understands what he reads at this level. Chip receives help with reading and language development in our resource room twice a week. There, and in class, we are working on building his functional vocabulary – stressing words that will help him get along in the community. We're taking a similar approach to building his spoken and written language skills.

Chip likes to use a computer and has acquired basic word-processing skills. He can now compose, format, and print a simple document. He is learning to use the spell checker. We work on developing lists of spelling words together so that Chip can learn words of interest to him and words that he needs to convey information effectively.

Chip has mastered a few words and phrases of elementary Spanish. He enjoys the group activities, and Ms. Gomez and I believe that they are helping to support his social skill development.

Chip's level of development in Mathematics is at the beginning third-grade level. As with Language Arts, I am taking a functional approach to teaching him mathematics, focusing on activities and skills that will be important to him in the community. He is enjoying the checkbook activity and is learning to manage and balance his account.

FIGURE 9.6 ■ **Artifact for Problem-Based Scenario 9.4 (continued)**

In Social Studies, Chip works on modified activities. In Art and Music, he enjoys the learning activities, but sometimes has problems functioning in these less structured, creative contexts. In P.E., Chip tries hard to keep up. His impulse control is more of a problem in the gym, and he often needs breaks to compose himself. He has difficulty following rules in games. However, relative to his own abilities, Chip is making average progress. We are working together to work out cues to help him function better in the gym and on the playing field.

A good start in the fifth grade, Chip!

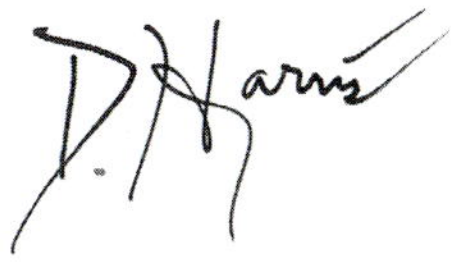

Science

Chip lacks understanding of basic science concepts. This makes it hard for him to cope with the grade 5 curriculum. While he concentrates well on individual note taking, he is inattentive and disruptive when the class works on experiments and projects. Chip will need to try much harder if he is to succeed in higher-level science.

FIGURE 9.7 ■ Artifact for Problem-Based Scenario 9.4

```
Date:     Tuesday, November 25, 2001
Subject: Chip's Science
To:       Dave Harris dharris@franklinsd.tx
From:     bknowles@franklinsd.tx (Barry Knowles)


Dave,

     I'd like your opinion about what to do with
Chip when I take your class for Science.  Up till
now, I've had him copy out sections of the science
text that we're using. He just can't handle the
group work.  He seems to enjoy copying out the text.
What do you think?



Barry Knowles
Grade 6 Teacher
Lincoln Heights Elementary
```

Understanding the Learning Context: The Supportive Classroom

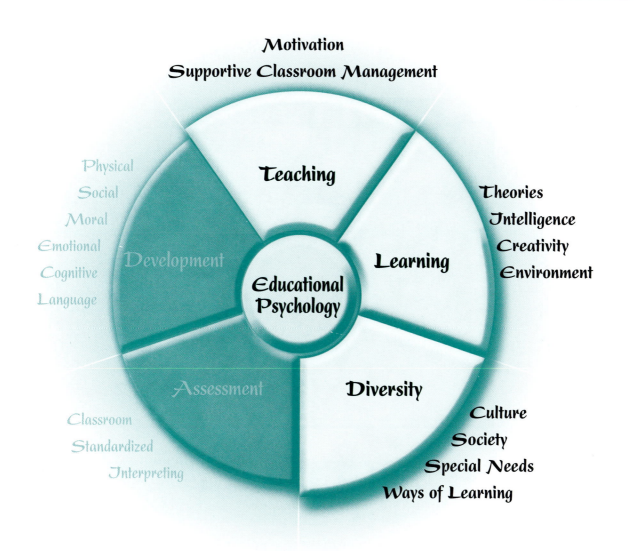

Motivation
Supportive Classroom Management

Teaching

Theories
Intelligence
Creativity
Environment

Physical
Social
Moral
Emotional
Cognitive
Language

Development

Learning

Educational
Psychology

Assessment

Diversity

Classroom
Standardized
Interpreting

Culture
Society
Special Needs
Ways of Learning

Throughout this book, we have discussed many things that go into creating a positive classroom that is supportive of all types of learners. Because of the complexity of human beings, planning the environment in which you will teach your students and learn from them is a multifaceted endeavor. It involves understanding your students not only in terms of their cognitive, physical, social–emotional, and moral development; their motivation to learn; the social–cultural influences on their development; and their intelligence and creativity, but in a number of other ways as well. The following are important considerations in creating a supportive classroom:

- How you organize the physical environment (Photo 10.1) of your classroom
- How you plan the daily timetable
- How you organize instructional groupings
- The types of learning tools you offer your students
- How you communicate with your students, their parents, and your colleagues
- How you encourage positive interpersonal interactions

PHOTO 10.1
The physical arrangement of the classroom supports student learning.

Psychological Needs: Building Competence, Autonomy, and Relatedness

Competence: To be competent is to be capable and effective at what one undertakes.

Autonomy: The sense that one has personal freedom.

Relatedness: A sense of being connected to other human beings.

To begin our discussion of the supportive classroom, we follow up on the discussion of motivation in Chapter 9. Eccles and Roeser (1999) found that when teachers incorporate several elements of the supportive classroom, students learn deeply and adopt a mastery approach to learning (see Chapter 9). To do this, a teacher should emphasize self-improvement and effort, provide choice and collaborative work, and "emphasize to their students that mastering new content, learning from mistakes, and continuing to try are all highly valued hallmarks of success" (p. 516).

Humans have three psychological needs: *competence, autonomy*, and *relatedness*. Satisfying these needs enhances intrinsic motivation, social development, and well-being (Ryan & Deci, 2000). Social context can foster or inhibit these psychological needs; this has obvious implications for education. The concepts of competence, autonomy, and relatedness are threaded throughout our discussion of the supportive classroom.

PHOTO 10.2
Children at play demonstrate competence, autonomy, and relatedness.

Making Thinking and Learning Visible

Giving students opportunities to discuss their thinking and problem-solving strategies with their classmates and teachers enhances learning and engagement in the classroom.

Reciprocal Teaching and Problem-Solving Strategies

Bruer (1994) argued that making thinking and problem solving "public and shared" in this way allows students to reflect on their own and others' thinking. (See our discussion of metacognition in Chapter 5.) This approach is used in *reciprocal teaching* (Brown & Campione, 1994; Hacker & Tenent, 2002) and computer networking that allows students to share their questions, strategies, hypotheses, and suggestions for solving problems (Scardamalia, Bereiter, & Lamon, 1994).

Bruer (1994) suggested one reason for the success of making thinking and learning visible is that it allows students who are experts to share their knowledge with those who are less skilled novices, making them aware of their own thinking and that of others. This awareness leads to increased competence.

> *Reciprocal teaching:* An instructional procedure that involves dialogue about predicting, clarifying, questioning, and summarizing text. Small groups of students and a dialogue leader (who can be a teacher or student) work toward gaining greater meaning from reading text (Hacker & Tenent, 2002).

Self-Directed Learning and the Benefits of Peer Tutoring

Biemiller, Inglis, and Meichenbaum (1995; see also Biemiller & Meichenbaum, 1992) used the expert–novice distinction just described and successfully increased grade 4 children's math-problem-solving ability. Less successful grade 4 students tutored grade 2 children in math. The fourth-graders were trained to look and listen to see who needed help and when, ask questions that would help them to find out what kind of help was needed, give hints (not answers!) to help the younger children find the solution, offer encouragement, and check out how successful learning and the help given were.

The older students' ability to do math increased, as did their ability to engage in task-directed speech. Task-directed speech contains statements that indicate the student is *self-directed*; they reflect conscious planning (e.g., first I'll think about what I already know, then I'll do some research on what I need to find out), conditional planning (if–then, choosing between alternative plans), and monitoring progress (Biemiller & Meichenbaum, 1992). Students who are not self-directed

Peer tutoring: An instructional strategy that involves students teaching other students. The student being tutored may be younger than the tutor or the students may be the same age.

make statements like, "Can you help me?" or "Do you know what I'm supposed to do?" These are general, unfocused statements that don't help them to reflect on the task at hand. Biemiller et al.'s (1995) approach to *peer tutoring* resulted in more competent, self-directed learners who knew how to talk about and seek help for their learning.

Classroom Management versus the Supportive Classroom

We deliberately use the term *supportive classroom* in this chapter, rather than *classroom management*. The latter term is a common one in the educational literature, and you will find useful information if you search the Internet using the term. The term *classroom management*, as used in educational research, has a much broader meaning than that often attributed to it in practice, where it often is used in reference to managing behavior, and a subtle (and sometimes not so subtle) connotation of control may accompany it.

We prefer the term *positive behavioral support* to classroom management. In essence, this means that teachers need to question *why* students are behaving the way they are and search for strategies that will support them to feel a sense of belonging in the classroom and will encourage autonomy. We introduced the concept of positive behavioral support in Chapter 4 when we discussed applied behavioral analysis and functional assessment.

Organizing and Managing Classroom Life

As you begin your teaching career, you will need to organize your classroom effectively and know how to manage it on a day to day basis. This organization and management include many details (Photo 10.3). Some examples are listed here in the form of guiding questions:

- Is there a smooth traffic flow into and within your classroom?
- Are books and supplies easily accessible for students?

PHOTO 10.3

Setting a positive tone and attitude for learning can start with making the classroom an organized and attractive space.

- Are routines like taking attendance, checking on absentees, and leaving the room understood and managed easily?
- Is the physical environment attractive and well lit?
- Are there well-defined spaces for individual and group work?

These questions do not require educational psychology to help you answer them, but they are nevertheless very important to setting a positive tone and attitude for learning in your classroom.

Five Features of Classroom Management

Educational psychology does provide background in a number of areas critical to successful classroom management, as you will see in the following list. Jones (1996; cited in Emmer & Stough, 2001) identified the following five main features of classroom management:

1. An understanding of current research and theory in classroom management and students' psychological and learning needs.
2. The creation of positive teacher–student and peer relationships.
3. The use of instructional methods that facilitate optimal learning by responding to the academic needs of individual students and the classroom group.
4. The use of organizational and group management methods that maximize on-task behavior.
5. The ability to use a range of counseling and behavioral methods to assist students who demonstrate persistent or serious behavior problems. (pp. 103–104)

Surfing Terms 10.1

Cooperative learning
Cognitive apprenticeship
Reciprocal teaching
Peer tutoring
Positive behavioral support
Classroom management
Responsive classroom
Classroom climate

The Importance of Effective Communication in Education

One of the most obvious, and yet overlooked, skills a teacher has is the ability to communicate effectively with students, parents, and colleagues. The entire sense of community that develops within a school is based on this ability to communicate with each other. Not only does effective communication develop a sense of belonging for students, but it also provides a sense of self-confidence that is related to student achievement (Bandura, 1986; She & Fisher, 2002).

Importance of Understanding the Community Culture

Since community is culturally based, it is important for you to know and understand the cultural setting of the community in which you are working. Culture affects parents' beliefs about education. It also influences the goals they set for their children and the way they interact with the school and teachers (McDermott & Rothenberg, 2001; Wentzel, 1999). These factors, in turn, influence the teaching and learning in a school along with the sense of community that teachers attempt to establish (Hildago, Siu, Bright, Swap, & Epstein, 1995). Communication is an ongoing skill; even veteran teachers find they can improve and learn new techniques for interacting with students and parents (Templeton & Johnson, 2001).

Working with Individual Education Plans

When working with students who have special needs, the ability to communicate becomes even more crucial. Although there are formal planning sessions,

PHOTO 10.4

A strong sense of community is
especially important for children
with special needs.

such as the writing of an Individual Education Plan (IEP), it is often day to day communication that provides more connection between the home and school. This does not mean the teacher necessarily has to provide written feedback. Communication can be far more informal. For example, one teacher of students with hearing impairments provides each student with a journal in which she jots down a brief note when she is working with the student. Then the journal is carried home for the parents to read. A brief phone call or short conversation at the beginning or end of the day can provide parents with ongoing information. Newsletters, open houses, and even picnics are effective means of providing parents and students with a sense of community, particularly important for students with special needs (Photo 10.4).

Communicating with Students: Clarity, Respect, and Encouragement

Research has shown that secondary teachers interact with approximately 150 different students in a day. And they tend to be unaware of the total number of encounters and often have trouble remembering specifics of the conversations or comments (Good & Brophy, 1991). Since we spend so much time working with students, the skill of communicating is taken for granted and it is assumed teachers are good at this. But all of us have had teachers who did not always communicate concepts and/or intentions clearly.

Developing the Ability to Listen

One of the most effective communication skills a teacher can develop is the ability to listen to what a student is telling him or her. A person who listens to what is being said respects the speaker. Earlier in this text we introduced the idea that by listening to what a student is saying you can gain considerable knowledge about the cognitive level of the student's understanding.

Developing a Teaching–Learning Style Based on Mutual Respect

If you are working within a communicative framework, the concept of *mutual respect* will become a natural extension of your teaching. It is only by listening and then responding with an appropriate comment or question that instructors construct knowledge in a teacher–student interaction. Mutual respect is an important component of any teaching situation. It forms the basis for most strategies in classroom management, and it allows learning to become a cooperative venture. It provides the forum for open discussions, allows for effective parent–teacher interaction, and enhances the sense of community detailed above.

Types of Teacher Communication

There are a number of different types of teacher communication formats, from formal questioning to the use of body language, that convey a range of messages to the student.

Verbal and Nonverbal Interactions

A traditional classroom management technique is for the teacher to move toward a student who is not paying attention. The proximity of the teacher is often all that is needed for the message "pay attention" to be conveyed. The differing teaching techniques for giving directions depend on the age level of the students and complexity of the instructions.

Kindergarten teachers usually start off by telling students to wait until they have given all the directions before getting up and moving. For instance, if the directions were "Go to the back of the room and pick up a piece of red paper," students would start to head toward the back before the sentence was finished.

In secondary school, students will wait until everything is organized before moving. Therefore, it is important to pay attention to how instructions, questions, and general verbal and nonverbal interactions affect the group of students you plan to teach and how your instructional style may influence how you communicate. (In Chapters 1 and 2, we discussed teacher-centered and child-centered instruction and how teachers' views of how their students learn affect their practice.)

Appropriate Encouragement and Praise

Academic achievement was found to be higher in classes where teachers provided encouragement and praise, used more nonverbal support, and were understanding and friendly (Good & Brophy, 1991). Attitudes toward the subject matter also improved when teachers provided students with challenging questions along with appropriate encouragement (She & Fisher, 2002). Students feel well supported when teachers believe in their ability to learn and become partners in helping students achieve their learning goals.

In Problem-Based Scenario 10.1, you meet Michael, an eighth-grade teacher. He faces a hurdle in teaching science the way he believes it should be taught. Some of his students are openly resistant to his teaching methods. This scenario provides an opportunity to think about instructional style and communication with students.

Communicating with Parents: Clarity and Openness

Most parents really only want what's best for their children. When we use the term *parent*, we extend that to include any primary caregiver (e.g., guardian, grandparent, foster parent). Parents tend to be more involved in schools during the elementary years and less so once students enter secondary school (Roderick & Camburn, 1999). It would be difficult to point to any one reason for this shift. As a teacher, you will find that families often have considerable time constraints. This affects the time that parents have for active participation in their adolescent's education.

Problem-Based Scenario 10.1

Student: *Jerry*

Teachers: *Michael and Mr. Finkel*

As the eighth-graders noisily bumped their way out of the room, Michael stifled a weary sigh. It was only October and already he was having problems with this group. After 3 years teaching science to grade 8s, you'd think he would have a good repertoire of ideas, but this one stumped him. Michael was trying to introduce the idea of scientific method and how to write a proper laboratory report. He felt it was important to supply reasonable rationales for each component of the lab report since students would be using this standard format for all science courses taught in the district. It seemed straightforward enough when he went over his lesson plan from last year and made some changes necessary for this class.

Jerry was an extremely bright student, but also very vocal. He seemed to be the leader among the group of boys in the class. The girls, much quieter, watched Michael expectantly each time Jerry raised his hand. Jerry challenged each item on the laboratory report, wanting to know why he, and everyone else in the class, needed to do that much writing. Finally, Michael clued into the fact that there was an underlying issue for Jerry and that he was a spokesman for several other students. Upon some close questioning, it became apparent that Jerry and several other students in the class had been in Mr. Finkel's class in grade 7 at Bays Elementary School. Apparently, Mr. Finkel taught science in a very different manner. In Mr. Finkel's class, things changed colors and made noises and smells. Sometimes lights flashed or there were small explosions. Mr. Finkel wore a lab coat and funny looking safety glasses whenever it was time for science. Everyone loved science in Mr. Finkel's class, and there was very little writing. By contrast, Michael's class seemed to be too much writing and boring labs. Jerry bluntly wanted to know when the science would begin.

Michael had tried his best to explain that science wasn't a "magic show." The class sat and listened quietly, but were obviously not convinced by his explanation. After they left, Michael thought about his next move. He would definitely like to discuss science teaching with Mr. Finkel, but felt it should be approached carefully in a collegial manner. But of greater concern was what to do now. The eighth-graders had a natural enthusiasm that he didn't want to stifle. How could he turn this around now that he knew what the students "thought science was"?

The lack of involvement does not imply that a family is not interested or concerned, but often family obligations, such as younger children, shift work, or day care, hinder a parent's ability to participate at the secondary level. This does not mean the teacher cannot communicate with parents, but rather a teacher should become more proactive, and sometimes creative, in contacting parents.

Ways to Defuse Problem Situations

There are instances when teachers can be hesitant to deal with parents, such as in the case of discipline problems or when they know a parent is unhappy with a situation. Babcock and Backlund (2001) offer some suggestions for defusing tensions:

- Talk about positive items first.
- Make the conversation student centered so that parents are aware that the focus is on a concern about the student as a person.
- Allow parents to "have their say" first so that any issues can be dealt with immediately.

Opportunities for Parent–Teacher Interactions

If a teacher opens a line of communication right from the beginning, it makes negative encounters less likely (Photo 10.5). Parents not only feel they know what

PHOTO 10.5
Open communication with parents is vital in strengthening the connection between home and school.

is happening at the school, but they also feel freer to contact a teacher to ask questions before issues develop into tense situations. Here are several common ideas for communicating with parents.

Parent–Teacher Conferences   These are often scheduled in the evening to accommodate working parents. While this is a good arrangement in many ways, there are often too many parents to see comfortably in a short period of time. It is nice to get to meet parents, but, particularly in secondary schools, there is often a level of confusion due to varying schedules, numbers of different teachers, and room changes. One of the authors remembers having 5-minute meetings in the gym where all the other teachers were also meeting with parents. A student would escort a parent to the teacher and then interrupt when the allotted 5 minutes had passed. It was unsatisfying for everyone. If possible, try to schedule a meeting that is mutually convenient and in relatively quiet surroundings, perhaps with the student as a participant in the discussion.

Written Communication   Short notes sent home are good ways to keep a dialogue open with parents. Instructors often use notes for students with special needs or for situations that require continuity of behavior or continuity of management strategies. Some teachers and schools have started to use newsletters to convey information, but these flyers often do not reach the parents (they end up in lockers or trash cans). Some teachers now set up e-mail lists for the parents of students in their classes. This is an easy and effective way to keep in touch with families. Digital technology can also be used to send photos of class projects and activities or to comment on an individual student's progress. Communication by e-mail does assume a computer in every home, however. Parents should have equal access to home–school communication. If any family will be disadvantaged by this approach, an alternative should be sought.

Web Sites   Many schools are now producing Web sites where material that once was sent home by way of a newsletter now appears on the Internet. Teachers are also supplying homework and extra information by posting it on links to the school's site. Although this is a good way to keep information available for a parent or student, it does not fulfill the one-on-one interaction so valuable to parents and teachers. This also assumes parents have a computer at home.

Telephone   Many teachers keep in contact with parents by telephone. This is a convenient way to contact parents when it may be very difficult to arrange a parent–teacher conference due to work schedules and the like. Many schools have automatic phoning procedures when a student is absent and the parent has not called or e-mailed a reason for the absence.

Parent Advisory Groups or Committees   Traditionally, these are groups of parents who organize support for the teachers and school. They participate in discussion regarding educational topics such as curricula or accreditation issues. This input assists teachers and administrators to understand community ideas and perspectives on a range of issues. These parents often run hot dog days or hold fund-raisers for extra school or sports equipment. Parent Advisory Groups or Committees help provide the connection to the community, especially for those parents who are unable to be more actively involved in the life of the school. Active, as opposed to passive, parental involvement in their children's education is critical to student success in school (Timmons, 2004). In Info Byte 10.1, we discuss the differences between these types of involvement.

Building Mutual Respect

In all these types of communication, it is important for teachers to build mutual respect. This is done by acknowledging the time constraints of the parents, attempting to work around their schedules, and speaking to both parents if possible. If necessary, take time to get some background from a counselor regarding any cultural information that may be important to your meeting; arrange for a translator to help with the meeting, if necessary; and have positive things to say, especially if there is a problem.

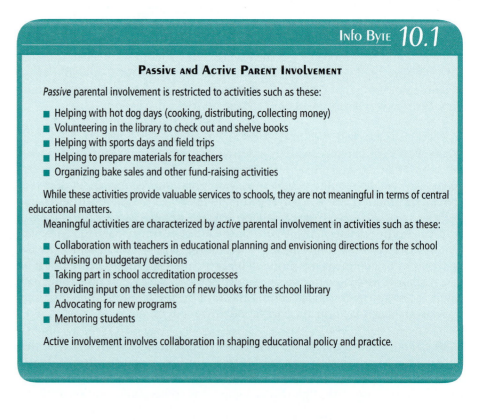

INFO BYTE 10.1

PASSIVE AND ACTIVE PARENT INVOLVEMENT

Passive parental involvement is restricted to activities such as these:

- Helping with hot dog days (cooking, distributing, collecting money)
- Volunteering in the library to check out and shelve books
- Helping with sports days and field trips
- Helping to prepare materials for teachers
- Organizing bake sales and other fund-raising activities

While these activities provide valuable services to schools, they are not meaningful in terms of central educational matters.

Meaningful activities are characterized by *active* parental involvement in activities such as these:

- Collaboration with teachers in educational planning and envisioning directions for the school
- Advising on budgetary decisions
- Taking part in school accreditation processes
- Providing input on the selection of new books for the school library
- Advocating for new programs
- Mentoring students

Active involvement involves collaboration in shaping educational policy and practice.

Keeping Lines of Communication Open

If there is a problem, try to supply some reasonable suggestions for rectifying the issue; listen to what parents have to say—they know the student the best; and always be courteous and friendly. With secondary students it is usually very effective to ask the student to join the meeting. Especially as students get closer to graduating, it becomes more important for them to help make decisions that may affect their progress and future. Joint parent–teacher–student conferences are also effective in elementary and middle schools. Some schools alternate student-led meetings with parent–teacher meetings. The student is central to the topics under discussion at a meeting with parents, and he or she deserves to have a voice in the meeting.

Knowing, Understanding, and Respecting the Culture of the Community

In many cultures, extended families are common. If appropriate, invitations can be given to include other members of a family to events such as open houses, plays, or evenings with a teacher. The rapport established by recognizing community traditions goes a long way to solidifying the teacher's connection to the student's education. Do not overlook the cultural influence on families. McDermott and Rothenberg (2001) found that low-income, urban African American and Latino parents "often felt alienated and unwelcome at school events" (p. 2). While the teachers worked hard to provide contacts with parents through newsletters and phone calls, there was still a problem in communicating that resulted in the parents feeling unwelcome.

As part of their study, McDermott and Rothenberg (2001) had preservice teachers develop a better understanding of the parents and the community. This was done through interviewing parents about the school and their children and by attending parent–teacher meetings. In the end this fostered greater communication between parents and teachers, and a greater sense of community.

Sometimes parents are reluctant to become involved in schools, even to the point of avoiding parent–teacher conferences, because their own school experiences were negative. Reentering a school environment can be extremely stressful for people who experienced failure and lacked a sense of belonging in school. As teachers, you need to be aware of possible reasons for parents' lack of involvement and look for ways to draw them into school life.

Communicating with Colleagues: Sharing Points of View and Teaching Strategies

Although teachers spend a considerable amount of time in individual classrooms, they also work in collaboration with other teachers and administrators. There are common objectives and shared strategies for student learning. When teachers work as a committed group, they find a sense of community developing (Photo 10.6). As mentioned before, an environment that is supportive and caring promotes student success. Students benefit from the consistency of a collaborative school staff. Teachers also benefit from this type of environment. When teachers collaborate, there is a greater sense of self-efficacy (Battistich, Solomon, Watson, & Schaps, 1997).

Both authors have worked within systems that exemplify this environment and can attest to the energizing nature of the collaborative teaching process. For a new teacher, this type of environment provides greater opportunities to become a more successful and effective teacher.

PHOTO 10.6
Students benefit from the consistency of a collaborative school staff and teachers feel a greater sense of self-efficacy.

Surfing Terms 10.2

School-based team
Special education assistant
Teaching assistant
School effectiveness
Teacher effectiveness

Teachers may find themselves part of a *school-based team* whose responsibility is to provide direction for the education of students with special needs. (Refer back to Info Byte 3.2. It provides an overview of the roles and responsibilities of school-based teams and the importance of effective communication in encouraging positive directions for students.)

Learning and Teaching Tools

Throughout this book we have attempted to focus on the student and his or her needs. This focus is a prerequisite for learning to occur. It provides an understanding of the learner as an individual with talents, interests, and personal goals. Then we looked at the classroom environment that provides the learner with a setting conducive to learning. Now we need to focus our attention on the actual planning of instruction.

Complementing Supportive Environments with Effective Instruction

In presenting our discussion of learning and teaching tools, we have decided to take an *instructional design* perspective. In your teaching career you will need to plan for a number of instructional situations, not all of them for your classroom. Teachers are often asked to put on parent workshops and participate in developing materials for a Teacher's Professional Day or Conference. By working through the steps in an instructional design format, you will find that the basic planning is adaptable for a number of situations and that some of the items often required in lesson plans by colleges and universities make more sense when viewed in the larger context of instructional design.

Instructional Design as a Tool for Planning

Instructional design is a broad term used to identify the process of planning, organizing, selecting materials, and evaluating some type of instructional situation (single classes to workshops) (Seels & Glasgow, 1998). Most of you will experience this process in the planning you are required to do for units of the curriculum and teaching individual classes.

Learner-Focused Planning   Instructional planning must be learner focused. You must understand *how* people learn. This has been covered throughout this book through our emphasis on the construction of knowledge. You must understand *why* people learn. This also has been covered as you worked through the material on motivation and self-esteem.

Holistic Human Development   Instructional planning must focus on, acknowledge, and enhance holistic human development. Thus, you must incorporate your knowledge of the different aspects of development to encourage change and growth in students.

Immediate and Long-Range Goals   Instructional planning must include immediate and long-range goals and objectives. You will need to know not only the immediate curriculum for a particular age group, but also what students have learned in the curriculum and what will be expected of them in the future.

Systematic Planning   Instructional planning must include not only some form of systematic planning, but also constant evaluation and reevaluation throughout the planning and implementation stages. For example, this may mean asking questions of colleagues or the students themselves, checking textbooks and/or curriculum guides, finding appropriate materials to enhance the lesson(s), and finding creative ways to introduce some enthusiasm to basic material and keep interest high (Photo 10.7). In every instance, you must ask whether your activities are allowing your students to learn effectively and enthusiastically.

PHOTO 10.7

Find appropriate materials to enhance the lesson and creative ways to introduce enthusiasm and keep interest high.

Student Development and Curriculum Goals

Since instructional design is such a large field, we will narrow our discussion to aspects that affect and influence children and adolescents in school. You should be aware that a number of designs are aimed at adults and training, such as those used by the military or fire departments. If you look at any of these, you will find that they all contain the same basic elements. The main differences are the result of the designer's understanding of the nature of the tasks being taught, the working environment, and the knowledge and skill level of the students (Dick & Carey, 1996; Gagne, Briggs, & Wager, 1992).

Instructional Design: From Educational Philosophy to Evaluation of Learning

The five elements of effective instructional design are outlined next. We have provided examples of how the process of instructional design would work in elementary and middle school.

The Mission Statement

This is a philosophical statement summarizing the beliefs, roles, and responsibilities about learning and education for a school or district. It is often fairly formal

TABLE 10.1

Examples of Instructional Design: Elementary and Middle School

	Unit	Needs Assessment	Goals	Objectives	Teaching and Learning Activities	Evaluation
Grade 3	Local Artisans	The use of local materials in fiber and ceramic arts	Students will gain knowledge of how local materials influence art forms.	Students will be able to identify local art. Students will be able to explain how the local landscape and materials influence art forms.	Visit local art galleries. Visit a local farm to buy fleece. Learn how to spin and weave. Gather local plants to dye wool.	Create a weaving in the local style.
Grade 8	The Early History of the Area	The influence of World War I on the local community	Students will gain background knowledge of the history of World War I.	Students will be able to identify the countries involved in WWI. Students will be able to explain why different countries decided to declare war. Students will be able to discuss the reasons why men volunteered to go to war.	Draw maps. Discuss borders and related disputes. Discuss how countries moved troops. Visit the local archives.	Test: Identify countries involved in World War I. Write an essay discussing border disputes. Create a model of troop movements.

and points to the underlying goals most citizens have for the educational process. If the school is private or religious, you will see the addition of statements reflecting the extended philosophy of the group the school represents. You should ask to see the mission statement for your faculty or the school where you do your practice teaching.

If you are planning a curriculum unit, the mission statement is more of a problem statement. This is the time to clarify exactly what you intend to teach, why it is necessary to teach this, and what the characteristics of the students are. Most teachers find the topics in the curriculum guides, but sometimes teachers have the opportunity to develop their own programs and materials. Most districts have locally developed materials that reflect some aspect of the community or its history.

The most important part of this phase is to be specific, since it provides the direction you will take in your planning. Let's use examples from grade 3 Art and grade 8 Social Studies to illustrate the instructional design process (see Table 10.1). Info Byte 10.2 reintroduces the performance and mastery goals and objectives discussed in Chapter 9.

INFO BYTE 10.2

Goals and Objectives

- An *educational goal* is a general statement that describes a characteristic that all students should possess after a specific amount of time working on the curriculum.

EXAMPLE:

> The students will master basic writing skills.

- A *performance* or *instructional goal* is a statement that describes a general characteristic that the student can demonstrate after working on the curriculum. As you can see, several performance or instructional goals would be necessary to achieve an educational goal.

EXAMPLE:

> The student will be able to write in paragraphs.

- A *performance* or *instructional objective* is a detailed statement that describes a very specific, concrete action that a student needs to demonstrate.

EXAMPLE:

> The student will be able to write a complete sentence (subject–verb–object).

It will take several performance or instructional objectives to achieve a performance or instructional goal. In this example, the student would need to know about structures such as topic sentences, concluding sentences, and indenting the first line to achieve the instructional goal.

- *Performance goals and objectives* describe an *observable* event the student must *demonstrate*. Be careful to make the underlying learning the objective, rather than the performance of a task. For example, a child may know $2 \times 2 = 4$ because he or she memorized flash cards, not because he or she understands that multiplication is a variation of addition.
- *Mastery goals and objectives* describe demonstrated events that reflect growth in a specific area, such as academic, personal responsibility, or physical capability. Success is based on multiple factors, such as ability, age, independence, and risk taking. For example, learning pottery skills requires numerous steps leading to mastery.

Needs Assessment: What, Who, and How?

This is a very necessary step, since the time you invest in asking questions will pay dividends later in your planning. It generally has three substeps:

- *Gather data on what already exists.* This may mean library research or asking questions of other teachers or experts in the field. A Web search may reveal interesting aspects of the topic that you were unaware of or even curricular materials available that would fit in perfectly with your intent.
- *Clarify who your learners are.* Exactly what level of experience do they have? Make sure you aren't assuming a level of cognition or competency beyond or beneath what actually exists.
- *Identify the physical constraints within which you work.* For example, if you need to have access to a computer, is one available? Or does the whole class have to use the same computer? How much time can you spend on this unit? Do you have any money for surplus or expendable materials?

While this part of the planning may seem picky, one of the authors had a student who developed an entire unit based on the belief that all children had access to computers at home. This was not the case. The student spent a tremendous amount of time revising the entire unit plan because this step was skipped.

Another example is the student who started to prepare an outdoor education program for a district that included a segment on sea kayaking. It wasn't until she was required to turn in a needs assessment for a course on instructional design that she found out that not only was another teacher in the same district halfway through planning an identical unit, but the teacher had already received funding from the school district to assist in its development. Knowing this in advance enabled the student to shift her focus to another aspect of outdoor education.

Constructing a Needs Assessment   A needs assessment clarifies several aspects of instruction planning, such as the following:

- What you know about the topic
- Where to find resources for it
- What resources are available
- Who the learners are
- What knowledge learners have of the topic
- What the constraints of the physical and supporting environment are
- What materials you need
- What permissions are required (and by whom)
- What supporting services are required

In many instances, all these issues are very straightforward, since a unit often requires an environment and materials readily available in a classroom. But if you get used to asking these questions at the early stages of development, it will become a natural part of your classroom organization and planning.

Now go back to your original problem statement and clarify or refine your wording so that it reflects any new information you have gathered. For example, for the grade 8 example, research of the sample topic revealed that the number of men who died during World War I influenced the community more than anything else.

Goals and Objectives: What Will Be Learned?

Researchers tend to identify the possession of goals as a desirable trait in a learner. Goals allow the learner to divide a problem into more manageable segments and focus on the important aspects that the student needs to understand or appreciate (Mager, 1972).

Types of Goals   In most instances, the goals in education are provided for teachers, as in this example: "All graduating students will have a basic understanding of the organization and functioning of the federal government." This is not only a fairly generic statement, but represents a desired and testable state. Often more noninstructional goals are not as easily tested: "All graduating students will become productive citizens." Both types of goals are valuable and should have a place in planning.

Forming Objectives   Once we get to objectives, we start to focus on the individual student and on specific learning outcomes. Often novice teachers use the objectives to write about what they intend to accomplish in the classroom. This actually forms a part of the learning process and has its place in the next section. The easiest way to avoid this mistake is to begin an objective with the statement, "Students will be able to. . . . " Thus the teacher emphasizes the skills the students will have acquired after they have finished the lessons in the unit. Specific objectives that use verbs indicating some action on the part of the student simplify the subsequent evaluation process.

Stating objectives does not mean we should use only what are known as *behavioral* or *performance* objectives (see Chapter 9). All instruction should acknowledge the nonbehavioral objectives required to work with students (Dick & Reiser, 1996). For example, "*Students will be able to appreciate the impact of the loss of loved ones on the families, irrespective of the soldiers' nationality.*" While this type of objective is hard to evaluate, it provides the kind of affective component desired for any instructional situation.

Evaluating Goals and Objectives   At this point you should go back to your original problem, and then to your goals and objectives, to determine whether these hold together and make sense. It is a good idea to ask another person to read over what you have planned to make sure you are keeping to your original problem and topic. It is very easy to stray into only one segment of the topic, and leave very little room for the original intent of the problem.

You will notice that in the examples provided the goals and objectives focused on the general topics of (1) available materials in art and (2) the history of World War I. However, the original intent was to work with a more local viewpoint. Goals and objectives should be rewritten to include aspects of the entire community.

As you organize your goals and objectives, it will become clear where to allot most of your time. While it is important to be able to identify the countries involved in the WWI conflict, according to your problem-topic, students also need to understand the geographic organization of the local community during that era. This automatically leads to goals and objectives reflecting aspects of the community at the time of the war.

Instructional Sequence: Teaching and Learning Activities

The instructional sequence is the actual organization a teacher plans and uses to achieve certain objectives; that is, it guides the learning process.

Learning about World War I: An Example   To learn about the countries of the world involved in World War I, students could participate in activities such as drawing maps and discussing border disputes and related issues, such as how countries moved troops (by ship, by land, with horses, etc.). A field trip could be used to gather information. Local archives can provide information for creating maps of the area, for example.

Understanding Artisans: An Example   To understand how local artisans work, students might visit studios and sites where local artists gather their materials. They could research the history of arts and crafts in the area or interview local artists. In secondary school, information is often conveyed in the form of a lecture or via a more passive format. How can you make your students more active learners? This is an example of a turning point at which a teacher has to make certain decisions.

What is the best way to convey the material that has to be transmitted? Is it direct instruction, discovery learning, lecture, and/or group work? From having done your needs assessment, you already know the constraints of time, materials, and environment. With this you can make appropriate decisions about the types of activities to plan.

Using Materials in Context   A word of caution should be given here. Very often, novice teachers are given lessons and materials in their entirety (worksheets, maps, readings, etc.). Goals and objectives are not necessarily included, so the materials stand alone. When others give you materials, realize that they are out of context. Teachers often wonder why lessons fail when they worked so well for another teacher. The reason is that goals, objectives, and the learning process have to be tied together to achieve positive outcomes.

One of the authors tells the story of the time when an elderly neighbor bought his first microwave oven. He complained that it was useless—it made terrible toasted cheese sandwiches. But he used a cooking process that was not appropriate to his objective. This happens in teaching too. We often are given what are said to be effective materials that turn out to be dismal failures and a waste of precious time.

In Problem-Based Scenario 10.2, you will meet two teachers who face different sides of a dilemma involving the use of prepared materials. This scenario will give you the opportunity to think about the practical implications of linking goals, objectives, and learning materials.

The opposite also occurs. Sometimes teachers planning projects for their class try very hard to write entire unit plans around these projects. This is extremely hard to do successfully. Often the teacher is so tied to a single idea that he or she fails to recognize that either the goals and objectives do not match the problem, or they are inappropriate for the students.

Instead, start off with what you want the students to learn, and then decide on the appropriate learning process to attain that goal. Now go back over your problem statement, goals, objectives, and learning process and see if they all make sense. Ask questions about logic and flow of ideas. Never be hesitant to change anything that does not belong or should be moved around.

Evaluation: What Was Learned?

In evaluating what was learned, the question should always be this: "Did the students achieve what they set out to learn?" If you have done a good job of writing your objectives, answering this question should be relatively straightforward.

You could give a paper and pencil test and ask students to "identify" or "define" the objective, or write a paper to "discuss" it, work with a group to

Problem-Based Scenario 10.2

Teachers: *Denise and Gloria*

When Denise began her job at Roosevelt Elementary, Gloria tried to help out. Denise was assigned to a grade 1–2 class where the seven first-graders were in need of considerable support in beginning school and the fifteen second-graders were academically capable. It was one of those ideas that worked on paper, but was very challenging to handle in practice. The thinking was that the second-graders would work independently, allowing the time needed to provide the support needed to the first-graders. The reality was that both groups needed specialized attention.

Gloria was an experienced teacher and she had lots of materials to share. However, she made it clear to Denise that the materials had to be used in a coherent fashion. They needed to be related to her teaching objectives. Denise visited Gloria several times during her first year at Roosevelt. Each time, she took away a stack of materials. Gloria began to get uneasy, especially after she began to see Denise heading down the hall every morning with a huge stack of paper. Was she giving her students a lot of "busy work"?

Two things happened in Denise's second year of teaching that upset Gloria. First, Gloria had some of Denise's former pupils in her third-grade class. Every now and then, they would say, "Mrs. Torres, we did this last year with Miss Chong." Second, Gloria overheard other teachers chatting in the staff room. They were very concerned that Denise had not returned the materials she had borrowed from them last year. Gloria resolved to stop sharing materials with Denise. She thought she was probably enabling her in failing to provide well thought out, integrated instruction to her students.

The next time Denise approached Gloria, Gloria was firm in saying she couldn't share materials any longer. She explained to Denise that it was affecting her own planning and she was concerned that the materials weren't being used in a cohesive way. Denise's face fell and she left Gloria's classroom in a huff. Following that, Denise refused to speak to Gloria. Gloria believed she had done the right thing educationally, but she worried about the effect on collegial relationships in the school. She was really in a quandary about what to do.

FIGURE 10.1

"build" it, go to the library to "find" it, or give a presentation to "show" it, and so on. The evaluation hinges on the action verb you used in your objectives.

For nonbehavioral objective verbs, such as "appreciate," you may want to select more informal evaluation techniques, such as noting whether students read topic items on the bulletin boards or pay attention to discussions of the topic that you overhear outside class. While these are subjective evaluations, they are often the only measures we have to understand the effect of the more affective goals and objectives.

As you go over this format for organizing a unit or lesson, you will note that after each segment you were told to go back over the whole plan to make sure it tied together. This means that the evaluation process is an ongoing, integral part of the instructional design-planning process.

Those in industry often hire outside consultants to review and evaluate plans as they go along. A teacher does not always have the luxury of having someone to read everything he or she plans. Therefore, you should get into the habit of reviewing your plans as you write them. Try to be as objective as possible. Remember not to fall into the trap of not changing something if it doesn't look right.

Instructional Media: Ensuring an Appropriate Match with Educational Goals

Technology provides teachers with the outstanding range of media available in most schools. Teachers often are encouraged to find ways to more fully use audiovisual equipment and computers. There are a few guidelines to be aware of when selecting media and/or materials for instructional use.

- Make sure the media or materials selected fit the goals and objectives of the lesson or unit.
- Make sure the media or materials are appropriate for the learner and the setting.
- Make sure the media or materials are appropriate for the content being presented (a stereo with bad audio is questionable for teaching music).
- Make sure the media or materials help in the learning, rather than detract from it (such as outdated materials in which adolescents focus more on the hair and clothes, rather than the message).
- Make sure you select the sequence of topics, rather than relying on prese-quenced media or materials.
- Make sure media or materials are available at the time you need them.

Developing a Teaching Repertoire

As you experience a variety of teaching opportunities, you will acquire a number of lessons and strategies that work with a range of different types of students. Over time you will develop your own teaching repertoire. All teachers have developed a repertoire. This repertoire is that "bag of ideas" so necessary for effective teaching. It is also what was referred to above in our discussion of lessons being given to novice teachers.

These lessons will only have value if they are accompanied by appropriate goals and objectives. Make sure you keep this in mind when you try something with a different group of students. All teachers have lessons that work well with one class and then go nowhere with the next class. This is because each class is made up of different individuals, with different talents, needs, and motivations.

Most teachers actually do a needs assessment without really identifying it as such. They look at a class and at the curriculum guide and come up with ideas that are appropriate and seem to work "magically." Veteran teachers also seldom write out lesson plans in the same detail as preservice teachers. This is because so much is done "in their heads" by relying on the "bag of ideas" they have developed through experience. It takes time for this ability to develop. In the meantime, preservice teachers are encouraged to write things down in a formalized manner.

Your university will probably have a format for planning lessons for you to follow. Compare it to the instructional design format above. Your university's format may omit the mission statement and the needs assessment; however, both of these are necessary. They underlie the philosophy of teaching and learning and the content and contextual analysis for the lesson. In Info Bytes 10.3 and 10.4, we present elementary and secondary lesson plans and compare them to the instructional design format.

In Problem-Based Scenarios 10.3 and 10.4, that follow, you have the opportunity to think about how to use effective communication skills and other strategies that help to maintain a supportive classroom environment.

INFO BYTE 10.3

ELEMENTARY LESSON PLAN
FOURTH-GRADE NOVEL STUDY—*Charlotte's Web* by E. B. White

Goals of the novel study

- Awareness of story structure, plot, setting, characters, and outcome.
- Appreciation of literature and language.

Objectives

- Students will learn how to predict content of a novel and test their predictions.
- Students will learn to raise questions about the sequence of story events.

Teaching and learning activities

- Introduce the reading response journal.
- Students record in their journals what they already know about *Charlotte's Web* or, if they have no knowledge of the book, make predictions about the novel.
- Students read the first chapter of the novel.
- Students meet in small groups to discuss their predictions and record questions.

Evaluation

- Students list the three most important ideas in the first chapter and explain why they are important.

INFO BYTE 10.4

SECONDARY LESSON PLAN

Women in Film: SUSAN SARANDON AND GEENA DAVIS

Goals and Objectives

- Construct an argument about a film or a body of work (IV-1).

Articulate a theme, strength, or weakness in a film or body of work (IV-1-1).

- Describe how film influences our thoughts and opinions (V-1).

Provide an example of a film that has influenced the way in which a group thought or acted and describe the effect of the film (V-1-1).

Identify techniques used to influence others through film (V-1-3).

- Describe how film influences our concept of gender (V-2).

Provide examples of films that promote a negative concept of gender (V-2-1).
Provide examples of films that promote a positive concept of gender (V-2-2).
Discuss the concept of gender in a film clip (V-2-3).

Opening Motivator

- Show some clips that project very negative images of women and start a discussion with a controversial comment about them (James Bond? *Beach Blanket Bingo*?).

Instructional Activity

- Small-group discussion (ask groups to make notes of their discussion) leading to full-class discussion.

Questions for Discussion

1. Should we be concerned about how women are portrayed in film?
2. Are images generally positive or negative?
3. What should we do to counteract negative images?

- Lecture and film clips

Rocky Horror Picture Show
Earth Girls Are Easy
A League of Their Own
Thelma and Louise
Dead Man Walking

- Return to discussion, if time.

Preparation

- Prepare film clips.
- Prepare lecture.

Evaluation

- Collect and review notes from small-group discussion.
- Monitor student input into class discussion.

Source: Reprinted with permission of author, David Nicks.

Problem-Based Scenario 10.3

Student: *Andrew*
Teacher: *Margaret*

Margaret had really liked her grade 8 class during the first term. She was even pleased when Mr. Goodhue, the principal, had asked her if she would take a new student in mid-January.

Andrew was a bit of a challenge since he had a mild form of autism, but Margaret felt she could work with him. She had attended the IEP meeting at the beginning of January to make sure she knew what to expect and to gain ideas for how to modify her science curriculum. It was at the IEP meeting that she met Mrs. Douglas. Mrs. Douglas was a Special Education Assistant (SEA) and would be working with Andrew in his classes. Mr. Goodhue felt Andrew should have a full-time SEA until they were sure there would be no difficulty having Andrew work in a regular classroom without an assistant. Apparently, there had been some previous incidents of punching other students when Andrew got frustrated with the work. Mr. Goodhue wanted to get things off on the "right foot," as he put it.

For Margaret, the problem wasn't with Andrew, but rather with Mrs. Douglas. At the beginning of each class, Margaret would give Mrs. Douglas a copy of the lesson plan and the highlighted work Andrew would do, along with any modified worksheets or handouts. Mrs. Douglas would thank Margaret and then proceed to talk to Andrew during the entire lesson. They ended up moving to the back of the room, and within only one week had set up a mini-work area for themselves. Margaret had tried to speak to Mrs. Douglas, but got only polite replies and agreements to allow Andrew to work with others in the class. Margaret didn't want to make a scene in front of the class, but she wasn't happy that Mrs. Douglas was essentially taking her student. Andrew had no contact with the other students and was not even really part of the classes Margaret taught. By the end of the second week, Mr. Goodhue spoke to Margaret in passing about how pleased he was with Andrew's progress in science. Apparently, Mrs. Douglas had been giving daily progress reports to the counselor.

This approach really wasn't working. Margaret was the teacher, and Mrs. Douglas was the SEA. Margaret needed to figure out how to tactfully approach Mrs. Douglas about the role of a SEA, without upsetting her, Andrew, or anyone else. This had to be done very carefully. But how?

Problem-Based Scenario 10.4

Student: *Jackie*
Teacher: *Samantha*

Cedar Grove Middle School prided itself on its approach to special education. The staff was committed to inclusion and was well known in the school district for their innovative approaches to supporting learners with special needs. Samantha Joseph had worked at Cedar Grove for 5 years, taking a leadership role in designing programs for students with learning disabilities and setting up a model school-based team. She had also expanded her knowledge of special education by taking courses on educating children with autism. In the last 4 years, she had successfully included three students with autism. Her relationship with the special education assistant who worked with her was a good one. Together they really seemed to help children progress. Samantha had encouraged Dorothy to take an active role in the Special Education Assistants' organization because she recognized her leadership and professional potential. All of this made what was happening to Samantha at the moment even harder to figure out and emotionally draining.

Samantha had just returned from a meeting with Dorothy, the local special education assistants' union rep, and the school principal that was focused on issues related to one of their students. Jackie had

(continued)

Problem-Based Scenario 10.4 (continued)

autism and had more difficulties settling into his seventh-grade classroom than other children with whom Samantha had worked. Samantha and Dorothy had had a number of meetings about Jackie to discuss strategies to support home–school communication and professional roles and responsibilities. Samantha felt that Dorothy had crossed the line in how she communicated to Jackie's mother and in some of the comments she had written in Jackie's homework book. However, Dorothy had received Samantha's feedback well and they seemed to be working things out. Now she sat alone in her classroom, shaken by a meeting at which she was accused of harassment.

She could hardly believe what she heard at the meeting. "Yes," she had agreed, "there are some differences of opinion about how to support Jackie, but we are working those out like professionals." She further agreed that she had discussed areas of responsibility with Dorothy and that, in her opinion, this was understood. She emphasized that there was always a professional, respectful tone to the discussions the two women had. Dorothy, however, adamantly refused to accept anything Samantha had to say. She insisted she had been treated with disrespect and humiliated. Moreover, this had happened so often, she really felt she had to contact her union.

Nothing Samantha or her principal said about due process made any impression. The meeting concluded in a vague fashion. Samantha knew a letter would arrive summarizing the meeting and there was mention of sanctions. She really had no idea what that meant. She had to talk to Ted, her principal, about how to proceed. Samantha truly believed in dealing with issues in a calm, professional manner, but now she felt hurt and angry. Didn't she have some rights too? (See Figures 10.2 and 10.3 on pages 304 and 305.)

Summary

In this chapter we introduced some of the most effective components of teaching. The concept of mutual respect forms the basis for effective classroom communities. It allows you to see beyond problem situations, since it implies knowledge and understanding of the community culture. It pays dividends in terms of communication between you, the teacher, and the students, parents, and cultural community. Teachers plan effectively when they provide relevant curriculum by taking into consideration the development of students, pertinent cultural considerations, and knowledge of how to enhance learning. Teachers plan classroom activities efficiently when they allow students the opportunity to learn in classes that support their autonomy and competence.

- Teachers need to understand that supporting student competence and autonomy builds mutual respect. This mutual respect for the student results in a relatedness to the classroom community and positive academic growth.
- Using a variety of teaching techniques that reflects knowledge of the student's capabilities and interests further develops respect.
- Positive behavioral support is a natural way to maintain an appropriate learning atmosphere in a classroom, rather than to control through a classroom management philosophy.
- Communication is an essential component for any classroom. This extends to communication between the teacher and the student, and with colleagues, parents, the administration, and anyone else involved in the education process.
- Effective instruction begins with detailed planning. It takes into consideration not only the "What do I do on Monday" issue but also answers questions such as "Where are we headed?", "Why do it this way?", "How can I reach everyone in the class?", "Did it work?"

■ All effective teachers build a repertoire of techniques and ideas that they adapt and apply to the range of student needs, interests, and abilities encountered in a classroom.

A Metacognitive Challenge

You should now be able to reflect on the following questions:

- ■ What makes competence, autonomy, and relatedness so important to learners?

- ■ How can I help students to become self-directed learners?

- ■ How can I organize my classroom for more effective learning?

- ■ What kind of classroom and students do I want? How can I make this happen?

- ■ How do communication skills and mutual respect interact?

- ■ What are the specific ways I intend to keep communication open with parents?

- ■ What are the assumptions and components of instructional design? Why are they important for planning?

- ■ Why is it important to develop my own teaching repertoire?

Artifacts for Problem-Based Scenarios

FIGURE 10.2 ■ Artifact for Problem-Based Scenario 10.4

Miss Joseph

I am really upset by what's happening to Jackie at school. You just don't know him like Dorothy does. She was his assistant from kindergarten to third grade and she's a really good friend. How dare you tell her that she can't make decisions about his homework? And what's this about her being told that the two of them can't just work by themselves all day? What do you know about autism? I live with it and I know what's best for Jackie. Leave Dorothy alone and let her get on with her job.

Margaret Lucas

FIGURE 10.3 ■ Artifact for Problem-Based Scenario 10.4

SPECIAL EDUCATION ASSISTANTS' FEDERATION
UNION OF PUBLIC EMPLOYEES
CEDAR GROVE LOCAL 119

November 14, 2002

Ms Samantha Joseph
Cedar Grove Elementary
Cedar Grove, WA

Dear Ms. Joseph:

This letter is to summarize our meeting of November 7, 2002.
Present were yourself, Dorothy Dan, Ted Emlich, and myself.
From the interactions described at the meeting, it is clear that
you have engaged in harassing Mrs. Dan, thereby preventing
her from fulfilling her responsibilities as a Special Education
Assistant. I have advised Mrs. Dan to file a formal grievance with
our union. Please note that you may be required to respond
formally to this grievance.

If you require further information about the grievance process,
please contact our office at 555-1172.

Yours sincerely,

Rose MacPherson

Rose MacPherson
Head, Local 119

Understanding the Learner in Context: Assessing Learning

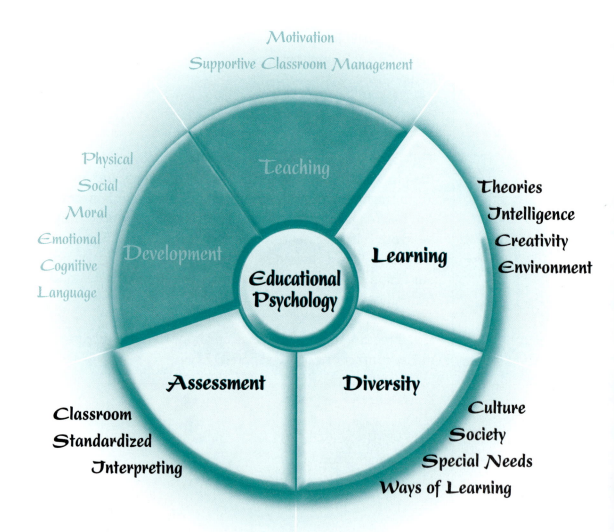

Motivation

Supportive Classroom Management

Physical
Social
Moral
Emotional
Cognitive
Language

Teaching

Development

Educational Psychology

Learning

Theories
Intelligence
Creativity
Environment

Assessment

Diversity

Classroom
Standardized
Interpreting

Culture
Society
Special Needs
Ways of Learning

This chapter is the first of two on the assessment of learning. As teachers, a significant part of your responsibility to both the learners in your classroom and their parents is the assessment and evaluation of how well students are learning and what levels of mastery they have attained. This responsibility has two components. The first is assessing and evaluating students on an ongoing basis in a way that is tied authentically to teaching, learning, and curricular objectives.

The second is reporting the results of assessment and evaluation to learners and their parents. We discuss both of these components in this chapter, with an emphasis on assessment and evaluation that focuses on describing the process and outcomes of learning in ways other than grades.

It is important to think about the ways in which we assess and evaluate our students because the way we teach affects the abilities that students demonstrate (Photo 11.1). In turn, what we think about the role of evaluation in education will influence how we teach. For example, if we teach primarily by lecturing with notes displayed on a projector, then our students tend to demonstrate their knowledge in the same way—through written and oral language. If we teach in a predominantly verbal fashion, then we usually assess that way. If we believe that the role of evaluation is to select for or eliminate students from something (e.g., a special program or scholarships), we will use strategies in our teaching to achieve that end.

The problem can arise that our assessment strategies may not allow students to demonstrate what they know and what they can do. Sternberg (1998a) argues that we need to break out of a vicious circle in which assessment predicts school success well, but not in a way that is inclusive of all our students. We need to broaden the scope of the way in which we teach and assess. This chapter offers strategies to meet the objective of inclusive assessment and evaluation practices.

PHOTO 11.1
The way we teach affects the abilities that our students demonstrate.

Assessment and Evaluation as Part of Teaching and Learning

Assessment and evaluation are linked both to each other and to curriculum and instruction. The goals of assessment and evaluation are to optimize engagement with learning. These goals are accomplished by knowing how children and adolescents understand the topics of the school curriculum; how their experiences and interests are relevant to the curriculum; and what teaching and learning strategies are most effective for each of them.

We want to emphasize how important it is to include the learners' points of view in the assessment process. Assessment and evaluation should be done *with* students, not *to* them (Wilson, 1996). We have probably all experienced a test that we thought was unfair or an evaluation situation in which we thought, "If only I could have explained how I was thinking about that question." When learners and teachers are engaged in a dialogue about the assessment of learning, the process becomes far less one-sided. The process also gives learners autonomy and insight into what they are learning, why they are learning it, and how they learn best. As we discussed in Chapter 9, this autonomy and insight make for engaged and motivated learners.

Making assessment and evaluation an integral part of teaching and learning requires *ongoing* assessment and evaluation of student learning by both teachers and students. Assessment and evaluation do not simply take place at the end of a unit, course, or term (*summative* assessment and evaluation); they are done throughout the year to inform instruction and program planning for individual needs (*formative* assessment and evaluation) (Wilson, 1996).

> **Summative** assessment and evaluation are done *after* a unit, course, or term is complete.

> **Formative** assessment and evaluation are done *during* a unit, course, or term to determine how students are progressing and to inform subsequent instruction.

A Note about Terminology

The terms *assessment* and *evaluation* often are used interchangeably because the two processes are interwoven. One can consider the assessment process to be data gathering—the collection of information by both teacher and student on the what and how of learning. The evaluation process involves the determination of how well a student is learning in comparison to himself or herself, to others, and/or to the curricular objectives. It reflects a judgment on the part of the teacher.

We use the term assessment to include *both* data gathering and evaluation, as the following definition implies:

> Assessment, broadly defined, is the process of collecting and interpreting information that is used (i) to inform students, and their parents/guardians where applicable, about the progress they are making toward attaining the knowledge, skills, attitudes and behaviors to be learned or acquired, and (ii) to inform the various personnel who make educational decisions (instructional, diagnostic, placement, promotion, graduation, curriculum planning, program development, policy) about students. (Principles for Fair Student Assessment Practices for Education in Canada, 1993, p. 2)

It is critical that all students benefit from thoughtful and fair assessment. However, for students with special learning needs the assessment process is especially important. Decisions that determine whether these students will receive special educational services are linked to assessment, as are educational objectives, instructional strategies, and effectiveness of programs (Pike & Salend, 1995). Thoughtful assessment helps to ensure success for all students.

The Teacher's Role in Assessment

Teachers play a central role in ensuring successful assessment (Earl & Cousins, 1996). The following three objectives can help you gather meaningful data in your classrooms. By meaningful, we mean data that will help you understand how, what, and how well your students are learning, gathered through a process that is characterized by reciprocity between student and teacher.

- Track student learning by observing and recording what students accomplish.
- Check on what has been learned by testing in a variety of ways.
- Find out what is "going on" with students by considering children's points of view, how they understand the lessons, and what they gain from instruction. (Neill, 1997)

Consider how this teacher prepares to find out what is "going on" with children:

> I remember you said that the man on the tractor made it turn by stopping one of the big wheels. Let's remember what you were thinking and try to figure out what you meant, the teacher begins as she invites the children to revisit their field trip to the farm. In regards to an experiment with shadows, "Here is a photograph of your jumping in the sunlight. Tell me what you were thinking just as you were in midair over your shadow." Here the teacher is asking two girls to confront their question about whether one's shadow is always attached to one's feet. Note that the teacher does not say, "Look at the photograph and tell me if your feet are attached to your shadow." The focus is on memories about the children's *thinking*, not photographic evidence of an answer. (Forman & Fyfe, 1998, p. 248, emphasis added).

The curricular goals and objectives for all these points should provide guidelines for the potential expectations of the teacher. For students with special needs, teachers should keep the individualized education plan (IEP) goals and objectives readily available for reference. Too often, teachers file away these goals and objectives and only bring them out for the yearly evaluations. Writing out, in point form on a single sheet of paper, the goals and objectives on which you are presently working is a good way to keep this information easily available. In this way you can check the items important to you as a teacher without working through an entire IEP document.

Learner-Centered Assessment

To ensure that one realizes the reciprocity between student and teacher, one should frame the objectives for gathering meaningful assessment data within a *learner-centered* perspective:

> Learner centered is the perspective that couples a focus on individual learners—their heredity, experiences, perspectives, backgrounds, talents, interests, capacities, and needs—with a focus on learning—the best available knowledge about learning and how it occurs and about teaching practices that are most effective in promoting the highest levels of motivation, learning, and achievement for all learners. This dual focus then informs and drives educational decision-making. (McCombs, 1997, p. 4)

Students' Perceptions of Their Learning and Achievement

Learners' own perceptions are powerful influences on learning. Learners' perceptions of classroom practices predict achievement and motivation far better than do teachers' perspectives (Eccles & Roeser, 1999). When teachers adopt a learner-centered perspective, this perspective influences student perceptions positively, which, in turn, boosts engagement with learning and achievement (McCombs, 1997) (Photo 11.2). When viewed in the context of life in an increasingly complex society, thoughtful assessment of one's own learning is critical.

PHOTO 11.2

When teachers adopt a learner-centered perspective, this boosts engagement with learning and achievement.

Students need to become their own best evaluators. In our culture they are faced with increasingly complex demands and are being asked at a very early age to ascertain their own position and to make personal decisions based on their assessment of the situation and their own skills. We want students to become lifelong learners; to internalize "seeking" knowledge, not to give that responsibility to others. To do this they must become their own question-askers and test-makers. (Earl & Cousins, 1996, p. 18)

For secondary teachers, the shift toward learner-centered assessment is a compromise between subject or curricular objectives and understanding the learner. All of us have had negative experiences with subjects that have influenced our willingness to do anything further in that field. On the other hand, with positive experiences, we may realize our limitations in talent, but still pursue an interest in the subject as adults.

Learners' Understandings of What Is to Be Learned

Unfortunately, it is rare that we consider how children and adolescents actually make sense of what it is they do in school. When elementary school children were asked what learning meant (Bickerton, 1994), several remarked that this was the first time anyone had ever asked them that question! Learning is central to the educational enterprise, and we need to know how children make sense of it.

Children's Changing Perspectives on the Learning Process   Bickerton finds that children in grade 1 typically reply that learning refers to "good work" or to specific activities like learning how to read, counting, or printing new words. Older children are increasingly more reflective, saying, "You get better at it if you try your hardest" (grade 3); "Learning means knowing how to do something without having any problems doing it" (grade 5); "Learning is knowing and understanding things you didn't know before" (grade 7) (Bickerton, 1994, pp. 6–8). (See Info Byte 9.2.) The perspectives children have of learning have implications for what they think they have to learn and how they will accomplish learning (Bickerton). Their perspectives change as they develop; these changing perspectives need to be respected and accounted for in instruction and assessment.

The Student's Point of View Is Primary   Vivian Paley (1986) emphasized, "The first order of reality in the classroom is the student's point of view. . ." (p. 127). Thus, we need to step back momentarily from the topic of assessment and consider how we teach. Think back to Chapter 2 in which we presented four models of mind (Bruner, 1996). If your goals as a teacher reflect your understanding that learners have important ways of making sense of the world and you use these ways of sense-making as starting points in instruction (models 3 and 4), you are honoring the first order of reality in the classroom. (Remember, though, that models 1 and 2 are not to be disregarded. There are times when direct instruction and modeling are important instructional strategies.)

Real-Life Teaching and Learning

If we include learners' perspectives on learning and the curriculum in our instructional design, we engage in *authentic pedagogy* (Meichenbaum & Biemiller, 1998; Newmann, Marks, & Gamaron, 1996) by ensuring that what we teach is *relevant* to our students.

Authentic learning tasks are real-life problems of relevance and value that encourage the development of conceptual understanding. As we discussed in the introduction to this book, engagement with educational psychology as it pertains to real teaching issues leads to learning that is more meaningful than learning that reflects memorization of facts about educational psychology. Wiggins (1997) argued that courses be designed "backward" from complex tasks that represent high standards of achievement rather than "forward" from a textbook or adult view of how a course should proceed (p. 56). This is why we emphasize real-life teaching scenarios in the process of learning to become a teacher.

Similarly, courses on mathematics, literature, science, and other subjects should be designed backward from complex tasks like the determination of the perimeter of the school playground, an excellent opening night at the theater, or the rediscovery of the principles of electricity (Photo 11.3). Course design could then move forward from the starting point of learners' initial understandings. This sort of instructional design engages students in real-life work, rather than simply hearing or reading about it (Pea, 1993).

PHOTO 11.3

Students learn more when they have opportunities to engage in authentic tasks in school.

From Authentic Pedagogy to Authentic Assessment

The principles of authenticity outlined above apply to assessment as well as to pedagogy. *Authentic assessment* supports classroom instruction; includes students in the assessment process; is multidimensional; assesses conceptual understanding, problem solving, application, and interpretation; and reflects local values and standards (Meichenbaum & Biemiller, 1998; Paris & Ayres, 1994; Pike & Salend, 1995).

Authenticity in Testing

Authenticity refers to "the extent to which a test, performance, or product used in an assessment bears a relationship to its real-world referent" (Wineburg, 1997, p. 62). Thus, tests are not excluded when discussing authentic assessment strategies. Tests are sometimes viewed as inauthentic, possibly because most of us tend to associate them with stress. However, there are good tests and tests that are not so good.

Tests can be very useful in assessment when they adhere to the following criteria:

- They have a good relationship to what has been taught (Wiggins, 1998).
- They are culturally sensitive (Smith, 2001).
- They can provide good and useful information.

For example, students might take a unit or chapter test *before* being taught the material in the unit to determine what they already know (a *pretest*). If they already know much of what is to be taught, their time is better spent learning the material in more depth, applying it creatively, proceeding to the next level of instruction, or working on an independent project of interest. (See Info Byte 11.1.)

INFO BYTE **11.1**

PRETESTING TO DETERMINE WHAT IS ALREADY KNOWN

Students who are able learners can benefit from assessment before instruction. For example, an A student in math could take unit or chapter tests before you teach the material, or a student who is reading material considerably above grade level could do tests associated with an advanced reader. If the student scores at 90% or better, it is obvious that they already know the material you are about to teach. At this point, you should continue testing, since the student may know considerably more than they have just demonstrated. Continue testing until the student demonstrates 75% mastery.

If students know most of what you have planned to teach, their curriculum can be "compacted" (Reis, Burns, & Renzulli, 1991; Renzulli, 1999). There are several options for compacting curriculum.

- Students could apply the material to be taught in more depth and/or creatively than the rest of the class.
- They could proceed to the level of instruction associated with the point at which they achieved 75% mastery. If this level is considerably above that of the rest of the class, other options may need to be considered such as these:

Accelerated instruction with an older grade and/or tutor
Individualized instruction in the regular classroom
Mentorship
Special program focused on the area of talent
"Replacement" of the time gained with study of another subject or topic of interest

Multiple forms of assessment, including testing, allow students to demonstrate what they know in different ways and provide a broader and deeper picture of a student's abilities than does only one type of assessment (Sattler, 1992; Sternberg, 1998b). We will have more to say about testing in Chapter 12.

In Problem-Based Scenario 11.1, you again meet Jessica and her teachers, Beth and Tanis. Beth is struggling to make sense of Jessica's test results in light of her class work. Consider how multiple forms of assessment may help all concerned to find an appropriate match between the curriculum and Jessica's abilities.

Problem-Based Scenario 11.1

Student: Jessica

Teachers: Beth and Tanis

The last couple of weeks had been stressful for Beth. Ever since Tanis had questioned just how gifted Jessica was, Beth had struggled to try to make sense of what appeared to be happening in class. First, it was unsettling to feel that she and Tanis were not on the same wavelength about Jessica. Their philosophies and intuitions about children were usually so in synch. Second, she thought back to what she had said about Jessica's math not being as strong as her other academic abilities. She realized that what she had said came from observing Jessica in class. Jessica's psychoeducational report showed math abilities at the 99.6th percentile. Beth knew the test Jessica took was not a perfect match to their local math curriculum, but she would have predicted that Jessica would do better in class than she was currently. Beth had placed her in fourth-grade math, thinking that would challenge her.

Questions swam in Beth's head. Was Jessica's math curriculum really challenging her? How could she find out? If her math curriculum was not a good match to her abilities, what about other areas of the curriculum? How could she start to make sense of all this?

FIGURE 11.1

Authenticity Increases Achievement

When students have opportunities to engage in authentic tasks in school and to participate in authentic assessment of their learning on such tasks, the level of their achievement improves (Meichenbaum & Biemiller, 1998). Furthermore, studies done by Case and his colleagues (Case, 1991; Case & Okamoto, 1996; Griffin & Case, 1996; Griffin, Case, & Siegler, 1994) and McKeough (1992) show that when children's current level of understanding is the starting point for instructional design their achievement is greater than when instruction is based on adult conceptions of knowledge. These studies validate Donaldson's (1979) important observation that, if we are to make a difference instructionally, we must "make the imaginative leap needed to understand the child" (p. 159).

Determining Baseline Knowledge

Teachers can gain understanding of children's knowledge of the curriculum by asking them what they know about a topic, having them define a topic or core concepts associated with a unit of study, and/or asking them what they'd like to find out about a topic. For example, "What do you know about civil rights?" "What are some things you'd like to learn about reptiles?" "What are questions you have about writing poetry?" Watson and Konicek (1990) described how the question "What is heat?" was posed to fourth-grade students before they began to study the concept. In this way, children tested their notions that sweaters and hats are hot by designing experiments, providing their teacher with an informed foundation from which to pose developmentally appropriate questions that helped them extend their knowledge.

> To the extent that one carries on a conversation with a child, as a way of trying to understand a child's understanding, the child's understanding increases "in the very process." The questions the interlocutor asks, in an attempt to clarify for herself what the child is thinking, oblige the child to think a little further also. (Duckworth, 1987, p. 96)

Avoiding Educational Overlays

For older students it becomes even more important to find their baseline knowledge. All too often secondary teachers assume that because something is in a curriculum guide it is part of a student's knowledge base. Everyone can remember a time when they memorized something that they really did not understand for a test. Take that knowledge as the base on which the next teacher builds his or her materials, and we can see why so many things are misunderstood. When this does happen, it is what one author calls an *educational overlay*; that is, it sits on top of a base, but never becomes part of the base knowledge. An example used in our classes is to ask those students who had high school biology (and are not science majors) to draw the Krebs cycle on the board. Students usually respond by laughing and shrugging their shoulders, indicating that they cannot remember it well enough to draw it. Most people had to know this as part of a secondary unit on energy transfer in the body, but it often had no meaning. It was learned for the test, but sits as an overlay of knowledge, never truly absorbed.

Authentic Assessment Strategies

A variety of assessment strategies exist to help teachers and their students reflect on learning. These are sometimes referred to as *performance-based assessments* or *curriculum-based assessments*.

PHOTO 11.4
Authentic assessment is
student-centered.

One of the most common is the portfolio, a collection of work assembled over the school year by the student in collaboration with the teacher (Photo 11.4). The contents of portfolios need not be limited to one school year. They can be cumulative, reflecting a student's development over a number of school years. By assembling a portfolio, students learn to reflect on their own learning by making judgments about what to include in their portfolios and why. This process encourages self-regulated learning, or "the direction and control of one's actions, thinking, and emotions to pursue and attain particular goals" (Paris & Ayres, 1994, p. 168).

Portfolios

Portfolios should contain not just final products, but work indicating the process of learning (e.g., Paris & Ayres, 1994; Wolf, 1987–1988), for example, drafts that led up to a short story or sketches preliminary to a sculpture. If we focus only on outcomes, the interesting and informative things that happen in the process of learning can be missed. "Directing interest to learning processes implies a shift from the results toward discourses about knowledge construction and meaning making" (Gandini & Kaminsky, 2004, p. 1).

Because of the importance of representing the process of learning in a portfolio, Gardner (1991) prefers the term *process folio*. Gardner stresses that initial ideas, working drafts, and critiques (by self and others) should be included in a process folio. Whichever term one chooses, portfolios or process folios should include a variety of products, for example, rating scales (also known as rubrics, discussed later), observations, videotapes of performances, drawings, self-reflections, photographs, and/or graphs (Photo 11.5).

Multiple ways of representing learning are especially important in addressing individual learning needs. For example, instructors can more adequately assess growth in students with writing disabilities if these students are given opportunities to show their learning through visual means or to show how a graphic organizer helped their writing (e.g., Day & Skidmore, 1996), rather than showing their learning through written work alone.

PHOTO 11.5

Portfolios or process folios should include a variety of products.

Students' Roles in Compiling Portfolios

Students have primary responsibility for choosing what goes in their portfolios. If teachers choose to add items, these should indicate that they were teacher chosen (Easley & Mitchell, 2003). Students need to be guided in selecting and reviewing the contents of their portfolios. Portfolios are not just collections of work; they need to be structured through reflections on growth and consideration of standards of excellence. To reflect on growth, students need concrete guidelines.

Choosing Products for a Portfolio   Questions or sentence stems can be used to help students choose and assess products in their portfolios.

- Paris and Ayres (1994) designed the "Why I Like It" sheet. Students complete two sentences: "I chose this piece of work to put in my portfolio because . . ." and "I would like you to notice . . ." (p. 68).
- Meichenbaum and Biemiller (1998) suggest having students ask themselves "Have I learned what I set out to learn?" "How did learning this skill (or strategy) make a difference?" (p. 133).
- Students also can formulate learning goals based on their reflections on portfolio products: "How does this new piece of work compare to others?" "Are there areas that need improvement?" (Easley & Mitchell, 2003).

Reflection on responses to these questions and/or sentence stems gives both students and teachers insight into thinking about thinking and thinking about learning, or *metacognition*, as discussed in Chapter 5.

Assessing Products for a Portfolio   Students should be directed to select items for their portfolios irrespective of the grade given by the teacher. All too often students feel the only items in a portfolio must be those with the highest grades or best comments. If it is your intention to have students select items irrespective of grades, you must also respect the student's decisions. Do not overrule a student's decision. Instead, if you feel something is more worthy than the item selected by the student, ask if you could include an additional item. Explain to the student why you would like to place this item into the portfolio, in addition to the one the student selected.

Portfolios for students with special learning needs follow the same principles. For example, Wesson and King (1996) described the portfolio of a student with serious behavioral challenges. His portfolio included a videotape of cooperative group lessons in which he participated. The videotape was added to from time to time to document progress. Also included were observations made by the teacher of the student's social interactions, observations of behaviors that needed support, and monthly parental reports about the student's attitude toward school. Taken together, this documentation allows student, teacher, and parents to reflect on specific concrete instances of behavioral challenges and to think together about what might support development.

Ensuring That Portfolio Assessment Is Valid and Reliable

As teachers, you may be called on to answer the question of how valid and reliable the contents of a student's portfolio are. Validity is important to ensure that what is in the portfolio is truly representative of what the student can accomplish. Reliability ensures that what is in the portfolio represents the student's ability on more than one occasion.

Validity Validity refers to whether what is contained in a student's portfolio is a meaningful representation of the student's learning. If you take an exam when you have the flu, the results are very likely not valid. You were not at your best, and you may have not written coherently about what you know well. Similarly, questions like the following could be raised about portfolios. Are the products and traces of process good indicators of a student's development? Do they give an accurate picture of what the student is capable of?

Paris and Ayres (1994) believe that authentic assessment has instructional and curricular validity because it is premised on relevant educational experiences. In other words, authentic assessment is meaningful, and therefore valid, because it relates to what was taught, how it was taught, and the content of the curriculum. However, other factors can affect validity even when every effort is made to ensure a good match between instruction and assessment, to follow learner-centered principles, and to include multiple forms of assessment.

Teachers need to be alert that students with diverse learning needs are given adequate and appropriate opportunities to demonstrate what they know. As with all students, a number of factors, such as motivation, stress, fatigue, physical disabilities, language proficiency, and cultural background can affect the validity of an assessment (Sattler, 1992). Children with attention deficit–hyperactivity disorder (ADHD), for example, demonstrate inconsistent patterns of performance. What they know on one occasion, they may not know on another (Smith, Polloway, Patton, & Dowdy, 1998). For assessments to be valid, they need to be collected on multiple occasions.

Reliability You may also be questioned about the reliability of the contents of a student's portfolio. For example, a parent might comment, "Those poems are not very good examples of what my son can write." The reliability of an assessment refers to its accuracy (Wilson, 1996). An assessment is reliable if there is reasonable confidence that similar abilities would be demonstrated on other occasions and if another individual evaluates a student's process or product in approximately the same way. The inclusion of multiple ways of representing knowledge and of multiple perspectives on the items in a student's portfolio (e.g., student, teacher, parent, and/or peer evaluations) ensures the accuracy of judgments about a student's growth. The parent's comment could indicate that the student is not demonstrating his full potential in class and/or that he needs writing opportunities with more scope.

Indicators of Quality

When one honors multiple means of demonstrating knowledge and learning in classrooms, assessment becomes more complex (Neill, 1997), as it should. When

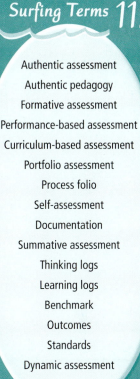

Surfing Terms 11.1

Authentic assessment
Authentic pedagogy
Formative assessment
Performance-based assessment
Curriculum-based assessment
Portfolio assessment
Process folio
Self-assessment
Documentation
Summative assessment
Thinking logs
Learning logs
Benchmark
Outcomes
Standards
Dynamic assessment

students are engaged in complex thinking, assessment needs to reflect that complexity. However, we would argue that with the complexity comes more meaning, for teachers and students alike.

Reflecting on Learning   Complex assessment goes beyond the "right answer" to uncover the meanings learners are making of the curriculum. Multiple ways of representing knowledge "make learning visible" (Project Zero & Reggio Children, 2001), allowing teachers and students to examine, interpret, and reflect on learning. For this process to work optimally, it needs a reference point. It is not enough simply to examine learning and development. Students and teachers need to understand what counts as excellence and then undertake their examinations within this framework.

Easley and Mitchell (2003) worked with their second- and sixth-graders to develop criteria for "what good math writers do" (p. 63) to help their students conceptualize mathematics and write reflections on mathematics for their portfolios. The grade 2 criteria were these

- Use drawings and diagrams.
- Use math language.
- Show you understand by giving examples.
- Make sure the work is correct.
- Use capitals and correct punctuation marks.
- Make sure the work makes sense.

The grade 6 criteria were similar but more detailed, reflecting the older students' experience and knowledge. For example,

- Describe it as if the reader doesn't know math.
- Try to tell it in more than one way.
- Relate it to real life.

Easley and Mitchell used "math talk questions" to help their students acquire a mathematics vocabulary with which to write. For example, prompts like "Pretend you are a (prime number, hexagon, . . .) and tell about yourself"; "Is there anything that puzzled you about (multiplication, fractions, . . .)?"; and "Explain why (multiplication is repeated addition)" (p. 64) strengthen mathematics understanding and help students to reflect on their own development.

Understanding Excellence   To understand and appreciate excellence, learners need to live with it. They need to hear and read good literature, play good music, and see good theater (Photo 11.6). Admittedly, judgments of what counts as good or excellent are subjective. However, teachers and students can use as guidelines recognized indicators of high-quality work in various professions, arts, and trades. State and provincial curricular scope and sequence charts help determine criteria for excellence, as well as local community standards. They will help you, as a teacher, to understand what is valued in the school community.

Rubrics

Once one determines the criteria for excellence, one can use rubrics as helpful tools in assessing where students fall on the path to excellence. A rubric is a rating scale that provides clear criteria for each point on the scale.

Rubrics allow for performance comparisons by spelling out different levels of quality along a continuum of achievement. They are often synonymous with performance or scoring criteria (Stiggins, 2001). For example, a rubric might describe a scale from 1 to 3 having the following categories:

- 1   Rudimentary understanding of a topic

PHOTO 11.6

Trips outside of the school environment can help shape students' ideas of excellence and what can be achieved.

- 2   Fundamental level of understanding in most students
- 3   Level of understanding that exceeds average expectations

Rubrics may form part of your provincial or state guidelines for education. In our province reading, writing, numeracy, and social responsibility all have performance standards. The performance standards describe the following categories within each grade level (British Columbia Ministry of Education, 2004):

- Not yet within expectations
- Meets expectations (minimal level)
- Fully meets expectations
- Exceeds expectations

Guidelines for Developing Rubrics

You also may need to develop rubrics as supplements to what is already available, or as your own resources if none exist. Here we outline some principles and examples to help with the development of rubrics.

Rubrics Should Address Skills and Conceptual Understanding   For example, an item on a rubric for mathematics might be "Understands the relationship between addition and multiplication," rather than "Knows addition facts to 15 and multiplication facts to 5." The mastery of conceptual understanding, rather than of specific tasks, should be emphasized.

Rubrics Should Be Tied to Instruction   For example, if you didn't teach the concept of relativity, it is not fair to assess students on their knowledge of it. Or, if you taught relativity through demonstration and followed up the demonstration with activities in which students tested their own hypotheses about relativity, then your rubric should reflect the degrees of sophistication involved in scientific problem solving.

Rubrics Should Be Brief Enough to Be Useful   When a rubric is chosen or designed by a teacher, one guideline should be practicality and ease of use. Descriptors need to be brief but to the point (Popham, 1997). As an example, the criteria for a first-grader who is fully meeting the expectations for writing from experience in the spring of grade 1, as determined by the British Columbia Ministry of Education (2004), are outlined in Table 11.1. These are succinct, focused criteria that help teachers in their assessment of children's emergent ability to write.

Once skills and/or conceptual understanding are determined, evaluative criteria are needed to assess students' responses. These criteria guide judgments about levels of student development. See Table 11.2 for an example in the domain of written language and Tables 11.3 and 11.4 for examples of rubrics to evaluate students' learning outcomes after studying the novel *Charlotte's Web* (see Chapter 10 for a lesson plan).

Criteria for Excellence: Domains

What has been described so far in reference to rubrics is thinking *in* a domain (Gardner, 1993) (e.g., thinking about progress in writing using criteria like those above). This is the most typical focus of rubrics. However, Gardner suggested two additional criteria for excellence that would enhance students' understanding of how they learn and teachers' ability to optimize development.

These additional criteria are thinking *about* a domain (e.g., awareness of literary style, abilities to discriminate genres and creative written work) and *approach to* working in a domain (e.g., immersion in work, methods of editing and revising, connections to other disciplines).

Here, too, a rubric may be helpful in evaluating progress. Students who are highly aware of literary style can, for example, write or tell stories that contain all the elements of a fairy tale, mystery, or tall tale. Psychologist David Feldman (1986) described a 5-year-old boy who wrote plays and novels and was very well aware of the differences in the genres. Similarly, one of the authors has studied young children's

TABLE 11.1

Assessment of Written Language Competence in First Grade (Writing from Experience)

	Meets Expectations (Minimal level)	Fully Meets Expectations
Meaning Ideas and information Details	Often retells another story Recognizable story situation Little development, few details	Some individuality Begins with characters and situation Has a problem and solution; few details
Style Clarity and variety of language Description	Conversational Repeats simple patterns, favorite words	Mostly conversational; may include some "story language" Repeats simple patterns; some simple description
Form Beginning, middle, end Sequence	May be very brief String of loosely related events— mostly "middle" Uses *and* to connect ideas Drawings may tell much of the story	Includes beginning, middle, and end Most events are in logical sequence Repeats the same connecting words Writing can stand alone
Conventions Capitals and small letters Spelling Use of phonics Punctuation Spacing Legibility	Mostly capital letters Some words spelled conventionally Many words spelled phonetically May experiment with punctuation Parts are legible	Both capitals and small letters Spells many familiar words correctly Uses phonics to spell new words Some punctuation Legible

Source: British Columbia Ministry of Education. BC Performance Standards: Writing Grade 1 (2005, p. 31). Describes student achievement in March-April of the school year. Copyright © 2005 Province of British Columbia. All rights reserved. Reprinted with permission of the Province of British Columbia.

TABLE 11.2

Rubric for Middle Years Essay Writing

	Absent 0	Undeveloped, Unclear 1	Partially Formed 2	Acceptable 3	Well Developed 4	Excellent 5
Focus of essay	No main idea or connection of ideas	Relates ideas to topic superficially Develops ideas randomly	Remains partially on topic Develops inadequate supporting ideas	Remains on topic Main idea stated only indirectly Three supporting ideas related only adequately	Says something about the topic Remains on topic throughout Main idea and three supporting ideas stated in introduction Conclusion related only vaguely to main idea	Says something new about the topic Remains on topic throughout Main idea and three supporting ideas stated in introduction Conclusion related directly to main idea

Source: Adapted from Carleton Board of Education, 1992; cited in Wilson, 1996, p. 52.
Similar descriptors were developed for the categories of support, organization, style, and mechanics in essay writing.

abilities in narrative and heard 6- and 7-year-olds relate well-developed fairy tales and use rhymed couplets for effect in personal stories (Porath, 1996).

All these children were fascinated by language and its power to entertain; they immersed themselves in writing and story telling. Their abilities constitute excellence in thinking in a domain and about a domain and their approach to working in a domain.

TABLE 11.3

Rubric for Evaluating Character Study (*Charlotte's Web*)

Rating	Criteria
Strong	Accurate description of physical characteristics; able to use adjectives to describe personal qualities, aptitudes, and interests
Good	Description of physical characteristics; able to use some adjectives to describe a few personal qualities, aptitudes, and interests
Satisfactory	Description of some physical characteristics; may have some difficulty describing personal qualities, aptitudes, and interests
In progress	Description of some physical characteristics with considerable difficulty describing any personal qualities, aptitudes, and interests

Source: British Columbia Ministry of Education. BC Education: Appendix D: Evaluation Example for English K to 7 (1996, pp. 3–4). Copyright © 2005. Province of British Columbia. All rights reserved. Reprinted with permission of the Province of British Columbia.

TABLE 11.4

Rubric for Evaluating a Letter to E. B. White

Criteria	Powerful	Competent	Developing	Not Evident
Follows friendly letter format (heading, paragraphs, closing)				
Body (logical, well developed, interesting)				
Presentation (spelling, mechanics)				
Handwriting (neatness, slant, correct formation)				

Source: British Columbia Ministry of Education. BC Education: Appendix D: Evaluation Example for English K to 7 (1996, p. 5). Copyright © 2005. Province of British Columbia. All rights reserved. Reprinted with permission of the Province of British Columbia.

At the opposite end of the rubric would be the absence of such competencies, with a category or categories in between that would describe growing competence in thinking in a domain and about a domain and developing an approach to work within that domain.

Observation

Your state or province may have guidelines for observations to determine if a child is meeting the educational, personal, and social goals for his or her grade level. For example, in our province the objectives for personal development in the area of mental well-being for children in grades 2 and 3 involve the degree to which they do the following:

- Avoid potentially hazardous situations
- Help others to overcome obstacles or problems
- Contribute to maintaining a clean environment
- Make efforts to be friendly
- Show respect for others
- Are considerate of the feelings of others (British Columbia Ministry of Education, 1999, p. 31).

You could develop an observation form that includes these criteria and an evaluation scale such as good, average, and needs improvement.

Teacher-designed observation guidelines that focus on individual student needs also are necessary. Teachers acquire complex knowledge of how personal, social, motivational, and academic factors interact by observing students carefully in their classrooms (Peterson, 1993). Teachers should note occasions in which a student reacts angrily to failure, has difficulty relating to peers, withdraws during group activities, arrives at school upset and distracted, or is frustrated by new learning (Photo 11.7). These are examples of behaviors that teachers need to think about, examine across contexts, and develop hypotheses about concerning possible causes. (Also see our discussion of functional assessment in Chapter 4.)

PHOTO 11.7
Careful observation can help teachers determine each student's particular needs in the classroom.

Problem-Based Scenario 11.2 gives you the opportunity to think about how observation may help Rick, a middle school teacher, to support a student with special learning needs.

For example, a student may appear frustrated by new concepts only in some subjects or in some teaching situations. Knowing this allows a teacher to test

Problem-Based Scenario 11.2

K-5   6-8   9-12   SpEd

Student: *Charles*
Teacher: *Rick*

At the end of the day, Rick left school quickly. "This was not one of my most stellar days as a teacher," he thought. In the last period, grade 8 English, things went particularly badly for Charles, a student with autism. Rick had just explained foreshadowing and the students were suggesting ways they could foreshadow events in a short story. Charles started to moan and rock back and forth. The students near him helped him settle down and the class got to work. When Rick went to check on him, he saw that Charles had scribbled all over his paper and the desk with a felt pen. He told Charles calmly to clean up his desk and take out a new sheet of paper. This prompted a temper tantrum that neither he nor students to whom Charles usually responded positively were able to quiet. Rick took a screaming Charles to the counselor's office. He felt shaken up and so did his students.

Rick thought he had a good relationship with Charles. There had been a few bumps in the road this term, but they were relatively minor. Rick knew the curriculum was challenging for Charles; however, he accommodated the level at which Charles could work and this usually worked well. He thought about the poem Charles had written a few months before. Charles had not grasped the idea of metaphor, but he worked so hard to make the poem rhyme. He had some system to put all the lines of the poem together and, in the end, it worked (see Figure 11.2 on page 328).

So, what was up? Was it the activity they did today? Something else like a problem at home or with one of the other kids? Another teacher? Rick wanted to come up with a plan to figure this out.

what he or she thinks may be the underlying reasons for the student's frustration. One of the authors tested different hypotheses about why one of her grade 4 students achieved poorly in Math:

> "Tyler was a very bright student, and he excelled in most subjects. He could be counted on to 'get' most new concepts almost before I finished explaining them, and he understood them at a deep level. He wasn't always the most cooperative of students; he could be stubborn and his behavior in class was often quite immature. In Math, Tyler never got the required work finished on time, didn't do his homework, and usually got marks in the C range.
>
> At first, I suspected a learning disability. Working with Tyler on basic facts and procedures for addition, subtraction, and long multiplication that required lining up of columns and understanding of place value indicated that he knew all this. There wasn't any evidence of an underlying processing difficulty.
>
> Then I thought he might not be sufficiently challenged by Math. The curriculum was individualized and he could proceed to more advanced work, but none of the more advanced opportunities that appealed to other equally capable children excited Tyler. Stubbornness and immaturity generalized across all activities, so those characteristics didn't really help me with addressing the Math issue.
>
> Finally, at a student-led conference, Tyler's mother asked him why he didn't do his work in Math. Tyler said, "I guess I just don't see the point of it." Hearing him say that was a big lesson for me as a teacher. How often did I actually make the point of learning clear? And Tyler, who had the capacity to see the big picture of learning, really needed to know the usefulness of what he was being asked to do."

Routines for Observation

Observations can be jotted down during the school day and reflected on later. In fact, Good and Brophy (1987) emphasized the importance of reflection after some time has elapsed. Interpretations made at the time of observation may be biased. Taking some time before interpreting the observations allows you to be more neutral and thoughtful about what you have observed.

Informal Observation

As beginning teachers, you may be wondering how you are going to find the time in the day to do observations. Building observations into your daily routine, rather than thinking of them as an add-on will help, as will starting slowly. Focusing on one or two students a day as a start will help you to find routines and strategies that work for you. Different systems are used for making observations including note cards, binders containing pages for individual students, notebooks with separate columns for observations and inferences, and plans to observe different students each day. You may find that a computer works best for you or a hand-held tape recorder.

For secondary teachers, observing individual students within short blocks of time and rotating schedules can be a challenge. A number of observational instruments are available, but the best ones are the ones you make yourself. The key is to have something that can be quick, reliable, and discrete.

One author found that file cards paper-clipped to her daily plan book worked the best.

> "Often the counselor would ask teachers to observe a particular student for things like attention, fatigue, or specific behaviors. With rotating schedules it was hard to keep track of students in different blocks. I found that if I set up a file card with the student's initials (mixed with mine to make sure a student couldn't be identified if the card got lost) at the top with the date it would serve as a memory aid. I would then put a shorthand notation of the specific item or behavior to be observed. Most often it

could be set up as a simple checklist of one or two things. For example, did he or she have the text and a pencil? Did he or she work cooperatively with the group? If it required a written comment, I would do it quickly when the students left the room. However, I never completed more than one file card for one student per day. At the end of a week I had a fairly accurate record over several days for the counseling department. You need to always keep things in code or shorthand in case some other student sees the file card. Confidentiality is very important."

Structured Observation

Informal observations can become the basis for more structured observations. As hypotheses are formed, you may want to develop checklists or rating scales or use existing instruments that allow for specific instances and levels of behavior to be recorded. For example, the Social Skills Rating System (Gresham & Elliott, 1990), Teacher Form, allows a teacher to rate how often a social skill or problem behavior is demonstrated (never, sometimes, very often) and how important the skill or behavior is (not important, important, critical) (Photo 11.8). In this way, teachers can reflect on what is important in their classrooms and how different students are developing in areas such as cooperation, assertion, and self-control (Gresham & Elliott).

If you decide to develop a rating scale for behavior yourself, first select an antecedent(s) associated with the behavior of concern (e.g., Ronnie has a temper tantrum when a spelling test is given or when the class prepares to go to the gym). Also, select consequences (e.g., Tomaso hits Ronnie when he has a tantrum). Your scale might look like this:

- When Ronnie has to do a spelling test, how often does he have a temper tantrum?
  1–almost always/ 2–frequently/ 3–sometimes/ 4–infrequently/ 5–almost never.
- When Ronnie has a tantrum, how often does Tomaso react by hitting him?
  1–almost always/ 2–frequently/ 3–sometimes/ 4–infrequently/ 5–almost never. (Sattler, 1992)

Surfing Terms 11.2

Anecdotal reports
Observation scales
Guided observation
Rating scales
Aptitude
Achievement

PHOTO 11.8

To develop a rating scale for behavior yourself, first select an antecedent(s) associated with the behavior of concern, then select consequences.

Considering Context

The context in which assessment takes place is important. Explicit guidelines and questions for consideration of context in informing assessment and instruction include the following:

- How might the student have interpreted the instructions?
- How might the students' background and prior experience have influenced his or her interpretation of this task?
- Would practice and support make a difference in performance? What kind of practice and support would be most helpful?
- If the student were allowed another avenue of expression, would he or she demonstrate understanding? (Porath, 1995)

Similar questions can be used to consider influences on behavior. Children may interpret others' behavior toward them in different ways and may react differently to adults than they do to children. They may behave differently with individual adults. They may behave very differently at home than they do at school or on the playground than they do in the classroom.

Reporting to Students and Parents

As a teacher you will need to be able to collect information on student progress and provide a report of this progress in the form of a report card of some type. Reporting involves summarizing the results of assessment and evaluation and representing them in an understandable format. While this seems straightforward, it really is not. It is often a subjective evaluation that represents a composite of pupil achievement. All schools must follow some criteria set out by the government to standardize the reporting procedure. As beginning teachers you need to find out the parameters under which you will need to report to the student, parents, and administration in your school.

Most report cards contain both grades and teacher comments. In many school jurisdictions, students in the primary grades (K to 3) receive comments only. In our province, students who have designated special needs also do not receive grades. Once letter grades are introduced, it is generally the expectation that the grades will be expanded on in written comments covering students' attitudes, work habits, effort, strengths, and areas needing improvement. Grades are discussed in Chapter 12. In this chapter we concentrate on written reports. However, one comment on grades needs to be made in the context of this chapter with its focus on learners' perspectives. One of the authors found that her grade 4 students were very stressed about getting their first letter grades.

"After talking to them a bit, I realized they had no idea what the grades represented. They heard about grades from their parents and older siblings and were excited about getting grades since they felt more grown-up. They had a vague understanding that an A was a good grade, but beyond that they were puzzled. The fact that C grades included C− and C+ complicated things further."

Explicit criteria for grades are as important as criteria for other assessment and evaluation procedures.

Clear and Concise Reporting

It is your responsibility as a teacher to write clearly about students' progress in school. Like many professions, teaching has a jargon all its own. Many parents are not familiar with educational terms. Just as students benefit from having clear indicators of quality, parents benefit from knowing exactly what their children have mastered and what they need help with. Each child's report should include statements of what he or she is able to do, areas that need further development, and ways to support his or her learning written in plain language. For example, write "help" rather than "assist" or "facilitate," "try" rather than "endeavor," and "soon" rather than "in the near future" (BC Education, 1996).

Many schools require informal reporting in addition to the formal process of report cards. The School Act in our province requires two informal reports each year. Informal reporting may include conferences with parents, student-led conferences, portfolio reviews, telephone conferences, written notes, e-mails, and/or interim reports. Interim reports are especially important when a student is experiencing academic or behavioral difficulties so that parents have regular updates. However, good communication about the progress of all the students in your class contributes to good home–school relationships and student achievement.

Summary

In this chapter, you learned ways of assessing and evaluating your students and the principles that inform authentic assessment. Both you and your students can learn from well-designed, thoughtful assessment processes. With all these tools, you will be well equipped to plan, interpret, and report on your students' progress.

- Assessment is done *with* students. They need to understand what is being assessed, how the assessment will be done, and what counts as excellence. They also need opportunities to reflect on their own progress.
- Having a repertoire of assessment strategies will help you to understand your students' learning in ways that can inform your instruction.
- Understanding what makes an assessment valid and reliable will help you to choose appropriate assessments.
- Including examples of the process of learning in a portfolio is equally important to sample products.

A Metacognitive Challenge

You should now be able to reflect on the following questions:

- What do I know about learner-centered assessment?
- How does my knowledge of authentic assessment help me plan teaching and learning activities?
- What do I know about valid and reliable assessments?
- How can I use my knowledge of different assessment strategies to help me meet the needs of individual learners?
- How does my knowledge of the context in which assessment takes place help me to plan appropriate assessments for the students in my classroom?

Artifacts for Problem-Based Scenarios

FIGURE 11.2 ■ Charles's Poem

foud
food

Everyone likes eating food
vegetables and fruit are good
but candy is better than grains and fish
it comes in chocolate and licorish
it has a really good taste
And all it wrappers go to waste

Sequence in which the poem was written:

Everyone likes eating food	2
Vegetables and fruit are good	4
But candy is better than grains and fish	6
It comes in chocolate and licorish	1
It has a really good taste	5
And all it wrappers go to waste	3

Understanding Test Results in Context

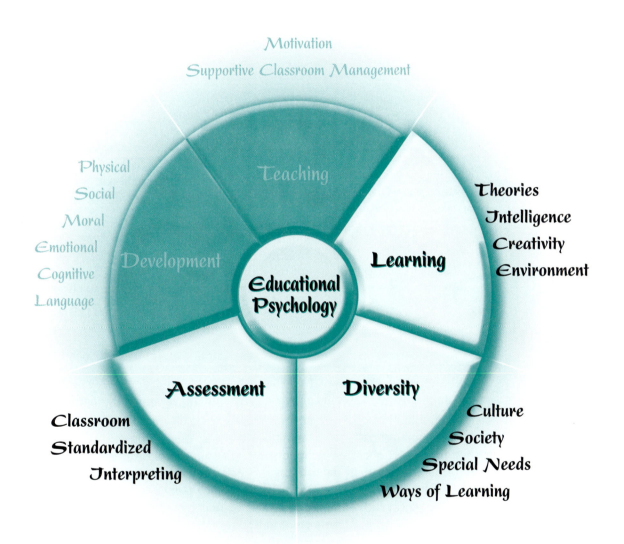

Motivation

Supportive Classroom Management

Teaching

Physical
Social
Moral
Emotional
Cognitive
Language

Development

Learning

Theories
Intelligence
Creativity
Environment

Educational
Psychology

Assessment

Diversity

Classroom
Standardized
Interpreting

Culture
Society
Special Needs
Ways of Learning

In this chapter we introduce you to basics for constructing tests in your classroom and background on standardized tests. Then we show you statistical methods for organizing and, more importantly, understanding the results from both types of tests.

Traditional teacher-made tests, if properly constructed, provide more authentic information for the teacher, parents, and school. As we saw in Chapter 11, we can use teacher-made tests to make informed decisions on various levels about the performance of students and the success of lessons. For standardized tests, your role as a teacher is determined by the type of test being given and the rationale behind its administration. Your role may consist of administering the test to your individual class, using an answer sheet to grade it, analyzing the results based on the materials supplied to you, making curricular decisions based on school results, and/or relaying results to students or parents.

For the results of teacher-made tests to be meaningful, we have to first make sure we design the best test possible. Next, we need to organize the results in a way that ensures we are getting the most accurate picture. This requires understanding some aspects of test construction and the basics of measurement and statistics.

Testing as a Component of Authentic Assessment

Testing is a valuable option in guiding instruction when it meets the standard of authenticity. That is, the test chosen or designed must be related to educational goals. It is important to remember that no one assessment should be used in isolation; a multiple assessment approach is essential. Thus, testing is *part* of the process of authentic assessment. It adds to our knowledge of students' abilities, acting as "a catalyst for improved instruction" (Popham, 1998, p. 384). There are a number of different kinds of tests. In this section of the chapter, we describe different categories of tests to help you make appropriate choices as a teacher.

Tests and Testing

All students are familiar with teacher-made tests. They are produced by the classroom teacher with specific objectives and students in mind. Standardized tests are usually used for larger groups of students or for comparisons to a larger group of individuals. These will be discussed later.

It is important to keep two key questions in mind when you consider testing:

1. Why are you giving the test?
2. What are you going to do with the results when you get them?

These questions may sound simplistic, but they provide guidelines for selecting the most appropriate test for your needs.

Why Are You Giving the Test?

Several things determine the purpose and form of a test.

- To determine readiness, placement, or planning for future instruction, you will need a *pretest*. These tend to be limited in scope (e.g., definitions, math facts) and are good to get a sense of a student's understanding of a proposed topic.
- To determine whether students understand instruction or to detect errors, you will need a *formative* test, something that will allow you to quickly tap into understanding. Teachers often use short quizzes for this purpose: true–false questions, fill in the blanks, or brief answers. The idea is to monitor ongoing learning.

- To determine specific problems, a *diagnostic* test is often used. Because these are very hard for a teacher to write, they are usually found under the category of *standardized tests*. For example, if you have a student who has difficulty with long division, you can use a standardized test that contains a number of very similar math problems. Each has a slight variation. Following the instructor's guide, you can quickly determine that the student has difficulty borrowing from another column. Although useful, these tests must be purchased from publishers and therefore tend to be expensive.
- To determine the extent of achievement at the end of instruction, you would use a *summative* test. These tend to be more extensive and not only require specific knowledge recall, but also application of ideas or concepts. They are used to verify mastery and/or assign grades.

Once you have decided why you are giving the test, this decision should direct you to the test format. For *formative* information, teachers usually like short, quick quizzes. They do not want to spend valuable class time, but do need to keep close track of learning. For *summative* information, teachers usually like to give students ample time to reflect on the topic. By utilizing the objectives for a unit or topic, the teacher can determine whether students can recall, identify, explain, analyze, understand, and so on. The questions asked should be directed by the objectives. For example, recall is easily accessed by a fill in the blank question, whereas understanding is perhaps better accessed by an essay question.

Criterion-Referenced and Norm-Referenced Tests

The purpose for giving the test will also determine the difficulty of the test items. If you are giving a *criterion-referenced* test, it means you are measuring against a set of standards you expect all students to be able to attain. For example, you might expect that students should be able to attain 80% mastery on each week's French vocabulary test. If instruction was good and students grasped the concepts being taught, you should expect high scores. That is, your students met the criterion. The difficulty of the question should be matched to the difficulty of the task. Do not under any circumstances change the difficulty of the question to get a range of grades. With criterion-referenced tests, the student is being tested against the set criteria, not against other students. The teacher determines exactly how much of a topic the student has mastered. It has nothing to do with anyone else in the class. As with other forms of assessment discussed in this chapter, criterion-referenced tests are linked to informing instruction. For this reason, it is important that the items be fair representations of the skill being assessed. The test must "ask the right questions" (Shapiro & Lentz, 1988, p. 90).

If a teacher needs to rank pupils, such as for receiving a scholarship award, they will select a *norm-referenced* test. The object here is to maximize differences between students. Questions should be selected for their range of difficulty to ensure that only those students who completely master the topic will obtain the highest scores. A consideration here is the upper limits of the difficulty of test questions. If a student can answer all the questions a teacher asks, the teacher never really knows the upper limits of the student's knowledge.

One of the authors once assessed a 9-year-old to see what his level of mastery was in mathematics. He was about to begin fourth grade. From the time he started school, this boy had been frustrated by a lack of challenge in math.

"Since I knew this child was advanced in math, I started to test him with standardized achievement tests at the fifth-grade level. He worked easily through fifth to eighth-grade tests, demonstrating mastery of all mathematical concepts tested except for

Criterion-referenced test: A teacher-made test for which the *criterion for mastery* is determined by the teacher and the curriculum.

Norm-referenced test: A test that has been *normed* on a large group of children of the same age and background as the children you plan to test.

geometry. He had never received instruction in geometry, but managed to figure out the concepts tested at the fifth- and sixth-grade levels. The point at which he began to have some difficulty with other aspects of mathematics was at the ninth-grade test. I recommended that his mathematics curriculum be modified to allow him to work at the ninth-grade level in math and the seventh-grade level in geometry, through mentorship."

Without testing to the limits, this student's level of ability would remain unknown. It was clearly above grade level, but just where exactly? Testing beyond age expectations allowed achieving an *optimal match* between development and curriculum (Keating, 1991).

It is always good to ask challenging questions of students that require thought to determine where they stand in their knowledge. Under no circumstances should trick questions be used. While you may get the range of scores you are looking for, the validity and reliability of the test will be compromised. Also, what you have just tested was not achievement, but rather the student's ability to detect tricks in questions. This introduces ethical issues.

What Are You Going to Do with the Results of the Test?

If the test is to determine awards, a norm-referenced test should be used. If you want to know what the students do not grasp, a criterion-referenced test should be used. However, teachers also need to give report cards or submit grades.

In many places, grades are not given to some groups of students. For example, primary children often receive report cards descriptive of learning achievements, or a student with special needs may be provided with an anecdotal comment card. However, for many classroom teachers, the actual giving of grades is a major component of their teaching. It is a way of conveying achievement and progress.

Understanding the Results of Tests

One problem for teachers is that not everyone can get A grades. This is why the distinction between criterion- and norm-referenced testing is difficult to reconcile. We suggest that you think of these two types of testing as ends of a continuum. Similar to what has been suggested before in this text, do not make topics distinct points that appear opposed to one another. The reality of a classroom is that students are compared not only to criteria, but also simultaneously to each other. Therefore, thinking of the continuum, if a teacher developed a formative quiz, it would be somewhere closer to the criterion end, but still have a normative component. For example, who already knows all the material? What needs to be retaught, if anything? If the teacher is giving a unit test, then the emphasis will slide toward the normative end. For example, who really knows the most or has the best grasp of the concepts? Did everyone at least attain the basics of the set criteria? In this way the reality of grading and evaluation can be acknowledged.

Some teachers use tests to create a range of scores. You will hear comments such as "My grades are too high. I just have to make the next test harder." If you find that the students have mastered the material and the resulting grades are too high or that they had difficulty and the grades are too low, the place to adjust this is *within the curriculum*. Either you are not providing enough challenge for students or you are teaching above their level of comprehension. Something should be adjusted, but within the classroom, not on a test.

Teacher-Made Tests

This test is the one we are most familiar with. It is the paper and pencil type of quiz or test usually given during a unit of instruction or at the end of an instructional unit. The intent of a formative test is often to determine level of understanding. It provides important feedback to the teacher regarding the clarity of the lessons and the comprehension of the topic. Teachers use formative tests to regulate their planning and provide a basis for decision making in lesson strategies. They use summative tests to determine the overall extent of student learning and understanding compared to the initial objectives and goals of a unit or topic. Since teachers use tests or quizzes to answer so many questions, they need to ensure that the results are providing accurate information. This means that tests must be not only reliable and free of error but valid to make sure we are making the correct decisions for students and programs.

Test Validity

For a test to be valid (a meaningful representation of the student's knowledge), the norm group should include children whose background and experience are similar to the children who will take the test (Sattler, 1992; Wilson, 1996). For example, tests normed on North American populations are not suitable for children who are recent immigrants. On the other hand, some children who are recent immigrants excel on tests normed on North American children, thus demonstrating their exceptional capacity to learn and to learn quickly. When considering whether standardized testing will help us understand a child's development, we need to consider the degree of match between the child and the test.

Stress, motivation, and fatigue also can influence the validity of standardized tests. With standardized achievement tests, the relationship of test content to local curricula is not perfect. The tests can provide valid and reliable indicators of *overall* achievement in school subjects, but will not always test the knowledge acquired in specific school curricula. After completing the science items on a standardized achievement test, an 11-year-old once told one of the authors, "Well, those items were OK but you didn't ask me about ants. I've spent the whole term studying about ants and I can tell you everything you want to know about them!"

Test Reliability

Reliability is an important consideration in standardized testing. It is an indicator of how consistent the results of testing are likely to be (Sattler, 1992), that is, how likely it is that a person will obtain a similar score on other testing occasions. Test developers use a variety of methods to ensure reliability. These include giving the same test to the same people on two occasions (test–retest reliability), giving alternative forms of the same test to two different groups in different order (i.e., one group does Form A, then B; the other does Form B, then A) (alternative form reliability), and examining the degree of consistency among comparable items (internal consistency reliability) (Sattler). Reliability indicators should be reported in test manuals; they range from .00 (complete absence of reliability) to 1.00 (perfect reliability). A reliability coefficient of .80 or higher indicates acceptable reliability.

A number of factors can affect the reliability of test results. If the same test is given to a student a short time after the first administration, reliability is likely to be high due to a *practice effect*. Guessing can lower reliability, as can misunderstood (or misleading) instructions, errors in scoring, and fatigue, stress, and degree of motivation (Sattler, 1992).

Construction of Teacher-Made Tests

Since all teaching strategies and lessons flow from goals and objectives, it is logical that this is where a teacher must begin when writing a test. By tying the goals and objectives to the testing, you can ensure that the results will inform you not only of student progress, but also of any needed adjustments in curriculum or planning. Goals and objectives should be based on the taxonomies of learning that show the progressions of difficulty and complexity when trying to learn something. Info Byte 12.1 lists several different taxonomies for learning.

Planning the Test

It is always a good idea to start planning for the evaluation of your objectives when organizing your lesson. Start by asking whether you would like to assess with a paper–pencil test or through some other demonstration of learning. Since

---

Info Byte 12.1

Taxonomies are classification systems used to describe learning behaviors. The bottom levels usually indicate the basic or simplest level, often related to some type of associative learning, such as naming something. The highest levels are related to complex tasks, such as evaluation. The taxonomies are for the cognitive, affective, and psychomotor domains (Bloom, 1956; Krathwohl, Bloom & Masia, 1964; Harrow, 1972).

Cognitive Domain

Type of Learning	Example
Evaluation	To argue, to contract, to compare
Synthesis	To plan, to design, to produce
Analysis	To classify, to distinguish, to restructure
Application	To generalize, to develop, to transfer
Comprehension	To paraphrase, to interpret, to conclude
Knowledge	To recall, to recognize, to identify

Affective Domain

Type of Learning	Examples
Characterization by value or value set	To revise, to resolve, to manage
Organization	To discuss, to theorize, to formulate
Valuing	To support, to debate, to relinquish
Responding	To comply with, to follow, to acclaim
Receiving	To accept, to listen (for), to respond to

Psychomotor Domain

Type of Learning	Examples
Nondiscursive communication	Body postures, gestures, facial expressions
Skilled movements	All skilled activities obvious in sports, recreation, and the like
Physical activities	Strenuous effort over time, quick precise movements
Perceptual	Coodinated movements: jumping rope, catching, and the like
Basic fundamental movement	Walking, running, twisting
Reflex movement	Stretch, extension, flexion

	Pre–WW I Europe	Leaders during WWI	US and Canada, WWI	Geography and Economics
Recall: names, dates, places	5 Multiple choice 10 Matching			10 Matching item/place on map
Explain: roles, etc.	1 Short answer	1 Short answer	3 Fill ins	1 Short essay
Compare: philosophic, etc.	1 Short essay		3 Multiple choice	2 Multiple choice

FIGURE 12.1

we have discussed other types of assessment tools in Chapter 11, we will continue with teacher-made testing. The easiest way to organize any test and to make sure you are actually writing a test that reflects what was covered in the class is to form a testing grid (Figure 12.1). For example, if you have an objective for students to know the capitals of European countries, you would list this as *recall*. If you want students to be able to understand and explain the causes of World War I, you would list it as *understanding* and *explain*, or maybe *synthesize*. In this way, you start to list the cognitive levels you hoped were attained during your lessons. Along the vertical axis you would briefly list the general topics you worked on in class. For example, if you spent a fair amount of time on the geography of countries before World War I, you could identify it briefly with *Geo–WWI*. Once your table is organized, keep track of questions as they are developed or selected from a test bank. In this way you can ensure that you are covering all aspects of the lessons for the unit or section. It is too easy to develop a test that actually misses some section of a lesson simply because you forgot about it. The grid will also make you aware of how many questions are being asked on one topic.

Writing Test Items

In general, there are two types of test items:

1. *Selection-type items:* The student selects from an option. These are true–false, matching, and multiple-choice.
2. *Supply-type items:* The student must supply the answer. These include short answers and essays.

The type of item you select should depend on the objective you are trying to assess. For instance, while essay questions are fairly easy to construct, they may not really be the most efficient way to determine if the student knows (recalls) the capitals of France and Italy. In this case, either use a selection-type item or a short-answer type. For example, The capital of France is ___. In this way you will know whether the student actually knows the answer, whereas it is statistically possible with the other types to get the answer by guessing. Supply items are great for objectives that include understanding, synthesizing, analyzing, and explaining. All types of questions have pros and cons to consider when making a selection or writing an item. Specific pointers for writing test items are given in Info Byte 12.2.

INFO BYTE 12.2

Popham (2002) suggests these guidelines for writing test items:

BINARY-CHOICE ITEMS

1. Phrase items so that a superficial analysis by the students suggests a wrong answer.
2. Rarely use negative statements, and never use double negatives.
3. Include only one concept in each statement.
4. Have an approximately equal number of items representing the two categories being tested.
5. Keep item length similar for both categories being tested. (p. 130)

MATCHING ITEMS

1. Employ homogeneous lists.
2. Use relatively brief lists, placing the shorter words or phrases at the right.
3. Employ more responses than premises.
4. Order the responses logically.
5. Describe the basis for matching and the number of times responses may be used.
6. Place all premises and responses for an item on a single page. (p. 141)

MULTIPLE-CHOICE ITEMS

1. The stem should consist of a self-contained question or problem
2. Avoid negatively stated stems.
3. Do not let the length of alternatives supply unintended clues.
4. Randomly assign correct answers to alternative positions.
5. Never use "all-of-the-above" alternatives, but do use "none-of-the-above" alternatives to increase item difficulty. (p. 135)

SHORT-ANSWER ITEMS

1. Usually employ direct questions rather than incomplete statements, particularly for young students.
2. Structure the item so that a response should be concise.
3. Place blanks in the margin for direct questions or near the end of incomplete statements.
4. For incomplete statements, use only one or, at the most, two blanks.
5. Make sure blanks for all items are of equal length. (p. 153)

ESSAY ITEMS

1. Convey to students a clear idea regarding the extensiveness of the response desired.
2. Construct items so that the student's task is explicitly described.
3. Provide students with the approximate time to be expended on each item, as well as each item's value.
4. Do not employ optional items.
5. Precursively judge an item's quality by composing, mentally or in writing, a possible response. (p. 157)

Source: W. James Popham, *Classroom Assessment: What Teachers Need to Know,* Third Edition. Published by Allyn and Bacon, Boston, MA. Copyright © 2002 by Pearson Education. Reprinted by permission of the publisher.

True-False or Binary-Choice Items

Although most of us know these items as true–false, there are several alternative options: yes–no, right–wrong, correct–incorrect, and so on. Basically, they provide a statement and ask students to select from two options.

Points to Note

- These items are good when you want to cover a large amount of material in a short time.
- They are subject to guessing, since you generally have a 50–50 chance of getting the correct answer.
- A student may know something is wrong, but not know the correct answer.
- Sometimes teachers ask students to write the correct answer when the statement is wrong. Use caution since the word *not* placed in a sentence can make the statement correct, even though the student doesn't really know the correct answer.

Matching Items

These items are excellent when you want to check understanding around concepts that group together, such as names and dates, events and places, and terms and definitions. Make sure you identify the basis for the matching and provide information in the directions to indicate whether an item can be used more than once.

Points to Note

- The column on the left should include the test number; the column on the right should be lettered.
- Entries or statements for which the student will try to find a match are called *premises*. Entries that contain the match are called *responses*.
- Do not have students draw lines from one column to another, unless this is in a primary grade where there are generally fewer items. So many criss-crossing lines are very difficult to correct.
- Have students write the answers in capital letters to avoid confusion over the letter.
- Give each column a title (even A or B).

Multiple-Choice Items

A multiple-choice item consists of two parts: a *stem* that states a problem and a number of options that contain the correct *answer* and multiple *distracters*. This type of item has a wide range of uses, from recall to evaluation. With careful wording, they can provide assessment of a great deal of material in a relatively short amount of time. For most teachers, a testing period usually consists of a maximum of one class period. Testing that goes beyond that compromises valuable classroom time. For this reason, most teachers use combinations of test questions, including multiple-choice items.

Points to Note

- Write clearly and accurately.
- Avoid long, complex sentence stems that confuse the student.
- A good distracter to add is a student's wrong answer given during a lesson. This will provide the teacher with information regarding students' understanding of the topic and a starting point to diagnose individual difficulties.
- Use caution to make sure hints aren't being given through grammar; for example, *a* or *an* should be written a(n), or the use of plurals, and the like.
- Make sure key words such as *all* or *not* are highlighted.

Short-Answer Items

These items can be in either the form of a question or an incomplete sentence. Either way the intent is to have a very short written response. Short-answer items work well for elementary students who do not necessarily have the skills to write longer essays.

Points to Note

- Write the item so that there is only one answer. Multiple answers make the question not only confusing for students but more difficult for the teacher to correct.
- Avoid verbatim material since it encourages rote memorization.
- Avoid grammatical clues.
- Keep blanks and blank space restricted or students will be triggered to fill in the space provided.

Essay Items

Essay items are excellent for providing students with an opportunity to provide critical analysis or evaluation of large amounts of important material. Since most essays require a considerable amount of time to answer, they have the disadvantage of being able to cover very small amounts of material during a testing period. For this reason, it is advised to limit this type of question to objectives that require more analysis from a student. Always ask yourself, "Does this question really provide me, as a teacher, with the kind of information I want?" If you find it doesn't do that, select another question type and save the essay question for the higher-level analysis of the topic.

Points to Note

- Provide sufficient time to answer the questions thoughtfully. Don't put too many essay questions on one test.
- If the question is too big, divide it into several smaller questions under one topic heading.
- Remember that some students have difficulty expressing themselves in writing. The added stress of the testing environment often compounds this difficulty.
- Make an answer rubric when you write the test; give each question a value, and then double-check it against the students' answers. Make any changes to your rubric *before* you start grading the essays.

Standardized Testing

Standardized achievement tests can inform teachers of students' level of academic ability as compared to other students their age, the *standard* for comparison. This is a *norm-referenced* comparison; that is, a child's performance on the test is compared to that of a *norm group*, other children who took the test for the purposes of determining the ranges of performance at different age and grade levels. Standardized intelligence tests can provide valuable information about a child's problem-solving abilities, verbal reasoning, abstract visual–spatial abilities, and mathematical reasoning. These tests sometimes are necessary to obtain and justify funding for special educational support. For example, in Canada, British Columbia's special educational guidelines include standardized testing in identification criteria for learning disabilities, intellectual disabilities, and giftedness (British Columbia Ministry of Education, 2002). From teachers' and parents' points of view, these tests often provide important validation of observations of a child's development. They also call attention to the realities of developmental differences and the need for program modification (Keating, 1991). Test data offer *starting points* for additional assessment based on the curriculum to provide an optimal match between the student and their educational program.

Standardized tests are available for a wide range of categories, including aptitude or ability, achievement, attitudes, personality, specific school subjects, vocational skills and knowledge, and general interests. Due to the extensive testing done with these instruments, items such as reliability, validity, age levels, and definitions (e.g., intelligence) are provided by the publisher. As a classroom teacher, you may be asked to help select a standardized test for your school within a particular area, such as a reading test. Make sure that the test selected not only tests what you want, but also check that the characteristics of the norming group are similar to those of your own students. In this way you can be more confident with an interpretation of the results, since you will be comparing your students to a group of students with similar background.

Making Sense of Measurement and Statistics

We need to go back to our two primary questions.

1. Why are you giving the test or quiz?
2. What are you going to do with the results?

To answer both questions, you will want information from the results of a quiz or test. The reason for giving tests or quizzes goes beyond giving grades. It usually informs you on a number of levels, for example, whether students are grasping concepts, whether the teaching strategy is appropriate to your objectives, how students understand concepts, and/or whether you are asking the right questions to determine their understanding of the topic. However, when we have a class of 20 to 30 students, it becomes hard to make sense of test results because they are confusing in their raw state. We need to have some way of grouping the results so that we can make sense of the results for the whole class *and* individual students. This is where measurement and statistics have their value. They provide a means to understand and interpret the results of tests or quizzes.

Measurement and statistics is a large field that should be carefully approached and studied. It is an extremely useful tool for teachers, allowing access to a lot of information from a test or quiz. Also, as a caution, it is very easy to use statistics to give information that can be misleading. An example would be this statement: 100% of the people in institutions for the criminally insane drank milk as a child. We could draw an inference about milk drinking and its effect on children from that statistic, if it was not such a ridiculous example. But the statement makes a point: caution should be used when interpreting statistical results. With this in mind, we would like to briefly discuss some aspects of trying to interpret test results.

The Normal Curve

The normal curve may be one of the most misunderstood constructs among teachers. Almost everyone has had a teacher who explained that the test results weren't "good," so the final grade was done on "the curve." Students accept this, and yet seldom is it explained. Even worse is the fact that teachers often use the term without knowing what it means.

Surfing Terms 12.1

Achievement tests

Aptitude tests

Authentic assessment

Cognitive assessment

Content-related validity

Construct-related validity

Criterion-referenced validity

Formative evaluation

Halo effect

Percentages

Portfolio assessment

Performance assessment

Reliability

Rubrics

Self-reporting inventories

FIGURE 12.2

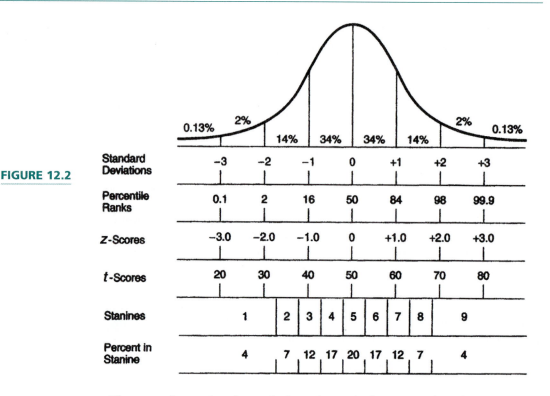

The normal curve is a theoretical, mathematical construct based on data from an infinite number of items. What this means is that the curve is constructed using an infinite set of items; thus, it is a theoretical structure. Nowhere can you get an infinite number of anything. If you look at Figure 12.2, you will see the ends of the curve never touch the line and that the total percentage indicated is 99.9%. Since it is infinite, it can never be 100%. Also, because it is theoretical, there are just as many items and variations on one side of the middle line as on the other. It is always a mirror image. The centerline is not only the average of all items, but the place where the most items cluster.

A Real-World Example of the Normal Curve

Let's use a real-world example to try to see how useful this curve is. If you wanted to measure the height of individuals aged 21 years, you would start off by measuring everyone in your class, then the university, then the city, then the state or province, then the country, and so on. You may find that the first set of data you place on the curve is grouped at one end. If the demographics of your area tend to be homogeneous, you will probably find quite a few similarities. If the demographics are heterogeneous, you might find the points on your curve are very spread out. But, basically, it will not look like the normal curve in the diagram. This is because the sample is too small. However, as you add more and more points as you collect data, you will notice the curve starting to become closer to the normal curve described above. You will eventually get to the point where you start to find data gathering an overwhelming task, so you should stop and see what the curve looks like, even though you have not acquired an infinite number of people (an impossibility).

If you have a very large sample, the curve will *approximate* a normal curve. That is, you will have pretty much the same number of people on either side of the middle, and most people will cluster at the midpoint. Now your curve could be represented with the diagram in the middle of Figure 12.2. The diagram is overly simplistic, but it may be helpful in understanding the normal curve. We include the curve itself as an alternative, since our intention is to have you understand how to *use* the tools of statistics. Select the version of the normal curve that is the most comfortable and understandable for you personally.

Central Tendency

We mentioned the clustering at the middle of the curve. This is called *central tendency*. There are three parts to this description of the clustering: *mean, median,* and *mode*.

1. The *mean* is the arithmetic average. If you take all the raw scores, add them up, and divide by the total number of items, it will give you what we know as an average.
2. The *median* is the number that separates one-half of the items from the other half. For example, the median of 2, 3, 6, 8, 9 would be the number 6. There are five items, so we find the one that represents the midpoint. If there is an even number of items, the midpoint is halfway between the items. The median for 3, 4, 5, 6, 7, 8 would be 5.5 (halfway between).
3. The *mode* is the item that occurs the most times. In the previous example, there isn't a mode since each number appears only once. But in a normal curve the item that occurs the most is the same as the mean and the median. This is because the curve is perfectly symmetrical, mirror images of each side, always the same.

The mean, or average, is the unit of central tendency we tend to be the most familiar with. Teachers always refer to class averages, and students use class averages to see how well they did compared to others in the class. But sometimes a mean can be deceiving. For example, we live in a city where there are several very expensive neighborhoods. When realtors want to advertise the city in a general advertisement, they often put not only the average sale price of a house, but also the median price. If realtors sold several multimillion dollar properties during a quarter and they advertised the average selling price, it would discourage people who feel they cannot afford to live here. The price of these high-end homes would pull the average higher than the actual price of a regular home. So realtors will mention the average (e.g., $300,000), but also include the median price (e.g., $100,000). In this way a buyer would know that, while the average is high, 50% of the houses are under $100,000 and 50% are above this amount.

The meaning of this discussion for you as a teacher is that you will need far more information about a test result than an average to make sense of the results. A few students who get 100% on a quiz may pull the average in such a way that you do not know how the rest of the class actually performed. The majority of students may be clustered around 50%, but the average is closer to 70% because of a few individuals. If we use only the average grade for comparison, we may think someone with a 60% did not do very well when he or she actually performed better than the majority of other students in the class. Even with the mean and median, there is still a problem. Not everyone got the mean or median scores (it is also possible no one got the mean or median scores). It would be good to find out how far away from the mean a particular score lies. This is where we can use the normal curve.

Since the normal curve is symmetrical, we could divide the area on either side of the midpoint into zones that capture a certain percentage of the population. These lines delineate an average distance from the midpoint. They are called *standard deviations* and mark set divisions or zones at specific distances from the mean. On the diagram (Figure 12.2) you will find that the zone between the mean and +1 or −1 standard deviation will encompass 34.13% of the population of items. This graphically stands for approximately 68% of any sample of items clustered around the mean. If you were to translate this into our previous example of height, we might find that the average height of 21-year-old females is 5′5″, with most of the population sampled being between 5′1″ and 5′9″. The reason we can say that most 21-year-old females are somewhere between 5′1″ and 5′9″ is because of the placement of the standard deviation lines. This is often written as follows: the average height of 21-year-old females is 5′5″ ±4″. Someone with a height of 5′2″ is still considered within the average range, even though they are not 5′5″ tall.

Going out further from the mean we find that between $+1$ and $+2$ and -1 and -2 standard deviations the zone contains 13.59% of the population. Again, going out further between $+2$ and $+3$ and -2 and -3, the zone contains 2.14% of the population. Beyond $+3$ and -3 there is a very small percentage of cases, as you can see on the diagram. Previously, we described what these small percentages mean in terms of IQ. We can now try to apply this understanding of the normal curve to a classroom, as a tool for teachers.

- When teachers say they aren't getting a normal curve within a class, this is very true. You should never expect to see a normal distribution since most classes have only 20 to 30 students. Remember, the normal curve is based on large (infinite) numbers. If your test was criterion-referenced and everyone understood the material, you will find that the grades will cluster toward the high end. This is great. It means you attained your objectives and students have grasped the material. We mentioned above how to get a range of scores with a test, if that is your intention (norm-referenced test).

- After taking a group reading assessment, the scores were reported to the teacher in the form of a standard score. Since every test has a unique mean and standard deviation (averages are always different on tests, and so are the standard deviations), it is easier for testing facilities or publishers to convert a raw score into a standard score. Below the normal curve on the diagram, you will find several common standard scores (Figure 12.2). It is important to realize that all the conversion does is change the numbers on the line along the bottom of the curve. If a raw score is placed "just a touch" above the mean when diagrammed with the raw scores, it will be "just a touch" above the mean when diagrammed with a standard score. Now all a teacher has to do is find the placement of an individual score along the standard score line and move up to the normal curve to understand what the student's score means. For example, if John gets a *T*-score of 55, go along the *T*-score line until you get to 55. (*T*-scores have a mean of 50 and a standard deviation of 10, so you know John did better than average). Place a ruler on the 55 and move up to the zone on the normal curve. John places midway between the mean and $+1$. It is within the average zone of students, but on the higher side. In Chapter 8 we discussed students who had WISC-III scores of 130. Looking along the deviation IQ line, we can find why these students were considered gifted. An IQ of 130 translates into $+2$ standard deviations above the mean. The student scored in the upper 2% of the population on this particular test.

- Since calculators usually have the option of providing a mean, median, and standard deviation, teachers should consider obtaining all these to answer questions about tests and quizzes. If all we rely on is getting an average for a student's grade, we may be doing the student an injustice. For example, Bill gets a 48% on a test. If the teacher has more information about the test, any conversation or interpretations of how well Bill performed on the test are more valuable. The average was 60%; the median was 40% with a standard deviation of 5. We can see that there were some high scores that pulled the average up, and Bill really did better than most of the students on this particular test. Sixty-eight percent of the students got between 35% and 45% on this test. Now we can go beyond our analysis of Bill's score to ask some questions about the test, the teaching strategy, students' understanding, motivation to learn the material, and the like. More statistical information has allowed us to become more informed about our assessment.

Surfing Terms 12.2

Assessment bias

Correction for guessing

Grade-equivalent scores

p-Value

Percentiles

Percentages

Stanines

Scaled scores

Skewed distribution

Standard error of measurement

T scores

z Scores

Problem-Based Scenarios 12.1 to 12.3 give you the opportunity to apply your knowledge of assessment and evaluation. In the scenarios, several issues related to testing, grading, and reporting to students and parents are presented.

Problem-Based Scenario 12.1

Teachers: *Alice and Ed*

As a new vice-principal, Alice had approached her position with great enthusiasm. The Professional Day had been a wonderful success. It was the conversation she had with Ed after everyone finished that made her wonder how she was going to handle this potential issue. The committee had invited a professor from the university in to discuss students with special needs.

When she asked Ed what he thought about it, she got quite a response. He thought it went pretty well. What had amazed Ed was the session on gifted and talented children. First, in 20 years of teaching Ed had never considered a student who was really bright academically as coming under the category of special needs. He had always figured these kids pretty much had it made. He remembered Edith Glover in particular. She had graduated from his grade 11/12 Advanced Biology class with the highest grade he had ever given. She was enrolled in a special program at the university that allowed advancement through premed and then medical school within a 5-year block of time. It was a trial program and did not get completely off the ground, but Ed was pleased one of his students actually made the cut and got into it.

But the speaker had said some other things that got him thinking. Ed felt that it was important to push students to really learn the subject. He believed in pop quizzes and took a half-credit off if a word was spelled wrong. All this motivated students to work hard in his class. He did not feel they worked as hard without the grading incentive. He knew he had a group of very bright students but he was not sure they were creative as well.

What bothered Ed was when the principal had announced at the end of the workshop that she wanted to see plans from each department on how the teachers were going to implement some of the ideas on creativity. The district was getting involved in part of a study from the university and the administration felt it was time to emphasize creativity. The big issue for Ed was he didn't want to change the way he graded. It worked. It weeded out those students who should not continue in Biology, particularly into the university.

The problem for Alice was the principal's memo (see Figure 12.3 on page 347). But after hearing what Ed said she started to wonder where to start and, in particular, how to approach Ed.

Problem-Based Scenario 12.2

Teacher: Barbara

Barbara thought this was a great opportunity. Teaching jobs had been very hard to come by lately, so when the school district offered her this chance she jumped at it. Mrs. Williams was going on a maternity leave. She had apparently worked up until the last minute, and when Barbara took over she indicated she did not really want to return, even after the leave was up.

Barbara knew she was a good teacher and was well liked by her colleagues and the students. She had three Social Studies 11 classes and two grade 8 Social Studies classes. If things continued to go well, she knew the job would be hers permanently.

Things had gone very well until yesterday. After only 2 weeks of teaching, it turned out the end of term grades were due in the office on Monday morning. Barbara had been talking to other teachers, so she did have some insight into her students that she felt would help when it came time to write comments after each grade. It seems Mrs. Williams was not a very good bookkeeper, however, and Barbara was having problems with the record of grades she had kept (see Figure 12.5 on page 348). She did not think it would be much of a problem and, with everything else

that needed to be done, she waited until Friday to call Mrs. Williams for help.

Mrs. Williams was not really pleased at the call; as a matter of fact she snapped at her. She told Barbara she was too busy with the new baby and said, "Besides, that's what they're paying you for." Now it was too late to ask for help from anyone else. If she wanted to make any kind of impression, she needed to have the grades ready on time on Monday.

The school worked on a three-term system, so Barbara knew that if she made some mistakes she still had a chance to make it up to the students. But it was also important to be seen as a fair marker, and she did not need to have any irate students or parents show up either. Also, the department head was watching her, and more than likely he would ask her questions about the report cards. The school used only grades of A, B, C, D, F, or In Progress for students who needed extra time to make things up, so Barbara figured that might make it easier. Now what she needed to do was figure out how to give grades to all the students.

FIGURE 12.4

Problem-Based Scenario 12.3

Teacher: *Sara*

Sara was overjoyed when she got a call asking her to take a long-term substitute teaching assignment. An elementary teacher was taking medical leave for the rest of the fall term, and there was a possibility he might need to extend the leave into the new year. Sara had been on call for 2 years and now, in late October of the third year, just when she was beginning to lose hope that she would ever get a permanent job, the district superintendent had called her. Well, this was not quite a permanent job, but the chance to prove herself might lead to one, and it offered some stability for the next few months. Sara was excited. She had received good reports on her substitute teaching and was respected in the school district. Now she had a chance to really make it all come together in a classroom of her own. And a fourth-grade classroom at that! This was Sara's favorite age group.

Sara began her assignment in the midst of Halloween excitement. It seemed like life was a swirl of orange and black as she got to know her students and balanced the day-to-day realities of teaching with trying to focus on long-term planning for the next several months. She was determined not to fall into a "just get through each day" way of thinking. It was important to her to be well organized and have a good sense of where she was headed with the curriculum and her students.

Still, before she knew it, the November reporting period was upon her. Now the demands on her were immense. Sara had three challenges: Make sense of the records left by her predecessor, integrate these records with her own observations and evaluations, and communicate grades and reflections on progress to her students and their parents in a meaningful way. The first challenge was the biggest. In poor health, Peter Garcia had not been able to keep up. Some grades and comments were available, but they were incomplete. In Language Arts, only reading and spelling records had been kept. Sara found no indicators of written language ability. For Science and Social Studies, stacks of unmarked projects were the only records. No indicators existed for Art. Sara was relieved that the school's gym and music teachers would submit grades for these subjects (see Figures 12.6 through 12.9 on pages 349–352).

Sara also realized that getting letter grades for the first time was a very big deal to her pupils. In her school district, letter grades were assigned beginning in fourth grade. Her students were excited and apprehensive at the same time, and Sara wondered how much they really understood about the meaning of As, Bs, and Cs.

Sara had only 2 weeks left in which to prepare report cards and organize the student-led conferences that were the norm in the school. She knew her principal would understand that she had taken on this position on very short notice and she hoped that the parents would equally understand. Still, this was not a situation she wanted to continue. She had to hit the ground running and come up with a strategy for assessing her students in a meaningful way.

Summary

In this chapter, you learned additional ways to assess and evaluate your students from teacher-made tests to standardized tests. Well-designed assessment procedures require adhering to the principles of reliability and validity in testing. You also learned basic measurement principles and some fundamental test statistics to help you interpret the results of testing. With all these tools, you will be well equipped to plan, interpret, and report on your students' progress.

A Metacognitive Challenge

You should now be able to reflect on the following questions:

- How can I plan and construct a test that reflects classroom objectives and activities?

- How does my knowledge of authentic assessment help me plan teaching and learning activities?

- What do I know about valid and reliable assessments?

- What are the appropriate conditions for the selection and use of standardized tests?

- What are standardized scores? What role do they play in education?

Artifacts for Problem-Based Scenarios

FIGURE 12.3 ■ Artifact for Problem-Based Scenario 12.1

MEMO

Alice,

I got a note from the superintendent today — he wants to have some plans for implementing creativity in place by the end of the month. He knows it might be hard for some teachers, but the Parent Advisory Group is becoming quite vocal about this issue.

Please see what you can do to help some of the teachers who might be having trouble with anything.

The workshop should be a good start.

Maria

FIGURE 12.5 ■ Artifact for Problem-Based Scenario 12.2

	Term 1	Unit 1 Test	Unit 2 Test	Unit 3 Test	Unit 4 Test	Quiz 1	Quiz 2	Quiz 3	% HW	Absent	Dept. z - Score	Mrs. W. Comments
G. Boucher	C+	90	95	80	75	80	60	69	12	8	0	polite
A. Carlson	B	90	85	80	80	89	73	62	100	0	0.5	doesn't like partners
P. Cheng	C	50	60	62	68	110	100	70	60	0	0.25	new to school
V. Chow	C	80	85	87	100	70	73	77	59	2	-0.3	very popular
D. Foulds	D	AB	37	65	70	70	69	82	70	1	-1.6	doesn't care
L. Herback	B	75	69	60	90	103	92	86	90	0	0.9	helpful
J. Hoogland	A+	100	78	115	100	110	87	92	95	0	1.8	social isolate
C. Ivey	A	90	82	110	95	105	110	98	90	0	1.5	obsessed with grades
J. Kadonoff	B	69	65	68	70	80	61	82	85	2	1.3	hard worker
R. Lacy	D	71	72	29	40	AB	72	77	83	0	-0.2	father just lost job
R. Lo	C	55	58	70	60	82	88	87	90	1	-1	esl
C. Mclellan	B-	62	75	79	89	91	76	78	90	1	2	quiet
V. Mala	C+	70	70	65	80	68	72	69	45	11	0	discipline problem
K. Martin	C	81	70	85	90	90		110	75	2	0.1	hard worker
A. Miester	D	32	0*	60	65	45	70	23	10	15	0	esl
G. Milne	F	60	50	40	30	60	65	AB	60	20	-1.5	LD
E. Opper	B-	65	70	75	75	59	60	57	80	0	1.8	usually late
I. Plaxton	C-	60	55	63	67		52	110	40	15	0.9	hates school
K. Proudlove	D	52	45	60	62	25	43	30	50	0	0.8	
W. Regan	B-	73	0*	60	61		115	80	55	0	0.5	caught cheating
D. Richardson	A	82	110	105	120	110	AB	73	20	4	2.8	has a tutor
L. Sawyer	C	76	74	70	62	41	23	55	70	1	-1	
P. Scott	C+	71	85	83	79	81	88	76	80	0	-0.3	
J. Smart	B+	90	92	95	110	60	102	93	10	0	0	esl/social isolate
A. Takahashi	C	85	72	69	81	60	14	19	63	0	-3	two part-time jobs
A. Tong	D	40	48	59	31	60	72	80	53	2	-1	
C. Vincent	B-	75	72	81	86		23	35	80	0	0.9	

*Caught cheating on tests

FIGURE 12.6 ■ Artifact for Problem-Based Scenario 12.3

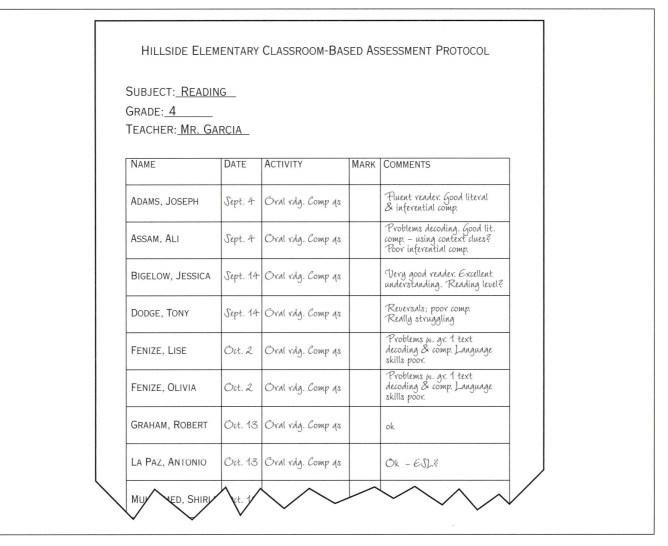

HILLSIDE ELEMENTARY CLASSROOM-BASED ASSESSMENT PROTOCOL

SUBJECT: READING
GRADE: 4
TEACHER: MR. GARCIA

NAME	DATE	ACTIVITY	MARK	COMMENTS
ADAMS, JOSEPH	Sept. 4	Oral rdg. Comp qs		Fluent reader. Good literal & inferential comp.
ASSAM, ALI	Sept. 4	Oral rdg. Comp qs		Problems decoding. Good lit. comp. – using context clues? Poor inferential comp.
BIGELOW, JESSICA	Sept. 14	Oral rdg. Comp qs		Very good reader. Excellent understanding. Reading level?
DODGE, TONY	Sept. 14	Oral rdg. Comp qs		Reversals; poor comp. Really struggling
FENIZE, LISE	Oct. 2	Oral rdg. Comp qs		Problems w. gr. 1 text decoding & comp. Language skills poor.
FENIZE, OLIVIA	Oct. 2	Oral rdg. Comp qs		Problems w. gr. 1 text decoding & comp. Language skills poor.
GRAHAM, ROBERT	Oct. 13	Oral rdg. Comp qs		ok
LA PAZ, ANTONIO	Oct. 13	Oral rdg. Comp qs		Ok – ESL?
MU___MED, SHIRL__	__ct. 1			

FIGURE 12.7 ■ Artifact for Problem-Based Scenario 12.3

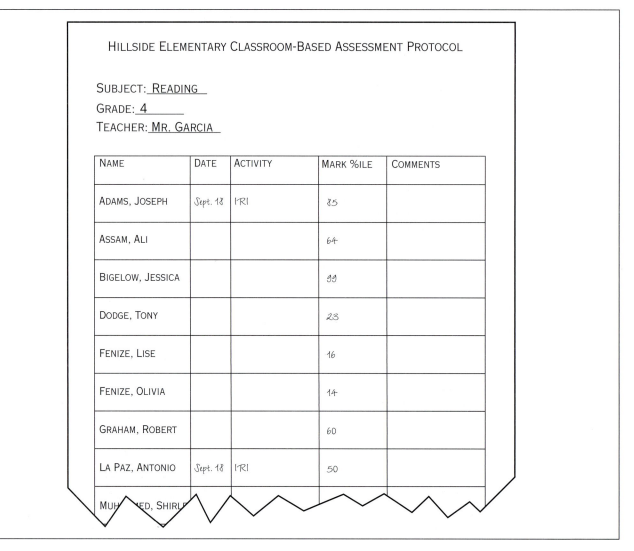

HILLSIDE ELEMENTARY CLASSROOM-BASED ASSESSMENT PROTOCOL

SUBJECT: READING

GRADE: 4

TEACHER: MR. GARCIA

NAME	DATE	ACTIVITY	MARK %ILE	COMMENTS
ADAMS, JOSEPH	Sept. 18	IRI	85	
ASSAM, ALI			64	
BIGELOW, JESSICA			99	
DODGE, TONY			23	
FENIZE, LISE			16	
FENIZE, OLIVIA			14	
GRAHAM, ROBERT			60	
LA PAZ, ANTONIO	Sept. 18	IRI	50	
MUHAMMED, SHIRLEY				

FIGURE 12.8 ■ Artifact for Problem-Based Scenario 12.3

SUBJECT: SPELLING FRIDAY TESTS/10

GRADE: 4

TEACHER: MR. GARCIA

NAME	Sept 5	Sept 12	Sept 19	Sept 26	Oct 5	Oct 10	Oct 17	Oct 24
ADAMS, JOSEPH	10	9	10	10	10			
ASSAM, ALI	5	6	6	4	7			
BIGELOW, JESSICA	10	10	10	10	10			
DODGE, TONY	3	4	2	4	3			
FENIZE, LISE	1	1	2	0	1			
FENIZE, OLIVIA	2	1	3	1	2			
GRAHAM, ROBERT	8	8	7	8	8			
LA PAZ, ANTONIO	6	7	7	8	8			
MUHAMMED, SHIRLEY	5	6	6	6	7			
NYCHAK, KENNETH	8	7	8	Abs.	6			
O'TOOLE, GILES	9	10	9	9	10			
PAOLO, FRANCES		10	10	10				

FIGURE 12.9 ■ Artifact for Problem-Based Scenario 12.3

SUBJECT: MATH

GRADE: 4

TEACHER: MR. GARCIA

NAME	Date CTBS math. Gr. 3	Date unit test Sept 26	Date think aloud + – probs	Date graphs	Date Oct. 10 chap 4 test	Date	Date	Date
ADAMS, JOSEPH	81	30	!	✓	10			
ASSAM, ALI	66	22	✓	✓	7			
BIGELOW, JESSICA	72	25	✓	✓	8			
DODGE, TONY	53	18	Can't do	X	3			
FENIZE, LISE	26	10	?	X	2			
FENIZE, OLIVIA	30	8	?	X	1			
GRAHAM, ROBERT	95	29	!	✓	10			
LA PAZ, ANTONIO	68	21		✓	8			
MUHAMMED, SHIRLEY	86	26		✓	9			
NYCHAK, KENNETH	69	20		✓	5			
O'TOOLE, GILES	98	30		✓	10			
PA___ FRANCE_								

Adaptive behavior: Age-appropriate social skills (e.g., being able to dress one's self; personal care; simple money management; communication).

Automaticity: When something is done automatically, without conscious thought (e.g., brushing your teeth, locking the door when you leave the house).

Autonomy: The sense that one has personal freedom.

Cephalocaudal principle: Top-down growth.

Cognitive science: The discipline that explains how the mind works as we think and learn.

Competence: To be competent is to be capable and effective at what one undertakes.

Competencies: Skills; areas in which a person is competent.

Criterion-referenced test: A teacher-made test for which the criterion for mastery is determined by the teacher and the curriculum.

Cultural competence: The ability to function competently in another culture and/or with people from other cultures; respect for and the ability and desire to learn about other cultures (Lonner & Hayes, 2004).

Developmental niche: The sociocultural context in which we develop—family, community, church, school, cultural traditions, national identity.

Didactic: Intended to instruct or explain.

Distal–proximal principle: Growth from the ends inward.

Egocentric: A viewpoint centered completely on one's self that ignores others' points of view (not to be confused with egotistic).

Expert: Learners who have developed a rich understanding of concepts.

Fairness and **Justice** are considered part of moral development (See Chapter 6).

Flexibility: The ability to adapt to a situation.

Fluency: The ability to understand abstract and novel relationships.

Formative assessment: and evaluation are done during a unit, course, or term to determine how students are progressing and to inform subsequent instruction.

General intelligence: A general ability to reason and solve problems believed to underlie all human thinking; sometimes referred to as g.

Heteronomy: Subjection to an external law. "Don't do that because it's against the rules!"

Hypothetical–deductive thinking: Thinking that involves forming a hypothesis and judging relevant evidence; the scientific method

Instrumentality: A factor that helps one reach a goal (e.g., "I have to spend a long time working on these proofs because I really want to be a math teacher, and I need to understand math concepts very well").

Interpersonal competence: The ability to understand others' points of view and to respond accordingly.

Learning community: A community that understands how people learn and provides the rich environments for learning to occur across the life-span.

Logical–mathematical thinking: Thinking that is structured and sequential or patterned

Mastery orientation: An orientation to learning that involves learning for learning's sake, rather than for the sake of performance (e.g., high marks on a test).

Mental states: Thoughts, feelings, desires, and intentions are mental states.

Models of mind: How we think learning takes place.

Niche: One's unique "place" in life; one's personal developmental space.

Norm-referenced test: A test that has been normed on a large group of children of the same age and background as the children you plan to test.

Norm-referenced: Tests that compare an individual's performance to a large group of individuals of the same age who also took the test. The larger group is called the norm group.

Novice: Learners who are encountering new material or who do not understand familiar material at a deep level.

Nurturant, resourceful environment: An environment that nurtures learners' needs through appropriate resources, stimulating experiences, encouragement, and support.

Originality: The ability to produce something that is new or that is not copied.

Peer tutoring: An instructional strategy that involves students teaching other students. The student being tutored may be younger than the tutor or the students may be the same age.

Perspective taking: The ability to comprehend a situation from another's point of view.

Positive behavioral support: Support that focuses on understanding behavior and providing a positive school environment.

Precocity: Developmental advancement (e.g., the ability to read several grade levels above one's age peers).

Proximodistal principle: Growth from the center outward.

Puberty: Age range during which an adolescent undergoes sexual maturation.

Reciprocal teaching: An instructional procedure that involves dialogue about predicting, clarifying, questioning, and summarizing text. Small groups of students and a dialogue leader (who can be a teacher or student) work toward gaining greater meaning from reading text (Hacker & Tenent, 2002).

Reciprocity: A balance in the relationship between two actions.

Relatedness: A sense of being connected to other human beings.

Social cognition: Knowledge and understanding of social situations. Cognition, in general, refers to how we perceive, remember, represent, and problem solve. Social cognition is cognition directed to social events and issues.

Social responsibility: Individual wants and needs are understood in the wider social context; responsibility is taken for the good of the community.

Summative assessment: And evaluation are done after a unit, course, or term is complete.

Theory of mind: The ability to understand our own and others' thoughts, emotions, and intentions.

Time-out: Placing a student in a separate area for a short period of time where there is no opportunity to interact with others.

Verbal reprimand: A scolding given due to some misbehavior; most effective when given quietly, unemotionally, briefly, and in a timely manner.

References

Ablard, K. E., & Lipschultz, R. E. (1998). Self-regulated learning in high-achieving students: Relations to advanced reasoning, achievement goals, and gender. *Journal of Educational Psychology, 90,* 94–101.

Alasker, F. D. (1995). Timing of puberty and reactions to pubertal change. In M. Rutter (Ed.), *Psychosocial disturbances in young people: Challenges for prevention* (pp. 37–82). Cambridge, England: Cambridge University Press.

Alderman, M. K. (1999). *Motivation for achievement: Possibilities for teaching and learning.* Mahwah, NJ: Erlbaum.

Alexander, C. N., & Langer, E. J. (Eds.). (1990). *Higher stages of human development: Perspectives on adult growth.* New York: Oxford University Press.

Ames, C. (1992). Classrooms: Goals, structures, and student motivation. *Journal of Educational Psychology, 84,* 261–271.

Anderman, E. M. (2002). School effects on psychological outcomes during adolescence. *Journal of Educational Psychology, 94,* 795–809.

Annett, M. (1973). Laterality of childhood hemiplegia and the growth of speech and intelligence. *Cortex, 9,* 4–33.

Archer, L. A., Campbell, D., & Segalowitz, S. J. (1988). A prospective study of hand preference and language development in 18- to 30-month olds: I. Hand preference. *Developmental Neuropsychology, 4,* 85–92.

Arlin, P. K. (1989). Problem solving and problem finding in young artists and young scientists. In M. L. Commons & J. D. Sinnott (Eds.), *Adult development, Vol. 1: Comparisons and applications of developmental models* (pp. 197–216). New York: Praeger.

Arlin, P. K. (1990, October). Teaching as conversation. *Educational Leadership,* 82–84.

Arlin, P. K. (1993). Wisdom and expertise in teaching: An integration of perspectives. *Learning and Individual Differences, 5,* 341–349.

Astington, J. W. (1993). *The child's discovery of the mind.* Cambridge, MA: Harvard University Press.

Atkinson, R. C., & Shiffrin, R. M. (1968). Human memory: A proposed system and its control processes. In K. W. Spence & J. T. Spence (Eds.), *The psychology of learning and motivation* (Vol. 2). San Diego, CA: Academic Press.

Babcock, S., & Backlund, J. (2001). Proactive parent communication. *Instructor, 110* (6), 34.

Bandura, A. (1977). *Social learning theory.* Englewood Cliffs, NJ: Prentice-Hall.

Bandura, A. (1981). Self-reliant thought: A developmental analysis of self-efficacy. In J. Flavell & L. Ross (Eds.), *Social cognitive development: Frontiers and possible futures.* Cambridge, England: Cambridge University Press.

Bandura, A. (1986). *Social foundations of thought and action: A social-cognitive theory.* Englewood Cliffs, NJ: Prentice-Hall.

Bandura, A. (1997). *Self-efficacy: The exercise of control.* New York: Freeman.

Barab, S. A., & Plucker, J. A. (2002). Smart people or smart contexts? Cognition, ability, and talent development in an age of situated approaches to knowing and learning. *Educational Psychologist, 37,* 165–182.

Battistich, V., Solomon, D., Watson, M., & Schaps, E. (1997). Caring school communities. *Educational Psychologist, 32,* 137–151.

Baumrind, D. (1971). Current patterns of parental authority. *Developmental Psychology Monographs, 4* (1, Pt. 2).

Baumrind, D. (1991). The influence of parenting style on adolescent competence and substance abuse. *Journal of Early Adolescence, 11,* 56–94.

Beins, B. (2002). Classes are a social affair. *Monitor on Psychology, 33*(10), 46.

Belenky, M. F., Clinchy, B. V., Goldberger, N. R., & Tarule, J. M. (1986). *Women's ways of knowing: The development of self, voice, and mind.* New York: Basic Books.

Bereiter, C., & Scardamalia, M. (1986). Educational relevance of the study of expertise. *Interchange, 17*(2), 10–19.

Bergman, C. S., & Plomin, R. (1989). Genotype-environment interaction. In M. Bornstein & J. Bruner (Eds.), *Interaction in human development* (pp. 157–171). Hillsdale, NJ: Erlbaum.

Berk, L. E. (1991). *Child development.* Boston: Allyn and Bacon.

Berndt, T. J. (1996). Exploring the effects of friendship quality on social development. In W. M. Bukowski, A. F. Newcomb, & W. W. Hartup (Eds.), *The company they keep: Friendship in childhood and adolescence* (pp. 346–365). New York: Cambridge University Press.

Berndt, T. J., Hawkins, J. A., & Jiao, Z. (1999). Influences of friends and friendships on adjustment to junior high school. *Merrill–Palmer Quarterly, 45,* 13–41.

Bickerton, G. (1994, June). *Narrative knowledge as revealed in children's perceptions of learning.* Paper presented at the Canadian Society for the Study of Education, University of Calgary.

Bickerton, G. (2000). *Children's understanding of scientific concepts: A developmental study.* Unpublished doctoral dissertation, University of British Columbia, Vancouver.

Bickerton, G., & Porath, M. (1997). Advanced scientific reasoning about buoyancy in middle childhood: An exploratory study. *Alberta Gifted and Talented Education, 11,* 5–13.

Biemiller, A., Inglis, A., & Meichenbaum, D. (1995, April). *Using peer tutoring to increase tutors' verbal self-regulation and problem-solving skills in mathematics.* Paper presented at the American Educational Research Association, San Francisco.

Biemiller, A., & Meichenbaum, D. (1992, October). The nature and nurture of the self-directed learner. *Educational Leadership,* 75–80.

Biro, F. M., McMahon, R. P., Striegel-Moore, R., Crawford, P. B., Obarzanek, E., Morrison, J. A., et al. (2001). Impact of timing of pubertal maturation on growth in black and white adolescents. National Heart, Lung and Blood Institute Growth and Health Study. *Journal of Pediatrics, 138,* 636–643.

Blair, C. (2002). School readiness: Integrating cognition and emotion in a neurobiological conceptualization of children's functioning at school entry. *American Psychologist, 57,* 111–127.

Bloom, B. S. (Ed.). (1956). *Taxonomy of educational objectives. Handbook I: cognitive domain.* New York: David MacKay.

Blumberg, P. (2000). Evaluating the evidence that problem-based learners are self-directed learners: A review of the literature. In D. H. Evensen & C. E. Hmelo (Eds.), *Problem-based learning: A research perspective on learning interactions* (pp. 199–226). Mahwah, NJ: Erlbaum.

Bransford, J. D., Brown, A. L., & Cocking, R. R. (2000). *How people learn: Brain, mind, experience and school.* Washington, DC: National Academy Press.

Brazelton, T. B., & Greenspan, S. I. (2000). *The irreducible needs of children: What every child must have to grow, learn, and flourish.* Cambridge, MA: Perseus.

Brinthaupt, T. M., & Erwin, L. J. (1992). Reporting about the self: Issues and implications. In T. M. Brinthaupt & R. P. Lipka (Eds.), *The self: Definitional and methodological issues* (pp. 137–171). Albany, NY: State University of New York Press.

British Columbia Ministry of Education. (1996). *Appendix D: Evaluation example for English K to 7.* Retrieved March 31, 2004, from www.bced.gov.bc.ca/irp/elak7/apdsam3.htm.

British Columbia Ministry of Education. (1999). *Personal planning K to 7. Integrated resource package.* Retrieved December 3, 2004, from www.bced.gov.bc.ca/irp/ppk7.pdf.

British Columbia Ministry of Education. (2002). *Special education services: A manual of policies, procedures, and guidelines.* Retrieved November 26, 2004, from www.bced.gov.bc.ca/specialed/ppandg/planning_4.htm.

British Columbia Ministry of Education. (2005). *BC Performance Standards: Writing Grade 1.* Retrieved May 14, 2005, from www.bced.gov.bc.ca/perf_stands/writeg1.pdf.

Bronfenbrenner, U. (1986). Ecology of the family as a context for human development: Research perspectives. *Developmental Psychology, 22,* 723–742.

Brooks-Gunn, J. (1988). Antecedents and consequences of variations in girls' maturational timing. *Journal of Youth and Adolescence, 9*(5), 365–373.

Brown, A. L., & Campione, J. C. (1994). Guided discovery in a community of learners. In K. McGilly (Ed.), *Classroom lessons: Integrating cognitive theory and classroom practice* (pp. 229–270). Cambridge, MA: The MIT Press.

Brown, L. M., & Gilligan, C. (1992). *Meeting at the crossroads: Women's psychology and girls' development.* New York: Ballantine.

Brown, R. (1973). *A first language: The early stages.* Cambridge, MA: Harvard University Press.

Brownlie, F., Close, S., & Wingren, L. (1990). *Tomorrow's classroom today. Strategies for creating active readers, writers, and thinkers.* Markham, ON: Pembroke.

Bruer, J. T. (1994). Classroom problems, school culture, and cognitive research. In K. McGilly (Ed.), *Classroom lessons: Integrating cognitive theory and classroom* practice (pp. 273–294). Cambridge, MA: MIT Press.

Bruner, J. (1986). *Actual minds, possible worlds.* Cambridge, MA: Harvard Press.

Bruner, J. (1996). *The culture of education.* Cambridge, MA: Harvard University Press.

Buhrmester, D. (1990). Intimacy of friendship, interpersonal competence, and adjustment during preadolescence and adolescence. *Child Development, 61,* 1101–1111.

Bukowski, W. M., Newcomb, A. F., & Hartup, W. W. (1996). Friendship and its significance in childhood and adolescence: Introduction and comment. In W. M. Bukowski, A. F. Newcomb & W. W. Hartup (Eds.), *The company they keep: Friendship in childhood and adolescence* (pp. 1–15). New York: Cambridge University Press.

Burns, D. E., Johnson, S. E., & Gable, R. K. (1998). Can we generalize about the learning style characteristics of high academic achievers? *Roeper Review, 20,* 276–281.

Byrne, B. M. (1996). *Measuring self-concept across the life span: Issues and instrumentation.* Washington, DC: American Psychological Association.

Carleton Board of Education (1992). *On your marks: Guide to the evaluation and improvement of writing in the transition years.* Ottawa, ON: Author.

Carpenter, S. (2001). Teens' risky behavior is about more than race and family resources. *Monitor on Psychology, 32* (1), 22–23.

Carr, E. G., Dunlap, G., Horner, R. H., Koegel, R. L., Turnbull, A. P., Sailor, W., Anderson, J. L., Albin, R. W., Koegel, L. K., & Fox, L. (2002). Positive behavior support: Evolution of an applied science. *Journal of Positive Behavior Interventions, 4,* 4–16, 20.

Case, R. (1985). *Intellectual development: Birth to adulthood.* New York: Academic Press.

Case, R. (1987). Neo-Piagetian theory: Retrospect and prospect. *International Journal of Psychology, 22,* 773–791.

Case, R. (1991). A developmental approach to the design of remedial instruction. In A. McKeough & J. L. Lupart (Eds.), *Toward the practice of a theory-based instruction: Current cognitive theories and their educational promise* (pp. 117–147). Hillsdale, NJ: Erlbaum.

Case, R. (Ed.). (1992). *The mind's staircase: Exploring the conceptual underpinnings of children's thought and knowledge.* Hillsdale, NJ: Erlbaum.

Case, R. (1995). Capacity-based explanations of working memory growth: A brief history and reevaluation. In F. E. Weinert & W. Schneider (Eds.), *Memory performance and competencies: Issues in growth and development* (pp. 23–44). Mahwah, NJ: Erlbaum.

Case, R. (1996). Introduction: Reconceptualizing the nature of children's conceptual structures and their development in middle childhood. In R. Case & Y. Okamoto, *The Role of Central Conceptual Structures in the Development of Children's Thought. Monographs of the Society for Research in Child Development, 61* (1–2, Serial No. 246), 1–26.

Case, R., Griffin, S., & Kelly, W. M. (1999). Socioeconomic gradients in mathematical ability and their responsiveness to intervention during early childhood. In D. P. Keating & C. Hertzman (Eds.), *Developmental health and the wealth of nations: Social, biological, and educational dynamics* (pp. 125–149). New York: Guilford Press.

Case, R., & Okamoto, Y. (1996). The role of central conceptual structures in the development of children's thought. *Monographs of the Society for Research in Child Development, 61* (1–2, Serial No. 246).

Ceci, S. J. (1996). *On intelligence: A bioecological treatise on intellectual development.* Cambridge, MA: Harvard University Press.

Chase, W. G., & Simon, H. H. (1973). Perception in chess. *Cognitive Psychology, 4,* 55–81.

Chomsky, N. (1965). *Aspects of the theory of syntax.* Cambridge, MA: MIT Press.

Church, M. A., Elliot, A. J., & Gable, S. L. (2001). Perceptions of classroom environment, achievement goals, and achievement outcomes. *Journal of Educational Psychology, 93,* 43–54.

Cole, M. (1999). Culture in cognitive development. In M. H. Bornstein & M. E Lamb (Eds.), *Developmental psychology: An advanced textbook* (4th ed.) (pp. 73–123). Mahwah, NJ: Erlbaum.

Cole, M., & Griffin, P. (1983). A socio-historical approach to remediation. *Quarterly Newsletter of the Laboratory of Comparative Human Cognition, 5* (4), 69–74.

Cole, M., Gay, J., Glick, J. A., & Sharp, D. W. (1971). *The cultural context of learning and thinking.* New York: Basic Books.

Cole, P. M., Bruschi, C. J., & Tamang, B. L. (2002). Cultural differences in children's emotional reactions to difficult situations. *Child Development, 73*, 983–996.

Committee on Youth. (1995). *Second Step: A violence prevention curriculum*. Seattle, WA: Committee on Youth.

Commons, M. L., Demick, J., & Goldberg, C. (Eds.). (1996). *Clinical approaches to adult development*. Stamford, CT: Ablex.

Connell, J. P., Spencer, M. B., & Aber, J. L. (1994). Educational risk and resilience in African American youth: Context, self, and action outcomes in school. *Child Development, 65*, 493–506.

Connell, J. P., & Wellborn, J. G. (1991). Competence, autonomy, and relatedness: A motivational analysis of self-system processes. In R. Gunnar & L. A. Sroufe (Eds.), *Minnesota symposia on child psychology* (Vol. 23, pp. 23–77). Hillsdale, NJ: Erlbaum.

Conry, J. & Fast, D. K. (2000). *Fetal alcohol syndrome and the criminal justice system*. Vancouver, BC: BC Fetal Alcohol Syndrome Resource Society.

Cooley, C. H. (1902). *Human nature and the social order*. New York: Charles Scribner & Sons.

Cooper, D., & Snell, J. L. (2003). Bullying—Not just a kid thing. *Educational Leadership, 60* (6), 22–25.

Covington, M. V. (1984). The self-worth theory of achievement motivation: Findings and implications. *Elementary School Journal, 85*(1), 5–20.

Covington, M. V., & Omelich, C. L. (1984). Effort: The double-edged sword. *Journal of Educational Psychology, 71*, 169–182.

Crain, W. (2000). *Theories of development: Concepts and applications* (4th ed.). Upper Saddle River, NJ: Prentice-Hall.

Crammond, J. (1992). Analyzing the basic cognitive-developmental processes of children with specific types of learning disability. In R. Case (Ed.), *The mind's staircase: Exploring the conceptual underpinnings of children's thought and knowledge* (pp. 285–302). Hillsdale, NJ: Erlbaum.

Cropley, A. J. (2003). *Creativity in education and learning: A guide for teachers and educators*. Sterling, VA: Kogan Page.

Cross, B. (1997). What inner-city children say about character. In A. Molnar (Ed.), *Construction of children's character. 96th yearbook of the National Society for the Study of Education, Part 2* (pp. 120–126). Chicago: National Society for the Study of Education.

Damasio, A. R. (1994). *Descartes' error. Emotion, reason, and the human brain*. New York: Avon.

Damon, W. (1977). *The social world of the child*. San Francisco: Jossey-Bass.

Davis, H. A. (2003). Conceptualizing the role and influence of student-teacher relationships on children's social and cognitive development. *Educational Psychologist, 38*, 207–234.

Day, V. P., & Skidmore, M. L. (1996). Linking performance assessment and curricular goals. *Teaching Exceptional Children, 29* (1), 59–63.

De Angelis, T. (2001). Punishment of innocents: Children of parents behind bars. *Monitor on Psychology, 32* (5), 56–59.

De Casper, A. J., & Fifer, W. P. (1980). Of human bonding: Newborns prefer their mothers' voices. *Science, 208*, 1174–1176.

Deci, E. L. (1971). Effects of externally mediated rewards on intrinsic motivation. *Journal of Personality and Social Psychology, 18*, 105–115.

Deci, E. L., Koestner, R., & Ryan, R. M. (2001). Extrinsic rewards and intrinsic motivation in education: Reconsidered once again. *Review of Educational Research, 71*, 1–27.

Deci, E. L., Ryan, R. M., & Koestner, R. (2001). The pervasive negative effects of rewards on intrinsic motivation: Response to Cameron (2001). *Review of Educational Research, 71*, 43–51.

Deegan, J. G. (1996). *Children's friendships in culturally diverse classrooms*. London: Falmer.

De Falco, K. (1997). Educator's commentary. In P. Salovey & D. J. Sluyter (Eds.), *Emotional development and emotional intelligence: Educational implications* (pp. 32–34). New York: Basic Books.

de Lisi, R., & Staudt, J. (1980). Individual differences in college students' performance on formal operations tasks. *Journal of Applied Developmental Psychology, 1*, 201–208.

Demetriou, A., & Efklides, A. (1988). Experiential structuralism and neo-Piagetian theories: Toward an integrated model. In A. Demetriou (Ed.), *The neo-Piagetian theories of cognitive development: Toward an integration* (pp. 137–173). Amsterdam: North-Holland (Elsevier).

DeVries, R. (1997). Piaget's social theory. *Educational Researcher, 26* (2), 4–17.

Dick, W., & Carey, L. (1996). *The systematic design of instruction* (4th. ed.). New York: Harper/Collins.

Dick, W., & Reiser, R. A. (1996). *Planning effective instruction* (2nd ed.). Boston: Allyn and Bacon.

Diekhoff, G. M., Brown, P. J., & Dansereau, D. F. (1985). A prose learning strategy training program based on network and depth-of-processing model. *Journal of Experimental Education, 50*, 180–184.

diSessa, A. (1988). Knowledge in pieces. In G. E. Forman & P. Pufall (Eds.), *Constructivism in the computer age* (pp. 49–70). Hillsdale, NJ: Erlbaum.

Dochy, F., Segers, M., Van den Bossche, P., & Gijbels, D. (2003). Effects of problem-based learning: A meta-analysis. *Learning and Instruction, 13*, 533–568.

Donaldson, M. (1978). *Children's minds*. London: Croom Helm.

Donaldson, M. (1979, March). The mismatch between school and children's minds. *Human Nature*, 155–159.

Donovan, M. S., Bransford, J. D., & Pellegrino, J. W. (Eds.). (1999). *How people learn: Bridging research and practice*. Washington, DC: National Academy Press.

Duch, B. J., Groh, S. E., & Allen, D. E. (2001). Why problem-based learning? A case study of institutional change in undergraduate education. In B. J. Duch, S. E. Groh & D. E. Allen (Eds.), *The power of problem-based learning* (pp. 3–11). Sterling, VA: Stylus.

Duckworth, E. (1987). *The "having of wonderful ideas" and other essays on teaching and learning*. New York: Teachers College Press.

Duffy, G. G. (1993). Teachers' progress toward becoming expert strategy teachers. *Elementary School Journal, 94*, 109–120.

Duncan, G. J., Ritter, P. L., Dornbusch, S. M., Gross, R. T., & Carlsmith, J. M. (1985). The effects of pubertal timing on body image, school behaviour, and deviance. *Journal of Youth and Adolescence, 14*, 227–235.

Durkin, K., & Barber, B. (2002). Not so doomed: Computer game play and positive adolescent development [Electronic version]. *Applied Developmental Psychology, 23*, 373–392.

Dweck, C. S. (1986). Motivational processes affecting learning. *American Psychologist, 41*, 1040–1048.

Dykstra, D. I., Jr. (1996). Teaching introductory physics to college students. In C. T. Fosnot (Ed.), *Constructivism: Theory, perspectives, and practice* (pp. 182–204). New York: Teachers College Press.

Earl, L., & Cousins, J. B. (1996). *Classroom assessment: Changing the face; facing the change.* Ontario Public School Teachers' Federation.

Easley, S. D., & Mitchell, K. (2003). *Portfolios matter: What, where, when, why and how to use them.* Markham, ON: Pembroke.

Eccles, J. S., Midgley, C., Wigfield, A., Buchanan, C. M., Reuman, D., Flanagan, C., & MacIver, D. (1993). Development during adolescence: The impact of stage-environment fit on young adolescents' experiences in schools and in families. *American Psychologist, 48,* 90–101.

Eccles, J. S., & Roeser, R. W. (1999). School and community influences on human development. In M. H. Bornstein & M. E. Lamb, *Developmental psychology: An advanced textbook* (4th ed., pp. 503–554). Mahwah, NJ: Erlbaum.

Eccles, J. S., Wigfield, A., & Schiefele, U. (1998). Motivation to succeed. In W. Damon (Editor-in-Chief) & N. Eisenberg (Vol. Ed.), *Handbook of child psychology: Vol. 3. Social, emotional, and personality development* (5th ed., pp. 1017–1095). New York: Wiley.

Eisenberg, N. (1992). *The caring child.* Cambridge, MA: Harvard University Press.

Eisenberg, N., Fabes, R. A., & Losoya, S. (1997). Emotional responding: Regulation, social correlates, and socialization. In P. Salovey & D. J. Sluyter (Eds.), *Emotional development and emotional intelligence: Educational implications* (pp. 129–163). New York: Basic Books.

Eisenberg, N., Losoya, S., & Guthrie, I. K. (1997). Social cognition and prosocial development. In S. Hala (Ed.), *The development of social cognition* (pp. 329–363). Hove, East Sussex, UK: Psychology Press.

Emmer, E. T., & Stough, L. M. (2001). Classroom management: A critical part of educational psychology, with implications for teacher education. *Educational Psychologist, 36,* 103–112.

Erikson, E. H. (1950). *Childhood and society.* New York: Norton.

Erikson, E. H. (1968). *Identity: Youth and crisis.* New York: Norton.

Evans, G. W. (2004). The environment of childhood poverty. *American Psychologist, 59,* 77–89.

Fatt, J. P. T. (2000). Fostering creativity in education. *Education, 120* (4), 744–757.

Feldman, D. H. (1986). *Nature's gambit: Child prodigies and the development of human potential.* New York: Basic Books.

Feldman, D. H. (1991). Why children can't be creative. *Exceptionality Education Canada, 1,* 43–51.

Ferrara, R. A., Brown, A. L., & Campione, J. C. (1983). *Children's learning and transfer of inductive reasoning rules: Studies of proximal development.* Unpublished manuscript. University of Illinois at Urbana-Champaign.

Ferrari, M. (Ed.) (2002). *The pursuit of excellence through education.* Mahwah, NJ: Erlbaum.

Ferrari, M., & Sternberg, R. J. (1998). The development of mental abilities and styles. In W. Damon (Ed.), *Handbook of child psychology* (Vol. 2). New York: Wiley.

Fischer, K. W. (1980). A theory of cognitive development: The control and construction of hierarchies of skills. *Psychological Review, 87,* 477–531.

Fischer, K., Hand, H. H., Watson, M. W., Van Parys, M., & Tucker, J. L. (1984). Putting the child into socialization: The development of social categories in preschool children. In L. Katz (Ed.), *Current topics in early childhood education* (Vol. 5) (pp. 27–72). Norwood, NJ: Ablex.

Fischer, K. W., Knight, C. C., & Van Parys, M. (1993). Analyzing diversity in developmental pathways: Methods and concepts. In R. Case & W. Edelstein (Eds.), *The new structuralism in cognitive development: Theory and research on individual pathways* (pp. 33–56). Basel: Karger.

Flavell, J. H., Beach, D., & Chinsky, J. (1966). Spontaneous verbal rehearsal in a memory task as a function of age. *Child Development, 37,* 283–299.

Flavell, J. H., Miller, P. H., & Miller, S. A. (1993). *Cognitive development* (3rd ed.). Englewood Cliffs, NJ: Prentice-Hall.

Forman, G., & Fyfe, B. (1998). Negotiated learning through design, documentation, and discourse. In C. Edwards, L. Gandini & G. Forman (Eds.), *The hundred languages of children. The Reggio Emilia approach—advanced reflections* (pp. 239–260). Greenwich, CT: Ablex.

Fried, R. L. (2001). Passionate learners and the challenge of schooling. *Phi Delta Kappan, 83,* 124–136.

Gagne, R. M. (1977). *The conditions of learning* (3rd ed.). New York: Holt, Rinehart & Winston.

Gagne R. M., Briggs, L. J., & Wager, W. W. (1992). *Principles of instructional design.* (4th ed.). Fort Worth, TX: Harcourt Brace.

Gambetti, A. (2001, February). *Lecture to the Canadian study group.* Reggio Emilia, Italy.

Gandini, L., & Kaminsky, J. A. (2004). Reconceptualizing assessment: An interview with Gunilla Dahlberg. *Innovations in early education: The international Reggio exchange, 11* (3), 1.

Gardner, H. (1983). *Frames of mind: The theory of multiple intelligences.* New York: Basic Books.

Gardner, H. (1985). *The mind's new science.* New York: Basic Books.

Gardner, H. (1991). *The unschooled mind: How children think and how schools should teach.* New York: Basic Books.

Gardner, H. (1993). *Multiple intelligences: The theory in practice.* New York: Basic Books.

Gardner, H. (1999). *Intelligence reframed. Multiple intelligences for the 21st century.* New York: Basic Books.

Gauvain, M. (2001). *The social context of cognitive development.* New York: Guilford Press.

Gazzaniga, M. S. (1998). *Cognitive neuroscience: The biology of the mind.* New York: Norton.

Ge, X., Conger, R. D., & Elder, G. H., Jr. (1996). Coming of age too early: Pubertal influences on girls' vulnerability to psychological distress. *Child Development, 67,* 3386–3400.

Gilligan, C. (1982). *In a different voice.* Cambridge, MA: Harvard University Press.

Ginsburg, H. P. (1997). *Entering the child's mind: The clinical interview in psychological research and practice.* New York: Cambridge University Press.

Giudici, C., Rinaldi, C., & Krechevsky, M. (Eds.) (2001). *Making learning visible: Children as individual and group learners.* Reggio Emilia, Italy: Reggio Children.

Glover, J. A., Ronning, R. R., & Reynolds, C. R. (Eds.). (1989). *Handbook of creativity.* New York: Plenum Press.

Goldberg-Reitman, J. (1992). Young girls' conception of their mother's role: A neo-structural analysis. In R. Case, (Ed.), *The mind's staircase: Exploring the conceptual underpinnings of children's thought and knowledge* (pp. 135–151). Hillsdale, NJ: Erlbaum.

Goleman, D. (1995). *Emotional intelligence.* New York: Bantam.

Goleman, D. (1997). Emotional intelligence in context. In P. Salovey & D. J. Sluyter (Eds.), *Emotional development and emotional intelligence: Educational implications* (pp. xiii–xvi). New York: Basic Books.

Golomb, C. (2002). *Child art in context: A cultural and comparative perspective.* Washington, DC: American Psychological Association.

Good, T. L., & Brophy, J. E. (1987). *Looking in classrooms* (4th ed.). New York: Harper and Row.

Good, T. L., & Brophy, J. (1991). *Looking in classrooms* (5th ed.). New York: Harper and Row.

Good, T. L., & Levin, J. R. (2001). Educational psychology yesterday, today, and tomorrow: Debate and direction in an evolving field. *Educational Psychologist, 36,* 69–72.

Gottfried, A. E., Fleming, J. S., & Gottfried, A. W. (2001). Continuity of academic intrinsic motivation from childhood through late adolescence: A longitudinal study. *Journal of Educational Psychology, 93,* 3–13.

Gould, S. J. (1981). *The mismeasure of man.* New York: Norton.

Gowan, J. C. (1981). Introduction. In J. Gowan, J. Khatena & E. P. Torrance (Eds.), *Creativity: Its educational implications* (2nd ed., pp. v–xiv). Dubuque, IA: Kendall/Hunt.

Graber, J. A., Lewinsohn, P. M., Seeley, J. R., & Brooks-Gunn, J. (1997). Is psychopathology associated with the timing of pubertal development? *Journal of the American Academy of Child and Adolescent Psychiatry, 36,* 1768–1776.

Grant, L. (1984). Black females' "place" in desegregated classrooms. *Sociology of Education, 57,* 98–111.

Greenberg, M. T., Kusche, C. A., Cook, E. T., & Quamma, J. P. (1995). Promoting emotional competence in school-aged children: The effects of the PATHS curriculum. *Development and Psychopathology, 7,* 117–136.

Gresham, F. M., & Elliott, S. N. (1990). *Social Skills Rating System.* Circle Pine, MN: American Guidance Service.

Griffin, S. (1992). Young children's awareness of their inner world: A neo-structural analysis of the development of intrapersonal intelligence. In R. Case, *The mind's staircase: Exploring the conceptual underpinnings of children's thought and knowledge* (pp. 189–206). Hillsdale, NJ: Erlbaum.

Griffin, S., & Case, R. (1996). Evaluating the breadth and depth of training effects when central conceptual structures are taught. In R. Case & Y. Okamoto, *The Role of Central Conceptual Structures in the Development of Children's Thought. Monographs of the Society for Research in Child Development, 61* (1–2, Serial No. 246), 83–102.

Griffin, S. A., Case, R., & Siegler, R. S. (1994). Rightstart: Providing the central conceptual prerequisites for first formal learning of arithmetic to students at risk for school failure. In K. McGilly (Ed.), *Classroom lessons: Integrating cognitive theory and classroom practice* (pp. 25–49). Cambridge, MA: MIT Press.

Grossman, H. (2004). *Classroom behavior management for diverse and inclusive schools* (3rd ed.). Lanham, MD: Rowman & Littlefield.

Guildford, J. P. (1959). Traits of creativity. In H.H. Anderson (Ed.), *Creativity and its cultivation* (pp. 142–161). New York: Harper.

Hacker, D. J., & Tenent, A. (2002). Implementing reciprocal teaching in the classroom: Overcoming obstacles and making modifications. *Journal of Educational Psychology, 94,* 699–718.

Halford, G. (1993). *Children's understanding: The development of mental models.* Hillsdale, NJ: Erlbaum.

Hamre, B. K., & Pianta, R. C. (2001). Early teacher-child relationships and the trajectory of children's school outcomes through eighth grade. *Child Development, 72,* 625–638.

Harris, J. R. (1998). *The nurture assumption: Why children turn out the way they do.* New York: Free Press.

Harrow, A. J. (1972). *A taxonomy of the psychomotor domain.* New York: David MacKay.

Harter, S. (1981). A new self-report scale of intrinsic versus extrinsic orientation in the classroom: Motivational and informational components. *Developmental Psychology, 17,* 300–312.

Harter, S. (1982). The perceived competence scale for children. *Child Development, 53,* 87–97.

Harter, S. (1985). *Manual for the Self-Perception Profile for Children.* University of Denver.

Harter, S. (1986). Processes underlying the construction, maintenance, and enhancement of the self-concept in children. In J. Suls & A. G. Greenwald (Eds.), *Psychological perspectives on the self,* Vol. 3 (pp. 137–181). Hillsdale, NJ: Erlbaum.

Harter, S. (1996). Teacher and classmate influences on scholastic motivation, self-esteem, and level of voice in adolescents. In J. Juvonen & K. R. Wentzel (Eds.). *Social motivation: Understanding children's school adjustment.* Cambridge Studies in Social and Emotional Development. (pp. 11–42). New York: Cambridge University Press.

Harter, S. (1999). *The construction of the self.* New York: Guilford Press.

Harter, S., & Jackson, B. K. (1992). Trait vs. non-trait conceptualizations of intrinsic/extrinsic motivation orientation. *Motivation and Emotion, 16,* 209–230.

Harter, S., & Pike, R. (1983). *Procedural manual to accompany The Pictorial Scale of Perceived Competence and Social Acceptance for Young Children.* University of Denver.

Harter, S., & Pike, R. (1984). The pictorial scale of perceived competence and social acceptance for young children. *Child Development, 55,* 1969–1982.

Hartup, W. W., & Abecassis, M. (2002). Friends and enemies. In P. K. Smith & C. H. Hart (Eds.), *Blackwell handbook of childhood social development* (pp. 285–306). Oxford, England: Blackwell.

Hatch, T. (1997). Friends, diplomats, and leaders in kindergarten: Interpersonal intelligence in play. In P. Salovey & D. J. Sluyter (Eds.), *Emotional development and emotional intelligence: Educational implications* (pp. 70–89). New York: Basic Books.

Heath, S. B., & McLaughlin, M. W. (1994). Learning for anything everyday. *Journal of Curriculum Studies, 26,* 471–489.

Helms, J. E. (1997). The triple quandary of race, culture, and social class in standardized cognitive ability testing. In D. P. Flanagan, J. L. Genshaft & P. L. Harrison (Eds.), *Contemporary intellectual assessment: Theories, tests, and issues* (pp. 517–532). New York: Guilford.

Hertzman, C. (2004, March). *Inequalities in early child development: The challenge to schools.* Paper presented in the lecture series, Building Capacity for Diversity in Canadian Schools, University of British Columbia.

Hightower, E. (1990). Adolescent interpersonal and familial precursors of positive mental health at midlife. *Journal of Youth and Adolescence, 19,* 257–275.

Hildago, N. M., Siu, S., Bright, J. A., Swap, S. M., & Epstein, J. L. (1995). Research on families, schools, and communities: A multicultural perspective. In J. A. Banks & C. A. M. Banks (Eds.), *Handbook of research on multicultural education.* New York: Macmillan.

Hitch, G. J., & Towse, J. N. (1995). Working memory: What develops? In F. E. Weinert & W. Schneider (Eds.), *Memory performance and competencies: Issues in growth and development* (pp. 3–21). Mahwah, NJ: Erlbaum.

Hoge, R. D., & Renzulli, J. S. (1993). Exploring the link between giftedness and self-concept. *Review of Educational Research, 63,* 449–465.

Horn, J. L., & Noll, J. (1997). Human cognitive capabilities: Gf-Gc theory. In D. P. Flanagan, J. L. Genshaft, & P. L. Harrison (Eds.), *Contemporary intellectual assessment: Theories, tests, and issues* (pp. 53–91). New York: Guilford.

Howes, C., & Tonyan, H. (2000). Peer relations. In L. Balter & C. S. Tamis-LeMonde (Eds.), *Child psychology: A handbook of contemporary issues* (pp. 85–113). Philadelphia, PA: Psychology Press.

Hunt, E., & Minstrell, J. (1994). A cognitive approach to the teaching of physics. In K. McGilly (Ed.), *Classroom lessons: Integrating cognitive theory and classroom practice* (pp. 51–74). Cambridge, MA: MIT Press.

Hymel, S., Comfort, C., Schonert-Reichl, K., & McDougall, P. (1996). Academic failure and school dropout: The influence of peers. In J. Juvonen & K. Wentzel (Eds.), *Social motivation: Understanding children's school adjustment* (pp. 313–345). New York: Cambridge University Press.

Inhelder, B., & Piaget, J. (1958). *The growth of logical thinking from childhood to adolescence.* New York: Basic Books.

Jackson, N. E. (2000). Strategies for modeling the development of giftedness in children. In R. C. Friedman & B. M. Shore (Eds.), *Talents unfolding: Cognition and development* (pp. 27–54). Washington, DC: American Psychological Association.

Jacobs, J. E., Lanza, S., Osgood, D. W., Eccles, J. S., & Wigfield, A. (2002). Changes in children's self-competence and values: Gender and domain differences across grades one through twelve. *Child Development, 73,* 509–527.

James, W. (1892). *Psychology: The briefer course.* New York: Henry Holt.

Jones, V. (1996). Classroom management. In J. Silula (Ed.), *Handbook of research on teacher education* (2nd ed.) (pp. 503–521). New York: Macmillan.

Kalchman, M., & Case, R. (1998). Teaching mathematical functions in primary and middle school: An approach based on neo-Piagetian theory. *Scientia Paedogogioca Experimentalis, 35,*(1), 7–53.

Kamii, C. (1984). Autonomy: The aim of education envisioned by Piaget. *Phi Delta Kappan, 65,* 410–415.

Katz, L. G. (1993a, Summer). All about me. Are we developing our children's self-esteem or their narcissism? *American Educator,* 18–23.

Katz, L. G. (1993b). What can we learn from Reggio Emilia? In C. Edwards, L. Gandini & G. Forman (Eds.), *The hundred languages of children: The Reggio Emilia approach to early childhood education* (pp. 19–37). Norwood, NJ: Ablex.

Keating, D. P. (1980). Four faces of creativity: The continuing plight of the intellectually underserved. *Gifted Child Quarterly, 24,* 56–61.

Keating, D. P. (1991). Curriculum options for the developmentally advanced: A developmental alternative to gifted education. *Exceptionality Education Canada, 1 (1),* 53–83.

Keating, D. P. (1999). Developmental health and the wealth of nations. In D. P. Keating & C. Hertzman (Eds.), *Developmental health and the wealth of nations: Social, biological and educational dynamics* (pp. 337–347). New York: Guilford.

Keating, D. P., & Hertzman, C. (Eds.). (1999). *Developmental health and the wealth of nations: Social, biological and educational dynamics.* New York: Guilford.

Kelson, A. C. M. (2000). Assessment of students for proactive lifelong learning. In D. H. Evensen & C. E. Hmelo (Eds.), *Problem-based learning: A research perspective on learning interactions* (pp. 315–345). Mahwah, NJ: Erlbaum.

Kitcher, P. (1996). *The lives to come: The genetic revolution and human possibilities.* New York: Simon & Schuster.

Klein, P. (1997). Multiplying the problems of intelligence by eight: A critique of Gardner's theory. *Canadian Journal of Education, 22,* 377–394.

Klein, P. (1998). A response to Howard Gardner: Falsifiability, empirical evidence and pedagogical usefulness in educational psychologies. *Canadian Journal of Education, 23,* 103–112.

Kohlberg, L. A. (1964). Development of moral character and moral ideology. In M. L. Hoffman & L. W. Hoffman (Eds.), *Review of child development research* (Vol.1). New York: Russell Sage Foundation.

Kohlberg, L. A. (1976). Moral stages and moralization: The cognitive-developmental approach. In T. Lickona (Ed.), *Moral development and behavior.* New York: Holt, Rinehart & Winston.

Kohn, A. (1993). *Punished by rewards: The trouble with gold stars, incentive plans, A's, praise, and other bribes.* Boston: Houghton Mifflin.

Kohn, A. (1994, December). The truth about self-esteem. *Phi Delta Kappan,* 272–283.

Kohn, A. (1997). The trouble with character education. In A. Molnar (Ed.), *The construction of children's character. Ninety-sixth yearbook of the National Society for the Study of Education, Part II* (pp. 154–162). Chicago: University of Chicago Press.

Krathwohl, D. R., Bloom, B. S., & Masia, B. B. (1964). *Taxonomy of educational objectives. Handbook II: Affective domain.* New York: David MacKay.

Krechevsky, M., & Seidel, S. (1998). Minds at work: Applying multiple intelligences in the classroom. In R. J. Sternberg & W. M. Williams (Eds.), *Intelligence, instruction, and assessment. Theory into practice* (pp. 17–42). Mahwah, NJ: Erlbaum.

Kuhl, P. K., & Meltzoff, A. N. (1997). Evolution, nativism, and learning in the development of speech. In M. Gopnik (Ed.), *The inheritance and innateness of grammar.* New York: Oxford University Press.

Kuhn, T. (1970). *The structure of scientific revolutions.* Chicago: University of Chicago Press.

Ladd, G. W. (1990). Having friends, keeping friends, making friends and being liked by peers in the classroom: Predictors of children's early school adjustment? *Child Development, 61,* 1081–1100.

Ladd, G. W., Buhs, E. S., & Troop, W. (2002). Children's interpersonal skills and relationships in school settings: Adaptive significance and implications for school-based prevention and intervention programs. In P. K. Smith & C. H. Hart (Eds.), *Blackwell handbook of childhood social development* (pp. 394–415). Oxford, England: Blackwell.

Ladson-Billings, G. (1995). But that's just good teaching! The case for culturally relevant pedagogy. *Theory Into Practice, 34,* 159–164.

Laird, R. D., Jordan, K. Y., Dodge, K. A., Pettit, G. S., & Bates, J. E. (2001). Peer rejection in childhood, involvement with antisocial peers in early adolescence, and the development of externalizing behavior problems. *Development and Psychopathology, 13,* 337–354.

Larivée, S., Normandeau, S., & Parent, S. (2000). The French connection: Some contributions of French-language research in the post-Piagetian era. *Child Development, 71,* 823–829.

Larkin, J. H. (1994). Foreword. In K. McGilly (Ed.), *Classroom lessons: Integrating cognitive theory and classroom practice* (pp. ix–xiii). Cambridge, MA: The MIT Press.

Leming, J. S. (1997). Research and practice in character education: A historical perspective. In A. Molnar (Ed.), *The construction of children's character. Ninety-sixth yearbook of the National Society for the Study of Education, Part II* (pp. 31–44). Chicago: University of Chicago Press.

Liben, L. S., & Bigler, R. S. (2002). The developmental course of gender differentiation. *Monographs of the Society for Research in Child Development, 67* (2, Serial No. 269).

Lickona, T. (1991). Moral development in the elementary school classroom. In W. M. Kurtines & J. L. Gewirtz (Eds.), *Handbook of moral behavior and development. Volume 3: Application* (pp. 143–161). Hillsdale, NJ: Erlbaum.

Lickona, T. (1997). Educating for character: A comprehensive approach. In A. Molnar (Ed.), *The construction of children's character. Ninety-sixth yearbook of the National Society for the Study of Education, Part II* (pp. 45–62). Chicago: University of Chicago Press.

Liddle, E., & Porath, M. (2002). Gifted children with written output difficulties: Paradox or paradigm. *Australian Journal of Learning Disabilities, 7,* 13–19.

Littlewood, W. (1984). *Communicative language teaching.* New York: Cambridge University Press.

Loftus, G. R., & Loftus, E. F. (1976). *Human memory: The processing of information.* Hillsdale, NJ: Erlbaum.

Lonner, W. J., & Hayes, S. A. (2004). Understanding the cognitive and social aspects of intercultural competence. In R. J. Sternberg & E. L. Grigorenko (Eds.), *Culture and competence: Contexts of life success* (pp. 89–110). Washington, DC: American Psychological Society.

Lorenz, E. H., & Lupart, J. L. (2001, May). *Gender differences in Math, English, and Science for grade 7 and 10 students—Expectations for success.* Paper presented at the Canadian Society for Studies in Education, Université Laval, Québec, Canada.

Lorenz, K. (1971). *Studies in animal and human behavior* (Vol. 2). Cambridge, MA: Harvard University Press.

Lott, B. (2002). Cognitive and behavioral distancing from the poor. *American Psychologist, 57,* 100–110.

Lucyshyn, J. M., Albin, R. W., & Nixon, C. S. (1997). Embedding comprehensive behavioral support in family ecology: An experimental, single-case analysis. *Journal of Consulting and Clinical Psychology, 65,* 241–251.

Lucyshyn, J. M., Kayser, A. T., Irvin, L. K., & Blumberg, E. R. (2002). Functional assessment and positive behavior support at home with families. Designing effective and contextually appropriate behavior support plans. In J. M. Lucyshyn, G. Dunlap & R. W. Albin (Eds.), *Families and positive behavior in family contexts: Addressing problem behavior in family contexts* (pp. 97–132). Baltimore: Brookes.

Lupart, J. L., & Pyryt, M. (2001, May). *Gender differences in science, math, and English, and adult life choices.* Paper presented at the Canadian Society for Studies in Education, Université Laval, Québec, Canada.

Marcia, J. E. (1966). Development and validation of ego-identity status. *Journal of Personality and Social Psychology, 3,* 551–558.

Marcia, J. E. (1980). Identity in adolescents. In J. Adelson (Ed.), *Handbook of adolescent psychology.* New York: Wiley.

Mager, R. E. (1972). *Goal analysis.* Belmont, CA: Fearon.

Marini, Z., & Case, R. (1994). The development of abstract reasoning about the physical and social world. *Child Development, 65,* 147–159.

Marsh, H. W. (1992). Content specificity of relations between academic achievement and academic self-concept. *Journal of Educational Psychology, 84,* 35–42.

Marsh, H. W. (1993). The multidimensional structure of academic self-concept: Invariance over gender and age. *American Educational Research Journal, 30,* 841–860.

Marsh, H. W., & Craven, R. (1997). Academic self-concept: Beyond the dustbowl. In G. D. Phye (Ed.), *Handbook of classroom assessment: Learning, achievement, and adjustment.* San Diego, CA: Academic Press.

Marsh, H. W., & Hau, K.-T. (2003). Big-fish-little-pond effect on academic self-concept: A cross-cultural (26 country) test of the negative effects of academically selective schools. *American Psychologist, 58,* 364–376.

Marsh, H, & Yeung, A. S. (1997). Casual effects of academic self-concept on academic achievement: Structural equation models of longitudinal data. *Journal of Educational Psychology, 89,* 41–54.

Maslow, A. (1970). *Motivation and personality* (2nd ed.). New York: Harper & Row.

Masten, A. S., & Coatsworth, J. D. (1998). The development of competence in favorable and unfavorable environments: Lessons from research on successful children. *American Psychologist, 53,* 205–220.

Matthews, D. J. (1997). Diversity in domains of development: Research findings and their implications for gifted identification and programming. *Roeper Review, 19,* 172–177.

Matthews, G., Zeidner, M., & Roberts, R. D. (2002). *Emotional intelligence: Science and myth.* Cambridge, MA: MIT Press.

Mayer, J. D., Caruso, D. R., & Salovey, P. (2000). Emotional intelligence meets traditional standards for an intelligence. *Intelligence, 27,* 267–298.

Mayer, J. D., & Salovey, P. (1997). What is emotional intelligence? In P. Salovey & D. J. Sluyter (Eds.), *Emotional development and emotional intelligence: Educational implications* (pp. 3–31). New York: Basic Books.

Mayer, R. E. (2001). What good is educational psychology? The case of cognition and instruction. *Educational Psychologist, 36,* 83–88.

McCloskey, L. A., & Stuewig, J. (2001). The quality of peer relationships among children exposed to family violence. *Development and Psychopathology, 13,* 83–96.

McCombs, B. L. (1997). Self-assessment and reflection: Tools for promoting teacher changes toward learner-centered practices. *National Association of Secondary School Principals Bulletin, 81* (587), 1–14.

McDermott, P. C., & Rothenberg, J. J. (2001, April). *New teachers communicating effectively with low-income parents.* Paper presented at American Educational Research Association Annual Meeting, Seattle, WA (ERIC Document Reproduction Service No. ED 454 207).

McHale, S. M., Crouter, A. C., & Tucker, C. J. (2001). Free-time activities in middle childhood: Links with adjustment in early adolescence. *Child Development, 72,* 1764–1778.

McKeough, A. (1992). A neo-structural analysis of children's narrative and its development. In R. Case (Ed.), *The mind's staircase: Exploring the conceptual underpinnings of children's thought and knowledge* (pp. 171–188). Hillsdale, NJ: Erlbaum.

McKeough, A., & Sanderson, A. (1996). Teaching storytelling: A microgenetic analysis of developing narrative competency. *Journal of Narrative and Life History, 6,* 157–192.

Meichenbaum, D., & Biemiller, A. (1998). *Nurturing independent learners. Helping students take charge of their learning.* Cambridge, MA: Brookline Books.

Milgram, R. M., & Hong, E. (1993). Creative thinking and creative performance in adolescents as predictors of creative attainments in adults: A follow-up study after 18 years. *Roeper Review, 11,* 135–139.

Miller, G. A. (1994). The magical number seven, plus or minus two: Some limits on our capacity for processing information. In

H. Gutfreund & G. Toulouse (Eds.), *Biology and computation: A physicist's choice. Advanced series in neuroscience, Vol. 3* (pp. 207–223). River Edge, NJ: World Scientific Publishing.

Miller, J. G. (2004). The cultural deep structure of psychological theories of social development. In R. J. Sternberg & E. L. Grigorenko (Eds.), *Culture and competence: Contexts of life success* (pp. 111–138). Washington, DC: American Psychological Society.

Miller, N. E., & Dollard, J. (1941). *Social learning and imitation.* New Haven, CT: Yale University Press.

Mistry, R. S., Vandewater, E. A., Huston, A. C., & McLoyd, V. C. (2002). Economic well-being and children's social adjustment: The role of family process in an ethnically diverse low-income sample. *Child Development, 73,* 935–951.

Moll, L. C. (1990). Introduction. In L. C. Moll (Ed.), Vygotsky and education: *Instructional implications and applications of sociohistorical psychology* (pp. 1–27). Cambridge MA: Cambridge University Press.

Molnar, A. (1997). Editor's preface. In A. Molnar (Ed.), *The construction of children's character. Ninety-sixth yearbook of the National Society for the Study of Education, Part II* (pp. ix–x). Chicago: University of Chicago Press.

Montemayor, R., & Eisen, M. (1977). The development of self-conceptions from childhood to adolescence. *Developmental Psychology, 13,* 314–319.

Moss, J., & Case, R. (1999). Developing children's rational number sense: A new model and an experimental paradigm. *Journal of Research in Mathematics Education, 30,* 122–147.

Mulvey, E. P., & Cauffman, E. (2001). The inherent limits of predicting school violence. *American Psychologist, 56,* 797–802.

Murray, B. (2000). Learning from real life. *Monitor on Psychology, 31,* 72–73.

Myers, I. B. (1962). *The Myers–Briggs Type Indicator.* Palo Alto, CA: Consulting Psychologists Press.

Nakamura, J., & Csikszentmihalyi, M. (2001). Catalytic creativity: The case of Linus Pauling. *American Psychologist, 56,* 337–341.

Neff, K. D., & Helwig, C. C. (2002). A constructivist approach to understanding the development of reasoning about rights and authority within cultural contexts. *Cognitive Development, 17,* 1429–1450.

Neill, D. M. (1997). Transforming student assessment. *Phi Delta Kappan, 79* (1), 4–40, 58.

Nelson, T. O. (1999). Cognition versus metacognition. In R. J. Sternberg (Ed.), *The nature of cognition* (pp. 625–641). Cambridge, MA: The MIT Press.

New, R. S. (2001). Italian early care and education: The social construction of policies, programs, and practices. *Phi Delta Kappan, 83,* 226–236.

Newcomb, A. F., & Bagwell, C. L. (1996). The developmental significance of children's friendship relations. In W. M. Bukowski, A. F. Newcomb, & W. W. Hartup (Eds.), *The company they keep: Friendship in childhood and adolescence* (pp. 289–321). New York: Cambridge University Press.

Newell, A., Shaw, J. C., & Simon, H. A. (1958). Elements of a theory of human problem solving. *Psychological Review, 65* (3),151–166.

Newell, A., & Simon, H. A. (1972). *Human problem solving.* Englewood Cliffs, NJ: Prentice-Hall.

Newmann, F. M., Marks, H., & Gamaron, A. (1996). Authentic pedagogy and student performance. *American Journal of Education, 104,* 280–312.

Nicks, J. D. (2000). *Secondary lesson plan.* Course assignment, EPSE 401. University of British Columbia, Vancouver, BC, Canada.

Noddings, N. (1995). Teaching themes of care [Electronic version]. *Phi Delta Kappan, 76,* 675–679.

Noddings, N. (1997). Character education and community. In A. Molnar (Ed.), *The construction of children's character. Ninety-sixth yearbook of the National Society for the Study of Education, Part II* (pp. 1–16). Chicago: University of Chicago Press.

Nowicki, E. A., & Sandieson, R. (2002). A meta-analysis of school-age children's attitudes towards persons with physical or intellectual disabilities. *International Journal of Disability, Development and Education, 49,* 243–265.

O'Donnell, A. M., & Levin, J. R. (2001). Educational psychology's healthy growing pains. *Educational Psychologist, 36,* 73–82.

O'Leary, K. D., & O'Leary, S. G. (Eds.). (1972). *Classroom management: The successful use of behavior modification.* New York: Pergamon Press.

Olweus, D. (2003). A profile of bullying at school. *Educational Leadership, 60* (6), 12–17.

Onwuegbuzie, A. J., & Daley, C. E. (1998). Similarity of learning styles of students and a teacher in achievement in a research methods course. *Psychological Reports, 82,* 163–168.

Osterman, K. F. (2000). Students' need for belonging in the school community. *Review of Educational Research, 70,* 323–367.

Owens, R. E., Jr. (1988). *Language development* (2nd. ed.) Columbus, OH: Merrill.

Owens, R. E. (1996). *Language development* (4th ed.). Boston: Allyn and Bacon.

Paley, V. G. (1981). *Wally's stories.* Cambridge, MA: Harvard University Press.

Paley, V. G. (1986). On listening to what the children say. *Harvard Educational Review, 56,* 122–131.

Paris, S. G., & Ayres, L. R. (1994). *Becoming reflective students and teachers with portfolios and authentic assessment.* Washington, DC: American Psychological Association.

Paris, S. G., & Paris, A. H. (2001). Classroom applications of research on self-regulated learning. *Educational Psychologist, 36,* 89–101.

Pavlov, I. P. (1927). *Conditioned reflexes.* New York: Dover.

Pea, R. D. (1993). Learning scientific concepts through material and social activities: Conversational analysis meets conceptual change. *Educational Psychologist, 28,* 265–277.

Pellegrini, A. D., & Blatchford, P. (2000). *The child at school: Interactions with peers and teachers.* London: Arnold.

Perry, N. E. (2002). Introduction: Using qualitative methods to enrich understandings of self-regulated learning. *Educational Psychologist, 37,* 1–3.

Peskin, H. (1973). Influence of developmental schedule of puberty on learning and ego functioning. *Journal of Youth and Adolescence, 2,* 273–290.

Peskin, J. (1980). Female performance and Inhelder and Piaget's tests of formal operations. *Genetic Psychology Monographs, 101,* 245–256.

Peterson, A. C. (1988). Adolescent development. *Annual Review of Psychology, 39,* 583–607.

Peterson, D. M., Marcia, J. E., & Carpendale, J. I. M. (2004). Identity: Does thinking make it so? In C. Lightfoot, C. Lalonde, & M. Chandler (Eds.), *Changing conceptions of psychological life* (pp. 113–126). Mahwah, NJ: Erlbaum.

Peterson, P. L. (1993). Toward an understanding of what we know about school learning. *Review of Educational Research, 63,* 319–326.

Piaget, J. (1932). *Moral judgement in children.* New York: Harcourt Brace Jovanovich.

Piaget, J. (1952). Autobiography. In E. G. Boring, H. S. Langfeld, H. Werner, & R. M. Yerkes (Eds.), *A history of psychology in autobiography* (pp. 237–256). Worcester, MA: Clark University Press.

Piaget, J. (1953). *The origin of intelligence in the child.* London: Routledge & Kegan Paul.

Piaget, J. (1972). Intellectual evolution from adolescence to adulthood. *Human Development, 15,* 1–12.

Piaget, J. (1981). *The psychology of intelligence.* Totowa, NJ: Littlefield, Adams.

Pianta, R. C. (1999). *Enhancing relationships between children and teachers.* Washington DC: American Psychological Association.

Pike, K., & Salend, S. J. (1995). Authentic assessment strategies: Alternatives to norm-referenced testing. *Teaching Exceptional Children, 28* (1), 15–20.

Pintrich, P. R, & Schunk, D. H. (1996). *Motivation in education: Theory, research, and applications.* Englewood Cliffs, NJ: Merrill-Prentice-Hall.

Plomin, R., & Rutter, M. (1998). Child development, molecular genetics and what to do with genes once they are found. *Child Development, 69,* 1223–1242.

Popham, W. J. (1997). The standards movement and the emperor's new clothes. *National Association of Secondary School Principals Bulletin, 81* (588), 21–41.

Popham, W. J. (1998). Farewell, curriculum. Confessions of an assessment convert. *Phi Delta Kappan, 79,* 380–384.

Popham, W. J. (2002). *Classroom assessment: What teachers need to know* (3rd ed.). Boston: Allyn and Bacon.

Porath, M. (1988). *Cognitive development of gifted children: A neo-Piagetian approach.* Unpublished doctoral dissertation, University of Toronto.

Porath, M. (1995). Classroom-based assessment for instructional planning at the elementary level. In J. Andrews (Ed.), *Elementary classrooms: Teaching students with diverse needs* (pp. 62–83). Toronto: Nelson Canada.

Porath, M. (1996). Narrative performance in verbally gifted children. *Journal for the Education of the Gifted, 19,* 276–292.

Porath, M. (1997). Gifted children's understanding of intelligence. *Roeper Review, 20,* 95–98.

Porath, M. (1998). Psychosocial development in girls of high ability. *International Journal for the Advancement of Counselling, 20,* 289–299.

Porath, M. (2001). Young girls' social understanding: Emergent interpersonal expertise. *High Ability Studies, 12,* 113–126.

Premack, D. (1959). Toward empirical behavior laws: I. Positive reinforcement. *Psychological Review, 66,* 219–233.

Principles for Fair Student Assessment Practices for Education in Canada (1993). Edmonton, Alberta: Joint Advisory Committee, Centre for Research in Applied Measurement and Evaluation, University of Alberta.

Project Zero & Reggio Children (2001). *Making learning visible: Children as individual and group learners.* Reggio Emilia, Italy: Reggio Children.

Purpel, D. E. (1997). The politics of character education. In A. Molnar (Ed.), *The construction of children's character. Ninety-sixth yearbook of the National Society for the Study of Education, Part II* (pp. 140–153). Chicago: University of Chicago Press.

Quiocho, A., & Rios, F. (2000). The power of their presence: Minority group teachers and schooling. *Review of Educational Research, 70,* 485–528.

Raver, C. C., Izard, C., & Kopp, C. B. (2002). Emotions matter: Making the case for the role of young children's emotional development for early school readiness. *Social Policy Report, 16* (3), 3–18.

Reddy, R., Rhodes, J. E., & Mulhall, P. (2003). The influence of teacher support on student adjustment in the middle school years: A latent growth curve study. *Development and Psychopathology, 15,* 119–138.

Reis, O., & Youniss, J. (2004). Patterns in identity change and development in relationships with mothers and friends. *Journal of Adolescent Research, 19,* 31–44.

Reis, S. M., Burns, D. E., & Renzulli, J. A. (1991). *Curriculum compacting: The complete guide to modifying the regular curriculum for high ability students.* Mansfield Center, CT: Creative Learning Press.

Renzulli, J. S. (1973). *New directions in creativity.* New York: Harper & Row.

Renzulli, J. S. (1999). What is this thing called giftedness, and how do we develop it? A twenty-five year perspective. *Journal for the Education of the Gifted, 23,* 3–54.

Renzulli, J. S. (2002). Emerging conceptions of giftedness: Building a bridge to the new century. *Exceptionality, 10,* 67–75.

Resnick, L. B. (1976). Task analysis in instructional design: Some cases from mathematics. In D. Klahr (Ed.), *Cognition and instruction.* Hillsdale, NJ: Erlbaum.

Rice, M. L. (1989). Children's language acquisition. *American Psychologist, 44,* 149–156.

Rinaldi, C. (2001). Documentation and assessment: What is the relationship? In C. Giudici, C. Rinaldi & M. Krechevsky (Eds.), *Making learning visible: Children as individual and group learners* (pp. 78–93). Reggio Emilia, Italy: Reggio Children.

Robinson, N. M., Zigler, E., & Gallagher, J. J. (2000). Two tails of the normal curve: Similarities and differences in the study of mental retardation and giftedness. *American Psychologist, 55,* 1413–1424.

Roderick, M., & Camburn, E. (1999). Risk and recovery from course failure in the early years of high school. *American Educational Research Journal, 36,* 303–343.

Rogoff, B., Bartlett, L., & Turkanis, C. G. (2001). Lessons about learning as a community. In B. Rogoff, C. G. Turkanis & L. Bartlett (Eds.), *Learning together: Children and adults in a school community* (pp. 3–17). Oxford, Oxford University Press.

Rogoff, B., Mistry, J. Goncu, A., & Mosier, C. (1993). Guided participation in cultural activity by toddlers and caregivers. *Monographs of the Society for Research in Child Development, 58* (8, Series No. 236).

Rosenholtz, S. R., & Rosenholtz, S. J. (1981). Classroom organization and the perception of ability. *Sociology of Education, 54,* 132–140.

Rowe, D. C. (1994). Genetic and cultural explanations of adolescent risk taking and problem behavior. In R. D. Ketterlinus & M. E. Lamb (Eds.), *Adolescent problem behaviors: Issues & research* (pp. 109–126). Hillsdale, NJ: Erlbaum.

Runco, M. A. (1987). Interrater agreement on a socially valid measure of student's creativity. *Psychological Reports, 61,* 1009–1010.

Runco, M. A. (2004). Creativity as an extracognitive phenomenon. In L. V. Shavinina & M. Ferrari (Eds.), *Beyond knowledge: Extracognitive aspects of developing high ability* (pp. 17–25). Mahwah, NJ: Erlbaum.

Runco, M. A., & Nemiro, J. (1994). Problem finding and problem solving. *Roeper Review, 16,* 235–241.

Rutter, M. (2001, November). *Biological and experiential influences on psychological development.* Paper presented to the Millennium Dialogue on Early Child Development, Ontario Institute for Studies in Education/University of Toronto.

Ryan, R. M., & Deci, E. L. (2000). Self-determination theory and the facilitation of intrinsic motivation, social development, and well-being. *American Psychologist, 55,* 68–78.

Saarni, C. (1999). *The development of emotional competence.* New York: Guilford.

Sadker, M., & Sadker, D. (1994). *Failing at fairness: How America's schools cheat girls.* New York: Scribner.

Salovey, P., & Sluyter, D. J. (Eds.). (1997). *Emotional development and emotional intelligence: Educational implications.* New York: Basic Books.

Santrock, J. W., & Yussen, S. R. (1992). *Child development: An introduction* (5th ed.). Dubuque, IA: William C. Brown.

Sattler, J. M. (1992). *Assessment of children* (3rd ed.). San Diego, CA: Jerome M. Sattler.

Scardamalia, M., & Bereiter, C. (1999). Schools as knowledge-building organizations. In D. P. Keating & C. Hertzman (Eds.), *Developmental health and the wealth of nations: Social, biological and educational dynamics* (pp. 274–289). New York: Guilford.

Scardamalia, M., Bereiter, C., & Lamon, M. (1994). The CSILE project: Trying to bring the classroom into World 3. In K. McGilly (Ed.), *Classroom lessons: Integrating cognitive theory and classroom practice* (pp. 201–228). Cambridge, MA: MIT Press.

Schon, D. A. (1983). *The reflective practitioner: How professionals think in action.* New York: Basic Books.

Scott, C. L. (1999). Teachers' biases toward creative children. *Creativity Research Journal, 12,* 321–328.

Scruggs, T. E., & Mastropieri, M. A. (1990). Mnemonic instruction for students with learning disabilities: What it is and what it does. *Learning Disabilities Quarterly, 13,* 271–280.

Seels, B., & Glasgow, Z. (1998). *Making instructional design decisions* (2nd ed.) Upper Saddle River, NJ: Merrill.

Shapiro, E. S., & Lentz, F. E. (1988). Behavioral assessment of academic skills. In T. R. Kratochwill (Ed.), *Advanced studies in school psychology, Vol. 5* (pp. 87–139). Hillsdale, NJ: Erlbaum.

Shaw, C. C. (1996). The big picture: An inquiry into the motivations of African American teacher education students to be or not to be teachers. *American Educational Research Journal, 33,* 327–354.

She, H. C., & Fisher, D. (2002). Teacher communication behaviour and its association with students' cognitive and attitudinal outcomes in science in Taiwan. *Journal of Research in Science Teaching, 39* (1), 63–78.

Shippen, M. E., Simpson, R. G., & Crites, S. A. (2003). A practical guide to functional behavioral assessment. *Teaching Exceptional Children, 35* (5), 36–44.

Simmons, R. G., & Blyth, D. A. (1987). *Moving into adolescence: The impact of pubertal change and school context.* Hawthorn, NY: Aldine.

Simplicio, J. S. C. (2000). Teaching classroom educators how to be more effective and creative teachers. *Education, 120,* 675–680.

Skinner, B. F. (1938). *The behavior of organisms.* New York: Appleton-Century-Crofts.

Smith, D. (2001). Is too much riding on high-stakes tests? *Monitor on Psychology, 32* (11), 58–59.

Smith, T. E. C., Polloway, E. A., Patton, J. R., & Dowdy, C. A. (1998). *Teaching students with special needs in inclusive settings* (2nd ed.). Boston: Allyn and Bacon.

Snow, C. E. (2001). Knowing what we know: Children, teachers, researchers. *Educational Researcher, 30,* 3–9.

Soby, J. M. (1994). *Prenatal exposure to drugs/alcohol: Characteristics and educational implications of fetal alcohol syndrome and cocaine/polydrug effects.* Springfield, IL: Thomas.

Spoehr, K. T. (1994). Enhancing the acquisition of conceptual structures through hypermedia. In K. McGilly (Ed.), *Classroom lessons: integrating cognitive theory and classroom practice* (pp. 75–101). Cambridge, MA: MIT Press.

Steinberg, A. (1993). *Adolescents and schools: Improving the fit.* Cambridge, MA: HEL Reprint Series.

Sternberg, R. (1985). *Beyond IQ: A triarchic theory of human intelligence.* Cambridge, MA: Cambridge University Press.

Sternberg, R. J. (1997). The triarchic theory of intelligence. In D. P. Flanagan, J. L. Genshaft & P. L. Harrison (Eds.), *Contemporary intellectual assessment: Theories, tests, and issues* (pp. 92–104). New York: Guilford.

Sternberg, R. J. (1998a). Ability testing, instruction, and assessment of achievement: Breaking out of the vicious circle. *National Association of Secondary School Principals Bulletin, 82* (595), 4–10.

Sternberg, R. J. (1998b). Principles of teaching for successful intelligence. *Educational Psychologist, 33,* 65–72.

Sternberg, R. J. (Ed.) (1999a). *The nature of cognition.* Cambridge, MA: MIT Press.

Sternberg, R. J. (1999b). A dialectical basis for understanding the study of cognition. In R. J. Sternberg (Ed.), *The nature of cognition* (pp. 51–78). Cambridge, MA: MIT Press.

Sternberg, R. J. (Ed.). (2000). *Wisdom: Its nature, origins, and development.* Cambridge: Cambridge University Press.

Sternberg, R. J. (2001). What is the common thread of creativity? Its dialectical relation to intelligence and wisdom. *American Psychologist, 56,* 360–362.

Sternberg, R. J., & Dess, N. K. (2001). Creativity for the new millennium. *American Psychologist, 56,* 332.

Sternberg, R. J., & Grigorenko, E. L. (2000). *Teaching for successful intelligence to increase student learning and achievement.* Arlington Heights, IL: SkyLight Professional Development.

Sternberg, R. J., & Grigorenko, E. L. (2004). Why cultural psychology is necessary and not just nice: The example of the study of intelligence. In R. J. Sternberg & E. L. Grigorenko (Eds.), *Culture and competence: Contexts of life success* (pp. 207–223). Washington, DC: American Psychological Association.

Sternberg, R. J., & Lubart, T. I. (1991, April). Creating creative minds. *Phi Delta Kappan,* 608–614.

Stiggins, R. J. (2001). *Student-involved classroom assessment.* Upper Saddle River, NJ: Merrill-Prentice-Hall.

Stipek, D., & MacIver, D. (1989). Developmental changes in children's assessment of intellectual competence. *Child Development, 60,* 521–538.

Strein, W. (1993). Advances in research on academic self-concept: Implications for school psychologists. *School Psychology Review, 22,* 273–284.

Streissguth, A., & Kanter, J. (Eds.) (1997). *The challenge of fetal alcohol syndrome.* Seattle, WA: University of Washington.

Strozzi, P. (2001). Daily life at school: Seeing the extraordinary in the ordinary. In C. Giudici, C. Rinaldi & M. Krechevsky (Eds.), *Making learning visible: Children as individual and group learners* (pp. 58–77). Reggio Emilia, Italy: Reggio Children.

Sugai, G., Horner, R. H., & Sprague, J. R. (1999). Functional-assessment-based behavior support planning: Research to practice to research. *Behavioral Disorders, 24,* 253–257.

Suizzo, M. (2000). The social-emotional and cultural context of cognitive development: Neo-Piagetian perspectives. *Child Development, 71,* 846–849.

Sullivan, K. (2000). *The anti-bullying handbook.* New York: Oxford University Press.

Super, C. M., & Harkness, S. (1986). The developmental niche: A conceptualization at the interface of society and the individual. *International Journal of Behavioral Development, 9,* 545–570.

Super, C. M., & Harkness, S. (1997). The cultural structuring of child development. In J. Berry, P. Dasen & T. Sarawathi (Eds.), *Handbook of cross-cultural psychology: Vol. 2. Basic processes of human development* (2nd ed.) (pp. 1–39). Boston: Allyn and Bacon.

Tanner, J. M. (1978). *Fetus into man.* Cambridge, MA: Harvard University Press.

Tatum, A. W. (2000). Breaking down barriers that disenfranchise African American adolescent leaders in low-level tracks [Electronic version]. *Journal of Adolescent and Adult Literacy, 44* (1), 52.

Templeton, R. A., & Johnson, C. E. (2001). *Playing the staff development game: Assessing a communications workshop to improve learning.* Technical Research Report. Peoria, IL: Bradley University (ERIC Document Reproduction Service No. ED 454 218).

Thorkildsen, T. A. (1993). Those who can, tutor: High-ability students' conceptions of fair ways to organize learning. *Journal of Educational Psychology, 85,* 182–190.

Thorndike, E. L. (1913). *Educational psychology (Vol.1). The psychology of learning.* New York: Teachers College Press.

Thorndike, R. M. (1997). The early history of intelligence testing. In D. P. Flanagan, J. L. Genshaft & P. L. Harrison (Eds.), *Contemporary intellectual assessment: Theories, tests, and issues* (pp. 3–16). New York: Guilford.

Timmons, V. (2004, February). *Supporting families to enhance children's learning.* Paper presented in the lecture series Building Capacity for Diversity in Canadian Schools, University of Prince Edward Island.

Todd, R. D., Swarzenski, B., Rossi, P. G., & Visconti, P. (1995). Structural and functional development of the human brain. In D. Cicchetti & D. J. Cohen (Eds.), *Developmental psychopathology: Vol. 1, Theory and Methods.* New York: Wiley.

Torrance, E. P. (1966). *Torrance test of creative thinking (Norms technical manual).* Princeton, NJ: Personnel Press.

Torrance, E. P. (1974). *Torrance test of creative thinking.* Lexington, MA: Ginn.

Trainor, L. J., Austin, C. M., & Desjardins, R. N. (2000). Is infant-directed speech prosody a result of the vocal expression of emotion? *Psychological Science, 11,* 188–195.

Underwood, M. K. (2002). Sticks and stones and social exclusion: Aggression among girls and boys. In P. K. Smith & C. H. Hart (Eds.), *Blackwell handbook of childhood social development* (pp. 533–548). Oxford, England: Blackwell.

Vaillancourt, T. (2001). *Competing for hegemony during adolescence: A link between aggression and social status.* Unpublished doctoral dissertation, University of British Columbia, Vancouver, British Columbia, Canada.

Valencia, R. R., & Suzuki, L. A. (2001). *Intelligence testing and minority students: Foundations, performance factors, and assessment issues.* Thousand Oaks, CA: Sage.

Vygotsky, L. S. (1978). *Mind in society.* Cambridge, MA: Harvard University Press.

Walberg, H. J., & Greenberg, R. C. (1997, May). Using the learning environment inventory. *Educational Leadership,* 45–47.

Walker, L. J., Pitts, R. C., Hennig, K. H., & Matsuba, M. K. (1999). Reasoning about morality and real-life moral problems. In M. Killen & D. Hart (Eds.), *Morality in everyday life: Developmental perspectives* (pp. 371–407). New York: Cambridge University Press.

Watson, B., & Konicek, R. (1990). Teaching for conceptual change: Confronting children's experience. *Phi Delta Kappan, 71,* 680–685.

Watson, J. (1925). *Behaviorism.* Chicago: University of Chicago Press.

Weiner, B. (1984). Principles for a theory of student motivation and their application within an attributional framework. In R. Ames & C. Ames (Eds.), *Research on motivation in education (Vol.1): Student motivation.* New York: Academic Press.

Weiner, B. (1986). *An attributional theory of motivation and emotion.* New York: Springer-Verlag.

Wentzel, K. R. (1993). Does being good make the grade? Social behavior and academic competence in middle school. *Journal of Educational Psychology, 85,* 357–364.

Wentzel, K. R. (1999). Social-motivational processes and interpersonal relationships: Implications for understanding motivation at school. *Journal of Educational Psychology, 91,* 76–97.

Werner, E. E., & Smith, R. S. (2001). *Journeys from childhood to midlife: Risk, resilience, and recovery.* Ithaca, NY: Cornell University Press.

Wesson, C. L., & King, R. P. (1996). Portfolio assessment and special education students. *Teaching Exceptional Children, 28* (2), 44–48.

White, B. (1975). *The first three years of life.* Englewood Cliffs, NJ: Prentice-Hall.

Wiggins, G. (1997). Work standards: Why we need standards for instructional and assessment design. *National Association of Secondary School Principals, 81,* (590), 56–64.

Wiggins, G. (1998). An exchange of views on "Semantics, psychometrics, and assessment reform: A close look at 'authentic assessments'."*Educational Researcher, 27* (6), 20–21.

Willms, J. D. (1999). Quality and inequality in children's literacy: The effects of families, schools, and communities. In D. P. Keating & C. Hertzman (Eds.), *Developmental health and the wealth of nations: Social, biological and educational dynamics* (pp. 72–93). New York: Guilford.

Wilson, L. M., & Corpus, D. A. (2001, September). The effects of reward systems on academic performance. *Middle School Journal,* 56–59.

Wilson, R. J. (1996). *Assessing students in classrooms and schools.* Scarborough, ON: Allyn and Bacon Canada.

Wineburg, S. (1997). T. S. Eliot, collaboration, and the quandaries of assessment in a rapidly changing world. *Phi Delta Kappan, 79,* (1), 59–65.

Winner, E. (1996). *Gifted children: Myths and realities.* New York: Basic Books.

Wolf, D. P. (1987–1988). Opening up assessment. *Educational Leadership, 45,* 24–29.

Yewchuk, C., & Lupart, J. (2000). Inclusive education for gifted students with disabilities. In K. Heller, F. Monks, R. Sternberg & R. Subotnik (Eds), *International handbook of giftedness and talent* (2nd ed., pp. 659–670). Amsterdam: Elsevier.

Youniss, J., & Damon, W. (1992). Social construction in Piaget's theory. In H. Beilin & P. B. Pufall (Eds.), *Piaget's theory: Prospects and possibilities* (pp. 267–286). Hillsdale, NJ: Erlbaum.

Yussen, S. R., & Kane, P. T. (1985). Children's conceptions of intelligence. In S. R. Yussen (Ed.), *The growth of reflection in children* (pp. 207–241). New York: Academic Press.

Zimmerman, B. J. (1989). A social cognitive view of self-regulated learning. *Journal of Educational Psychology, 81,* 329–339.

Zimmerman, B. J., & Bandura, A. (1994). Impact of self-regulatory influences on writing course attainment. *American Educational Research Journal, 31,* 845–862.

Zins, J. E., Travis, L. F. III, & Freppon, P. A. (1997). Linking research and educational programming to promote social and emotional learning. In P. Salovey & D. J. Sluyter (Eds.), *Emotional development and emotional intelligence: Educational implications* (pp. 257–274). New York: Basic Books.

Index

The abbreviations *t* and *f* stand for table and figure, respectively.

A

ability, *versus* capability, in schools, 199
academic competence, 138, 248–249, 258–259, 280
    and attribution theory, 251–253
    and authentic tasks, 314
    and culture, 157
    and emotional development, 53, 159–160
    and encouragement, 285
    and extracurricular activities, 206–207
    and gender, 155–156, 204–205
    and high expectations, 199
    and intersubjectivity, 138–139
    perception of, 153–159
    and poverty, 189–192
    and prosocial behavior, 138
    rationales for, 251–253
    and school environment, 199
    and self-concept, 153, 158–159
    and self-esteem, 154–159, 251
    and self-worth, 253–254
    and social development, 52, 138
achievement. *See* academic competence
adaptability, 202, 220
ADD (attention deficit disorder), 123
"added value" schools, and development, 199
ADHD (attention deficit disorder with hyperactivity), 123
adolescence. *See also* children; friendship; peer relationships
    and curriculum matching, 73
    decline of motivation in, 255–256
    friendship in, 147, 149
    and memory, 122
    physical development in, 29–31
    and risk-taking behavior, 18
    and self-concept, 152, 154–155, 157, 249
    and sense of belonging, 203–204, 208
    and social cognitive development, 139–140
African American parents, and alienation, 289
African Americans, 289
    and culturally relevant teaching, 192–193
    and IQ test biases, 216
aggression, 143
AI (artificial intelligence), 118
American Sign Language (ASL), 34, 197
Ames, C., 260
Anderman, E. M., 201, 203
animal communication, 31–32
Annett, M., 37
aphasia, 37
applied behavioral analysis, 104–106, 111. *See also* behaviorism, and learning
    and functional assessment, 105–106, 111
    and positive behavioral support, 105–106
    and problem behavior, 104–106
artificial intelligence (AI), 118

ASL (American Sign Language), 34, 197
assessment and evaluation, 298, 306–308, 320*t*. *See also* intelligence quotient (IQ) and testing; standardized tests; teacher-made tests
    assessing excellence, 318–320
    authentic, 312, 314–315
    complex assessment, 317–318
    context of, 326
    of creativity, 231
    and intelligence testing, 221–222
    learner-centered, 309–310
    needs assessments, 292*t*, 294–295
    and observation, 322, 324–325
    and portfolios, 316–317
    pretesting, 312, 330
    and rating scales for behavior, 325
    and report cards, 326–327
    reporting of, 326–327
    and rubrics, 318–322, 321*t*, 322*t*
    and speech community, 39
    teacher's role in, 308–309
    terminology, 308
    and testing, 329–330
    of writing, 320*t*, 322*t*
association, and learning, 98
Attention Deficit Disorder (ADD), 123
Attention Deficit Disorder with Hyperactivity (ADHD), 123
attribution theory, and motivation, 251–253. *See also* rationales
authentic pedagogy, 311
authenticity, and increased achievement, 314
automaticity, and learning, 99
autonomy, 164, 280
Ayres, L. R., 316–317

B

Babcock, S., 286
Backlund, J., 286
Bandura, Albert, 110, 250–251
baseline knowledge, determining, 314
basic activity, 91
basic skills, 91
Baumrind, D., 185–187
behaviorism, and learning, 97–98, 100–106, 110–111. *See also* applied behavioral analysis
belonging, and adolescence, 203–204, 208
best practice, 6
Bickerton, G., 41, 310
Biemiller, A., 83, 281–282, 316
Bigler, R. S., 204
Binet, Alfred, 43
Blair, C., 190
Blatchford, P., 147
Bloom, Benjamin, 48

369

Photo Credits